THE DIAGNOSIS OF REASONING
IN THE MENTALLY RETARDED

THE DIAGNOSIS
OF REASONING IN THE
MENTALLY RETARDED

BÄRBEL INHELDER

Professor, Institut des Sciences de l'Education,
Université de Genève

Prefaces by JEAN PIAGET

Translated from the French
by Will Beth Stephens and Others

JOHN DAY BOOKS IN
S E
SPECIAL EDUCATION

THE JOHN DAY COMPANY

NEW YORK

Translated from the French, *Le Diagnostic du raisonnement chez les débiles mentaux,* © 1943 by Delachaux and Niestlé, Neuchâtel (2d ed. 1963).
This translation was prepared by Will Beth Stephens with the assistance of Katherine Cavanaugh, J. L. Delcourt, Philippa Harverson, Patricia Moran, and Eleanor Duckworth, Translation Editor. It was supported in part by a fellowship from the Vocational Rehabilitation Administration, U. S. Department of Health, Education, and Welfare.

Library of Congress Catalogue Card Number: 68–15247
PRINTED IN THE UNITED STATES OF AMERICA
BY AMERICAN BOOK–STRATFORD PRESS, INC.

To My Father

Contents

Preface to the First Edition

The work of Mademoiselle Inhelder needs no introduction. The clarity of her thought and of the ideas which she develops, the abundance of data, her skill in examining children, and finally her ability to write clearly of difficult matters—these qualities are found on each page of this volume, and they make a preface superfluous.

Nonetheless, Mlle. Inhelder had the kindness to ask me to write a preface. While I thank her for associating me with this fine book, which only she could have written, I must say that there are at least two reasons why I feel uncomfortable in doing so. For one thing, a chapter on psychopathology in the present book draws heavily on *Le Développement des quantités physiques chez l'enfant* (1941), which we wrote together. Secondly, Mlle. Inhelder has brought my hypothesis of intellectual operations to bear in her work on mental diagnosis and oligophrenia. In these areas, therefore, it is impossible for me to have an impartial opinion.

From among the numerous new contributions that the work makes, I will limit myself to comments on the original position that Mlle. Inhelder adopted in using the hypothesis of intellectual operations in the analysis of mental development in all its complexity.

In *Le Développement des quantités physiques chez l'enfant,* the two of us sought to explain the manner in which children from four to twelve years construct the principal notions of physical quantity and the weight and volume of bodies. We found that for each of these notions, the child went through a rather long period during which he based his judgments on simple perceptions or on intuitions centered on his own activity (lifting, for instance). Later he succeeded in de-

9

centering his judgment and depended on rational and experimental procedures. This progress was always accomplished in the same manner: instead of following the irreversible course of his actions or of perceptual transformations, the child began to be able to retrace his action backward. Such is the operation: an action which has become reversible is inserted into a system of similar, coordinated actions. For example, at one point, a child will claim that a pellet of clay changes in weight when stretched into a sausage shape, flattened into a cake, or divided into bits. At about nine years, he will affirm that the weight remains the same because you can get back to the original form by compensating for each of these actions by its inverse; he thus understands that the relations form a system in which each transformation is compensated by others. Such a system of relations and of operations is what we have termed a "grouping," and the criterion for the presence of a "grouping" is the notion of conservation (conservation of matter, of weight, or of volume).

One might consider these results as pertinent only to the mechanisms of conceptual or reflective intelligence. Seen as characterizing a special domain, like a game limited to the arena of rational thought, they would have a certain importance for cognitive psychologists, educators, or teachers of mathematics, but they would not go beyond the confines of this purely intellectual universe.

However, Mlle. Inhelder firmly believed in the reality of operations, not only in the finished products of thought but in the mechanism of its development, and dared to hypothesize that retardations and anomalies of this development ought to be discernible as retardations or fixations in the elaboration of the operations themselves and their "groupings." She even dared to suppose that a method originally conceived for the analysis of operational groupings in normal children accustomed to verbal intelligence and school situations could be applied without change to diagnostic research and even to prognosis in the very complex field of mental deficiency.

When the Department of Public Instruction in the canton of St. Gallen asked her to organize its school psychology service, with the essential task of identifying and orienting abnormal or retarded children, Mlle. Inhelder decided to give these children the same examinations that she had skillfully used with normal children. Although we were pleased with the possibilities of scientific interest in such a comparison, we must admit that we did not suspect that this method would become central in her everyday practice.

The first surprising discovery—and if Mlle. Inhelder had expected this outcome, others were perhaps less convinced in advance—was that the stages observed in the operational development of the normal also were found with impressive regularity in the retarded. From more than 150 subjects, not one understood the conservation of weight without having the conservation of substance, nor the conservation of volume without both weight and substance, while the conservation of substance *was* found without the other two, and the conservation of weight was found without the conservation of volume. This finding alone would justify the study.

But there was more. In a canton where the service was set up on an experimental basis, Mlle. Inhelder was able to achieve a large measure of professional success in the difficult problem of identifying retarded children. Above all, the determination of their exact intellectual level (the determination on which all their future school learning is based) was achieved by the author in a way that clearly justified the experiment, while making no compromises with the logic of the system.

As previously stated, it is not our place to judge this system, but let us take note of the unexpected consequences for the development of intelligence itself. The first is the discovery of a new criterion of mental deficiency. We know how the determination of retardation has given rise to various interpretations and how crudely empirical are the indices used to distinguish the imbecile from the moron or from the simple retardate. By hypothesizing a fixation in the stages of operational development, Mlle. Inhelder has arrived at a criterion which has among other things the special merit of utilizing natural cut-off points within an apparently continuous evolution. The imbecile remains refractory to all thought operations; his approach is purely intuitive and perceptive. On the other hand, the retardate can reach the level of concrete operations, i.e. those organized in "groupings," which must, however, be accompanied by manipulations. The retardate is still not capable of "formal operations," which go beyond physical experience and are organized on a hypothetico-deductive level. A person who is capable of these formal operations has to be classified simply as a slow learner.

Briefly, then, mental deficiency may be characterized by the possibility of an incomplete "operational construction," and the reader will note how subtly the author develops the consequences and the many implications of this thesis.

Among these implications is a final point which we wish to emphasize. The fact that in mental development some constructions are completed and others remain incomplete surely attests to the existence of laws of equilibrium comparable to those governing organic growth, laws that make it possible to distinguish an adult state from a normal state in the process of formation and from a pathological state of arrested growth or pseudo-equilibrium. Here again, Mlle. Inhelder's research has brought an unforeseen importance to the concept of operations. It is easy to hazard theoretical comparisons and to conceive of operational groupings as laws of equilibrium whose reversibility recalls the classical definitions of the notion of equilibrium as it first appeared in the physical sciences. Thanks to Mlle. Inhelder, this theory has acquired a real coefficient of probability: if in fact an individual whose operational equilibrium will always remain incomplete is for that reason mentally deficient, then operations and their groupings appear as components, not only of an abstract structure of a system-building theoretician but of a vivid reality, full of significance for the dynamism of concrete development.

Mlle. Inhelder is to be congratulated on her fine effort and on the results now available for the consideration of psychologists and psychopathologists; she has succeeded in getting the operational hypothesis out from behind the boundaries of pure theory construction into the field of effective reality.

JEAN PIAGET

Geneva, Switzerland
April 1943

Preface to the Second Edition

If it was useful to give a preface to this work at the time of its first edition, the number of volumes that Mlle. Inhelder and I have published together since then prevents me now from eulogizing my collaborator as I might wish. Nonetheless, I may be permitted to point out the importance of that portion of her research which goes beyond my own domain. In addition to her work in pure developmental psychology, which has gained her a wide reputation, particularly in Great Britain and the U. S. A., Mlle. Inhelder has continued her investigations in the direction of possible applications to education in general and to the problems of mental deficiency. In the first of these two fields, it is evident that the various studies we have done on the development of operational structures, both logico-mathematical (number, space, chance, logic of classes, relations, and propositions) and physical (notions of quantities and induction of elementary physical laws), suggests numerous didactic applications, as has been recognized in several different countries where Mlle. Inhelder has been called upon quite regularly. The most outstanding example is the commission created in 1959 by the National Academy of Science of the U. S. A. for the reform of American programs for teaching mathematics, physics, and elementary biology. The commission included recognized American specialists in these fields and in psychology, plus one invited European, Bärbel Inhelder. We have read with interest the report of the first symposium of this commission, held at Woods Hole, Massachusetts, which was published by J. S. Bruner under the title *The Process of Education* (1961). This work is still going on, moreover, and still with Mlle. Inhelder's collaboration.

In the area of mental deficiency, the comprehensive introduction which Mlle. Inhelder has written for the second edition of this work makes it unnecessary for me to elaborate on the many developments which have issued from the method inaugurated with her first edition. The idea of applying to the diagnosis and prognosis of mental retardation and to problems of child psychopathology in general the results of the studies on the development of operational structures in normal children turned out to be fruitful and even indispensable, inasmuch as these studies deal with the dynamism of intellectual development in its broadest sense. The close collaboration between Mlle. Inhelder and our colleague J. de Ajuriaguerra, Professor of Psychology, University of Geneva, has already borne fruit in this regard, in the general area of scholastic difficulties and even in the analysis of specific disturbances, of language for instance, in which detailed understanding is particularly difficult. Some of these disturbances are correlated with deficiencies in the handling of intellectual operations, while others are completely independent of this sector of cognitive functioning and seem to be more closely connected with the insufficiencies in the figural aspect, including spatial or spatial-temporal representation.

What with her educational concerns and her interest in mental deficiencies, and still inspired by her central involvement in developmental psychology, Mlle. Inhelder has, in recent years, given additional attention to a group of questions that have great importance for all three of these areas. These questions concern the possibilities and limiting factors involved in trying to accelerate the acquisition of operational structures.

Stimulated by the symposium at Woods Hole, the psychologist J. S. Bruner, of Harvard University, had the idea of relating our results in developmental psychology to the attempts being made by noted physicists (including J. Zacharias and the late F. Friedman of M. I. T.) to introduce young children to experimental science. Bruner felt that the adequate organization of an environment (experimental material, etc.) would permit facilitation in encoding information and unlimited acceleration in the acquisition of operational structures. Having created with G. Miller the Center for Cognitive Studies at Harvard University, he invited Mlle. Inhelder there for several months of collaboration. With the assistance of Magali Bovet, she began by confirming in Bruner's presence—in a progressive school—the same structures of thought in children between five and seven years of age as had been established in Genevese children of the same age (the same preoperational reactions of nonconservation, etc.). This confirmed the wisdom and necessity of taking account of a certain rhythm of development; environment alone was not enough to do the whole job. An ensemble of complementary research resulted, which was aimed at deciding between (and synthesizing, if possible) the two points of view—American functionalism and Geneva structuralism. This research still continues, carried on by research assistants at Harvard and Geneva, with periodic conferences on the methods and the results (for the Atlantic is crossed more and more rapidly). A great deal can be expected from such research, because the study of learning—in the American sense of neo-learning—is not at all restricted to the problem of possible (but not unlimited) acceleration of development: above all, it represents a method of analyzing the passage from one structure to the next and the very mechanisms of this transition. This is the problem Mlle. Inhelder undertook to study in her longitudinal research with G. Noelting, and she is extending it now in controlled experimentation which characterizes learning research.

If we have tended to provide information here which appears somewhat removed from the diagnosis of reasoning in the mentally deficient, it is to show the continuity of interest in Mlle. Inhelder's work since this first study. The central idea is to reinforce the analytical power of developmental psychology by posing the same problems of progressive structuration in all areas of practical application, where the facts clarify one another, passing from the normal to the pathological or from spontaneous thought to school assimilation. Thus it is of great value to publish a new edition of the work that did so much to stimulate research in these many areas, apparently quite separate, but in fact admirably convergent.

JEAN PIAGET

Geneva, Switzerland
September 1963

Foreword to the First Edition

Charged in 1939 by the Department of Public Instruction of the canton of St. Gallen with the identification and mental diagnosis of abnormal children, we had recourse at first to the usual tests of general development and to a series of tests then used in psychological consultations. However, the need to construct a more specialized test for the diagnosis of reasoning soon became apparent.

Most of the cases were children with scholastic difficulties, who had been referred to us either by teachers or by the medical staff of the schools. Often we had to decide whether a child should be admitted to regular classes, placed in a special education class, or discharged from compulsory schooling. It goes without saying that a decision which recommends institutional placement must be based on a precise clinical study of mental equilibrium. In certain cases the nature and degree of the mental deficiency are quickly determined, for example when the subject is an idiot incapable of learning or an imbecile who should be placed in an institution for retardates. However, to distinguish between the imbecile and the retardate is a more difficult problem, and to distinguish between the retardate and the slow learner still more so. Such cases often require a more penetrating diagnosis. Things become still more complicated when it is not a matter of simple retardation, but of affective and intellectual equilibrium.

The psychologist in charge of academic placement of these children is often called upon, if not to assess their complete mental organization, then at least to make a differential diagnosis of retardation, *i.e.,* to discern which of the abnormal manifestations stem from an intellectual deficiency and what are the possibilities for subsequent development.

Classical tests of general development, whether they establish mental ages, intellectual quotients, or psychological profiles, measure performance rather than analyze the processes themselves, and for this reason they seem to us insufficient to diagnose mental retardation. André Rey's excellent clinical tests of learning and of adaptation do, on the other hand, provide valuable psychofunctional indices. However, these tests are oriented toward memory acquisitions, affective processes, and practical intelligence, and it seemed to us useful to complement them with diagnostic tests of reasoning.

Having previously studied, with J. Piaget, the genesis of operational mechanisms in which successive stages are constructed by differentiation and integration, we believed it would be possible to adapt this genetic research to mental diagnosis. The operational stages could furnish a model of development against which deficiencies could be seen as arrestations and abnormal fixations. We have selected the tests from our work *Le Développement des quantités physiques chez l'enfant* (1941). Just as in that work we questioned normal children on the conservation of matter, weight, and volume—when a clay ball is transformed or a sugar cube dissolved—we are using the same tests now to study reasoning in the mentally retarded.

The operational tests suppose a certain minimum of comprehension and intellectual exchange, and for this reason they are most appropriate in the diagnosis of upper-level deficients. The subjects diagnosed in this work are usually termed "mentally retarded." Although we were mainly interested in school-age retardates, we also examined a number of adults who function at this level.

In studying more than a hundred subjects, all of them designated by doctors and specialist teachers as retarded, we were struck by the vagueness of the current definition of deficiency. Some authors base diagnosis on physical or psychomotor indices. Others rely on scholastic deficiencies or on difficulties in social integration; while still others use mental ages or intellectual quotients. Even in quantitative evaluation large margins of variability still exist from test to test. We can hope that one day these various indices will be systematized enough to determine a general syndrome of deficiency. But already it seems to us imperative to single out some precise symptoms which characterize deficiency in the area of mental functioning. Our diagnostic experience has led us to the following statement: reasoning of the mentally deficient is characterized by incomplete operational construction. The idiot and the imbecile are incapable of operational thought (they remain preoperational, using either perceptual or intuitive modes); the slow learner arrives, sooner or later, at the stage of formal operations. By contrast, the retardate appears to be able to reach the level of concrete operations, but never attains the level of formal or hypothetico-deductive operations. The present work seeks to substantiate this statement.

However, we must ask whether it is legitimate to isolate one mental function—one as limited as reasoning—from the ensemble of mental organization, particularly when current psychopathological investigations suggest that this organization is a unified totality. Instead of engaging in global valuations or the determination of general factors under the pretext of directly attaining this totality as such, in our opinion it is better to attempt a finer dissection whose results, even if partial, can at least be integrated in a general diagnosis.

The analogy with anatomical dissection will perhaps make it possible to understand the difference between the conception defended here and that which has inspired most tests up until now. Suppose that one attempts to figure out the anatomy of a complicated region of an organ, and the regressions or reintegrations that could take place in it. Two methods are possible: either you proceed randomly to make all possible cuts, in the hope of tying them together by a simple summation of results, or you follow, one after another, each nerve, each nerve bundle, or each element. Perhaps the first method will succeed in some cases, but when it fails because the totality is too complex, only the second method will permit a precise determination. In other words, how can you examine a child in order to dissect, in the whole group of possible psychopathological troubles, those which stem from deficient intellectual construction?

If we limit ourselves to transversal cuts, we do obtain different levels, but we do not know if these are stages of construction. To isolate the framework of the construction as such, we must cut around its very shape, and this is possible only with a method of free conversation which enables us to pursue the operations one by one, and to place them in their natural context.

Of course, results which are limited to the study of reasoning cannot assume full meaning until they are seen in relationship to all aspects of mental life. When seen in the context of total mental organization, the signs of intellectual retardation that are brought out in the course of this research furnish some precise indications for a complete diagnosis.

It goes without saying that the diagnosis of reasoning as described in Chapters 2, 3, and 4 cannot take the place of a total diagnosis that takes into account all the factors in play. But when the diagnostic method reaches the point where all the clinical signs complement one another in a detailed tableau, it is certain that operational diagnosis will have its place, complementing and being complemented by the other aspects of the analysis.

Permit us to acknowledge our debts to the teachers in pedagogy and in psychology to whom we owe the inspiration for this work. Bovet and Descoeudres trained us in functional education and the pedagogy of abnormals. Rey initiated us in the problem of mental diagnosis, and we benefited from a number of methods which he inaugurated in the medico-pedagogical service of L'Institut des Sciences de l'Education. By his counsel and example, Lambercier has made it possible for us to understand the demands of the scientific technique of psychology laboratories. The influence of Piaget's thought on the conception of our work is so evident that it does not seem necessary to emphasize it here. The present research brings to light the value of his genetic theory for mental diagnosis. May the writer express her profound gratitude for the kind support that he has shown throughout her studies.

At L'Institut des Sciences de l'Education, founded and inspired by Edouard Claparède, we have been privileged to find surroundings that foster research in developmental and clinical psychology.

Finally, we would like to thank Messrs. Plüer, Grob Niedermann, and Kläui for their cooperation in giving us access to subjects in the institutions they direct.

BÄRBEL INHELDER

Translator's Introduction

In her Foreword and in Chapter 1, Bärbel Inhelder compares her work to other approaches concerned with the diagnosis of mental retardation. No attempt is made here, therefore, to redo what she has done. Nonetheless, some background information about her and the Geneva school appears to be in order.

After she received her Ph.D. (*summa cum laude*) from the University of Geneva in 1943, Bärbel Inhelder remained to serve as Director of Research at the Institute of Educational Sciences, a post she continues to hold. In 1948, the University of Geneva also appointed her Professor of Developmental Psychology and of Educational Psychology. Recognition of Inhelder's work by other universities was indicated when she served as guest lecturer at the University of Zürich in 1951, when she was awarded a Rockefeller Fellowship in 1954 for study and conferences in the United States, when in 1961 she served as Senior Research Fellow at the Harvard Center for Cognitive Studies, and when in 1964 she was lecturer for the Faculty of Humanities at the University of Aix-en-Provence, which awarded her an honorary doctor's degree. In 1962 she was chosen to be president of the Swiss Psychological Society. Major contributions which she has coauthored with Jean Piaget, also of the University of Geneva, include: *Le Développement des quantités physiques chez l'enfant* (1941), *The Child's Conception of Space* (French 1947, English 1956), *The Child's Conception of Geometry* (French 1948, English 1960, with Alina Szeminska), *La Genèse de l'idée de hasard chez l'enfant* (1951), *The Growth of Logical Thinking from Childhood to Adolescence* (French 1955, English 1958), *The Early Growth of*

21

Logic (French 1959, English 1963), *L'Image mentale chez l'enfant* (1966a), *La Psychologie de l'enfant* (1966b), and *Memoire à intelligence* (in press).

When the present work was first published, almost twenty-five years ago, the use of metric intelligence scales was widespread and unquestioned for most diagnostic purposes. At that time one of the book's major contributions was a comprehensive analysis of the inability of intelligence tests to diagnose cognitive processes, an analysis that remains timely. Inhelder also noted that psychologists tended to pay attention to verbal logic only and often failed to be concerned with nonverbal abilities and insufficiencies.

By 1941, Piaget had already published the general lines of his theory of development. *The Origins of Intelligence in Children* in 1936 (English 1952) and *The Construction of Reality in the Child* in 1937 (English 1954) described the development of sensory-motor intelligence during the first two years of a child's life. *The Child's Conception of Number* by Piaget and Szeminska and *Le Développement des quantités physiques chez l'enfant,* coauthored by Inhelder, had their original French publications in 1941. In the latter work, Inhelder and Piaget provided evidence to support the view that the genesis of logical operations is rooted in actions rather than words, a discovery that has provided a common thread throughout all of the Geneva work. The theoretical position of the development of operational structures dominated that book. As the various structural levels were described in these early works, the first outline of Piaget's famous stages of cognitive development were presented. An outline of this stage theory is provided by excerpts from Inhelder's discussion of it:

Whereas somatic and perceptual development seem to be continuous, intellectual development seems to take place in stages, the criteria of which can be defined as follows:

(1) Each stage involves a period of formation (genesis) and a period of attainment. Attainment is characterized by the progressive organization of a composite structure of mental operations.

(2) Each structure constitutes at the same time both the attainment of one stage and the starting-point of the next stage, of a new evolutionary process.

(3) The order of succession of the stages is constant. Ages of attainment can vary within certain limits as a function of factors of motivation, practice, cultural milieu, and so forth.

(4) The transition from an earlier to a later stage follows a law of implication analogous to the process of integration, preceding structures become a part of later structures. . . .

Three operational structures can be distinguished in the cognitive development of the child; each one characterizes the attainment of a major stage of development; and within each one, sub-stages can be distinguished. . . .

The first major stage of sensory-motor operations occupies approximately the first eighteen months. It is characterized by the progressive formation of the schema of the permanent object and by the sensory-motor structuration of one's immediate spatial surroundings. The observations and longitudinal studies carried out by Piaget on his own children indicate that this progression originates in the functional exercising of mechanisms that are reflexive in origin, and leads gradually to a system of movements and of displacements. In this way the child's conception of the permanence of objects is brought about. This sensory-motor system is made up of displacements which, if they are not reversible in the mathematical sense, they are nonetheless amenable to inversion (*renversables*). The displacements made in one direction can be made in the inverse direction; the child can return to his starting point; he can attain the same goal by different routes. In the co-ordination of these movements into a system, the child comes to realize that objects have permanence: they can be found again, whatever their displacements (even if these be outside the field of vision). Piaget has compared this system, which has the characteristics of a group structure to the structure of Poincaré's model of the geometric "group of displacements."

One can distinguish six sub-stages in the course of this first major stage of development; their continuity is assured by schemata [schemas] of action. These schemata [schemas] are transposable or generalizable actions. The child establishes relations between similar objects or between objects which are increasingly dissimilar, including relations between those objects and his own body (for instance, the extension of the schema of graspable objects to that of invisible objects). Thus a schema can be defined as the structure common to all those acts which—from the subject's point of view—are equivalent. . . .

. . . The second developmental stage of concrete thinking operations extends approximately from the middle of the second year until the eleventh or twelfth year. It is characterized by a long process of elaboration of mental operations. The process is completed by about the age of seven and is then followed by an equally long process of structuration. During their elaboration, concrete thought processes are irreversible. We observe how they gradually become reversible. With reversibility, they form a system of concrete operations. For example, we can establish that although a five-year-old has long since grasped the permanence of objects, he has by no means yet any notion of the elementary physical principle of the conservation of matter. . . .

After a period of gradual construction, and at about seven years of age, a thought structure is formed; as a structure it is not yet separated from its concrete content. In contrast with the sensori-motor actions of the first stage—which were executed only in succession—the various thought operations of the second stage are carried out simultaneously, thus forming systems of operations. These systems, however, are still incomplete. They are characterized by two forms of reversibility (a) negation, as expressed in the [well known] plasticine experiment, in which a perceived change in form is cancelled by its corresponding negative thought operation; and (b) reciprocity, as expressed in the child's discovery that "being a foreigner" is a reciprocal relationship, or that left-right, before-behind spatial relationships are relative. At the concrete level, these forms of reversibility are used independently of one another; in formal thought, they will form one unified system of operations. . . .

Thus during the course of this second period of development, we can follow the genesis of thought processes which—at about seven years of age—issues in the elementary logico-mathematical thought structures. Nevertheless it still requires years before these structures are brought to bear on all possible concrete contents. It can be shown, for example, that the principle of invariance (constancy, conservation) is applied to the quantity of matter earlier than to weight, and to volume still later. In every case, as earlier schemas are integrated into later ones, they are altered in the process. Thus the process seems indeed to be one of genetic construction—a gradual process of equilibration within a limited system of concrete operations. Equilibrium within this system is attained at about eleven or twelve years of age. This operational structure, in turn, forms the basis of the development of the formal thinking operations. . . .

. . . The third stage, that of formal thinking operations, begins, on the average, at about eleven or twelve years of age and is characterized by the development of formal, abstract thought operations. In a rich cultural environment, these operations come to form a stable system of thought structures at about fourteen or fifteen years of age.

In contrast to the child in stage two whose thought is still bound to the concrete here and now, the adolescent is capable of forming hypotheses and of deducing possible consequences from them. This hypothetico-deductive level of thought expresses itself in linguistic formulations containing propositions and logical constructions (implication, disjunction, etc.). It is also evident in the manner in which experiments are carried out, and proofs provided. The adolescent organizes his experimental procedure in a way that indicates a new sort of thought structure. . . .

In analyzing these thought structures, Piaget found that they come more and more to approximate formal models as the subject's experimental procedures become more and more effective. The combinatorial method, for example, corresponds to a lattice structure and the method of proportionality, to the structure of a group. Above all, the formal thought structure, as compared to the concrete, is marked by a higher degree of reversibility. And in this case, the two forms of reversibility already constituted—negation and reciprocity—are now united in a complete operational system. We can say that the new operational abilities formed during this third stage are the abilities that open up unlimited possibilities for the youth to take a constructive part in the advancement of scientific knowledge—provided that his setting offers him a suitable practice-ground and a favorable intellectual atmosphere. . . .

Piaget postulates that each organism is an open, active, self-regulating system. Mental development would then be characterized by progressive changes in the processes of active adaptation. The fact that, in healthy children and adolescents in our civilization, this continual mental transformation tends nonetheless toward order and not toward chaos, would indicate—according to this hypothesis—the influence of self-regulating processes, such as those involved in a principle of equilibrium. Operational structures—both concrete and formal—are a special case of this principle of equilibrium. A change in perception, for instance, can be seen as a disturbance of the equilibrium; operations can restore this equilibrium by compensating or cancelling the change.

The . . . [stages] of . . . [cognitive] development thus represent a constant progression from a less to a more complete equilibrium, and manifest therein the organism's steady tendency toward a dynamic integration. This equilibrium is not a static state, but an active system of compensations—not a final conclusion, but a new starting-point to higher forms of mental development [Inhelder 1962: 23–28].

Certain of the above levels were more fully developed in Piaget's *The Psychology of Intelligence* (French 1947, English 1950b) and in *The Growth of Logical Thinking from Childhood to Adolescence* (Inhelder and Piaget: French 1955, English 1958), but the outline existed when Inhelder undertook her work with retardates in the St. Gallen school system. While Piaget was still primarily interested in the nature of intelligence per se, Inhelder recognized that this work could be significant in the diagnosis of individual differences.

Inhelder's work proved useful in two respects. First, the type of clinical assessment that Piaget used to study the development of intelligence proved to be a useful approach in the practice of diagnosis of individual children. The procedure is more penetrating than are standardized responses to traditional intelligence test items. Second, the theoretical formulation of stages held promise for the categorization of different levels of mental retardation. Clinically, Inhelder found that insufficiency in reasoning in mentally retarded children could be identified as a fixation at one or another of the early stages of development.

The utility of this stage concept as outlined by Inhelder and Piaget, while not fully realized at the time of the first edition of the book, has, however, been demonstrated in the last twenty-five years, both by Inhelder and by others. She has summarized this work in the introduction to the second edition.

Some words of preparation for American psychologists of the 1960s may be in order. For one thing, the research methodology that characterizes the work of the Geneva Group lacks the precision to which American readers are accustomed. Piaget and Inhelder have often been charged with methodological shortcomings, a charge which may to some extent be justified. It is, however, important to realize the merits of their methodological approach in the early exploratory stages of an investigation. Important findings rarely are quantifiable at the onset, and whereas a rigid methodological structure may produce comprehensible numbers, this may occur at the expense of hiding complex and real phenomena. Flexible exploratory work can reveal aspects which merit and demand a great deal of scrutiny before it is clear just what ought to be measured and how. Inhelder has discussed this in a brief section of the introduction to the second edition, "Statistical Procedures of Standardization and Evaluation." These pages deserve particular attention. A more specific point, which may take contemporary readers by surprise, is the reference to homogeneous development of the retarded. It is important to realize, as Inhelder herself insists, that she is concerned with homogeneity only within the area of reasoning.

Evaluation gains accuracy when afforded the luxury of retrospection. After twenty-five years, Inhelder's *The Diagnosis of Reasoning in the Mentally Retarded* remains the major research effort to relate Piaget's theory of the development of intelligence to the area of retardation. The enduring value of this work lies in its detailed demonstration of the use of Piaget's theory of cognitive development to assess the intellectual development of a retardate and in its delineation of the diagnostic techniques involved. Findings from this initial study continue to serve as the framework for research in the area of retardation which draws from Piaget's theory of the development of intelligence.

WILL BETH STEPHENS

Temple University
Philadelphia, Pennsylvania
April 1968

References in Translator's Introduction

Inhelder, Bärbel
    1962   "Piaget's Genetic Approach to Cognition," *in* "Thought in the Young Child," William Kessen and Clementina Kuhlmann, eds., *Monographs of the Society for Research in Child Development, 83,* 27, 2.

Inhelder, Bärbel, and Piaget, Jean
    1958   *The Growth of Logical Thinking from Childhood to Adolescence.* (French 1955, English 1958), New York, Basic Books.
    1963   *The Early Growth of Logic.* (French 1959, English 1963), London, Routledge and Kegan Paul.

Piaget, Jean
    1950b   *The Psychology of Intelligence.* (French 1947), New York, Harcourt, Brace.
    1952   *The Origins of Intelligence in Children.* New York, International Universities Press.
    1954   *The Construction of Reality in the Child.* New York, Basic Books.

Piaget, Jean, and Inhelder, Bärbel
    1951   *La Genèse de l'idée de hasard chez l'enfant.* Paris, Presses Universitaires de France.
    1956   *The Child's Conception of Space.* (French 1947, English 1956), London, Routledge and Kegan Paul.
    1962   *Le Développement des quantités physiques chez l'enfant,* 2d ed. Neuchâtel, Delachaux and Niestlé.
    1966a   *L'Image mentale chez l'enfant.* Paris, Presses Universitaires de France.
    1966b   *La Psychologie de l'enfant: Collection "Que Sais-je."* Paris, Presses Universitaires de France.
    (In press)   *Mémoire à intelligence.*

Piaget, Jean, Inhelder, Bärbel, and Szeminska, Alina
   1960   *The Child's Conception of Geometry.* (French 1948, English
          1960), London, Routledge and Kegan Paul.
Piaget, Jean, and Szeminska, Alina
   1952   *The Child's Conception of Number.* (French 1941, English
          1952), London, Routledge and Kegan Paul.

Glossary*

Accommodation, or outer adaptation, serves as a complement to assimilation and occurs when environmental conditions require coping which necessitates a modification, revision, or rearrangement of existing mental structures or schemas.

[It] refers to an activity; although the modification of assimilatory schemas is admittedly brought about by resistance of the objects, it is not simply dictated by the object but rather by the subject attempting to overcome this resistance (this can therefore come about as either an immediate reaction or through trial and error, etc.). But secondly, even if accommodation is an activity serving to differentiate assimilatory schemas, it has only a derived or secondary status vis-à-vis assimilation [Piaget and Gréco 1959; 44].

Assimilation corresponds to inner organization and occurs when an organism incorporates something from his environment into his cognitive structure.

[It] implies the transformation of perceptions in such a way as to render them identical to one's own thought, that is to say, with prior schemes. To assimilate is therefore to conserve and in a certain sense to identify [Piaget 1956a: 142].

Concept Formation (concept and scheme)

A concept is simply a scheme of action or operation, and it is in carrying out actions engendering A and B that one will be concerned as to whether or not they are comparable [Piaget 1947: 41].

Decalage, time lag, or temporal displacement, is a downward dropping movement from one plane to another and is used to refer to aspects of cognitive development which appear at a stage subsequent to the one at which they normally are expected.

* By Will Beth Stephens. Acknowledgment is made of Michael J. Chandler's assistance in the preparation of the portions of the glossary that are derived directly from Piaget's writings.

31

(vertical)

. . . decalages in comprehension refer to passage from one to another plane of activity. For example: from the plane of action to that of representation [Piaget 1950a: 330].

. . . the child appears at the onset not to reflect, in words or in notions, the operations which he already knows how to execute in acts and if he cannot reflect on them, he is obliged . . . to carry out once again the work of coordination between assimilation and accommodation already accomplished in his previous sensory-motor adaption to the physical and practical universe [Piaget 1950a: 317].

(horizontal)

. . . horizontal decalages occur at a common level of development but between different systems of actions or ideas. For example: conservation of the notion of quantity of material before the conservation of the notion of weight, where the same groupments of actions are in play (simple addition or variants of parts) but which are applied to qualitatively different contents (substance and weight) [Piaget 1941b: 263].

Decentering makes possible the coordination of different viewpoints. As organization and coordination develop, it becomes possible to consider two relations, such as height and weight, at the same time rather than centering on one aspect only.

. . . the decentration of an ensemble is a . . . recasting of a system of perspectives or evaluations [Piaget 1956b: 68–69].

. . . progressive decentering of actions, that is to say, an elimination of egocentrism . . . stemming from the fact that initial actions become reversible and operatory [Piaget and Inhelder 1962: 339].

Groupment

From a genetic point of view, logical and infralogical operations precede numerical and metric operations. These primitive operations are based upon the structure of a groupment. Concrete psychological operations present a groupment structure in the same sense that formal operations present an "INRC Group" structure (propositional-combinatorial) . . . the psychological criteria of groupment properties is the discovery of the conservation of totalities independent of the arrangement of their parts [Piaget 1949a: 85].

INRC Group

[INRC] is the system of operations known to logicians as the INRC group . . . The letters I, N, R, and C in the name for this group have the following referents:

(1) Identity operator (I) is an operation which, when performed on any proposition, leaves it unchanged.

(2) Negation or inverse (N) refers to the relationship between the operators in symbolic logic. Thus *dysjunction* is the inverse of *cojoint negation,* and *conjunction* is the inverse of *incompatibility.*

(3) Reciprocal (R) refers to the relationship between the operators *disjunction* and *incompatibility* on one hand, and between the operators *conjunction* and *cojoint negation* on the other.

(4) Correlate (C) refers to the relationship between *disjunction* and *conjunction* on one hand, and to the relationship between *incompatibility* and *cojoint negation* on the other . . . [Hunt 1961: 233].*

Juxtaposition refers to the cognitive habit of linking one thought element to another without regard for causal or logical relations.

This phenomena refers to the inability of the child to produce a thoroughly coherent narrative or explanation and, on the contrary, a tendency to break down the whole into a series of fragmentary and incoherent statements. These statements are juxtaposed to the extent that neither causal nor temporal relations exist between them [Piaget 1956b: 123].

Logico-Mathematical

Piaget states that logic "is the basis of all elementary structures, and particularly those which antedate mathematization" [Piaget 1949b: 99]. In this sense Piaget uses the term logico-mathematical to refer to all those structures characterized either by mathematical principles or by more primitive or elementary principles of logic [Chandler 1967].

Operation may be defined psychologically as an action which can be internalized and which is reversible; thus, addition, subtraction, multiplication, and division are operations. Operations are coordinated into systems which are characterized by laws which apply to the system as a whole.

. . . psychologically an operation is an interiorized action which becomes reversible through its coordination with other interiorized actions in a structural whole possessing certain laws governing that totality [Piaget, Beth, and Mays 1957: 35].

Reversibility is the capacity of inversing an operation of mind or the ability to study a problem from two opposite viewpoints.

We will define reversibility as the capacity to execute a particular action or annul it while remaining cognizant that it constitutes the same action [Piaget, Apostel, and Mandelbrot 1957: 44].

Scheme is the part of an action that is transferable to the same situations or is generalizable in analogous situations. In genetic psychology, a scheme

* Reprinted with permission from J. McV. Hunt, *Intelligence and Experience* © 1961, The Ronald Press Company, New York.

is an active mental structure which deforms and reforms by assimilating the environment or accommodating to it.

The schème of an action is, by definition, the structural ensemble of the generalizable characteristics of that action, that is to say, those which permit the repetition of the same action or its application to new concepts. The schème of an action is, however, neither perceptible (one may perceive a particular action but not its schème) nor directly available to introspection. One becomes aware of its implications only through repeating the action and comparing its successive results [Piaget and Beth 1961: 251].

Structured Whole refers to the movement of thought toward the construction of a whole; relationships between its parts are separable as well as integrated.

We speak of a structure . . . when elements are joined into a totality possessing certain wholistic properties and when the properties of the elements depend entirely or partially on the characteristics of the totality [Piaget, Apostel, and Mandelbrot 1957: 34].

Syncretism

It is the spontaneous tendency of children to perceive through global visions rather than through the discerning of details, to find, without benefit of analysis, immediate analogies between objects or unfamiliar words, to link naturally heterogeneous events, even fortuitous ones.

In brief it is the tendency to relate everything with everything. Syncretism is therefore an excess [Piaget 1956a: 13].

Transductive refers to mental processes which pass from one particular case to another particular case without using general information. The term implies passage from singular to singular or special to special without evoking general laws or comprehending the reciprocity of relations.

Stern has baptized this reasoning process transduction as opposed to induction and deduction [Piaget 1956a: 154].

References in Glossary

Chandler, Michael J.
1967 "Definition of Terms Found in Piaget's Writings" (personal communication). Geneva, University of Geneva.

Hunt, J. McV.
1961 *Intelligence and Experience.* New York, Ronald Press.

Piaget, Jean
1941b "Le Mécanisme du développement mental et les lois du groupement des opérations: Esquisse d'une théorie opératoire de l'intelligence," *Archives de psychologie, 28,* 215–85.
1947 *La Psychologie de l'intelligence.* (English 1950), Paris, A. Colin.
1949a *Introduction à l'épistémologie génétique: 1. La Pensée mathématique.* Paris, Presses Universitaires de France.
1949b *Traité de logique: Essai de logistique opératoire.* Paris, A. Colin.
1950a *La Construction du réel chez l'enfant,* 2d ed. (English 1954), Neuchâtel, Delachaux and Niestlé.
1956a *Le Jugement et le raisonnement chez l'enfant,* 4th ed. (English 1928), Neuchâtel, Delachaux and Niestlé.
1956b *Le Langage et la pensée chez l'enfant,* 4th ed. (English 1926), Neuchâtel, Delachaux and Niestlé.

Piaget, Jean, Apostel, L., and Mandelbrot, B.
1957 "Logique et équilibre," *Études d'épistémologie génétique, 2,* Paris, Presses Universitaires de France.

Piaget, Jean, and Beth, Evert W.
1961 "Épistémologie mathématique et psychologie: Essai sur les relations entre la logique formelle et la pensée réelle," *Études d'épistémologie génétique, 14,* Paris, Presses Universitaires de France.

Piaget, Jean, Beth, Evert W., and Mays, W.
　　1957　"Épistémologie génétique et recherche psychologique," *Études d'épistémologie génétique, 1,* Paris, Presses universitaires de France.

Piaget, Jean, and Gréco, Pierre
　　1959　"Apprentissage et connaissance," *Études d'épistémologie génétique, 7,* Paris, Presses Universitaires de France.

Piaget, Jean, and Inhelder, Bärbel
　　1962　*Le Développement des quantités physiques chez l'enfant,* 2d ed. Neuchâtel, Delachaux and Niestlé.

THE DIAGNOSIS OF REASONING
IN THE MENTALLY RETARDED

1. Developmental Theories and Diagnosis of Mental Development

Whatever their causes, children's mental troubles are essentially of two forms: (1) retardations, which are comparable to what psychiatry frequently terms "hypo" troubles, and (2) states of disequilibrium, such as an exaggeration of certain traits (*e.g.,* emotional overreaction), functional difficulties (*e.g.,* lack of interest or inattention), or various types of instability, all of which can be called "para" troubles. In general psychiatric theory, mental troubles have been conceived of for some time as fixations at some early stage of development. We are making the same hypothesis for intellectual troubles: we see "hypo" troubles as simple arrestations; "para" troubles, also fixations, we see as being due to difficulties in effecting the integrations which under normal conditions assure functional continuity from one level to the next.

If this general hypothesis is right—and as a first approximation it seems to us well founded—then diagnostic procedures must attempt to compare a given trouble with characteristics of a certain level of normal development. "Comparing" in this context means establishing differences as well as resemblances, of course.

Although the formulation is simple, its application is not because of disagreement concerning the laws of development. Each diagnostic system depends on its underlying idea of normal development. It is clear that development cannot be described by a collection of raw facts. It requires interpretation. Each author of a diagnostic system conceives of mental development in his own way, and his interpretation is clearly reflected in his method. Therefore, it is necessary to set forth the developmental theory implied in each.

Moreover, as we shall see below, there are sometimes considerable differences between a developmental theory and the practical procedures inspired by it. Often an author has more subtle ideas about development than his applied psychology would lead one to suppose, or conversely, his practice may imply a theory of development to which he has in fact given very little formulation. We must keep in mind these differences between a theory and its application.

It is impossible to analyze all the systems of mental diagnosis in this brief summary, which is intended only to place our own work with respect to other systems and to point out the problems. We limit ourselves to discussing authors who have contributed distinctive views of mental development and precise methods of diagnosis. Moreover, we limit ourselves to the diagnosis of development, without looking at the diagnosis of aptitudes. We do not of course go into questions of techniques.

The aim of this first chapter, then, is to show the main possible approaches to mental development among which authors have oscillated. We see three such approaches, which can be ordered on a continuum, along which there are, of course, many intermediate stages.

1. MENTAL DEVELOPMENT CONCEIVED AS A SIMPLE ADDITION OF SUCCESSIVE ACQUISITIONS (without any hypothesis as to the mechanism of such acquisitions). This conception supposes the existence of a ready-made mental structure, in which the contents alone are acquired progressively by personal experience or by education. The internal mechanism of evolution, therefore, is simply the unfolding of this structure.

Such a theory has scant acceptance at the present time, because there is general recognition of some active construction in mental development. Reducing development to the simple sum of successive acquisitions is in fact a denial of this activity. Although almost no contemporary author completely denies the active and constructive character of the evolution of mental functions, there are many who refuse to define the mechanism of this evolution. Out of scientific caution, they believe that it is possible to study only exterior results, *i.e.,* acquisitions. Alfred Binet, for one, did not deny that mental structures change as they develop, but he did not think he could usefully study the transformations, and therefore he held himself to the study of performance in terms of age, as though it were simply a question of summation, without qualitative change. Whether you deny progressive structuration as an explanation of mental development or whether you simply decide not to study its detail, the practical result is the same. This situation can be compared with that frequently found in the exact sciences. Positivism made a principle of refusing to study causes. Others, such as Galileo, Newton, and those whom Leon Brunschvicg called "positivists in spite of themselves" simply put off this study and were concerned only with the laws of phenomena considered as effects. In the study of human development there are also many "positivists in spite of themselves." Alfred Binet serves as a prototype. Binet's approach consists in studying mental development only by its results and neglects the search for causes (structural development).

We shall see later how this approach to mental development gives rise to the classical method of testing, aimed at finding a solution to a specific practical problem.

2. MENTAL DEVELOPMENT REGARDED AS A LINEAR AND CUMULATIVE SUCCESSION OF STRUCTURES. According to this interpretation, new acquisitions are not considered in isolation as inexplicable facts or as simple products of experience, but as elements determined by the mental structure of the subject at a given level. These structures follow one another in a regular order, although later ones do not necessarily grow out of earlier ones. Each structure characterizes a stage or a natural period, and these stages succeed each other linearly. Each new mechanism integrates the preceding ones, thus giving rise to the possibility of simple arrestations and troubles of integration. Different successive types of thought described by Janet under the names of "assertive belief," "reflective belief," "sense of reality," etc., are examples of these stages, as are the different systems of cortical integration described by Wallon.

In this view of development, diagnosis consists of determining clinically the stage corresponding to the trouble, or the level at which integration was inadequate.

3. MENTAL DEVELOPMENT REGARDED AS A PROGRESSIVE ORGANIZATION OF AN OPERATIONAL MECHANISM. New mechanisms are not simply superimposed and integrated after the fact, but are successive

forms of equilibrium of a common internal process of organization. This third interpretation, like the second, posits a succession of qualitatively distinct mental structures, but in addition it posits a law of construction whereby the stages are related to each other by the same operational mechanism. Furthermore, there are no general stages. In any one area, there are linear stages of development, but these do not necessarily correspond to the progression of stages in another area.

The diagnostic method that corresponds to this third interpretation is the clinical method in its most general sense. Specifically, the diagnosis of reasoning processes consists of attempting to ascertain the thought mechanisms and the successive operations which constitute them.

In the following analysis we will give only one or two examples to illustrate each of these views, without trying to be exhaustive. In order to place our position in perspective, we will emphasize the points on which there is greatest divergence, rather than look at intermediate points of agreement.

1. Mental Development Conceived as a Simple Addition of Successive Acquisitions

We must of course start with Alfred Binet, whose "metric scale of intelligence" (Binet and Simon 1917; see also Binet and Simon 1905) was the first precise instrument for the diagnosis of mental development. No procedure of psychological examination has known such great success, nor given rise to such varied adaptations, but at the same time none has provoked such lively criticism. While recognizing the obvious objections of principle and of method, it is not possible to contest Binet's merit: he opened the way for a scientific diagnosis of inferior stages of intelligence (Rey 1935).

In judging this ingenious method, it is necessary to remember Binet's aim, of which certain disciples and adversaries of the method appear to have lost sight. For Binet, the measure of intelligence was not an exact translation of a theory of mental development. He was a cautious experimentalist, on guard against formulating, or at least against publishing, a complete system; his instrument was to be used for detecting and sorting out mental anomalies.

How Binet was led to elaborate this instrument is a matter of common knowledge (Binet and Simon 1917). Very early in his career he was interested in the physical signs of intelligence. At that time he took head measurements and sought to determine whether a correlation existed between mental and physical development. In his attempts to see whether there was a relationship between variations in head measurements and variations in intelligence, he realized how vague and inadequate were the psychological and psychiatric classifications of that period. There was clearly a need for more precise means of investigation.

At the same time, French school authorities were starting to plan a program of instruction for slow and retarded children. Binet was given the task of identifying these children. The need to identify retarded children brought him back to his first problem: to establish for all age groups the characteristics of normal intelligence.

With these two goals in mind, Binet and his collaborator, T. Simon, presented a great many problems, experiments, and questions of all sorts to a large group of children of different ages. The average success or failure among children of a given age was taken as normal intelligence for that age (Binet and Simon 1908). Binet distrusted single tests. This is evidenced, for example, in his criticism of Biervliet's attention test (Binet 1913). He did not see intelligence as the product of one particular function, but rather as a composite in which interest, attention, and savoir faire, as well as reasoning, play separate roles. It is the totality of these reactions to the external world that gives an individual his intellectual value. To examine intelligence, one must furnish the subject with many opportunities to show what he can do, but at the same time eliminate as much as possible strictly scholastic acquisitions.

Even if the choice and scaling of tests can be established only on the basis of experience, and even if they need to be continually controlled by this experience, they are not fortuitous and arbitrary. The simplicity of Binet's metric scale leads us too often to forget that he was a subtle psychologist. In his well-conceived experimental studies (Binet 1903), he shows that children differ from adults not only in degree but in quality, and more specifically in a weakness of invention, of comprehension, and of censure. Intelligence tests must, then, get at development in these areas and omit others which are less important developmentally. Thus, scattered among the items, we find problems in invention and comprehension. It is regrettable that the psychological analysis of these tests had to give way to the demands for a global measure.

As Binet examined children whose mental retardation had already been clinically established, he obtained results that were comparable in every way to those of younger normal children. The greater the retardation, the younger the normal child of comparable performance. This supported the conclusion that age level was one good interpretation to give to performance on a test.

This does not mean, as a superficial interpretation of Binet's thought too often tends to imply, that the mentality of a retardate is exactly the same as that of a younger child. His interesting observations on imbeciles (Binet 1909) show how misleading such an affirmation would be. Binet merely says that, given the same problems as a normal child, a retardate can solve ones which can be solved by a normal child X years younger. Mental age thus becomes the measurable index of intelligence.

But let us remember what that means: these "measurements," even for Binet, did not have a true mathematical value. They simply give an order or a scale. Just as a child can be physically taller or shorter than the average child of his age, so can he be more or less advanced intellectually in relation to the average. But, whereas the difference of height can be measured directly by comparing the height of the subject to the average height of his contemporaries, the difference in intelligence can be expressed only by the number of years or months of intellectual advance or retardation. The "metric scale" is nonetheless an original and practical method of mental evaluation and has become the prototype of all tests of development.

Although the Binet-Simon test is an excellent means for the rapid detection of mental anomalies, it cannot meet the demands of a psychological "diagnosis" of thought because:

A. Binet's tests do not take into consideration structural, or even functional, questions. What is this intelligence he attempts to measure? This question has been asked ever since the appearance of the "metric scale" and has been the focus of discussion in all the critical studies. In reality, the test tells us only what a child in a given situation can or cannot do, compared with standardized results of groups of children of different ages, and this makes it possible to place the child on a chronological scale. So it actually measures the results of previous activities and acquisitions—that is, the algebraic sum of successes and failures. There is no attempt at causal analysis. It remains a very tricky problem to go further and conclude from this summation of results anything about the way the child arrived at them, the intellectual constructions that enabled him to do so, or the nature of the deficiencies from which his failures stemmed. Of course, the alert experimenter will see qualities that cannot be measured numerically. One must anticipate, with any test, a fairly large margin for clinical intuition. But this means that the value of the diagnosis will depend on the skill of the clinician, and the fact remains that the instrument itself lacks the power of analysis that alone assures adequate knowledge of thought development and its pathology.

B. One inadequacy gives rise to another; the genetic problem remains unsolved. Does the intelligence scale express a natural development? Can levels of mental age be considered as stages of a real evolution? Let us recall that the notion of mental age was defined as the algebraic sum of successes and failures and simply represents an average output. It does not necessarily express the dominant characteristics of a level of development. This is evident in view of the fact —which Binet himself pointed out—that success on any one test does not imply success on all tests for lower age groups. However, the integration of previous acquisitions seems to us to be the first criterion of a genuine evolution. Far from being worried by this, Binet, along with all supporters of synthetic or global tests, was quite happy with the rather unusual idea that a child can make up for his failures by success in other areas. For example, failure at the fifth-year level will be compensated for by a success in the tests for higher ages, or inversely, a success can be canceled out by a negative result in quite a different test. This compensation takes place not only among tests of the same kind, so that a failure due to inattention can be made up by a success on the same problem presented in another form, but among qualitatively different tests. One cannot help being concerned by an empiricism so like that of school examinations. Must an individual's intelligence be judged by this interplay of compensations? Are there not deeper signs of how his intellectual operations are functioning? The idea of mental age cannot as such be considered a genetic stage. The first deals with performance, the second with underlying construction, and even if the study of performance is useful as a first approximation, it cannot replace the study of construction.

C. Obviously, a test which measures only acquisitions cannot deal with the laws of transformation that tend to characterize and to explain successive levels of mental evolution. Some of the Binet tests reduce the idea of progress to a simple juxtaposition of knowledge and techniques, like counting change, giving the days of the week in reverse order, etc. Some of them measure the increase in attention or memory span: *e.g.*, an eight-year-old can retain a larger string of numbers or can reproduce more syllables than a four-year-old. Some of them, however, measure real and qualitative transformations, such as the transition from enumeration to description and interpretation of pictures, or the development of different types of definitions, or reactions to absurd sentences. But these few really revealing tests are mingled with the others, so the stages they mark cannot be scaled.

In general, the relation between the "scale of intelligence" and the ensemble of Binet's psychological conceptions is paradoxical. His genetic studies have such subtlety and depth that it is hard to understand such a surprising simplification where it comes to measurement, though admittedly it was due to practical demands.

Nevertheless, Binet's inspiration in the domain of mental diagnosis has been most fruitful. General treatises like those of Stern (1928), Claparède (1924), Decroly and Buyse (1928), and many others are ample testimony to this fecundity. In the specific area of our interests —the genetic diagnosis of reasoning—we shall discuss two of the principal ideas that stem from Binet: (1) the quantification of global and specific levels and their relation to actual age, and (2) the analytic profile of development.

(1) Some psychologists have tried to estimate intellectual age in a more precise and detailed manner by seeking to determine the levels at which particularly revealing aptitudes or notions appear. We find some clear examples in the tests that Alice Descoeudres (1920) developed by drawing on the ideas of Binet and his successor Decroly. Decroly's *Etudes de psychogenèse* (1932) studies the development of notions of quantity, time, and color, of questions asked, of different forms of competition, etc. His studies of the beginnings of enumeration and quantification are particularly interesting. These observations furnish tableaux of development in which the acquisitions for each age in each of the domains are presented. Yet Decroly did not extend his study to the point where he could speak of stages of evolution characterized by changes in the intellectual structure of the notions or operations he was examining.

Alice Descoeudres, as she followed the development of each pupil in her classes, felt the need to know and even to measure normal development in a more searching way than had been done up until then, in order to place retarded children with respect to a developmental scale. She established a variety of tests that included language, manual skills, and observation. By far the most highly developed was the examination of language. It was composed of twenty-five questions pertaining to comprehension, vocabulary, knowledge, and judgment, arranged in a certain order, and each child was given all of them. A child's total number of successes determined his linguistic level. Mental or intellectual age was established by averaging several tests, so that it was the result of a combination of partial values. The correlation between these averages and the levels of the Binet-Simon tests seems to have been relatively high.

There is no question that such meticulous observation and measurement of a particular function (*e.g.,* spoken language and verbal comprehension) have much to contribute, both to general psychology and to diagnosis. They permit comparisons of the development of children of different social environments, languages, sexes, and races.

However, from the point of view of the relations between developmental theories and their application to diagnosis, whatever the progress of these differentiated tests over the Binet-Simon tests, they remain measures of acquisitions, and not of the operations that make the acquisitions possible. They are clearly less heterogeneous than the Binet-Simon tests, but they do not go any further in the direction of describing the mechanism of mental evolution. The quantification of successive outputs can never adequately express the internal dynamism of development.

It was Stern who introduced the notion of intellectual quotient. As the word indicates, the quotient expresses a relation between mental age and actual age. This notion corresponds to the observation that the degree of retardation, which since Binet had been expressed in terms of years, is not absolute, but relative to the level of development. For example, a retardation of two years is a great deal more serious at five years than at twelve years. The intellectual quotient proved to be just about constant. This is interesting because it underlines the relativity of any new acquisition with respect to the sum of previous acquisitions. Thus, a retardation of two years in the acquisitions of a twelve-year-old corresponds to a retardation of one year in the acquisitions of a six-year-old, etc., so that making up a year for a six-year-old is equivalent to making up two for a twelve-year-old.

(2) Besides questions of mental age, psychological diagnosis has also dealt with the diagnosis of specific aptitudes, as explored by Claparède (1924). Although not of direct concern in the diagnosis of retardation, the problem of measuring individual differences has indirect relevance insofar as it contributes to the study of development.

After Rossolimo (1926) and Claparède (1917), Vermeylen (1922) made use of the analytic method of profiles by combining it with the global measure of mental age. Vermeylen singled out functions of acquisition, of elaboration, and of execution in mental activity. He established fifteen series of tests for the principal mental functions, with ten levels of difficulty in each series. A diagram linked the highest levels attained by the subject within each area, and the total number of points indicated the global mental level. This method made it possible to link three types of data: the partial level for each function, the relation between the functions, and finally the global age.

The use which Vermeylen made of these tests in classifying types of mental deficiency is well known. We are indebted to him for having verified experimentally what until then had been only a clinical observation, namely that mental functions do not progress in a regular manner, and that the relations among them can vary even within the same global result. The mental profiles translate the variety of different types of mental retardation.

Nevertheless, the fact is that this comparison of particular functions remains imbued with a certain empiricism, accepting without question the possibility of juxtaposing partial mental activities and measuring the performance of each one, without taking into account their internal mechanisms or coordination.

In the same direction, Charlotte Bühler and her collaborators (Bühler and Hetzer 1932) provided more precise measures of early childhood development. She developed a group of tests designed to meet the needs of schools. For Binet, the task had been limited to an identification of retarded children; for Stern and the Americans it had expanded to the selection of the gifted, and for that reason it needed prognostic indices. In both cases, the maximum output of an individual is measured. But it is quite a different matter to uncover an inadequacy and to make a diagnosis that includes recommendations for treatment. Here the psychologist needs a global view of the child in his free and full unfolding.

Such a diagnostic procedure must be based on preliminary knowledge of psychological behavior in its most general sense. To have understood this necessity and undertaken this preparatory work with great experimental ingenuity and remarkable statistical precision appears to us to be one of the great merits of Charlotte Bühler. Similar efforts have been made by Gesell (1925), but the resulting diagnostic instrument was neither as practical nor as precise as that of Charlotte Bühler.

In the total picture of the child's behavior, everything is not equally symptomatic either of the child's individual character or of his level of development. Observation requires direction. However, the directions or dimensions of the observation cannot be determined a priori; they are established by a complete inventory of behavior in the course of the first year. This systematization, based on the observed frequency of diverse types of action, led Bühler to distinguish the following six "dimensions": sensibility, movement, sociability, learning, manipulation of objects (*Materialarbeitung*), and intellectual activity. Once the first kinds of behavior have been noted, it becomes relatively easy to see what is in each of the dimensions. The age level can then be determined experimentally. The tests are scaled by months for the first eight months, by intervals of two months until the end of the first year, and then by intervals of six months.

The different observational dimensions become modes of description. In addition to intellectual level (modeled on Binet-Simon), the descriptive and graphic representation of the profile gives an analytical picture of behavior. In a harmonious development, all the dimensions are at equal levels. In more heterogeneous cases, the partial advances or retardations are marked by oscillations in the profile. Of course this is only a descriptive picture and does not give the etiology of the mental troubles. Such are the advantages of Bühler's approach over the simple measure of global level or age averages. It represents undeniable progress in psychological analysis.

Although the tests deal with general behavior, and not the results of learned acquisitions, they are still based solely on successes or failures, and neglect the underlying mental processes. Despite Charlotte Bühler's impressive work on stages, age levels still appear to be defined more by output on test items than by actual stages of thought or behavior. This is due to the fact that the dimensions among themselves do not form a homogeneous entity. Describing static states of different simultaneous processes is not the same thing as understanding their internal relations and developmental laws. This absence of unity within levels, the static description of independent elements, poses an interesting problem, which Bühler herself was the first to see. In her *Kindheit und Jugend* (Bühler 1928), she sought to sketch the beginnings of consciousness as rhythmic movement back and forth between subjectivization and objectivization, and between differentiation and synthesis.

A newborn infant is enclosed in a state of pure subjectivism. During the first year he starts to become oriented toward the external world, taking hold of objects and establishing means-end relationships among them. In a second phase, between the second and fourth years, he subjectivizes the external world. This is the period of the first symbols and conscious volition, as he starts the pursuit of goals. During a third phase, between the fifth and eighth years, an important transition takes place from fiction to reality, from play to building and work. Objective interests are aroused at the same time, as he begins to submit to the rules of the community. A fourth phase, between the ninth and thirteenth years, marks the beginning of a dissociation between the ego and the external world, as he becomes conscious of himself as an individual distinct from the universe. Finally, during a fifth phase, this oscillation between subjectivity and objectivity achieves a synthesis in the form of a personality situated in the universe.

Thus, each phase is determined, not by the appearance of acquisitions or isolated functions, but by the dominance of a formal principle; each phase develops from the preceding phases by differentiation and synthesis.

Here Charlotte Bühler's work raises a curious problem: why is this evolutionary principle, designed to explain the principal stages of consciousness, so hard to detect in these tests? Is it because the mechanism of intellectual evolution cannot be detected by specific, precise experiments? Or, if it could be, would the stages so discovered be without any practical significance for mental diagnosis? What is the reason for the discontinuity between the developmental theory and the accompanying techniques? Perhaps the answer is that the theory and the diagnostic tests really stem from two different positions; that when psychologists construct testing scales, they behave like "positivists in spite of themselves," renouncing genetic explanation and temporarily seeing development as a gradual cumulation of acquisitions, while remaining ready to change their attitude and to refine their ideas when they return to the realm of theory.

It does not serve our present purposes to try to answer this thought-provoking question, but it may gain the attention of future historians of experimental psychology. Perhaps a study of the stages of cumulative functions (second conception) and of operational organization (third conception) will prove to be the best way to approach the significance of this question for diagnostic theory. The remarkable thing is that here again in Bühler's work we find the dualism that appears to characterize all test authors to the present time, the dualism between a general theory of development and a diagnostic instrument adapted for the needs of practical psychology.

In summary, the first point of view (development equals the sum of acquisitions) appears to stem above all from a preoccupation with measurement. In each of the authors cited above, there is a general tendency to express mental diagnosis—like all findings of experimental psychology for that matter—by means of mathematical indices. This need for precision is easy to understand, and has always been reinforced by the positivist notion that there is no exact science without measurement and that, furthermore, laws expressed in metric values do away with the need for any other explanation. From this belief were born metric scales such as Binet's, wherein test results are expressed in terms of a time difference from the average age of performance; or aptitude tests, wherein results are expressed in dispersion tables (Galton's ogive, percentiles, etc.); or various procedures designed to portray psychological profiles graphically or to calculate correlations among various sets of data.

Two comments are necessary; the first is that in psychology one tends too often to take measurements whose significance is unknown. Even so fervent a supporter of measurement as Claparède (1924: 83): "You must test the tests," *i.e.,* determine their exact psychological meaning. No measurement can dispense with the search for causes that science constantly pursues—in spite of the false positivist ideal. Second, since psychological measures are always based on averages and correlations, *i.e.,* on statistical facts, the genetic mechanism itself always remains out of reach. The products of intellectual operations are measured, not the operations themselves. We might ask, then, if the operations are not impossible to measure, and if the most exact way to describe them does not consist in analyzing their "groupings" or "groups" as Piaget has tried to do, and as this author has tried to do with him in a study of the development of quantities in the child (Piaget and Inhelder 1941). In this case it is the "grouping" of possible operations that determines the level of development, and not the statistical frequency of the results. Again, we are studying only those operations which are put into use, that is to say results, but in "groupings" we are able to get at the formation of the operations as well as their products.

2. Mental Development Regarded as a Linear and Cumulative Succession of Structures

Another conception of development that is highly instructive for the present research was supplied by Pierre Janet. This author, instead of using developmental psychology as a point of departure for pathology, moved in the opposite direction. Clinical observations of psychoneurotic adults (see in particular, Janet 1894 and 1926, *1*) inspired his famous hierarchical table and led to his general interest in developmental studies.

His original conception of the mind was as a hierarchical synthesis of systems, of which the highest was the conscious ego, and the lower consisted of different kinds of actions which could break out unconsciously as "automatisms." From this conception, Janet deduced his famous idea of mental "oscillations": mental activity could adopt successively either higher or lower forms, the lower forms being the only ones possible in various states of illness. This hypothesis of oscillations was still static, but Janet went on to a clearly developmental point of view by translating his various "levels of activity" into stages of development. In so doing, he came in line with a classical notion of French psychiatry. According to most French psychiatrists—Blondel (1914) being a notable exception—mental illness is understood as an arrestation of development or as a regression. In his studies of neurosis, Janet pointed out the temporary or permanent disintegration of higher tendencies, giving free rein to lower functions. Similarly, in his conception, retarded subjects never go beyond the lower functions. Janet goes so far as to find in epileptic convulsions the diffuse agitation of the most primitive systems (impulsive reflex movements).

As an example of this parallelism between developmental stages and pathological states, let us take Janet's comparison between hysteria and psychoasthenia, each characterized by unrealistic beliefs. There are two distinct types of beliefs: the beliefs that are not based on reflection and those that are. Hysteria is characterized by the first kind of belief, while the beliefs of psychoasthenia are thought out, and reflect a loss of the higher functions (the sense of reality is abolished in the "disease of doubt"). Belief in the imaginary, then, characterizes an early stage, and considered belief stems from a more evolved system. In fact, an hysteric patient believes in what he desires or fears. There is immediate, uncritical affirmation, inspired by the strongest impulse of the moment. For Janet, this belief in the imaginary is an intermediate stage of development between inconsistent language, which precedes it, and reflection, which follows. According to Janet, this mentality is similar to the egocentrism that Piaget sees as a predominant characteristic in children under seven or eight years of age.

The stage of reflection comes about through the confrontation of various elementary beliefs, so that reflective belief is essentially a social product. Again, Janet points to the parallel with Piaget's description of children from seven to eleven years becoming capable of an ever-increasing collaboration. However, reflection is not everything. Observation of psychoasthenic states in which the patient is quite capable of logical thought but still does not adapt himself to experience indicates a breakdown of the sense of reality, which undermines the logical reflection.

In order to base diagnosis on a rational principle of development which corresponds in reverse order to the levels of disintegration in different mental illnesses, Janet established a hierarchical table of all psychological tendencies. Here is a brief summary of that table:

TABLE I

Janet's Hierarchy of Psychological Tendencies	
Lower Tendencies	Reflex or explosive stage Perceptual or suspensive stage Socio-personal stage
Middle Tendencies	Intellectual stage (elementary operations) Stage of inconsistent language Stage of imaginary belief Stage of reflection
Higher Tendencies	Stage of the function of reality Experimental stage Progressive stage

Such a hierarchy makes it possible to think in terms of a series of evolving stages; the main idea derives from Ribot's law, which holds that the most recently acquired functions are the ones that are most readily destroyed. This seriation of functions makes it possible to establish an order of destruction in mental illnesses, using as a frame of reference the absence or presence of these functions in the various forms of retardation. In mental retardation, the idiot would be at the level of lower functions, while the imbecile can attain the level of elementary operations or that of inconsistent language. With a normal person, all the tendencies are integrated, and their genesis corresponds to an order of increasing difficulty and complexity from reflex to reasoning, the criterion of difficulty being the quantity of energy spent for each action.

After having constructed a genetic psychology that was, in a sense, deduced from this hierarchy of tendencies in patients, Janet sought to study the successive stages directly and to analyze them one by one. His last works—such as *L'Intelligence avant le langage* (1936), *Les Débuts de l'intelligence* (1935), *L'Évolution de la mémoire et la notion du temps* (1928), *L'Évolution psychologique de la personnalité* (1929)—are truly developmental books of great interest, in which his various theories of affective and intellectual development are condensed. There is no need to discuss these conceptions in detail; the central idea is enough for the present discussion on diagnostic significance.

However coherent this system may be, Janet's final theory of stages still presents certain difficulties. If each stage is characterized by the appearance of new function, does this not force us to deny the existence of the function prior to the appropriate stage? For example, there would be no memory before the language stage (Janet emphasized that memory is due to language, or more precisely that memory is the coherent narration of events), and no reflection before a certain form of socialization of thought, and, above all, no sense of reality before the internalized discussion which constitutes reflection. This succession of heterogeneous functions reveals a linear conception of development that can be reduced to a simple addition of independent, irreducible mechanisms. It is not, as was the case with Binet, Decroly, and others, a simple summation of observable results, since these results are seen as subordinate to the evolution of mental structures; but it is still a cumulative addition of the structures as such.

The order of stages is imposed by the facts—and we are not questioning this order—but it does not constitute an explanation of those facts. To refer to the amount of energy spent in maintaining the synthesis at every level assuredly does not explain the appearance of new behavior, and as a hypothetical explanation it does no more than echo the observations. Even adopting the idea of an increasing complexity of mental functions, it is difficult to understand how a new function integrates the preceding ones without some law to account for the transformation. For example, according to Janet's hierarchy, the sense of reality and of experimental thought come only after the stage of reflection. These types of behavior certainly do exist in many higher forms of action, but is it not arbitrary to deny that there is any sense of reality or submission to experience in lower forms? In the elementary intellectual operations to which Janet attributes such importance, there is certainly a sense of reality, adaptation to the external world, and a sensory-motor mode of experimentation. They are different, perhaps, from the higher equivalents, but the continuity poses a problem Janet did not resolve.

In constructing hierarchies by an accumulation of elements, one runs a double danger: either one emphasizes the difference and loses sight of the continuity that alone explains the coherence; or one attempts to identify elements and tends to forget that manifestations that appear to be the same can arise from different functions, depending on the level at which they appear. Although Janet avoided the second of these dangers, he was perhaps not as successful in avoiding the first.

The practical difficulties of such a system are apparent in what Piaget terms "decalages." Certain problems which are resolved on one level of development reappear in another form at a higher level, and then require a new solution. There are "vertical" decalages when the same problem must be resolved twice, first at the sensory-motor level, and later through reflection. An example is the discovery of spatial relations, first in action and then through mental representation. "Horizontal" decalages occur when different related notions are elaborated successively by the same operational mechanism. (Horizontal decalages in the construction of the notions of quantity, weight, and volume of matter will be discussed in Chapters 2 and 3.) Such decalages, which mark both the continuity of intellectual elaboration and the successive levels of equilibrium, seem to be neglected by

Janet. Janet shows, for example, with great ingenuity, the early construction of intellectual objects, such as "the road," and "the village square" (Janet 1935: Chap. 2), the former based on a sense of direction that has become in some way mobile and reciprocal, and the second on a sense of relative position. The reversibility of movements and the reciprocity of positions and points of view are operations which in practical terms constitute the notion of space, and Piaget has shown their genesis during the first two years of the child's life. But this practical notion has to be reconstructed on the verbal and reflective plane. There is also the problem of the relativity of right and left and the coordination of spatial perspectives. So there does exist continuity between the first intellectual objects and rational notions. To account for both this functional continuity and the different methods of intellectual elaboration requires some conception of an internal law of genetic construction. Janet suggests theoretically that each stage represents a reorganization and a new synthesis of the preceding ones. But in fact he is assuming a hierarchical seriation in which new functions appear and are integrated after the fact.

The diagnostic method implied by his theory would consist in placing the subject at the appropriate stage, which would be ideal if it could be done in detail. However, when we deal with reasoning, this simply cannot be done unequivocally, since comparable mechanisms are found at different levels; we need a theory of the decalages. For example, we ask a retarded child the relation between a weight A and a weight C, if $A = B$, and $B = C$, and he cannot tell us. We might say, then, that he does not have the higher functions, or even "reflective behavior." But if we pose the problem with respect to quantities of matter, instead of weights, he has no trouble knowing that $A = C$. Does this mean that he does have the functions that we just decided he did not have? Where do you mark the exact beginning of the "stage of reflection"? These problems will arise at each step of the way, as long as we do not try resolutely to base the diagnosis on the development of the evolutionary mechanism itself.

The internal mechanism of evolution is the central problem in Wallon's work. His research focuses on psychomotor development, and here he finds laws that are analogous to Sherrington's laws of integration in neurology. Let us look at the principal traits of his developmental conception as it relates to pathological diagnosis.

Like Janet, Wallon started from abnormal children: "The normal child can be discovered in the pathological child" (Wallon 1925: 309). Definite synchronisms are hard to find in normal evolution, since there are always overlaps from the past and future, but in abnormal children all the functions are arrested at approximately the same point. By meticulous and cautious comparison it is possible to fix their time of appearance.

At the most primitive level there is only preconscious or impulsive activity. This is the level of reflexes or automatisms. During a permanent or temporary absence of higher mental functions, this is the only form of action possible. If we can observe the transition away from this primitive state, we will have observed the beginnings of consciousness.

The first stage is characterized by the play of emotions. Wallon differs from many other psychologists in thinking that the various emotive manifestations do form a stage of development that depends on an organized system of cerebral centers, notably optic-striated centers. Emotions are of primary importance for mental life, and in a way form the source of subjective consciousness. Optic-striated or postural systems start by being independent from the functional systems that supplant them later. And even when the subordination to higher centers has taken place it remains fairly fragile; the neurological connections between the cortex and the optic-striated system are indirect. But despite the initial antagonism between automatisms and emotions, and between emotions and mental representations, all the transitions can of course be made.

The second level, the sensory-motor stage, is characterized by the development of motor and sensory systems and differentiations among them. The act as felt is coordinated with the act as effector, and these sensory-motor coordinations come to integrate the emotions, through the progressive predominance of the hemispheres over the subcortical centers. This development dominates the mental activity of the first year.

Wallon's third level, the projective stage, comes between these subjective stages and objective representation. This stage is difficult to recognize in the course of normal evolution, but it is clear in cases of hypertrophy or insufficiency of the frontal lobes, conditions found in certain forms of epilepsy. The affected person is capable of intentional motor acts, but he does not have objective goals. Lacking representations that go beyond his egocentric activity, he is asymbolic, His consciousness remains projective and concrete, and he is unable to carry out any plans outside the field of immediate activity.

Wallon's final stage marks the achievement of consciousness; "mental" or "virtual" space supersedes sensory space.

The pattern of these stages seems to show clearly the evolutionary principle which determines them. According to Wallon, "There is no better way to know the great stages and the general plan of mental life than to relate each function to a moment of cerebrospinal development and to the corresponding anatomical formations" (Wallon 1934: 67). In addition, these functions are progressively integrated, so that they assure increasing equilibrium through the course of mental development. And each level would correspond to a new, irreducible physiological system which integrates the preceding functions.

Here is how such a system of integration lends itself to the diagnosis of psychomotor deficiencies. For Wallon, diagnosis of a pathological state consists not of establishing the corresponding level of mental development, but of identifying the dystrophies of the nervous apparatus corresponding to the mental level. It is not a question of determining mental age, and surely not of using one sign as an indicator of a complex mental problem, but rather of finding the inadequacies in the integration of the nerve centers. Certainly, anatomy and histology alone do not reveal mental structures. Clinical observation and psychophysiological experimentation have to substantiate them. Since children's psychological difficulties on the whole do not come under the psychopathological classifications used with adults, it is necessary to look for more appropriate procedures.

The importance of knowing the conditions of psychomotor anomalies cannot be denied, and it is to Wallon's great credit to have disclosed them. But the investigation of deficiencies in higher mental functions, especially reasoning, remains to be done. This genetic and pathological theory, related to the evolution of the nervous system, is of great interest not only in itself but because of the host of questions that it raises. We would like to retain the idea that pathological levels, defined by inadequate integration, mark the successive stages of mental evolution better than normal development does, and also to heed the warning contained in this idea, namely, to distrust oversimplified identifications between normal and pathological development. But there are difficulties with the theory. We have been struck by two in particular. The first is related to the transition from lower functions to proper intellectual functions; the second is related to the general question of the transition from any one stage to the next.

In reference to the first difficulty, a theory which explains the integration of mental function by the maturation of nerve centers is certainly persuasive when the phenomena in question are directly dependent on these nerve centers, but it runs into serious trouble when it is applied to higher functions. In fact, in reading Wallon's work one is struck by the contrast between the precise analysis at the lower stages and the more evasive, almost metaphoric character of his descriptions when he deals with behavior in which the interdependence of mental functions and nerve centers is not as clear. The full development of the frontal lobes does not explain consciousness, and the transition from the sensory-motor stage to representation remains a major problem. Wallon speaks of "transposition" and of "sublimation of underlying activities." Body positions are "the indispensable foundations of abstract intelligence." Spatial intelligence "must gradually replace its own instruments with others taken from the external world. It starts by annexing them, incorporating them, and ends by being subordinated to their combinations." The first instrument is only a support of automatisms; then "the instrument takes over . . . The intuition of one's own body in space is replaced by the possibility of imagining positions and contacts independent of the subject himself." "At that point the transfer has been made from the psychomotor plane to the mental plane . . . This is the moment when the notion of space is freed from one's own body and its movements, and seems to be sublimated in systems of place, contact, position, and relations independent of oneself" (Wallon 1937: 106, 121).

The construction of this mental space might, then, give us the key to the transition from lower to higher functions. But it is just here that Wallon substitutes simple description for explanatory analysis. He even writes that "this power of intellectual schematization corresponds to levels of nerve structures that are independent of motor structures" (Wallon 1937: 121).* How, then, can his developmental theory and his ingenious method of diagnosing disintegration syndromes be gen-

---

* Wallon's last book, *De l'Acte à la pensée* (1942), shows, still more clearly than those preceding, this gap in his conception of mental development; in order to explain the development of thought he is obliged to invoke the social factors of sign, myth, and rite.

eralized to the study of troubles of reflective intelligence or of reasoning itself?

This first difficulty leads to a second, which is more general and more profound. Wallon's stages are far more neurological and biological than Janet's, and again they appear as superimposed structures, integrating lower functions into higher functions after the fact, leaving the transition from one stage to the next unexplained. Wallon demonstrates the initial antagonisms between levels, but he offers no explanation for the development from one level to the other. The following quotation illustrates this: "All motor evolution consists in the superposition of new structures, rather than the replacement of one by the next. Early ones are integrated by later ones, so they lose their autonomy and become partial or intermittent mechanisms (Wallon 1937: 105).

On one hand, then, structures are superimposed, and do not develop out of earlier ones; on the other hand, an irreducible new system which cannot be correlated to nervous development can only be a creation *ex nihilo,* discontinuous from preceding functions. Continuity demands not only the superposition and later integration of heterogeneous functions, but progressive integration inherent to the development.

However, perhaps an interval law of development will be more apparent if, keeping in mind his valuable insights, we now return to the study of normal development. As we have seen, Wallon's study of pathology does have the advantage of preventing a too easy identification of pathological levels with stages of normal development. In so doing, we find two fundamental groups of facts:

First, in the transition from one stage to another, not only is the first integrated into the second but the second is in part determined by the first. Let us take Wallon's spatial intelligence as an example. It is impossible to break up the construction of spatial coordinations during the first two years into various superimposed levels and to go from movements of the body to "combinations of contacts independent of the subject" without seeing that this evolution is determined from the beginning by a tendency toward decentering that takes the child from the egocentrism of initial perceptions of space, to the "grouping" of the displacements of his own body and of objects, and then from this organization of displacements and objects to the organization of anticipations and representations (Piaget 1954). If it were simply a question of integration after the fact, it would be hard to understand how this gradual organization would result in the schema of the permanent object, and the various translation, rotation groups, etc. (Piaget 1952). It is much easier if we see the behavior at each stage as determining the following ones and then being integrated into them.

Secondly, we must somehow keep some notion of functional continuity to explain how the behavior at one stage can influence the next stage, even though the neurological systems at these stages are different. The model of the assimilation of objects to activity and the accommodation of schemas to the facts of experience, which Piaget describes in *The Origins of Intelligence in Children* (1952) is an example of such functional continuity. This same functional continuity is found again in his description of the progressive "grouping" of operations at the level of thinking.

3. Mental Development Regarded as a Progressive Organization of an Operational Mechanism

So far, we have sketched two conceptions of development. We have seen that one of these, based on progressive acquisition of independent elements, gave birth to the idea of mental age and to the diagnostic method of testing. The other, derived from psychopathological levels, brought to light the hierarchy of mental functions, and thus lent itself to a clinical diagnosis of oscillations and disintegrations. A third point of view, based on a model of operational organization, will now be considered.

This point of view becomes clearer and clearer in the psychological writings of Jean Piaget. There were signs of it in his first book, *The Language and Thought of the Child* (1926), but it is developed much further in his more recent works, *The Child's Conception of Number* (Piaget and Szeminska 1952), and *Le Développement des quantités physiques chez l'enfant* (Piaget and Inhelder 1941). Since the principal objective of this present work is to see whether such a theory of development and the method it implies could be used as a model and as an instrument of analysis in the diagnosis of reasoning in retardates, we hope we will be forgiven for spending more time on it than on the first two.

There is no reason for a detailed discussion of this entire genetic theory of reasoning, as it is elaborated in several of Piaget's well-known works. We would, however, like to mention one aspect which has special relevance to the present problem, namely: how does diagnosis based on operational analysis compare with other possible conceptions and methods? We shall not discuss Piaget's epistemological point of view, although it can indeed not be dissociated from his genetic psychology. The most useful approach for us to take is probably to sketch a few of the major themes and to trace briefly the chronology of their development.

Right at the beginning of his psychological career, Piaget started to focus on the subject that has since become the center of his investigation, the genesis of logic. Whether it was through the language accompanying the free activity of young children, or in their spontaneous questions, or by an analysis of their grammar, or in formal problems in the tests of Binet or Burt, he has been interested not in the individual content of the thought of each child but in its structure and functioning (Piaget and Inhelder 1941 and Piaget 1928a).

It was Claparède who said that this mental structure had so far remained like "a puzzle for which some essential pieces are missing while other pieces seem to be borrowed from another game, and cannot be placed" (Piaget 1926: viii). Piaget's explanation began by positing two antagonistic planes of thought, one dominated by egocentrism, the other determined by norms of social exchange. The development of reasoning which takes place from the age of three or four to the age of eleven or twelve marks the gradual disappearance of one plane of thought in favor of the other.

Let us look at egocentrism, the original structure and functional kernel of the child's thought until he is seven or eight years old, and a characteristic, as we shall see, of the thinking of certain retardates. This notion enables us to see children's thinking as unified and coherent, differing in nature and not only in degree from adult thought. Up until now, it has been considered in negative terms—incapable of formal thought, of deduction, and of synthesis; insensitive to contradictions; impermeable to experience; rarely conscious of its own processes. However, the notion of egocentrism gives a positive significance to this type of mentality. These characteristics can be seen as interdependent and complementary aspects, evidence of a *sui generis* structure of thought.

Functionally, egocentrism is characterized by the predominance of the search for immediate satisfaction. This characteristic is manifested, for instance, by the absence of a need for verification. There is already an attempt at intellectual adaptation, but it remains permeated by playful tendencies. From this point of view, the child's mode of thought can be placed between socialized thought and what Bleuler and the psychoanalysts have called autistic thought. In addition, egocentric thought is unconscious of itself, so that objective reality, instead of being confronted, is assimilated to the subject.

As for its structure, egocentric reasoning does not conform to the norms of discussion and of intellectual exchange in general. Piaget, in his first writings, defines this way of thinking as being essentially irreversible, in complete contrast to equilibrated and reversible operations of logical thought. The irreversibility of the process can be seen in the incapacity to form hypotheses, since each idea presents itself to the child in the form of a belief (Janet's stage of imaginary belief). Once started in a certain direction, even if this direction is recognized as false, the child cannot return to the point of departure in order to start again. An excellent example is found in children's ordering of events in a narrated story (Piaget and Krafft 1925).

Secondly, the irreversibility of the contents of the child's thought at this stage is illustrated by the absence of physical constancies. The external world is conceived as a succession of purely transitory states, without any underlying permanency.

A third manifestation of the irreversibility of the structure is transductive reasoning, which differs from both induction and deduction; it proceeds by a syncretic fusion of judgments and conclusions, without any link of logical necessity.

Thus the thought of the child constitutes a coherent system whose most general expression is egocentrism. What is the course of the evolution which finally achieves a mobile equilibrium of logical operations? Obviously neither the accumulation of acquired facts nor the sudden appearance of new functions can explain such a transformation. Some organizing process is needed, such as Piaget started to describe in general terms as "socialization of thought." Whether it is a question of norms of logic, or moral norms, or a deductive system of causality (to the extent that this is rational), thought is always the fruit of mental cooperation of the child with his surroundings. It is only by free intellectual exchange that children, and in general man, can free themselves from their initial egocentricism. The change consists in "placing oneself," and thus approaching the ideal of reci-

procity. Mental cooperation has, therefore, three essential consequences for the thought of the child. First, as he becomes conscious
of his subjectivity he constructs objective representations; he no
longer considers his point of view to be universal, but sees it as a particular point of view among many; he understands the relativity of
ideas and relations. Second, only the mutual respect growing out of
cooperation assures moral autonomy, while unilateral respect leads to
moral constraint of one form or another (Piaget 1932). Third, for
logic, the importance of exchange in the form of discussion is undeniable; as the child is obliged to justify his point of view, he seeks to
verify his statements, to consolidate his beliefs, to think in terms of
unequivocal and stable concepts, and to respect the principle of noncontradiction; then, left alone, the child's logical thought respects the
same rules and takes the form of an internalized discussion.

Such is the first aspect of intellectual evolution; thought proceeds
from egocentrism to socialization; rational norms are elaborated as a
result of mental cooperation. Let us look now at the second aspect,
which is complementary to the first—the internal mechanism of this
process.

This internal development can be seen best of all in the analysis of
children's thinking about reality and causality (Piaget 1929). Through
the original "clinical" method which he used, conversing with children
on questions concerned with animism and realism, or having them
reflect on a physical experiment appropriate to their level, Piaget was
able to detect different modes of representation and explanation. He
observed, in the course of development, the decline of three characteristics: realism gives way to objective representations; physical law
becomes detached from moral law; and egocentric and phenomenistic
causality change to rational deduction. He noticed in general the
same succession of types of thought for each one of the problems and
experiments, so he considered them as stages in a common evolutive
process, having the same qualitative thought content and mental
structure.

Up to that point, one might believe that thought began in the purest
subjectivism and progressed toward objectivity. However, in Piaget's
own words, "This research is in some sense hanging in mid-air until
we go back to the source of reasoning to analyze preverbal intellectual
behavior" (Piaget 1952: Introduction). The idea that thought is prepared by action, and constitutes in some sense an awareness of this

action, is current nowadays in psychology, thanks in no small part to Janet's fine research.

But we must study the nature of the relation between these different levels of psychological activity. In *The Child's Conception of Physical Causality* (1930) and in a paper given to the French Society of Philosophy (1928b) Piaget has approached this relationship by examining children's predictions and explanations of physical phenomena. While predictions and explanations are more or less on the same level at the earliest stages, there are intermediate levels where prediction is clearly in advance of explanation. The child is able to generalize his previous experience and to construct inductively a law that enables him to make certain predictions, but he is unable to give correct explanations. Finally, explanation catches up again with prediction. For example, when a solid object is immersed in water, the amount of water rise is first predicted and explained on the basis of weight. At an intermediate level it is predicted correctly, on the basis of volume alone, differentiated from weight, but the explanation continues to be based on the more primitive notion of weight. Finally, volume is used as the basis for both prediction and explanation.

These facts are doubly instructive. There is evidently a continuity between sensory-motor or practical intelligence and rational thought. But the latter is not a direct prolongation of the former, as the positivists would have it. Between these two systems comes a third, namely, egocentric thought, which assimilates external experience to the subject before establishing objective relationships. Let us examine each of these aspects, the functional continuity of intelligence and the variation in the structures which it creates as it develops.

What mechanisms assure the continuity of intellectual evolution? Piaget's answer to this question is of central significance for any developmental theory. It expresses his biological point of view. Intelligence is defined as a process of adaptation, at first more restrained than biological adaptation but later outstripping it. Its function essentially is structuring the universe. The functional invariants common to biological structures, and therefore to psychological structures, too, are organization and adaptation. The first assures the preservation of the organism, and the second its interactions with the environment by means of two complementary mechanisms, assimilation and accommodation. *The Origins of Intelligence* (Piaget 1952) describes one such continual process of adaptation, beginning with hereditary mechanisms and ending with the ability to invent new means to attain given goals. From reflexes to the first intellectual operations, assimilation organizes the sensory-motor schemas, and accommodation differentiates them, so that these two processes—at first antagonistic—come to complement one another, finally achieving the equilibrium of a reversible system of schemas of action.

The functional continuity observed at the sensory-motor level is extended to the level of reflective thought. For example, at the sensory-motor level, during his first two years, a child slowly develops the notion of a permanent object. At first, the universe is only a series of tableaux, appearing and disappearing one after another, but gradually the child is able to introduce constancies into this universe. Finally, he is able to recognize objects from different points of view, to follow their spatial displacements, and to remove obstacles in order to get at them.

Between the ages of four and eleven or twelve, the child goes through exactly the same steps in reflective thought. Instead of having to find a hidden object, he has to postulate its constancy throughout variations in its form. Until six or seven years, he believes that sugar disappears when it is dissolved in water, but during the next five years he comes to realize that the sugar retains the same quantity, weight, and volume, even when it is dissolved. By this time, the mechanisms of assimilation and accommodation take the form of interaction between deduction and experience.

Why is this development not linear? Once a given difficulty has been overcome at the sensory-motor level, why does it reappear at the level of conceptual intelligence? Precisely because there are different levels of intellectual elaboration, and because the functional invariants change their structure from one level to the other. The task that Piaget has set himself is that of determining the particular forms of equilibrium at each level, and the laws which govern their succession. He has already achieved results in the areas of qualitative logic, number, and physical quantities.

On the basis of his insights into the first manifestations of sensory-motor intelligence, Piaget is now examining the notion of operativity. What is an operation in terms of adaptive action? It is an action which has become reversible through the achievement of an equilibrium between assimilation and accommodation. Piaget is studying the mechanisms of logical reasoning from a double point of view—intellectual development and axiomatic analysis. One initial discovery has opened new perspectives for the psychological significance of logic and its relations with mathematics. This is the finding that the operations on which classes, relations, and numbers are established always form "groupings" or groups (Piaget 1941a, 1942). A logical operation never appears in isolation. On the one hand, it is always accompanied by its inverse, so that any operation can be "undone" again in thought; and on the other hand it always forms part of a system of operations. These two aspects, reversibility and a total system, insure the rigor and fecundity of reasoning. The whole of *Le Développement des quantités physiques chez l'enfant* (Piaget and Inhelder 1941) shows that conservation principles are based on the operational "groupings" of positioning and partitive composition, made up of the following four mechanisms: the direct operation, the inverse operation, associativity, and the identical operation.

But if each grouping has achieved a state of equilibrium, why does any further evolution take place? Piaget attempts an answer to this central question in a theoretical article (Piaget 1941b) in which he suggests that the different levels succeed each other according to the differentiation of their equilibrium states. At the sensory-motor level there is only one system of groupings, that of means and ends; at the level of reflective thought, this one primary system becomes differentiated into practical, logico-arithmetical, and physical groupings. Similarly, within each level the content is gradually differentiated. A grouping does not necessarily operate on any given content; it structures the content progressively, as exemplified by the time lag between the notions of the conservation of substance, of weight, and of volume. A grouping is the end product of an evolutive process, but at the same time it is the internal law of this process.

Such a theory has already given direction to a body of research which may make possible a more precise description of the steps involved in psychological development. It also has the advantage of reconciling the functional continuity of the developmental process with the discontinuity presented by different complete structures at different levels. Contrary to the conception of development as a progressive accumulation of acquisitions, this conception finds continuity not only in the results but in the operational unfolding of development. On the other hand, instead of having to see new functions as being created *ex nihilo,* or as owing their successive integration to the maturation of neurological systems, this theory seeks to grasp the internal law of development. Certainly, this conception, which Piaget developed on the basis of many investigations, is still more of a working hypothesis than a detailed explanation of the process of development. For as Piaget says at the end of the article *"Le Mécanisme du développement mental et les lois du groupement des opérations"* (Piaget 1941b), the study of groupings necessarily introduces the study of regulations, a study which is far from being complete (Piaget 1943). However, on the level of logical operations, this conception has proved fruitful and has obtained precise results, so it seems to us of great interest to put it to test in the domain of the diagnosis of reasoning.

One major question remains. The conception of operational groupings is clearly useful in describing the development and the equilibrium states of rational or logical thought. But is it useful as a general principle of mental development? Specifically, do the stages in the development of the notion of the conservation of matter correspond to general psychological levels, or just to stages in the development of rational thought? That is the question which this work attempts to answer. Can the operations of which an individual is capable be taken as an index of his mental level and his intellectual equilibrium? If they can, we could expect to find retarded children fixated at lower operational stages.

An established parallelism between rational development and general mental development would seem to have two major implications. From the point of view of the theory, if pathological arrestations fixate at certain stages, we can have a clearer picture of the groupings at these stages than we can obtain from the transitions and fluctuations of normal development.

The other implication is the practical one. As we have suggested, operational analysis might provide a diagnostic method whereby clinical signs of reasoning deficiencies could enable us to ascertain different types or levels of mental deficiency. Moreover, this analysis might be both rich and clear enough to be one element in a total diagnostic picture.

The most suitable method for pursuing these possibilities seems to be the one we used in our previous work published in collaboration with Piaget. As we previously did with normal children, we should engage the retarded children in experiments which require some operational thinking: elaborating the principles of conservation of substance, weight, and volume, for instance, or constructing equal quantities. To study the development in normal children it was necessary to use a variety of experiments, each one analyzing a particular aspect of physical quantification, and all of them together serving to show the coherence of the operational construction. In individual diagnosis, however, we must choose among the possible experiments. We have chosen three, in which the required operations seem to have general significance:

1. The transformation of clay balls, in which the operational groupings and the stages of integration are clear.

2. The dissolution of sugar in water, an interesting experimental context in which to examine operational construction, experimental reasoning, and representation.

3. Only as a countertest, the experiment termed "the bars," which requires a deductive composition of objects of equal weights but different volumes.

The three tests in combination, with similarities and differences in their results, may furnish indications of intellectual equilibrium.

It is likely that other tests, such as those used in "The Child's Conception of Number," would lead to similar results, provided they are used in a clinical manner; we have simply chosen to start with tests from the area of physical quantity.

Our diagnostic procedure is based on free conversation as developed by Piaget and adapted by us for the study of the notions of conservation and atomism (Piaget and Inhelder 1941). The principles of the "clinical" method and the precautions it entails are well enough known (Piaget 1929: Preface), so that we need not discuss them here. A presentation of actual conversations with the subjects will illustrate the diagnostic procedure better than any methodological discussion.

To summarize, there are three principal points of view on mental development, each one giving rise to a diagnostic method: corresponding to the idea of development as a series of acquisitions is the test method, which, as we have seen, assesses the results of intellectual work, but not the dynamism itself; corresponding to the idea that progressive stages are the methods which define retardation either by an equivalent stage of normal development (Janet) or by the syndrome corresponding to this stage (Wallon). However, either the diagnosis is too general or the natural entities that the syndromes define remain completely distinct from each other at the different levels. In adopting operational psychology, we are hoping to achieve both detailed analysis of the different levels, and their integration in successive total systems.

2. Reasoning Fixations at the First Stage*

At the end of the previous chapter, it was noted that it is the operational development of thought which leads a child progressively to the ideas of conservation of substance, then of weight, then of volume, as it simultaneously leads to atomistic explanations and to a generalized idea of the conservation of quantity. As this logical evolution passes through four developmental stages, it obeys the immanent law of "grouping." If clearly defined stages of logical construction do exist (Piaget and Inhelder 1941), the problem posed is: can these stages be seen as the levels of mental development at which mentally retarded children remain when they fail to attain complete maturity of reasoning?

The problem would be less difficult if true retardation could be regarded as a simple halting or retardation of mental development, showing itself simultaneously and equally in all psychological functions. Unfortunately this is not so, as mentioned in our critique of tests. The current notion of simple retardation is based on an artificial conception of mental evolution; such an idea implies that evolution can be determined by the summation of graded results. Some time ago, Binet drew the attention of clinical psychologists to the existence of paranormal phenomena which play as important a role in the psychology of the retardate as do the phenomena of simple retardation. Since then, research in the area of developmental and pathological diagnosis has provided evidence of an integration of psychological functions which, rather than following a linear development in their

* The word "fixations" is used for fixations which are momentary as well as those which are final.

totality, consist of systems of integration whose internal mechanisms must be determined.

In the diagnosis of mental retardation, it is impossible to set forth clinical indices by simple conversion to a certain mental level on a linear scale, a level which would be traced and scaled on the normal curve for normal children. The question may be simplified if, instead of trying to measure or determine qualitatively a general intellectual level encompassing all the intellectual functions, the area is limited to the study of the retardation or the development of a particular function, such as reasoning. Then we can make an effort to establish the levels of reasoning as such through their isolation, insofar as possible, from other mechanisms such as memory, habit, perception, etc. In the first chapter, certain authors were mentioned who have attempted to combine the global level and the psychological profile. However, even in such a delimited field there is risk of again finding a simple reduction of the difficulties as they relate to a global psychological level and to linear stages. To evaluate the level of reasoning attained by a subject is also complex if the inquiry is not limited to particular types of logical operations which follow step by step the evolution throughout mental growth. If a series of reasoning problems chosen at random according to the usual methods of selection are used as tests, there is a risk of being unable to dissociate the variables of language, attention, memory, representation, etc. from the logical problem itself. These variables can be controlled if the research is limited to certain well-planned studies, but if it proceeds at random, control is difficult. The principal obstacle is that reasoning in all psychological mechanisms, and especially in the system of formal operations, consists in an arrangement of structures in which the functioning can be brought about only by contacts with experience or active participation. The elaboration of physical formulas or the construction of operations is inseparable, then, from the individual experience of the subject. Thus, to proceed empirically and not in relation to a previous developmental analysis makes it impossible to distinguish the part played by acquired experience from that played by operatory mechanisms in the success or failure of a given subject. The normal child of seven, the moron of twelve, or even the imbecile assimilates an enormous number of varied experiences which are usually found to be qualitatively irreducible from one level to the other.

For these reasons, our system of experiments is limited to those referred to in the previous chapter. In such experiments, the relation of normal evolution to acquired experience is as well known as its relation to operatory development. This tight delimitation, rather than breaking down the diagnosis into a multitude of isolated and juxtaposed determinations, must rejoin the essentials of thought, *i.e.,* the functional nucleus or core common to all reasoning. Our hypothesis supposes that at a certain level of analysis one discovers not an undefined multiplicity of operatory mechanisms, but a certain number of fundamental and general operations which are found in all intellectual constructions and whose stages of development are the same for all problems. However, there will be varied decalages and integrations according to the domain and contents. To grasp the operation in a circumscribed domain is not to lose oneself in extreme specialization, but simply to substitute finer analysis of an important part for general examination of the overall system upon which this part is dependent. This means that the general will be obtained from the particular, rather than from simple generalities.

Even though the reasoning of the retarded child seems to be difficult to measure developmentally, it is possible through analysis to grasp the norms common to all coherent thought. Should our previously stated hypothesis be correct, the study of the notions of conservation in mentally retarded children will make it possible to determine a certain level of reasoning in their mental development. Data which deal with the intellectual reactions of a group of retarded children of different age levels is presented in the second chapter. To verify the hypothesis, structured conversations are presented with mentally retarded children from institutions, from special classes, or referred to us by doctors or teachers. All these children are classified as retarded, although the method of diagnosis may have differed from the one employed in this study. The diagnoses were made by doctors, psychologists, or specialized teachers. Besides our own interview processes, techniques used in medico-pedagogic consultations were also applied.

1. The Assessment of Conservation of Substance

The test termed "Conservation of Substance" has been useful in clinical interrogation because the questions in it interest the children and make a minimum demand on acquired knowledge or memory effort. The technique, which is set forth in detail in *Le Développement des quantités chez l'enfant,* includes presenting the child with two identical balls of clay. By comparison, he finds them equal in both weight and volume. Weight, or qualitative identity, can be verified by scales, provided he understands the use of scales. All that is necessary is that the child be able to make the correspondence between "heavier" and the lowering of the platform of the scales, and, inversely, between "lighter" and the raising of the platform, as well as the correspondence between equality of the levels of the two platforms and equality of weight. The capacity for making such an intuitive correspondence is a limiting condition for the use of our tests, and it also serves as a criterion for distinguishing the severely retarded. No profound imbecile is able to attain such comprehension. In morons, however, one is struck by the almost immediate comprehension of the weighing after a few preliminary illustrations. In order for the children to establish equality of volume, it is necessary to resort to indirect comparison, such as the level of water displaced. For example, they see that if two identical balls of clay are emerged in two identical beakers which contain the same amount of water, an equal rise in water level occurs, reaching "the same height," because the same amount of space is occupied.

Once the child is convinced that the two balls contain equal amounts of clay, that they are the same weight, and that they occupy the same amount of space, he is asked to use one of the two balls either to make a sausage or a pancake or to break it up into small pieces. When the sausage is made, the examiner has a discussion with the mentally retarded youngster to determine if he understands the principles of conservation. The child not only answers but also is required to justify his expectations, to compare them with the results of the test experience, and to state precisely his often implicit notions. What is important is to determine not just simple verbal notions but also the operatory mechanisms of thought. Is this retarded child incapable of "groupments," and will he remain entirely dependent on immediate experience obtained from preception, or will he attain a partial and limited operatory construction? What are the possibilities of ulterior developments, and what are the limits of his reasoning? These are questions for clinical investigation. Therefore, the examiner's conversation with the retarded child, although centered on the problems to be solved, must also, as far as possible, follow his spontaneous reflections. In order to know the logical structure of acquired notions, it is indispensable to place them in their natural context.

Consideration is now given the facts, which, better than all diagramatic description of the method, familiarize the reader with structured conversation. First cited are six cases of subjects who were questioned concerning the deformation of a clay ball. For the sake of anonymity their names are abbreviated and sex is distinguished by M for male and F for female.*

<h2 style="text-align:center">OBSERVATION 1—STA., F, 13.0†</h2>

This young girl was in an institution for abnormal children. The doctor classified her retardation as endogenous, and the case history revealed severe deficiency in psychomotor and mental development. Entrance into school was delayed a year, but even then, the child was incapable of meeting the requirements of the program. When transferred to a special class, some academic skill was acquired, which included the ability to engage in elementary mathematical operations, but not the ability to think independently. Because she was highly verbose and had no apparent physical handicaps, her intelligence was overestimated. Results of the Stanford-Binet indicated a retardation of only four years (IQ 70), but her intellectual behavior, and in particular her scholastic failure in spite of adapted methods, proved the retardation to be more profound. A diagnosis of borderline functioning between imbecile and moron was indicated. Later inquiry (at fifteen years) showed that Sta. had made little or no progress after fourteen years, and subsequently she was placed in a closely supervised rural environment, where she engaged in farm tasks.

Spontaneous interest in the problems submitted to her remained superficial and emotion-laden. Sta. sought approval rather than the correct answer. Because of this need for approval, she made continued efforts to concentrate and to respond, although she was unable to pass beyond the first level of operatory reasoning.

Sta. equalizes the two balls and verifies that they are of equal size and weight. She understands the use of scales and knows when weight is balanced.

---

* Questioning was done in St. Gallen or Zürich dialect; translation into French (and then from French into English) has obviously resulted in a loss of the style of the subject's expression.

† 13:0 = 13 years and no months of age.

And now you are going to transform one of the balls into a long sausage. (*She manipulates the ball with care and enjoyment.*)

If you put the sausage on the scales, would it have the same weight as the ball? *Oh no, the ball is heavier. That* [*the sausage*] *is stretched out, but the other is a ball.*

Is there as much clay in the sausage as in the ball, or is there more in one than in the other? *In the ball, there is more; the ball is heavier.*

And why do you think the ball is heavier? *Because when it is stretched into a sausage it is lighter.*

And why is there more clay? *It's less when it's stretched.*

Could you make it into a ball again? *Yes, then the ball would be the same, just as large and just as heavy.*

And why? Are you sure? (*She laughs.*) *Because before it was just as large.*

Now you can break the ball into little pieces, and then we will ask what they weigh in relation to the ball. *It's easy: the little pieces are lighter because they are stretched then cut into pieces, and it* [*the ball*] *is heavier because it hasn't been touched.*

Is it always the same amount of clay or has that changed also? *In the little pieces there is less clay, and in the ball more.*

Are you really sure there is less. Look at it! *Yes, less clay.*

Could you make a ball again? *Of course, it would be the same as before, but now it is lighter.*

We are going to weigh it and see if what you thought is right. (*She takes a lengthy, astonished look.*) *But there is more clay in the ball; it can't be the same thing.* (*She looks at it laughingly as though she suspects a joke.*)

But you see that it is the same weight. Can you explain how it is possible? *It is you who makes it balance and stop now.* (*She looks attentively and is impervious to the experience.*)

You make the ball again and then flatten it into a pancake. (*She does it with enjoyment and answers spontaneously.*) *The ball is heavier because the pancake was squeezed and pressed and it is flat.*

And compared to the clay, is it the same amount? *There is always more in the ball.*

Could you make the ball again out of the pancake? *Yes, the same as before, but there is less clay now.* (*Again the two amounts are compared on the scale and again the child refuses to admit equality.*)

OBSERVATION 2—CLE., M, 10:9

When tested, this boy was under observation at a psychiatric clinic. The medical-psychological examination revealed retardation, endogenous in nature, accompanied by symptoms of epilepsy. In the area of intellectual development, a striking contrast was found between defective reasoning and practical application of knowledge. Thus, the child showed considerable difficulty in an academic setting, particularly in elementary mathematics, but he performed well in manual tasks adapted to his age level. The Stanford-Binet Test showed a retardation of only 1.7 years (IQ 88), with highly irregular performance, whereas Vermeylen's Test indicated a retardation of approximately three years.

Throughout prolonged observation, the child had shown instability and marked fluctuations in mental activity. The psychiatric prognosis was poor, and possible increase of the gap between mental and physical development was noted.

Reasoning, as revealed during conversation, indicated a profound deficiency in the operatory mechanisms of thought. Here the boy's reflections indicated great interest in practical manipulations and in problems based on these activities. It seemed that clinical interrogation as well as the choice of tests might momentarily stabilize the fluctuation in attention habitually present in this child when he was confronted with academic problems.

Cle., after having verified the size and weight of two balls and after having transformed one of them into a sausage, spontaneously remarks: *The sausage is lighter: it is not like the ball; it is squeezed more.*

Is there still as much clay, or how much do you think there is? *There is more clay in the ball because the ball is squeezed more; it takes more space because the other one is like a thin sausage.*

Now you can make lots of little pieces out of it. (*He does so quickly.*)

Are they the same as the sausage or the ball? *No [in a positive tone] it is not the same thing. The ball is heavier.*

How do you know it is heavier? *It is harder, squeezed more. These [indicating the little pieces] are lighter because they aren't squeezed very much.*

Is there as much clay here as there? *If I make a ball again, then it is the same.*

And when it is in little pieces as now? *No, it is not the same thing.*

There are so many little pieces.

Then which one has more? *When it is in the ball it is larger.*

And if you make a pancake? (*He makes it immediately.*) *The pancake* [*weighing it in his hand*] *it's lighter. It's not hard like the ball.*

Is there as much clay or not? *Oh, there's more because that* [*pointing to the pancake*] *is bigger and wider.*

Again the examiner makes two identical balls and immerses one in a beaker of water. The child is asked beforehand to predict what will happen. If I drop this ball into the water, will the water stay at the same level or will it rise? (The examiner marks the water level on the beaker with a rubber band.) *It won't do anything to the water: the water stays the same.*

As the ball is dropped into the beaker the child observes the rise in water level. *It has gone up: it's heavy and that made the water go up.*

Why does the water go up when it is heavy? *That* [*indicating the ball*] *goes to the bottom and makes that* [*the water*] *go up.*

The other ball is immersed and the identical water level verified. *It goes up just the same with two balls.*

Show me where it will go if we put the pancake in. (*He shows a much higher level.*)

Why didn't it go as high as you said? *Because it's thin: it swims in the water. It can't go down! It's light.*

The child is given another trial, but he remains unable to determine the exact level. *It goes up a bit, but it is not the same thing; it is too thin.*

And the sausage, and where would it make the water rise to? *The water would move a little but not much.*

Will it rise also, or not? *A little, but with less than the ball.*

And with the little bits? *Not at all, they are too little.*

OBSERVATION 3—BLA., F, 11:2

Examination of Bla. was made at the psychiatric clinic for children. The diagnosis was retardation of an endogenous nature. The coexistence of several somatic indices—microcephaly, syndactlylia, and rickets—indicated a state of general deficiency. From childhood there had been physical and mental retardation. For three consecutive times, entry into primary school was delayed a year. Finally, at nine years, the child entered a preparatory class. In addition to mental retardation, various behavior problems—particularly a lack of sexual control—were noted. Therefore Bla. was placed in an institution for retardates, where she now follows the special class program. Psychological tests revealed a retardation of 3.65 years, or an IQ of 68. The child's capacity for observation was good, but she had difficulty in comprehending abstract problems, particularly in arithmetic. When she was observed three years after the initial examination, she experienced difficulty in adapting to new situations, and her development continued to show marked retardation. However, the girl was not destitute of originality nor of vivacity, and notable progress had occurred. Between her thirteenth and fourteenth years, an arrestation in her capacity to function constructively was noted, but there was a perfecting of acquired techniques.

Unlike the two children mentioned above, Bla. understood and appeared to consider each answer. She comprehended the process of weighing and the function of scales.

Bla. observes carefully the two balls of clay, one red and one green. *It's the same size—same size.*

And then you weigh them, you see they are the same weight. (*She observes the scales.*) *Yes, it's just the same thing.*

Then you make a sausage with one of the balls. (*She makes it carefully.*)

Then the ball and sausage are compared. (*Without being prompted, she speaks spontaneously.*) *The ball is heavier because that is a ball. This is a sausage.*

And why do you think it is heavier when it is in a ball? *When it is round it is heavier.*

Is there the same amount, or is there more clay in the green ball than in the red sausage? *More of the green ball because it is squeezed, shaped.*

And the two balls, how were they at the start? *The same weight, just the same in everything.*

You can break the sausage until you have lots of little pieces. (*She reflects during the breaking process.*) *The little pieces are heavier.* (*She starts laughing.*) *It makes many little birds.*

Why are they heavier than the ball? *Because they are so stretched; the clay is torn into pieces.*

And when you put them all back into a ball again [the examiner indicates by gesture]? *The same weight then because it's all in one piece.*

And the clay, is it the same thing or not—when it is in small bits and when it is all in one piece?

(The child is permitted to make a pancake after reassembling the little bits.) Is there as much clay in the pancake? *There is more in the ball because the pancake is like that. (She gestures to signify its spreading.)*

And as for the weight, how much do you think it will weigh? *The ball is heavier.*

Scales are used to verify the equivalent weight of the two. (*Amazed, the child declares:*) *It's just the same.*

How do you explain that it weighs so much? *Because there is the same thing of clay.*

How do you know there is the same amount of clay? *No, no, not the same clay now, because it is spread out. It's no longer the same weight, I think!*

But what do you see? Look carefully at the scales. (*She takes a prolonged look without arriving at a solution.*)

Try to explain! *Perhaps it's because it is not so stretched out.*

Observation 4—Schmi., M, 13:0

A variety of reasons were given for Schmi.'s referral for scholastic observation. He was enrolled in a third-year remedial class, but his teachers considered him incapable of following instruction. His intellectual development, which had been very retarded since early childhood, seemed to have become fixated. In all tasks requiring operatory comprehension, and in arithmetic and grammar in particular, the child failed completely. In addition, his behavior showed signs of instability and disturbance. School no longer interested him, and he played hookey every time he had the opportunity. Also, he was undisciplined at home and ran away for short periods. The parents, conscious of their inability to supervise the child, voluntarily requested that he be placed in a home.

Doctors and specialized teachers had observed a state of retardation that approached imbecility. Our examination, which measured both reasoning and learning ability, indicated that the child's performance was unstable and retarded. Lack of sufficient guidance had contributed to the instability. Schmi.'s behavior became more stable when he was placed in a home for retardates with behavior problems. When appropriate methods were utilized, and discipline was consistent and kind, he became interested in manual work. Nevertheless, his intelligence continued to be deficient, and his reasoning ability did not improve. The examination indicated retardation in operatory development.

Upon entering the room, Schmi. hurried to a toy, let it drop a few seconds later to pick up another, and moved things about without being able to settle on any one thing. Little by little during the examining session he became interested in the problem posed by the changing shape of a clay ball. Our questions succeeded in maintaining his intellectual efforts.

He made two clay balls and by weighing found they were equal. Then he transformed one into a long sausage.

What would the sausage weigh if you put it on one platform of the scales and the ball on the other? Show me what the scales would do. *The sausage is lighter because it is a sausage and because there is less clay. The platform where the sausage is put would be higher.*

Is there less clay here than there? *Yes [makes a circle of the sausage], but it's longer than the ball.*

Then there is more or less clay in the ball? *(He hesitates.) I don't know, it isn't the same thing.*

Now you can make lots of little pieces with the sausage. *Now they are very small. There is not so much as there was before.*

And how is it when compared with the weight of the balls? *Much lighter than the ball.*

Are you sure? *Yes, they are so small.*

Could you make a ball again with all the little pieces? *Yes, perhaps it would be like the other, perhaps larger. (He hesitates and is not able to decide.)*

Then why larger? *No, perhaps the same thing. I'm not sure.*

The scales are used again. *It's exactly the same thing. I don't understand. The ball is heavier. Ah! It's because with these [the little pieces] you can make a ball too.*

A ball the same as the other? *No, quite a bit smaller.*

Why would it be smaller? *Because if the little pieces are put together it doesn't still give as big a ball as the other one. In the other ball there is more clay.*

Would you like to make a pancake? (*While manipulating the clay he says:*) *First I'll make a ball.* (*He observes and then says to himself again:*) *It is as big as the other.* (*Then he flattens it into a pancake.*)

If the ball and the pancake were weighed now? *The pancake would be lighter.*

Are you sure? *Yes.*

Why? *It's made like that. It's made so that it is lighter.*

And when the ball was weighed with the little pieces how was it? *The little pieces were lighter.*

Was that what we saw? Do you remember? *Yes, it's true. It was the same weight.*

And now if we compare the ball with the pancake? *The pancake is lighter than the ball.*

And if we compare the pancake with the little pieces? *The pancake is a little heavier. It would be just in the middle—it is lighter than the ball and heavier than the little pieces.*

Scales are again used to verify weight. *They are the same weight, that is because there is as much clay. But no, there can't be as much in the pancake.*

Observation 5—Tus., M, 10:7

Unlike Schmi., this boy had no physical indices of retardation, nor did he have obvious behavioral problems. He possessed certain practical skills, such as milking and caring for dairy cattle. These tasks require a degree of motor coordination usually not possessed by imbeciles. Furthermore, he came from a very poor social environment (the father was retarded, and because of her behavior the mother had been placed under the observation of local authorities). Tus. supervised the education of his younger brothers and sisters, all of whom were retarded. At school, however, his intellectual retardation was apparent. Although he worked with zeal, he was unable in four years of schooling to make the progress usually expected in two. He lacked the capacity to understand elementary arithmetic and to develop logically a sequence of reasoning. Slightly higher levels of ability were noted in the areas of memory and graphic expression, and his motor development approached normal.

At first it appeared that academic retardation due to environmental deprivation prevented a maximum level of performance. However, his case history revealed that he had been late in walking, in verbalization, and even in dentition. Two years after the first examination, his parents changed their residence to prevent the child's being placed in a special class. At this time, Tus. was found to have made minimum progress in operatory capacity, although he continued to perform farm chores well.

During clinical conversation the boy showed an infantile affectivity. Everything amused him. A lack of inhibition and self-criticism was noted. He adapted quickly to the test situation and made the two balls with pleasure and precision. Scales were used to establish the weight equivalence of the two.

You can make one of the balls into a long, thin sausage. (*He does and laughs loudly.*) *It's not the same thing.*

Not the same thing as what? *It doesn't weigh the same thing.*

Which one do you think is heavier? *The ball, because the sausage is longer and thinner and lighter than that* [*the ball*] *because that is— how do you say it—unrolled.*

And the clay, is there as much or not? *In the sausage there is more clay because it is longer.*

And how were the two balls at the start? *The same thing heavy. The same in everything.*

And now? *There are more things in the sausage.*

And which one do you think is heavier? *The ball is heavier.*

We are going to break the sausage into little pieces. (*He does it immediately.*)

Do you remember in the beginning the balls were the same thing, now that you have made little pieces of one, how would they compare with the ball if you put them both on the scales? *The little pieces are lighter because they are separated.*

Why are they lighter when separated? *It isn't all in one piece.*

And why are they lighter when they are no longer in one piece? *I don't know, it's lighter when it is so little when it is separated.*

And is there still the same amount of clay? *No, no longer the same thing. There is more in the ball because it* [*the little pieces*] *is separated, and not this.*

Then the child is asked to make a thin pancake. (*He puts the little pieces into a ball and flattens it into a pancake.*) *The same thing heavy because that is together, like the ball.*

Exactly the same heavy. It doesn't make any difference if it is flat?

(*Laughter.*) *Ah, it's the ball which is heavier. I know! Because it is a ball and the other is a pancake, and in the ball there is more clay.*

Why do you think there is more? *Because it is a ball and the ball is heavier.*

Can you make a ball again with the pancake? *Yes, it will make the same thing as the other; you only have to squeeze it.*

Will it again be the same weight as the other? *Oh, no, when you make a ball with the pancake the ball is larger when you put all that together again.*

The scales are used to establish weight equivalence. (*He is astonished at the equivalence between the two balls and can give no explanation.*)

And now let's compare the ball with the pancake. *The pancake is lighter.* (*Equivalence of weight is again verified by the scales, and the child still remains confused.*)

These examples could be multiplied. Although our research is limited to the diagnosis of younger retardates, it would be interesting to use the same method to examine retardates termed "adult." In fact, the reactions of the morons and the imbeciles of twenty, thirty, and forty years of age do not differ from those already presented in this chapter. An example follows:

OBSERVATION 6—WID., F, 24:3

Wid. was referred by a social worker in her community because of refusal to work. Her pretext was limited vision or blindness. Examination proved this claim false, but established mental retardation. Her vision troubles were greatly exaggerated, and the answers she gave to questions concerning her sight were contradictory. Information from former schoolteachers confirmed the diagnosis of mental retardation. As a child, Wid. was obliged to repeat each class, and an elementary knowledge of arithmetic, spelling, and reading was acquired with difficulty. An optical examination verified the examiner's belief that visual troubles were willfully exaggerated, and that retardation made it difficult for her to comprehend and respond correctly to the examining situation. These troubles would not prevent the successful performance of manual tasks. The psychiatrist also noted a tendency to confabulate and a definite retardation.

The manner in which such a subject reasoned in the test situation was interesting, and her unwillingness to read was in contrast to her naïve interest in the transformation of a ball of clay.

Wid. immediately understood the concept of weighing and carefully made two identical balls.

You are going to transform one of the balls into a long sausage. (*While manipulating the clay she says:*) *It isn't the same thing. It was a ball before and now it has become lighter.*

Is there as much clay in the ball as there is in the sausage? *No, it is not the same thing. There is more in the ball. You take clay away from the ball to make the sausage. There is less; you lose some. (Continues spontaneously:) If you put the clay into a ball again you would have a ball like before.*

A ball of the same size? *No, not as big. It would be a little smaller.*

Why would it be smaller? *Because now it is spread out* [*i.e.,* the sausage is spread out].

And if, instead of stretching it, you broke the ball into little pieces? (*Hesitates a moment.*) *Maybe the same weight. Oh, no, it isn't! It's a little lighter, the little pieces. There is less clay. Some has been lost.*

How do you know there is less? *Perhaps some of it stuck to my hands. (She looks at her hands, but sees none.) No, there isn't any.*

Then how much do the little pieces weigh if you compare them to the ball? *Less, because there are lots of little pieces.*

And the amount of clay? *There isn't less because there was none lost, but it doesn't weigh the same thing.*

Equivalence of weight is established by the scales. (*She still believes in the equality of weight and will not let herself be persuaded. For some time she attempts to find an explanation, but finally gives up and says:*) *It still hasn't become lighter.*

These conversations seem to classify each of the above persons examined as retarded, but even though each is retarded, he presents certain individual pathological traits which distinguish him from other retardates. Although only six cases are cited, there is variation with respect to age, case history, general behavior, and reaction to the psychological examination. The ages of the subjects varied from ten or thirteen years to adults of over twenty years. Some had several years in special education classes, whereas others had only repeated their first years of primary school. Some could adapt to practical tasks, whereas others were prevented by instability from performing tasks which required only elementary processes. Some had accompanying physical deficiencies, while others were completely normal in appearance. Even with these variations, all those examined were either retarded or slow learners and had accompanying paranormal phenomena.

These phenomena were evidenced in the attitude adapted by the retardates in the testing situation. Each understood the given facts of the problem and had sufficient motivation to seek a solution. The only major variation from subject to subject was in the nature and consistency of this motivation. The first child's desire to succeed stemmed from a desire to appear adequate, *i.e.,* the affective contact stimulated him more than the problem itself. When Sta. was presented a delimited aspect of a problem, his interest quickly diminished, whereas conversation with the examiner held his intellectual interest. In the second subject, interest was aroused by the test itself. The child adapted rapidly, but later showed difficulty in continued concentration on the same object. The third subject reacted more slowly but became increasingly interested during the course of the test situation, whereas the fourth had a short attention span and poor retention. The fifth case could make precise observations, but showed perseveration. The sixth and final case, although more advanced in age, reacted more naturally to our questions and responded without tiring; her language structure was complex in contrast to her naïve thought content.

In certain instances, these individual characteristics can influence reasoning. A case discussed in Chapter 4 oscillated between several levels of reasoning. The discussion centers on the difficulties experienced by the individual in relating to his social group, on the one hand, and on the unstable nature of his operatory development on the other. Surprisingly enough, in spite of the individual paranormal phenomena, a common logical structure and identical psychological functioning remained in most of the cases. Because of this, an effort was made to establish the fact that the forms of reasoning presented in the first group of cases pertain to the same well-defined developmental stages. The stage was homogeneous to the first stage in conservation of substance, as shown in Piaget's genetic studies of the normal child.

The indices which center on the quantity of substance, weight, and volume (and which characterize a stage) changed with transformations or divisions of two identical clay balls. In most cases, although the contrary was also observed, the ball that had not been transformed was considered greater in quantity. Illustration is found in a review of the subjects' responses (in italics).

Observation 1: *In the ball there is more [than in the sausage]. The ball is heavier . . . because when it is stretched into a sausage it is lighter. In the little pieces there is less clay,* and also, in the case of the pancake, *there is always more in the ball.*

Observation 2: *There is more clay in the ball [than in the sausage].* After seeing the clay broken into pieces: *No, it is not the same thing. There are so many little pieces. It is not the same thing, the ball is heavier.* One reference to the pancake was *Oh, there's more because that is bigger and wider.*

Observation 3: *More of the green [clay] in the ball than in the sausage,* and *the little pieces are heavier,* and the same *there is more in the ball [than in the pancake].*

Observation 4: In the sausage, *there is less clay.* And when the clay is broken into pieces, *Now they are very small. There is not so much as there was before.* In the pancake, *it's made so that it is lighter [less clay].*

Observation 5: *In the sausage there is more clay . . . there are more things in the sausage,* after it is broken into pieces, *there is more in the ball. When you make a ball with the pancake the ball is larger when you put all that together again.*

Observation : *You take clay away from the ball to make a sausage. There is less. You lose some.* When the clay is broken into pieces, *It's a little lighter, the little pieces. There is less clay.*

The additions and subtractions anticipated by the subjects in successive transformations of the clay ball are set forth in the following table:

TABLE II

TRANSFORMATIONS ANTICIPATED BY SUBJECT

	Lengthening	Division into Small Pieces	Flattening
Observation 1	Subtraction	Addition	Addition
Observation 2	Subtraction	Addition	Addition
Observation 3	Subtraction	Subtraction	Subtraction
Observation 4	Subtraction	Addition	Subtraction
Observation 5	Addition	Subtraction	Addition
Observation 6	Subtraction	Subtraction	Not questioned

All the subjects believed in subtraction at one time and in addition in the quantity of substance at another. The one exception revealed a transitory belief that was unrelated to the basic aspects of operatory reasoning. Tus. (Observation 5) appeared to acknowledge momentarily that each of the two objects appeared "the same thing heavy" or "the same," whereas the little pieces had less clay because they were "separated." When the question was asked, he, like the other individuals at this level, said that the ball contained more clay "because it's a ball and the other is a pancake."

The following identical reactions are noted in the conservation of weight:

Observation 1: *The ball is heavier. That [the sausage] is stretched out, whereas the other is a ball. . . . When it is stretched into a sausage it becomes lighter. . . . The little pieces are lighter because they are stretched and then cut into pieces, and it [the ball] is heavier because it hasn't been touched . . . the ball is heavier because the pancake was squeezed and pressed and it is flat.*

Observation 2: *The sausage is lighter; it is not like the ball; it is squeezed more.* For the little pieces: *No it is not the same thing. The ball is heavier . . . it is harder, squeezed more. These [the little pieces] are lighter because they aren't squeezed very much. The pancake, it's lighter. It's not hard like the ball.*

Observation 3: *The ball is heavier because that is a ball. This is a sausage . . . when it is round it is heavier . . . the little pieces are heavier . . . they are so stretched; the clay is torn into pieces. There is more in the ball because the pancake is [gestures to signify spreading].*

Observation 5: *The sausage is longer and thinner and lighter than that [the ball] because that is—how do you say it—unrolled. . . . The little pieces are lighter because they are separated. . . . It isn't all in one piece . . . it's lighter when it is so little when it is separated.* After having anticipated briefly that the pancake was the same as the ball: *It's the ball which is heavier. I know! because it is a ball and the other is a pancake, and in the ball there is more clay.*

Observation 6: *No, it's not the same thing. It was a ball before and now it has become lighter.* For the division (after a slight hesitation), *Maybe the same weight. Oh, no it isn't! It's a little lighter, the little pieces. . . .*

A table presenting types of variation of weights believed by the subjects to occur follows:

TABLE III

VARIATION OF WEIGHT

	Lengthening	Division into Small Pieces	Flattening
Observation 1	Subtraction	Subtraction	Subtraction
Observation 2	Subtraction	Subtraction	Subtraction
Observation 3	Subtraction	Addition	Subtraction
Observation 4	Subtraction	Subtraction	Subtraction
Observation 5	Subtraction	Subtraction	Subtraction
Observation 6	Subtraction	Subtraction	Not questioned

Conservation of volume will be discussed in the following chapter. Attention is addressed now to the portion of Observation 2 in which the subject gave consideration to the little pieces—"they are too little" (to make the water rise)—after observing that the ball made a considerable rise in the water level.

The comments regarding substance, weight, and volume are surprisingly homogeneous. In fact, the above-mentioned retardates refused to acknowledge conservation in its earliest genetic form, substance, or consequently that of weight or volume.

The regularity of these reactions may be established statistically and standardized through testing. Such an approach risks overlooking the essential question, however: why are retardates unable to solve problems which are solved with ease by normal children of the same chronological age (the conservation of substance is usually discovered between seven and eight years of age, weight at approximately ten years and volume at approximately eleven years)? In order to answer this question, one must analyze the subject's elaboration and justification of their opinions concerning the nonconservation of matter.

A methodological difficulty is noted. Retarded subjects do not volunteer their opinions. Perhaps this is not due to their faulty mental functioning, but without doubt it constitutes a trait characteristic of their mentality, which can result from an inferior level of development. According to Piaget, egocentrism makes it difficult for a child to justify his opinions when they are compared with those of others or when their validity is questioned, because he believes the whole world thinks as he does. Neither does he realize the need for coherence between different viewpoints, nor can he be motivated to do so. To obtain proof by a simple recording of responses becomes impossible. The clinical approach is utilized, because it encourages the child to justify his beliefs, to formulate perceptions, and to make intuitive comparisons.

At this level of development, however, even skillful interrogation meets with difficulty. Because it is self-evident to him, the child is frequently unable to explain his nonconservation.

Examples of spontaneous and elicited replies regarding the nonconservation of substance given in italics:

There is addition or subtraction of substance because *it's less when it is stretched* (1); *there is less, you lose some* (6); or *in the little pieces there is less clay* (1); *the little pieces are heavier* (3); *they are so small* (4); or, in the case of the pancake, *the ball is heavier because the pancake is squeezed* (1); *the ball is larger* (5); or simply, *there can't be as much* (4), or again, *there is always more in the ball* (1).

The reasons most frequently given show the primacy of perception over intellectual operations. The child conceives only absolute and irreversible relations, such as bigger-smaller, or longer-thinner. Sometimes he is surprised that there are "so many little things" or that they are "so little." Incapable of operations of composition and reversibility, the child is bound by perceptive illusions, in which the substance appears to expand or contract.

Sometimes a subject explains the absence of conservation of substance by invoking the increase or the decrease of weight. Perhaps lack of conservation of weight makes him unaware of conservation of substance. In fact, at this level of development these two notions are still undifferentiated in the child's thought and are not distinguishable from that of volume. In future stages there is progressive differentiation, and the first to be attained is conservation of substance.

One could ask why the perception of differences dominates over the equivalence of the quantity of matter that was verified carefully by the child at the beginning of the experiment. Can this be attributed to a simple lack of memory? Because the subjects are abnormal children, possessed of varying degrees of retardation, the question demanded close examination. To accomplish this, the following questions were posed: "Do you remember how the balls were in the beginning?" or "Could you make a ball again?," etc. The responses were:

Observation 1: Anticipates that the ball can be remade. *Then the ball would be the same.* Why? *Because before it was just as large.*

Observation 2: Spontaneous anticipation: *If I make a ball again, then it is the same.*

Observation 3: And how were they at the start? *The same weight, just the same in everything.*

Observation 4: Visualizes the possible return to the initial state, but without being sure the ball will again be the same size as before.

Observation 5: And how were the two balls at the start? *The same thing heavy.*

Observation 6: Says spontaneously, *If you put the clay into a ball again you would have a ball like before.*

Each was capable of recalling the equality that was verified at the beginning and of visualizing a possible return to the initial state. Therefore, their belief in nonconservation of substance after transformation cannot be attributed to difficulty in memory, but essentially to deficiency in reasoning. They were incapable of a system of reversible operations which supposes more than a simple return to the starting point. Reversibility implies a coordination of relations which is capable of inverse as well as forward composition, and it is the absence of this reversible coordination that characterizes thought at this level of development.

The operatory aspect of the notions of conservation has been discussed in another work, *Le Développement des quantités physiques* (Piaget and Inhelder 1941), which examined the group of reactions just cited to determine whether they formed a coherent whole which could be called "mentality." In some cases, it was interesting to let the child verify the predictions by using scales and to observe the discrepancy between his predictions and reality. The fact that a subject was capable or incapable of integrating the new experimental data into his scheme of reasoning and of making them correspond to actual facts helps us to judge his development in reasoning. As it happened, none of the above subjects, after having verified experimentally the equality of weight between the transformed clay and the initial ball, knew how to interpret the fact in terms of the conservation of substance.

Observation 1: *It's you who makes it balance and stop now.*

Observation 3: Momentarily forecasts the correct interpretation, but immediately contradicts herself: *It's no longer the same weight, I think.*

Observation 5: An explanation is not found, and he remains disconcerted.

Observation 6: States simply, *It still hasn't become lighter,* without being able to deduct from this the permanence of substance.

Such impermeability to experience (which is limited to a simple reading of facts that either contradicts these facts or tries to justify them by subjective reasons) clearly shows that a child of this level is far from understanding the invariance of the quantity of substance. Although faulty, the group of responses are not the result of chance reactions, but reveal a consistent, clearly determined type of reasoning. In view of this fact, how can these reactions be interpreted in terms of the diagnosis of the mentally retarded? As is shown by the commentaries on each case, these subjects, in addition to their retardation, were possessed with diverse troubles. It seemed possible, therefore, that their reasoning in this testing situation would also differ, but this was not the case. The reactions to these tests of reasoning were homogeneous. Is it pure chance that all the subjects were incapable of constructing notions of conservation of substance, weight, or volume? Does the similarity denote a common mentality, fixed at an inferior level of thought development? Does the incapacity to comprehend conservation, even that of substance, constitute a sign of lesser ability?

Two methods exist which can be used to verify the second hypothesis. The first one is termed extrinsic and locates the particular results in a larger general investigation of mental organization. This procedure is necessary if a complete diagnosis is desired. The second method, termed intrinsic in relation to the study of reasoning as such, consists in locating the pathological reasoning in the overall picture furnished by a study of the development of normal thought. The advantage of the second method is that it delimits our research to the area of reasoning and encourages us to look within this area for operatory and genetic factors which can give indications of mental retardation.

The subjects included in this study were not only inept in solving problems accomplished by normal children of seven to eight years but also presented, almost word for word, the same judgments and reasoning found in normal children between five and seven years in reply to the same tests. Not only has the absence of several isolated logical operations been noted but also the presence of a type of reasoning whose characteristics must be specified as applying to a particular intellectual level.

In children of eleven, twelve or thirteen years, and even in adults, a type of reasoning characteristic of normal children under eight years is an indication of fixation at an infantile level or of mental retardation. In other words, each of the above-mentioned subjects had a reasoning structure well below that of his chronological age. The severity of the retardation appears to be related to the age of the subject. The method of determining retardation by the relation of the mental age to the chronological age has some value, but this relationship could never assume mathematical rigor, because mental evolution, even though continuous, includes neither regular growth nor a qualitatively homogeneous unfolding. In child logic, the fundamental notions appear to be acquired at approximately twelve years. If a child of fourteen has the reasoning processes of a ten-year-old, the relation $10/14$ does not necessarily have the same relationship that a relation of $5/7$ would have when observed in a child of seven years.

The test of the transformation of a clay ball permits a diagnosis of retardation in reasoning for all the previously cited cases, and it is easy to determine the qualitative level of this retardation, since none of the subjects exceed a stage of reasoning common to normal children of seven years. Moreover, to establish a genetic diagnosis concerning the level of thought development is not always sufficient; often a prognosis is indispensable. Here analysis of some essential operations of thought gives the more important indications. In Observation 4, the school had stated that the child could no longer follow the regular program, and that he had particular difficulty in understanding elementary mathematical problems. Because the child was unstable, difficult, and the product of an unfavorable environment, the causes of his scholastic deficiency probably were numerous. A test of general intelligence based on scholastic ability cannot identify true intellectual inferiority. An analysis of reasoning does make this differential diagnosis and is the rational starting point for a prognosis and for planning a remedial program.

In the case of the young epileptic, Observation 2, it is important to determine whether the intellectual operations have been impeded in their development. The prognosis could be completely different in a case of a child with normal thought function, whose problem was merely the retention of signs of excessive fatigue.

In order to take a professional and scholastic view of our retarded subjects it is important to know, as in Observation 5, that this boy is retarded even though his physical appearance is that of a normal child. To increase the number of hours he is in school is useless; it is also useless to have him repeat the same academic training. Practical training would be more suitable.

If these examples were multiplied, one would see the value of genetic and qualitative diagnosis of reasoning. However, an objection immediately arises. Care must be taken not to exaggerate the clinical significance of reasoning as indicated by conservation of matter in subjects who are above the normal age for this process. If important indications can be derived from reactions in a limited area, it is because an operatory and genetic analysis of reasoning, as measured in the conservation of substance, made it possible to show how the operations utilized in such reasoning relate to the entire thought processes in normal subjects under seven years of age. Thus by analysis of the reasoning pertaining to the invariance in the quantity of substance, it becomes possible to extricate an operatory process common to all elementary intellectual activities. These indices may be used as criteria for retardation of reasoning.

The study of the development of normal thought shows that the discovery of the conservation principle, even in examples as elementary as the conservation of substance or quantity of matter, requires in reality the construction of a closed and reversible system of operations. In the area of qualitative logic, Piaget called the system a "groupment," by analogy to the "groups" used in mathematical operations. For example, in the transformation of the clay ball, an understanding of the notion of conservation requires: (1) recognition that the whole is comprised of a reuniting of the parts (composition), (2) realization that any arrangement of the same parts results in the same whole (associativity), (3) awareness that all transformations, such as the changing of a ball into a sausage, can be annulled by the inverse transformation (reversibility), and (4) comprehension that each part retains its identity (identical operation by reunion of the part to itself). The construction of the unvarying whole requires logic. Moreover, such a process is general. To reason correctly and to make any coherent representation is impossible without the notion of conservation, for without conservation, the logical framework of thought would lack structure. However, if all conservation is based on grouping, the operatory process that constitutes the "grouping" will be found in all classification, in seriation, and in all numbering as it is encountered in all experimental activity which is concerned with thought that is adapted to the physical world. In the clinical situation, the discovery of conservation signifies a more comprehensive intellectual activity than is indicated by the special problem on which questioning is centered.

Although the presence of a groupment is symptomatic of an activity that is logical in nature, the absence of groupment, *i.e.,* the lack of a certain form of conservation discussed elsewhere in this chapter, does not constitute a simple negative sign which indicates a breach in the subject's intelligence. When the relations entering into the thought processes are not grouped, *i.e.,* when they do not constitute closed and reversible systems, as was shown in the above example, they are not completely disorganized. Instead of being centered in relation to reasoning activity (groupment), they are centered on the activity itself. The opposite of groupment is egocentrism of thought, which, according to Piaget, forms the general basis of earlier prelogical thought. If subjects deny that there is conservation of quantity when the clay ball is stretched into a sausage, it is because from their visual perception and motor activity, or sensory-motor schemes inherent in their activity, the ball appears to be heavier and to contain more material than the sausage, in that the sausage is stretched out, or thinner. The primacy of perception on intellectual construction is in fact the primacy of subjectivity on the object, or of egocentrism on the logical grouping.

The fact that children aged ten to fourteen years, or even some adults, deny the conservation of substance, which normally occurs at seven years, does not signify that these subjects are incapable of groupment logic. However, these retardates are assigned to a category of intellectual egocentrism which includes events concerned with representation of the world and causality, and which is their attitude toward experience in general. Not only did the above subjects contest a priori the conservation of matter but—even more important—they were not able to profit from the experience of seeing objects weighed which they believed to be of unequal weight. This impermeability to experience is a clear manifestation of egocentrism, which is contrary to the construction of logical groupments.

2. Experiment Concerning the Dissolution of Sugar

If the experiments on the transformation of clay balls permit the diagnosis of certain difficulties, the following experiments furnish concrete information about previously diagnosed troubles of operatory functioning. In these experiments, the subjects were presented with a problem involving synthesis, the solution of which required a more complex effort of adaptation. Logical construction was required, as well as certain representations and experimental attitudes. In these tests, one or more cubes of sugar were dissolved in a glass of water. The retardates were then asked if the sugar which disappeared perceptively was conserved qualitatively and quantitatively in the solution. If there was an idea of conservation, it was interesting to note under which of these two forms the subject imagined the invisible permanance of the sugar in the water.

Prior to the study, 100 normal subjects, ages four to twelve, were interrogated. Genetic analysis revealed the same stages of conservation as were found in the transformation of the clay ball; furthermore these were characterized by a progressive development of atomistic representations as schemes of composition of matter. During normal development there is a synchronization among (1) development of operations, (2) atomistic explanations, and (3) experimental attitudes. This synchronization, although interesting, does not reveal anything surprising in normal children whose thought processes develop harmoniously. From the psychological, as well as from the diagnostic, point of view (which is the one used in this research) it would be instructive to find the same synchronization and the same relationships among these three distinct processes in the mentally retarded. Conservation of substance, weight, and volume of sugar requires only the reversible construction referred to earlier as Piaget's operatory "groupment." In addition, the atomistic representation also constitutes a sort of groupment, because the unseen grains of sugar are conceived of as a real element of composition. Besides simple logical operations, such construction supposes a detailed spatio-temporal representation, which seems to require psychological functions other than simple deduction leading to conservation. The lesson the subject gains from the experiment arises from very different functions, because it brings into play the subject-object relation more than the coherence, among themselves, of the subject's judgments. If we do not admit a priori that groupment constitutes the opposite of egocentric thought, we cannot see immediately the relation of interdependence that can exist among these three processes of physical reasoning.

It is possible that in a retardate, advanced in age but arrested at an inferior level of reasoning, the atomistic representations (to the extent that they are based on intuitive facts) will be (1) ahead of, (2) at the same level, or (3) at a lower level than his logical operations. The question regarding the child's experimental reasoning may be concerned with type rather than mental level. The analysis of observations will provide interesting points and, in fact, show a high similarity to normal development.

The dissolution of sugar test, desirable because it utilizes everyday experience and observations accessible to all, is administered in the following way: the subject is presented with two glasses filled with the same quantity of water. The water level is marked with a rubber band and the equality of weight is established by scales. Then the examiner asks what will happen when cubes of sugar are put into one of the glasses of water. The question is intentionally vague at first, in order to permit the child to approach it in his own manner. The interrogation must be extremely flexible and must follow the individual course of reasoning. The correct method respects spontaneity and individuality of thought, but leads the interrogation toward the essential points of the analysis. For example, it is necessary to know: (1) whether the subject does or does not believe in substance conservation and in the variance of weight and volume, (2) what his atomistic representations are, and (3) up to what point he can interpret the intuitive and experimental facts of conservation. The method is illustrated by excerpts from interrogations.

With few exceptions all the subjects interviewed on the transformation of the clay ball and also questioned concerning the dissolution of sugar in water gave corresponding results. Additional cases are cited, however, in order to give the reader a more adequate idea of the multiplicity of types of deficiencies found among retardates. It is surprising to find in this psychological analysis the same primitive functioning of thought.

OBSERVATION 7—LUB., F, 9:5

At the time of the examination Lub. was in a class for slow learners. She suffered neither from instability nor hyperactivity, was docile and conscientious in her work, and presented no behavior problems in the classroom. Immediate retention of learning approached that of the normal, but processes of acquisition were abnormally slow. She was a bradypsychic. A mournful expression or a blissful smile accompanied all her mental activity. Affectivity was infantile and uninhibited; self-appraisal was not well developed, and scholastic achievement was inferior. Observations made by her teachers and test results both indicated borderline mental retardation, characterized by a slow, complacent attitude. The same level of retardation was evident in all her constructive activity. Her chronological age was nine years and five months; her mental age appeared to be seven years, therefore retardation was not severe. When seen three years after the examination her development had continued, but still at a retarded rate.

Close analysis of the reasoning of a child whose mental age does not differ greatly from her chronological age is interesting. As noted in the following illustration, Lub. quickly understood the problem and successively examined different hypotheses. The little girl attempted to supply answers to her own questions. If she was unable to give the solutions expected for her age, it was because her operative development was two or three years retarded.

What will happen if I put this sugar in the water? *It will rise higher . . . no the sugar would be melted.*

And why did you think that the water would rise? *Because the sugar takes up room. . . . But instead it melts. It doesn't rise . . . [reflects].*

Which is more correct: to say that the water rises or that it doesn't rise? *Both, first it rises and then it goes back down.*

What happens to the sugar when it is soaked in the water? (*Reflects.*)

Does it stay as it is now, or what happens? *No, it melts.*

To melt, what does that mean? How can you say that another way? *Afterward there will be no sugar. It will all be gone away.*

Does it still have a taste or not? *Oh, it's sugar, that's for sure.*

But why? *Because the sugar has already been inside.*

And if you keep the glass for several days, does the water stay sugared? *Not any more because you think when it is left like that the water cannot keep the taste. The taste alone cannot remain.*

We are going to drop the sugar in and see what happens, O.K.? First, we will mark the water level exactly in order to see if it moves. (The level is marked by means of a rubber band. *The child immerses the sugar.*) *It has risen, you see. I told you that it takes up room, but it can't stay like that. It goes down again as soon as the sugar melts.*

We are going to remember what you have just said and try it afterward. Now we are going to weigh. (Scales are used to establish the weight equivalence of the two glasses of water.)

And if you put a piece of sugar in? *That doesn't matter much. Once it's melted it's not heavy any more at all; it's like it was plain water again because the sugar disappeared.*

After the complete dissolution of the sugar, the level is noted. *The water stayed up high.*

Why? How do you explain that? *Because we put sugar in there.*

And now is it still there? *Because the sugar . . . no it's no longer inside.*

Then why does the water stay elevated? *Because the spoon is still inside* (the one that was used for stirring).

We will take out the spoon. (*Expresses astonishment as she closely observes the contents of the glass.*) *There, there are several little particles which float.*

They take up room, these several little particles? *No, now there is nothing more. It is all clear.*

OBSERVATION 8—BUC., F, 10:5

The physical appearance and mental behavior of Buc. differed greatly from the preceding case. First, her mental retardation was more accentuated. When she was six years of age a psychiatrist determined her IQ to be 69, and her case history emphasized the congenital character of her retardation and the general deficiency of mental organization. At eight years the same test, Stanford-Binet, resulted in an IQ of 82. Had the child made this mental gain in two years? Review of her academic record did not confirm the hypothesis. A program of special instruction was followed with great difficulty. Her teachers reported very conscientous work and her scrupulosity bordered on the pathological. Although the child performed better in work demanding concentration, she was almost completely incapable of personal reflection. For these reasons Buc. did not seem merely a case of retardation. Added to her mental deficiency were emotional problems and affective disequilibrium. Did the child's awareness of her intellectual incapacity make her easily discouraged? Rather than the emotional problems hampering mental development, the mental retardation seemed due to heredity and intellectual difficulties which persisted despite special methods for learning.

In spite of her initial inhibitions, the child quickly became familiar with the nonscholastic task and showed no anxiety.

What will happen if you put two pieces of sugar in the water? *They melt slowly.*

Why do they melt? *Because they are white, and when they get wet they melt.*

And then what? *That makes sugared water.*

Is there still some of the sugar in the water? *No, it isn't there any longer.*

Then what is in the glass? *Water.*

Does this water have a taste? *A sugared taste.*

And when you leave the glass of water like that for several days, does it keep the taste? *Yes.*

Will you see some of the sugar when it is melted? *No, no, you see nothing more.*

Do you think the water level will rise or lower when the sugar is put it? *The water doesn't rise. The sugar isn't heavy.*

It only rises when something heavy is put in? *Yes, it must really weigh something.*

We will go on to the experiment after we see that the water level and the weight of the two glasses are equal. *It has risen just the same.*

Why do you think so? *Well, the sugar is a little heavier.*

Once the sugar is melted, where will the water level be? Show me the place. *The water goes back down because you can't see the sugar any more when it is melted, and then it doesn't weigh anything any more.*

Why doesn't it weigh anything any more? *But it isn't there any more [astonished that such a question could be asked]. It is simply gone, it goes away when it melts.*

A check is made following the dissolution. Does the water go back to its first level? *Not completely.*

Why not completely? *It's still heavy; the water that has something inside.*

Where does this water come from that's heavy? *But it's water from the faucet.*

But why is it heavier than the other? Look at the scales. *That, I don't understand.*

Tell me, is there any way to get back the sugar that was put in the inside? *No, it's no longer there. It's simply gone.*

OBSERVATION 9—WIES., F, 11:1

Syndactylism was noted in this girl, who was very small in stature. After several years of failure in a primary school she was placed in an institution for retardates. Psychological examinations reported that an IQ of 70 was accompanied by hyperactivity and psychomotor difficulties. The following information was contained in her school record: scholastic performance was irregular; attention span was short; there was failure in problems of formal reasoning; behavior was that of an uninhibited, talkative, hyperactive child who desired, but probably did not have, social contacts.

When the child was seen three years later she had made some scholastic progress in courses adapted to her level of ability. Some of her classwork was at the fourth-grade level, but she was assigned to lower classes for spelling and arithmetic. While there was some progress in verbal and written expression, her thoughts remained quite immature. Further intellectual progress could not be expected. The question was: should her academic training be continued or should she learn household work?

Reaction to the test and the examiner was immediate. She jumped around gaily, ready to be amused, or even to work.

What do you think will happen when the two pieces of sugar are put in the water? *The water becomes sweet.*

Why? *Because the sugars are sweet themselves.*

And does the sugar stay in pieces? *No? They are going to melt.*

What does that mean exactly, to melt? *At first the sugar is whole, and then when you put it in the water and you wait . . . After several hours it is all melted.*

And how does it become when it melts? *Very small.*

And when you wait a long time? *Oh, after some time it has all melted. It is no longer inside.*

Is there anything more at all? *No, nothing.*

You can't get the sugar back? *Well no, it's gone.*

Will the water stay at the same level it is now when you put the sugar inside or will it move? *It rises, no, it stays the same because the sugar melts.*

(The two glasses are compared and equality of weight demonstrated.) How much will the glass weigh when the sugar is put in? *Since you put sugar in it's a little heavier.*

And when it is melted? *It's light again. As light as plain water.*

(The sugar is dropped in the water.) (*The child observes that the level rises when the sugar is immersed.*)

Why does the water rise? *Because you put the sugar in.*

And when the sugar is melted does that change something about the level or does the level move? *The water goes down again. The sugar melts and in the end it is no longer inside.*

Why is it still sweet when the sugar is no longer there? *Because before there was sugar inside. You put it in there and the taste is still there.*

(Demonstration.) Look at the two levels. Has the water gone back down like you thought? *It is still up high.*

But meanwhile the sugar has melted. *I don't understand: It's because of the rubber band.* (*The levels were marked by rubber bands.*)

And when the rubber band is taken off, the water goes down? *I think so. It can't stay. The sugar isn't there any longer.*

Now we are going to weigh the two glasses. How will the scales be? *Oh, the same. It's like the other glass again.*

(Demonstration.) (*She sees the inequality. After a long reflection:*) *There is more water inside, you see!*

Where did this water, that there is more of, come from? *From the fountain.* (*She does not understand the relation of the sugar and is astonished by the question.*)

But you remember in the beginning there was just the same amount of water; they weighed the same. *Yes, yes, weight, but you put the sugar in . . . But now the sugar isn't there any more.*

OBSERVATION 10—RUE., M, 12:0

Rue.'s academic achievement had been closely observed. Because his physical appearance was normal, the school physician had permitted him to enter primary school. There it soon became evident that he was incapable of following routine classes. The first grade was repeated without success. Following this his peasant parents decided to place him in an institution. When he was interviewed at the age of nine years he could count up to ten on his fingers and recognize some letters, but he lacked word recognition and was unable to compose simple words or to add. He spoke little at school and preferred to play preschool games. There was a noticeable lack of motivation. During four years of special instruction the elementary techniques of reading and writing were acquired. He evidenced interest in the growth of plants and animals and he was enthusiastic over farm work. Because of his scholarly application and his memory ability he was even able to learn part of the multiplication tables. However, his incapacity to analyze simple arithmetic problems or to master a situation requiring thought continued.

Immediate and sustained interest was noted for tests such as the dissolution of sugar. However he was not able, through reasoning, to comprehend that the sugar substance remained in the water although it was invisible. The two glasses of water were weighed, and the child had no difficulty in confirming the equality of weight and of level.

And if you put two pieces of sugar in the water what will happen? *The water is sweet.*

Why? *Because the sugar you put in is sweet.*

And what happens to the pieces of sugar? *They melt.*

Can you still see the sugar when it is melted? *No.*

But it will still be in the water? *No, it is no longer inside.*

And the taste? *It stays.*

And how can the taste stay when there's no longer any sugar there? *That gives taste to the water, I don't understand how the taste remains.*

Will the level rise or go down when you put the sugar in the water? *The water rises a bit.*

Why does it rise? *Because it hasn't much room when you put the sugar in.*

(*The child puts the sugar in and is delighted with his correct prediction.*)

And when the sugar is melted? *The water goes down again because the sugar has melted and the water has room again.*

And what is the weight of this glass that has the sugar in it when it is weighed again with the plain water? *Now it is a little bit heavier, but when it is melted it is like it was before.*

Is it as light as plain water now or heavier? *Yes, like completely plain water. The same as the other.*

We are going to see. Watch what happens to the sugar. *It's like little threads. (Watches the process of dissolution into particles. After several moments:) You don't see anything any more. It is gone.*

Look; has the level gone down again? *Not completely yet. The sugar hasn't melted yet like it must.*

And then when it has all melted like it must, you think it will go down? *Yes, it's sure to.*

(Demonstration of weight.) *It's heavier. (Laughs.) It is because the sugar inside hasn't all melted yet. We have to wait.*

The water remained up high and it is heavier than the plain water, but we can't see the sugar, how can this be? *I don't know, maybe there is still some of the sugar inside.*

The impression may have been given that the retardates included in this study reply with the same eloquence as younger normal children. If advanced word usage and sentence structure are quite striking in some of them, there are others who express themselves with difficulty and from whom responses are elicited only because of the examiner's skill in following detours and repetitions. Such a pattern is noted in the following case:

OBSERVATION 11—MUG., M, 16:5

The mother of the child was schizophrenic and had been confined to an institution for fifteen years. Since early childhood, Mug. had displayed diverse psychotic problems, of which mental retardation was the predominant deficiency. Retardation, but not of the same degree, was evidenced in all functions. Language was particularly hampered. At sixteen and a half the boy still expressed himself in incomplete sentences. Grammar and spelling comprised his main areas of difficulty. There was no question of maladaptation to the primary program. Mug. had repeated each of his elementary classes two or three times. Later, when placed in the understanding atmosphere of a special class, he was able to make some progress, particularly in manual work, which he performed accurately. He also had a good memory for numbers and mechanically adapted the rules of calculation to arithmetic problems, but he did not understand their logical structure.

Moreover, Mug. was very withdrawn, suspicious, and timid. Only in a sympathetic atmosphere did he respond to social contacts and take an interest in what went on around him.

He demonstrates the equality of weight and levels of the two glasses of water.

What happens if I put these pieces of sugar in the water? *They melt.*

What does that mean? *They melt.*

Do they stay in whole pieces? *Oh, no.*

Will you still see the sugar when it is melted? *No.*

Will the level of the water change when the sugar is dropped in? *It stays where it is; it melts in the water [the sugar].*

Will the weight change when the sugar is put in the water? (The glasses are on the scales.) *Heavier.*

(He observes the demonstration.) *It rises.*

Why does the level rise? *Because it is heavier.*

Why is it heavier when the sugar is added? *I don't know very well.* (*Observes the scales.*) *You see it is heavy.*

And when it is melted will it still be the same? *No, it lowers.*

Why will it lower? *No more sugar.*

Because there isn't any sugar in the water any more? *No, it isn't inside any more, still a little powder and then nothing else.*

How were the two glasses on the scales when the sugar was put it? *Not just as heavy after that. Heavier when the sugar was put in.*

And now how will the two pans be on the scales? *The same again —like the other glass, like plain water.*

Look at the water level; has it gone down like you thought? *No, it has risen because you put in the sugar.*

Then it has stayed up high. How do you explain that? *Don't know. The sugar isn't there any more.*

And if the level stays up high, what weight will the water have now? *The same. (Indicates the glass which contains plain water.)*

(Weight equality is demonstrated on the scales.) *Heavier because you had thrown in two pieces of sugar.*

But now no more of the sugar is seen and you thought that there wasn't any more. *The glass is thick* [*the glass which contains the water*].

If you drank the contents of this glass, would it have a taste or not? *It's sweet.*

Why is it still sweet? *Because you put two sugars in.*

But are they still there in some sort of way? *Not any more.*

Then there is nothing at all left of the sugar? *No, only the taste.*

OBSERVATION 12—DOR., F, 52

In conclusion, the interview of an adult fifty-two years of age is presented. This trainable retardate had been referred for examination prior to placement in an appropriate institution. The first grades of primary school had been repeated. Dor. knew how to read and write, and she could converse on familiar subjects without betraying her mental subnormality, but the inferiority was quite evident in intellectual tasks. After several years of school she remained at home, unoccupied. At the death of her parents her brothers and sisters tried to locate employment for her. At this time the degree of her mental retardation was perceived. Up until then it had been hidden by a verbal façade. She proved unable to adapt to any job. Dor. could barely understand the most simple instructions; she lacked initiative and perseverance and could not handle responsibility. Employment was located in a hospital where the supervisor taught her simple techniques of house cleaning and food preparation, but at the end of several months she was rejected because of lack of training and intelligence.

Her responses concerning the dissolution of sugar in water follow:

Certainly you have already seen sugar melting in water? *Oh, when I take tea and stir it there are grains in the bottom of the cup, but when I stir well there isn't anything.*

Then we are going to do it, but with pure water in order to see clearly what happens. First we weigh the two glasses. (*Observes weight equality.*)

And since there is the same amount of water in both, the level is equally high, and in order to remember it we are going to mark the levels with these two rubber bands. (*Follows attentively all the details of the experiment.*)

And now tell me what will happen if we put all the sugar in? *It melts, I don't know, it gets smaller. It falls apart, and then finally you can't see it any more.*

When you don't see anything any more, is it because there isn't anything left or can it be that some sugar remains? *Nothing more; you know no one has ever asked me that, but I don't know how there could be anything there.*

This water still has a taste even when you can't see any more sugar? *Of course, it's sugared water.*

But where does this taste come from if there isn't any more sugar as you said? *The taste always remains. It always stays longer.*

And if we leave this glass for several days like that would it keep the taste? *Oh, well I'm not very sure about that.*

While waiting, we will put the sugar in. Will the level always stay as we marked it or will it move? *It splashes a little, that's all.*

We will immerse the sugar. *Oh, it rises.*

We will mark the second level. Why do you think it rose? *The sugar is a little heavy, but when it melts it's like it was before.*

It doesn't stay at the upper rubber band? *No, it lowers.*

And about the weight? You watched; what did the scales do when the sugar was put in? *It goes down. It is a very little bit heavy now.*

How will it be when the sugar is melted? *Oh, like before. It is clear water.*

(*She stirs the solution and watches what happens.*) *See there is small grains, like particles . . . It's like powdered sugar. You know, like people use for jam. Now you see, they are very small . . . I don't see anything more.*

(During the dissolution the glass with the marked level and the scales were hidden behind a screen.) Now we are going to see if the water goes down again like you thought. *No, it's funny, there's the rubber band; then it stayed up high.*

And if you took away the rubber band? *Perhaps it goes down.* (*Watches the level with curiosity.*)

We take it off. Did it move? *Maybe a little.*

But all in all it doesn't go back to the lower rubber band? *No.*

Why not? *I don't know.*

How do you think the scale will be now, still heavier on the side where the sugar melted? *No, it is light. It is completely melted. You don't see anything. It is plain water.*

The screen is removed to reveal the two glasses on the scales. (*Stupefaction.*)

As illustrated by these interviews, all the subjects, although beyond the age of six to seven years, *i.e.,* the period characterized by egocentrism in reasoning, retain their ideas of the complete disappearance of substance. Several of the subjects' suppositions will be listed. These subjects did not know how to express clearly the belief in the quality of nonconservation. At this level of significance the term "melt" denotes an irreversible process. Subjects give it the following interpretations:

Afterward there will be no sugar. It will all be gone away (7). *No, it isn't there any longer* (8). *After some time it has all melted. It is no longer inside* (9). Again, *It is no longer inside . . . It's like little threads . . . You don't see anything any more. It is gone* (10); or *No, it isn't inside any more, still a little powder and then nothing else* (11). *It melts, I don't know, it gets smaller. It falls apart, and then finally you can't see it any more.* Can some of it still remain? *I don't know how there could be something there* (12).

Retardates who predicted addition or subtraction of the quantity of substance in the transformation of the clay ball deny in the dissolution of sugar that there can be qualitative permanence. They state there is a complete disappearance of substance. Their thought, which errs in constructing an operative groupment or in assessing reversibility, follows the physical process of dissolution and remains dominated by facts supplied by sensory perception. The same errors are noted in questions of weight and volume; the latter is measured by the quantity of displaced water. All the above-mentioned subjects assumed the disappearance of substance and predicted the equality of weight in the control glass and the glass containing the sugar solution. Several of these responses follow in italics: *Once it's melted it's not heavy any more at all . . . it's like it was plain water again because the sugar disappeared* (7). *You can't see the sugar any more when it is melted, and then it doesn't weigh anything any more* (8). *Then light again. As light as plain water* (9). *Now it is a little bit heavier, but when it is melted it is like it was before . . . like completely plain water. The same as the other* (10). *The same again, like the other glass, like plain water* (11). *Oh, like before. It is clear water* (12).

Similar responses are given for volume. All predicted that the level that marked the height of the water at the moment of the immersion of the sugar would descend to the former level during the dissolution.

Observation 7 said: *It can't stay like that. It goes down again as soon as the sugar melts.* Observation 8: *The water goes back down because you can't see the sugar any more when it is melted.* Observation 9: *The water goes down again. The sugar melts and in the end it is no longer inside.* Observation 10: *The water goes down again because the sugar has melted and the water has room again.* Observation 11: When it is melted, will it stay where it is now? *It stays where it is, it melts in the water . . . no it lowers . . . no more sugar.* Observation 12: *But when it melts it's like it was before . . . it lowers.*

The above responses demonstrate a perfect coherence in the beliefs of nonconservation of material. From the operatory viewpoint the same absence of groupment that was previously revealed (ball of clay) and the same primacy of immediate and subjective perception are noted. In addition, the sugar experiment questions in a new and more precise way the relations between reasoning and the experiment.

Reasoning operates as a function of an intuitively determined content, which consists, in the first instance, in the dissolution of a piece of sugar into small grains, visible at first, but then seeming to disappear; and, in the second, in the fact that the substance under consideration is qualified by a permanent taste. The direct experiment simultaneously offers facts of disappearance and indices of continuation of substance, and it is of great interest to examine more closely how the subject assimilated the facts.

All the retardates (probably because they are more advanced in years than normal children at this level) have already observed that water with melted sugar in it becomes sugared, and they did not remember it spontaneously, questions were asked to call their attention to this fact. However, and this is curious, they managed perfectly well to reconcile the absence of sugar (as a subtraction of substance) with the permanence of taste, or they simply imagined that the taste they observed would disappear in its turn, or they considered it sweetened by an independent permanence. Several of their thoughts on this subject are given:

Observation 7: *It's sugar, that's for sure . . . Because the sugar has already been inside.* And if you keep the glass does the water stay sugared? *Not any more, because you think when it is left like that, that the water cannot keep the taste. The taste alone cannot remain.*

Observation 8 knows that the sugar taste remains when the sugar is no longer visible in the water. Observation 9: Why is it still sweet when the sugar is no longer there? *Because before there was sugar inside. You put it there and the taste is still there.* Observation 10: How can the taste stay when there's no longer any sugar there? *That gives taste to the water, I don't understand how the taste remains.* Observation 11: *It's sweet because you put two sugars in.* . . . Then there is nothing at all left of the sugar? *No, only the taste.* Observation 12: *The taste always remains. It always stays longer.*

None of the subjects had the idea of interpreting the presence of taste as witness to a permanence of substance. On the contrary, they assimilated this intuitive fact, taste, into their scheme of nonconservation. This is an example of the transformation known to be characteristic of the egocentric mentality of children of four to seven or eight years.

The conclusion these subjects drew from the physical process of dissolution was not the sort of atomism by which normal children of approximately twelve years explain the conservation of substance in the solution, nor can such a conclusion be expected of retardates at this level. However, all of them have closely observed the decomposition of some form of substance into small grains or dust, or they have watched the pulverization of sugar and have been able to recover deposits of sugar or salt in a saturated solution. Here is another fact indicative of one of their mental traits, and one that initially appears to be the antithesis of egocentrism, but in reality is only a particular aspect of the surface reasoning of the subject which cannot surpass actual fact. The phenomenon of pulverization and dissolution is thus registered as such without being interpreted as an index of the permanence of substance.

Observation 7: *There are several particles which float . . . now there is nothing more. It is all clear.* Observation 8: *They are white, and when they get wet they melt.* Observation 9: *At first the sugar is whole, and then when you put it in the water and you wait . . . After several hours it is all melted . . . very small . . . It is no longer inside.* Observation 10: *It's like little threads . . . you don't see anything any more. It is gone.* Observation 11: *Still a little powder and then nothing else.* Observation 12: *There are grains in the bottom . . . but when I stir well there isn't anything . . . it melts . . . it gets smaller. It falls apart, and then finally you can't see it any more.* During the dissolution he observes: *See there is small grains, like particles. . . . It's like powdered sugar . . . now you see they are very small . . . I don't see anything more.*

These facts, as well as the reflections pertaining to taste, prove that these subjects observed phenomena which bring normal individuals of their age to the idea of conservation of substance. However, these retardates are quite far from interpreting them as a principle of conservation and consider them instead to be indices of the disappearance of substance. It is, then, evident—but not a proven psychological fact —that the belief in conservation or nonconservation of substance does not result from the observation of facts, but from the intellectual structure by means of which these facts are assimilated by the subject, whether he be normal or pathological. A child at the level now being discussed will have assimilated over the years a series of observations (persistence of taste, dispersion of particles of sugar in liquid, clouds formed in the water by sugar in suspension, etc.), but will not be capable of relating these observations logically into a coherent system. A subject at a higher level, in turn, needs only a fact from experience, which is assimilated immediately to schemes of conservation, and any other conception seems illogical to him.

Registered experiences cannot be said to be prolonged without reasoning occurring. All experience has to be interpreted, and this process of assimilation offers during the present stage this double character of dwelling on the exterior of things (*e.g.,* the observation of the dissolution of sugar into particles), and of transforming the observed facts (*e.g.,* the evidence that the taste either evaporates or continues to exist without relation to its supportive substance). This assimilation of intuitive facts into the reasoning of the subject may be due to chance, but is one aspect of the prelogical mentality of young children. Consideration is given again to previously made observations concerning operatory functioning. If the absence of conservation of substance is explained in part by default of "groupment," it has just been shown that it results also from an egocentric assimilation of qualitative facts. The behaviors of reasoning under their most operative aspect, and those of observation or of experience under their most intuitive aspect, are then indissociable and complementary, and, as just observed in the analysis of retarded reasoning, are subject to the same accidents or arrestation of development.

Moreover, nothing is more instructive in the elucidation of the general relations between reasoning and experience at different levels of mental retardation than the examination of the experimental reasoning of the subjects in its active functioning, *i.e.,* the analysis of their reactions to demonstrations made experimentally during the interview and which bear on the constancy of level and of weight in spite of the dissolution of sugar. Can these facts be considered illustrations of the conservation of sugar, or does their observation shatter their conviction of the disappearance of matter? An examination of the subjects' reactions may provide an answer.

The subject cited in Observation 7 at first seemed to establish a relation between the constancy of the level and the permanence of the sugar:

Because we put sugar in there . . . Because the sugar [pauses] *no, it's no longer inside.* As he seeks another explanation, he sees the spoon, which serves to elevate the water level, but once the spoon is removed he fails to interpret it in relation to the permanence of substance. Subject 8, seeing the constancy of the level, concluded: *It is still heavy, it's the water that has something inside,* but without conceiving how, as certain normal children of the same age would, there is a transformation of the substance into liquid. For him, *It's water from the faucet,* and when he compares the weight he finishes by saying, *I don't understand.* Similarly, Subject 9 says: *I don't understand, it's because of the rubber band,* and he believes that if the rubber band is removed the level will again descend. Subject 10 concludes simply that the process of the dissolution of sugar is not yet finished: *The sugar hasn't melted yet like it must,* and continues to believe it will go down in proportion to the melting of the sugar. Likewise, when considering the weight, he shows the same tendency to disregard the fact of dissolution: *The sugar hasn't melted yet like it must . . . We have to wait,* and realizes only at the end that there could be a relation between the demonstrated weight and the substance of the dissolved sugar. The next subject (Observation 11) invokes the thickness of the glass to explain equality of weight between the glass of plain water and that containing the solution of sugar. Subject 12 simply shows stupefaction, without trying to interpret the fact that is contrary to her prediction.

We can see that these subjects present different reactions when they observe facts of the experiment which do not correspond to their expectations. Some remain astonished without being able to form new hypotheses. Others refute the facts, convinced that the experiment sooner or later will accommodate their idea. Then there are those who, by faulty deduction, establish links that could be called purely phenomenalistic no matter what is invoked as the cause, provided that it occurs in the same perceptive field (thickness of glass, rubber band, etc.).

What these attitudes have in common is an impermeability to experimental facts and an incapacity to modify a belief or prediction in relation to the experiments. This imperviousness recalls, though to a lesser degree, the pathological phenomena of perseveration and obstinacy. A type of mental attitude characterizing paranormal reactions is evident. It may be demonstrated that this impermeability is part of a functional totality which is normal when evident below seven years, and is shown by a type of reasoning that is centered on itself, *i.e.*, assimilates the facts to subjective schemes instead of elaborating them according to the rules of a groupment which is both operatory and experimental. The genetic analysis of reasoning in the normal child permits consideration of this functional totality as characteristic of a determined mental level—that of children below six to seven years. We observe in them on the one hand the same incoordination of relations previously referred to in connection with the nonconservation of substance in the experiment of the balls. On the other hand we observe the same incapacity to take into account experimental results as was shown in the examples concerning the dissolution of sugar. These two symptoms of deductive and inductive insufficiency are interdependent and indissociable, because they both result from the same general operatory insufficiency (difficulty of groupment), and both indicate mental level. The existence of this mental level is perfectly normal during early childhood, since egocentric schemes carry it on to constructions of reasoning, but it is abnormal and gives evidence of retardation when it is characteristic of the individuals ten to fifteen years old or older who are included in this study.

3. Tests of Logico-Arithmetical Compositions

In the preceding tests, there has been an insistence on the relations between operatory reasoning and the influence on the retardate of experiences gained during the testing situations. By contrast, a test is now presented in which the experimental and intuitive aspects are reduced to a minimum in order to determine, in a more rigorous and general aspect, the formal mechanisms of thought.

From a large number of possible tests of logic on the contents of the preceding experiments, the compositions of equivalence of weight in the following form was chosen: The subject is presented with a set of brass bars of the same weight and dimensions, and distinguishable one from the other only by color (red, blue, and yellow). The set also includes other objects: pieces of lead and pieces of charcoal, the substance and dimensions of which differed, but which were equal in weight to the bars. After having the child verify $A = B$, $B = C$, $C = D$, $D = E$ (then A, or B, or C, = the brass bars D or E, or the lead or charcoal), problems were presented in the following way:

If $A = B$ and $B = C$, how about A and C? The same thing was done by substituting for one or several elements of the composition the unlike object. Finally, additive compositions of this nature were possible: Let $A = B = C = D$, $A + B =$ or $>$ or $< C + D =$ etc.

The test of equivalence of weight seemed more useful in the diagnosis of reasoning than formal tests. Its principal advantages over other tests of reasoning are:

1. The test procedure is very simple. A minimum demand is made on the subject's memory in order to keep the test procedure in mind. In addition, memory can be supplemented by demonstration.

2. The tests of equivalence of weight constitute a particular case of factors present both in the transformation of the clay ball and in the atomistic composition of sugar dissolving in water. The subjects failed previous tests concerning the conservation of matter, and as a result were reported as being in the first stage of conservation of matter. It is interesting to examine the logical operations of which certain retardates are incapable. One question can be asked: does such a failure reveal a limited mental level, and at the age of the subjects in this study can it be symptomatic of mental retardation?

3. In the test of the bars, reasoning is observed which is based on precise perceptual facts which are optical or weight illusions: two bars of equal dimensions appear longer when placed in a nonparallel position. In the illusion of weight, a piece of lead held in the hand seems heavier than either a piece of charcoal or a brass bar, even though the three are equal in weight. The illusion is so strong that all the subjects, whatever their level of retardation, were mistaken. This fact was originally established in an explanatory study and later became the basis

of the tests. Since Demoors' work, the absence of weight illusion is considered a sign of retardation, but this is present only in the severely retarded (Rey 1930). The retardates questioned in the present research showed slightly reduced weight illusions.

The test of the composition of weight, which was previously studied in the development of the normal child, permits a better understanding of operatory reasoning which is based on some well-determined perceptive data. Subjects who have affirmed with such conviction the addition or subtraction of the clay substance or the disappearance of the sugar may be equally incapable of comprehending operations as simple in appearance as these: If A = B and B = C, then A = C. If the elements of the composition are like objects, differing only in color, will they be mistaken when an unlike object is substituted for one of the like objects or when additive compositions are involved?

Some of the interrogations follow, all showing the same difficulty in comprehending elementary logical compositions.

OBSERVATION 13—LUB., F, 9:5

Lub.'s reactions to the dissolution of sugar are found in Observation 7.

What do you think, will those two bars [red and yellow] weigh the same? *I think so.*

Why? *They are the same size.* (Scales are used to demonstrate weight equivalence.)

And the yellow and the blue? *Equal too.* (*Demonstrates.*)

The blue and the red haven't been tried yet. What do you think they will show on the scales? (They are placed at angles to each other on the table.) *The red a little bit heavier: it is a little bit bigger.* (*Uses scales for demonstration.*) *They weigh the same too.*

Why? *They are the same size, same width.*

The lead and the red bar, what will these two show? *The lead is heavier.*

Why? *Because it's made of lead, because like that it's a big piece and the other a stick.*

(Weighs to demonstrate equality.) And now the lead and the red bar? *Perhaps the same too. The stick isn't wood.* (*Weighs them in her hand.*) *No, the lead is still heavier. It's such a heavy piece.*

And the yellow and the lead? *All of that is iron, it's the same thing. But the lead is still heavier.*

(Demonstrates weight equality on scales.) Yellow + blue and red + lead? *There, there are two things and there also. Maybe it is the same thing.*

And among the objects themselves, are they all the same? *No, the one with the lead is heavier.*

(Demonstrates the weight equality of charcoal and bar.) The bar was the same thing as the lead, do you remember? And now the bar was weighed with the charcoal, and if you compared the charcoal and the lead? *It's the lead which is heavier. After all it's lead.*

OBSERVATION 14—CLE., M, 10:9

This boy's responses to the transformation of clay were listed in Observation 2.

Cle. demonstrates successively the weight equality between the red and yellow bars and the red and blue; the demonstration is done with attention and precision.

And what are the yellow and the blue like (placed at angles on the table)? *The blue is heavier.*

Why do you think so? *It seems heavier.*

(Uses scales to demonstrate equality.) (*Astonishment without explanation.*)

Will the lead and the blue be the same weight or will one be heavier than the other? *The lead is heavier.*

We will see. (Demonstrates their equality.) *After all it's the same weight.*

And the lead with the red? (*Weighs them in his hand.*) *Not the same.*

It weighed the same as what bar? *As the blue.*

And now the lead with the red? *It is the lead which is heavier, because all the same it's lead.*

OBSERVATION 15—BAL., F, 11:2

Bal.'s responses to the transformation of clay are listed in Observation 3.

(Demonstrates immediately on the scales.) *The red and the blue are just as heavy; the blue and the yellow are the same weight too.*

And these two that we haven't weighed together yet (the red and yellow are placed at angles)? *They are not just as heavy; the red is heavier and the yellow is lighter. You can see it easily.* (The equivalences are repeated.)

The red equals . . . *the blue bar.*
The blue equals . . . *the yellow bar.*
And now the red and yellow, if you put them on the scales? *Not as heavy. (She had no idea of putting them together to measure them, and is dumbfounded when the examiner demonstrates their equality on the scales.)*
What do you think the lead and the red bar will show if we weigh them on the scales? *That [indicating the lead] is heavier because it's stone.*
We'll see. *(Demonstrates equality on the scales.)*
And the lead with the blue bar? *(Hesitates a minute.) Not as heavy. The lead is heavier. I can weigh them, see? (Demonstrates with astonishment their equality.)*
And if I put the red + the yellow in one pan of the scales and the blue with the lead on the other? *There, where the lead is, is heavier, because there is heavy iron in the lead and that weighs on the scales.*
(During demonstration she is astonished without trying to analyze the additive composition.)

OBSERVATION 16—MUG., M, 16:5

Demonstrates the following equality on the scales: The red = the yellow; the blue = the red.
And blue and yellow [placed at angles]? *The blue heavier, the yellow lighter. The blue is longer (without showing a desire to measure them). (Demonstrates on the scales and observes the equality attentively.)*
The blue and the lead; how do you think they will be on the scales? *Oh, it is the lead which is heavy! (Demonstrates on the scales: refuses at first to admit the fact.) All the same the lead weighs more; it pulls it down. (Finally admits:) it's just as heavy.*
The lead with the yellow; how would that be on the scales now that you know how it was with the blue? *(Takes only the lead in his hand.) Oh, the lead is heavy. It's heavier.*
But you remember the lead and blue bar were the same . . . *The lead is still heavier.*
Red and lead? *(Same reaction.)*

OBSERVATION 17—WID., F, 24:3
(See Observation 6)

Demonstrates equalities: Red = blue, blue = yellow.

And now the red bar and the yellow—does that weigh the same too, or not (still placed at angles)? *The red is heavier because it has more iron.*

(She is required to demonstrate the double equality of volume and weight by comparing the bars and weighing them.)

The lead and the blue bar? (*Predicts*) *The lead is heavier because it's made of lead.*

(Demonstrates on the scales and carefully observes the equality.)

The yellow bar and the lead? (*Hesitates, then weighs in her hand*) *The lead is heavier.*

The yellow was as heavy as which of the bars? *The blue or the red.* (*Puts them one beside the other.*)

And the lead is the same as which bar? *Oh, the lead is heavier.*

But you remember it was weighed. *Yes, it was the same.*

The lead = the blue; the lead and the yellow, how are they? *The lead is heavier.*

OBSERVATION 18—WIES., F, 11:1
(*See Observation 9*)

(*Immediately takes the bar; asks what are they for, and how they can be played with.*)

(The bars are weighed successively.) The red = blue, blue = yellow, and now if we weigh the red and yellow (placed at angles on the table)? *The yellow is heavier.*

Why do you think so? *It is a bit bigger.*

We are going to see if you worked it out. (*Demonstrates their equality.*) *Oh, it's the same weight after all.*

The red bar and the lead? (Equality of weight is immediately shown.) They weight the same, and if instead of the red bar, we put the blue? (*Weighs in her hand.*) *Oh, the lead is heavy. The lead is heavier.*

(*Demonstrates on the scales.*) *Oh, it's equal after all. That's funny.*

And now we put two bars on one side, and on the other one bar with a piece of lead. What does the scale show? (*Without hesitation*) *There, where the lead is, it's heavier.*

What is striking in the reactions of these subjects is the incapacity to effect this fundamental composition of all logic, which consists of concluding that A = C when it is given that A = B and B = C, and of understanding that $A + B = C + D$, if it has been established that $A = B = C = D$. The following is a close examination of how the subjects conduct themselves when the problem is to compose simple equalities whose elements are homogeneous among themselves and can be distinguished by color.

Observation 13: *The red a little bit heavier; it is a little bit bigger.*

Observation 14: Does not seek to justify it: *The blue is heavier . . . it seems heavier.*

Observation 15: *They are not just as heavy; the red is heavier and the yellow is lighter. You can see it easily.*

Observation 17: *The red is heavier because it has more iron.*

Observation 18: *The yellow is heavier . . . it is a bit bigger.*

Observation 14: *Not the same . . . it is the lead which is heavier, because all the same it's lead.*

Observation 15: *Not as heavy. The lead is heavier;* and for the additive composition: *There, where the lead is, is heavier because there is heavy iron in the lead and that weighs on the scales.*

Observation 16: Does not attempt to compare them, but is impressed: *Oh, it is the lead which is heavy!* and persists even after he recalls the equality of weight in another bar: *The lead is still heavier.*

Observation 17: Hesitates, but after weighing them in his hand says: *The lead is heavier.*

Observation 18: *Oh, the lead is heavy. The lead is heavier.* The same opinion is given for the additive composition: *There, where the lead is, it's heavier.*

Thus all these subjects are victims of perceptive illusions, and make no attempt to correct them, either by deductive reasoning or by an actual substitution. Because homogeneous elements are involved, *i.e.,* elements of the same density and spatial congruence, the deductive reasoning could be strengthened by a material arrangement which consists in substituting the elements one for the other after having established their equality by spatial superposition or by juxtaposition. (Children of approximately seven years who function at a superior mental level proceed with the given facts in this manner.) If subjects in this study are not able to deduct a third equivalent relation from two others, nor to substitute one element for another, it is because they do not consider the objects as measurable quantities, nor even as qualitatively equivalent (from the viewpoint of qualitative operations), but consider them from a purely perceptive viewpoint. It is recalled that the same subjects were incapable of comprehending the quantitative invariance of substance after transformation or dissolution, because they were influenced by perceptions without applying reasoning to the situation. The same phenomenon is now observed. The tests are simplified because there are no physical changes of matter.

This childish mode of reasoning, in subjects the age of those included in this study, reveals a deficiency in the functional mechanism of thought. The deficiency is more pronounced if, instead of limiting the composition to like elements, one of them is replaced by an unlike object, with or without additive composition.

Some responses from subjects who have verified the equivalence of weight between bar A and the lead and who have been asked if this lead is equivalent to bar B are recorded below:

The subject described in Observation 13 showed some hesitation, which reveals the mode of reasoning at this mental level. After having given incorrect responses on the equality between like elements, she supposed for a time that the lead and a bar were of equal weight: "Perhaps the same too. The stick isn't wood," but she changed her mind afterward. "No, the lead is still heavier. It is such a heavy piece." The same thing happened when the yellow bar was substituted for the red; she started by affirming that "all of that is iron, it's the same thing," only to contradict herself immediately afterward; "But the lead is still heavier." Lub. supposed equality of additive compositions in the same way: "There are two things and there are two also. Maybe it is the same thing." Then she contradicted herself; "No, the lead is still heavier." Finally, when the piece of charcoal was substituted for the bar, she was completely persuaded that the lead was still heavier; "No, the one with the lead is heavier," although she had stated earlier that the two equaled a bar.

This case is cited in order to underline the fact that the retardate who lacks genuine reasoning will, under systematic questioning, have recourse to automatic verbal responses which in appearance are superior to their thought level. Observation 13, after having given incorrect responses to compositions with homogeneous elements, foresaw as possible the equality of lead to bar B (given that the lead equals bar A and that A = B). By taking this response out of context, one could think that it is deductive reasoning and question the clinical significance of her failure and by consequence the value of the test.

With a more extended clinical interrogation, however, it is easy to determine the part played by reasoning and the part attributed to verbal automatism. Let us examine how the child justifies her statement of equality: "Perhaps the same too. The stick isn't wood" or, further on, "All of that is iron, it's the same thing." These responses seem to signify that the bar is not as light as one might think, and that all the things are believed to be made of the same substance, "of iron." The child, far from realizing relations of equality or of substituting equivalent elements, depends on purely qualitative judgments. And immediately afterward she contradicts herself: "No, the lead is still heavier. It's such a heavy piece." Even when a piece of charcoal is substituted for the second bar, her opinion does not change; she clings to the idea: "After all, it's lead." If the child were capable of deductive composition, these judgments would be generalizable to all objects. The extent to which she clings to a subjective judgment of facts is proved when she predicts the equality of the additive composition for the simple reason that "there are two things and there two also," and sometimes predicts inequality by "the lead is heavier."

When a person is not limited to a simple registering of contradictory propositions and will try to analyze the psychological structure of reasoning, then this person will always know how to attain through various verbal automatisms the true functioning of thought. All the same, when it becomes necessary to determine a child's level of reasoning, it is preferable not to base the diagnosis solely on the results of a test of this kind, but to insert the clinical signs into a more synthesized picture of all the facts for which the experiments of conservation have furnished a sample.

As a countertest and an instrument of diagnostic differential, this test of "the bars" provides precise indications of deficient reasoning. What is the significance of these revealed failures? The subjects described in this chapter are found to be incapable of understanding that two quantities equal to a third are necessarily equal to each other. In other words, they do not know how to constitute a groupment of equivalence, either by abstract deduction or by a practical substitution. An attempt made previously to explain their incapacity to substitute one element for another by explaining that the retarded subjects listed in this chapter consider only objects as absolute qualities and that the objects are not, therefore, coordinated. These persons do not know how to surpass the perceptual phenomena. Moreover, the test termed "the bars," far from simply repeating tests of physical conservation, reaches reasoning in its purest and most general form. If from the point of view of physical or experimental reasoning these subjects refused to understand the invariance of physical quantity from the logical viewpoint, which is the view now under consideration, they still show an incapability of postulating that an element remains identical to itself when it is compared with others. To believe that $A = C$ once it is admitted that $A = B$ and $B = C$ is to suppose that one of the elements has changed in the course of the composition, and to believe also that $A + B = C + D$ (being given the equivalence of all the elements) supposes that these changes occur because they are added. The necessity for considering the elements as unvarying and identical to themselves during a period of reasoning is not particular to compositions of equality of weight as just shown, but is the conditioning of all reasoning. No matter what, deduction supposes the invariance of premises—otherwise the conclusion is contradictory. It is this disregard for noncontradiction, this unconcern with respect to the invariance of propositions, that seem to characterize the mentality of the young retardates now under consideration. Perhaps it could be admitted that some subjects (having never before thought of problems of conservation of substance, weight, and volume) do not succeed at the outset in conceiving of such an invariance without attributing clinical importance to such an incapacity. However, it remains striking that these same subjects reveal themselves incapable of achieving an operation as fundamental as that of postulating identity of "logical conservation" (as opposed to physical conservation) of a fact in the course of some type of reasoning. This incapacity, which in various forms is a trait characteristic of the reasoning of normal children below six or seven years, seems to signify in our mentally retarded cases a fixation of thought functioning at a clearly determined prelogical level.

If an effort is made to separate the information resulting from the three tests that have been used in the diagnosis of retardation, there must be insistence on the double convergence that the subjects' reactions show in spite of differences in the tests and in spite of the differences of individual circumstances. First, in regard to the tests themselves, a synthesized problem has been utilized—that of the transformation of clay, which calls to mind both a logical construction (the conservation of substance in spite of the change of form) and an experimental induction (the observation of the constancy of weight and sometimes volume). By contrast, the second test insists on the utilization of facts from experience. There is also a logical construction (the conservation of sugar substance), but the second test cannot be applied to a series of facts that the child already knows (permanence of taste) or demonstrates gradually (permanence of the level and of the weight). The third test emphasizes the operatory mechanism, while maintaining connection with the verification of facts.

In spite of this diversity, the obtained reactions are generally perfectly coherent. A retardate who is incapable of believing that the totality of clay is conserved cannot believe in the conservation of dissolved sugar and does not manage to compose the equality of weight, height, or substance in the test of the bars.

The following chapter sets forth examples of decalages which witness the fact that an individual can occupy an intermediate position between two successive stages. However, a subject seldom responds correctly to all the questions pertaining to the sugar and to the bars who does not conceive the conservation of the quantity of clay. The inverse is also noted. There is, then, an intrinsic coherence of the intellectual operations observed in relation to these tests, and this coherence maintains an essential unity of the operations of groupment. To say that the subject does not know how to "group" the logical relations necessary to assure the conservation of substance in the test of the balls is in effect to admit that instead of objectively coordinating the transformations of length, thickness, etc., the subject attaches himself only to the subjectively significant relations, such as the impression of weight which the transformed ball will exert on the hand, etc. All these subjective reports are either contradictory among themselves or else they cannot be objectively coordinated. They evidence a manner of thought remaining egocentric because it is linked more to practical perception than to reasoning, or more to the child's own activity than to relations exterior to the ego. However, the reactions of the child to the test of the sugar or to that of the bars do nothing other than to reproduce this same mental attitude with slight variations. In the case of the composition of weight, the subject trusts perception and does not reason, thus showing a surprising incapacity to effect the most elementary logical groupment. In the sugar test, instead of taking into account the experimental facts that are offered to his perception during the interview, he prefers to ignore rather than to correct his initial ideas, and this maintains in spite of the contrary appearance. The reason is that the objective reading of the facts supposes a previous renouncement of egocentric perception and a logical groupment of the relations necessary for interpreting the perceived items. Operatory mechanism and submission to experience reveal a similar experimental attitude of mind which is not attained by these subjects and which is opposed to the egocentric attitude, whose sole means of linking new ideas to old ones is the assimilation to schemes of subjective activity.

A convergence appears in the structure of reasonings analyzed during the three different tests, but it is surprising to be able to establish from the reasonings revealed in the test that these subjects belong precisely to the same mental level. In each instance, the case history or medical records indicate profound diversity. Not only do their chronological ages vary between ten and twenty years or over but their social and scholastic behaviors vary from one case to another. Some compensate by verbal facility, memory, or character, while others seem to evidence greater intellectual decline than actually exists. Indeed, it is surprising that all these individuals are found to be at an equivalent level on the three tests, and even more surprising that they reproduced almost word for word the reactions observed in normal children of four to seven years.

It is less astonishing to encounter a fifteen-year-old retardate who fails to define a word, to interpret an image, to retain series of numbers, to repeat a sentence, etc., than to see him reasoning like a six-year-old for half an hour, slowly constructing his thoughts, little by little, when a new problem is encountered. The resumé of these retardates' reactions in this chapter authorizes the placement of their reasoning at a determined stage of the normal evolution of thought, instead of defining their mental level in terms of failures or negative results. In this way, it becomes possible to describe their mentality in a positive manner.

It is more instructive to know that the subjects are at the five-to-seven-year stage for the operations of reasoning than it is to establish through tests that they are at a corresponding mental age. Instead of simply providing the examiner with results attained by the subjects in a metric examination, the tests used in this present research describe the subjects' thought development as adaptation occurs. *To classify these subjects as being in the first stages of conservation is to attribute to them a certain mentality whose operatory structure and whose links with the functioning of intelligence are known through previous genetic studies.*

3. Fixations of Reasoning at the Second and Third Stages

The previous chapter discussed the cases of certain retarded subjects who showed a mentality comparable to the level of thought characteristic of children between four and seven years, both from the viewpoint of their reasoning (absence of grouping) and of their contact with experience (which showed the dominance of perception over deductive and inductive interpretation of reality). Even among the mentally retarded, however, there exist a number of subjects who progress beyond this mentality, and who are distinguished from it by more or less well-developed logical constructions. Is it necessary to find (with several years of decalage) exactly the same evolution of thought in relation to the development of quantities as was described previously in normal children? In this event, can we assign to the thought of the retarded fixations which are clearly limited to evolutionary stages? Even though they proceed at a slower rate, does the reasoning of the educable retarded pass through the same phases of development as that of normal children? If not, is it necessary to foresee instead another possibility which resembles the first: once the most elementary stage, which is characterized by systematic belief in nonconservation, has been passed, does it become impossible to distinguish subsequent levels? One might expect, after the first stage, to discover either paranormal traits, which cannot be classified by stages, or a mixture of traits belonging to the normal at different stages.

Such are the two possible directions in which reasoning in the mentally retarded could develop. Analysis of the facts will show that the second must be rejected, and that the first will be confirmed by the operatory unfolding itself. Retardates neither progress at the same rate as the normal nor do they present an equally stable system of thought. It is possible to consider phenomena which are paranormal and which complicate the development. Within the classification of retardation, growth is not entirely uniform; therefore it will be necessary to foresee states of pseudo-equilibrium characterized by fixations, or premature stops and oscillations between two operatory levels.

Because Chapter 4 is devoted to the phenomena of paranormal oscillations, present consideration is given to the fixations that define retarded reasoning at the genetic stages of operatory mechanisms. First, however, it will be necessary to establish how the distinct phenomena of Stage I can be situated in a genetic scale which also includes Stages II and III (notions of conservation and of compositions of equality). It will also be necessary to determine whether these reasoning processes really show the mentally superior levels that were described in the preceding chapter.

The first section of the chapter deals with modes of thought characteristic of the second level of reasoning. The second section is concerned with the educable retarded (or morons) who reach the third level but who do not attain the complete equilibrium of adult thought.

First Section: Stage II

The interrogations will be analyzed in the order of the three tests utilized in the first chapter: transformation of balls of clay, dissolution of sugar, and transivity of length. These interrogations serve as samples of the abundant material that has been collected in institutions for the retarded, in special classes in public schools, and in school counseling.

Transformation of the Ball of Clay

Reasoning in relation to the transformation of the ball of clay that exceeds Level I shows an operative capacity sufficient to assure the conservation of substance. Nonetheless, the reasoning of these retardates is unlike that of normal subjects of their age who attain the superior levels of permanence of weight and of volume.

OBSERVATION 19—AND., F, 10:10

When examined, this girl was in the second year of a special class, where she had acquired the elementary techniques of reading and writing. In areas concerned with the comprehension of mathematical operations and logical thinking, And. had acquired by means of practical manipulations the mechanisms of addition and subtraction, but she had continuing difficulty in understanding that division was the inverse operation of multiplication.

After classifying her as a retardate, the local school psychologist advised placement in a special class. The retardation, two and one-half years as determined by the Stanford-Binet, placed her at an eight-year level of performance, and assigned her an IQ of 67, which corresponded to her level of scholastic achievement.

And.'s performance on tests of drawing and learning served to confirm the diagnosis. Work was slow, academic tasks were difficult for her (25th percentile), and she always evidenced the same inadequacies (Rey 1934). Due to lack of mobility, rigid schemes were utilized; for example, her drawing was a faithful reproduction of school models. Imitation dominated her work; the characteristic is typical of docile and conscientious retardates.

These indices left no doubt concerning her retardation, but And., as much by her acquired knowledge as by her actual conduct, showed a mentality superior to that described in Stage I. A follow-up study showed that in time the girl's development continued beyond the level achieved in the tests reported in the study. Notable progress was made during the ensuing four years as she continued in special classes.

Reactions to the transformation of a ball of clay were characteristic of reasoning at the second stage in tasks of conservation. In this stage, the invariance of the substance is affirmed, but the weight and the volume are considered variable when the substance is either lengthened or broken into pieces. And. compared the two balls with care and confirmed their equality in size and weight.

Now you are going to make one of the balls into a long thin sausage. (*She does it.*)

And if you put it on the scale, how much will it weigh? *The ball is heavier because it is all round.*

Why does it matter if it is round? *But it is heavier!*

And is the clay more or less when it is in a sausage? *The same, it only has to be rolled into the ball, now it is just longer.*

We are going to make a ball again and break it into little pieces. (*Says spontaneously*) *The ball is heavier because it is always the same thing, big and thick.*

And the pieces? *They are quite small and thin.*

And if you compare them to the clay? *Oh, always the same because you only made little ones from it.*

You see, you make a thin pancake, and you look again to see if it is the same thing or not. *There (pointing to the ball) all the same, it is heavier.*

Why do you think that? *It is still a big piece, still thick, and there it is quite thin.*

Could you make a ball again from the pancake? *Yes, and then it would be the same thing big.*

Why do you think just the same thing and not more or less? *Because you haven't taken anything away or added anything.*

What will happen if I put each of the balls in a glass of water? Will that make the level of the water move? *No, the water stays the same height, the ball simply stays on the bottom.*

We are going to see if you figured that out right. *(Demonstrates that the level rises.)* Why did it rise? *Because it just now rose.*

But why did it rise just now when I put the ball in? *It is the ball that made it rise.*

And if I took the ball out again? *The water will go down as before, because the piece of clay won't be there any longer.*

And how does the ball make the water rise? Look, it is just the same thing for both balls. The water rises exactly the same. *Well, I don't really know.*

The ball takes up space in the water. It chases the water out, then the water has to rise, rise just as much as the ball is big. *Oh, yes, when I lift out the ball the water goes back into its place.*

That's it, and if in place of the ball you put the pancake, is that going to make the level of the water rise the same or not? What do you think? *The water rises too, the pancake takes the place of the water, but much less. It is thinner.*

And if you put the sausage in place of the pancake? *That makes it rise more than the ball (she points to the higher level) because the sausage is longer than the ball and then it takes up more room in the water.*

And with the little pieces? *That rises the least because they are the smallest.*

And why does that rise least when they are so small? *Because they take up less space when they are small.*

And when one weighs the small pieces with the ball, what happens then? *The small pieces are lighter. (Demonstrates by weighing.)*

What do you think? (*Shows great astonishment.*) *The same weight.*
How did this happen? You thought it was lighter? *Yes, but the weight is the same.*

And if the little pieces were made into a sausage and the sausage was compared with the ball? *I don't know, maybe also the same weight.*

Why did you change your mind? *Oh, I'm not real sure. Maybe the ball is still heavier, but in any case it's the same clay.*

OBSERVATION 20—STR., F, 11:10

If the preceding case was one of simple retardation, the present one presents a more irregular mental development. Retardation in the area of reasoning is only one of the more salient manifestations.

Str. was under psychiatric observation at the time she was seen by the examiner because of seizures which had prevailed since early childhood. According to the case history, her intellectual development was retarded. However, the Stanford-Binet indicated an IQ of 92, which is within normal limits, but a detailed analysis of the results indicated irregular development. Language and memory were above average for her age group, whereas self-control and imaginative or diverse thinking were at a lower level. The misleading indication of an almost normal IQ was due to her verbal facility and was in striking contrast to her deficiencies in constructive or creative activities.

Irregularity of performance also was evident in her academic work. Her successes occurred in the areas of reading, language, and copy work, but she had difficulty in adapting intelligently to new situations. Thus she was unable to follow arithmetic instruction in a second-year special class. To compose new problems was impossible for her, and she was also completely unable to solve practical problems encountered in daily living. Her drawing was primitive, and her imagination was limited.

Prognosis was difficult because the usual criterion for mental retardation could not be used with Str. The possible continuation of seizures had to be considered. Nonetheless, as a reference point for future observation, it was important to determine as precisely as possible the actual level of operative development. Had test results revealed an attitude of indifference, one of the goals of the examiner's discussion would have been to sustain her attention. However, once her interest was gained, the subject concentrated on the problem at hand. Her reasoning was found to be superior to that of subjects performing at Stage I, but she did not attain the level that was considered average for her chronological age.

The following exchange illustrates her immediate comprehension in a problem of conservation: she made two balls of clay, confirmed their equality, and then transformed one of the balls into a sausage.

The sausage always has the same weight as the ball? *The ball is heavier than that. It is a sausage; it is lighter.*

And the clay; there is as much of it, or does that change also? *Just the same thing because before the two balls were the same size. The one the sausage was made of was just as big.*

And if the ball and the sausage were weighed, are you sure they would not weigh the same? *The sausage is lighter.*

Why lighter? *Yes, why? (She asks herself.) . . . I don't know.*

You can make little pieces with one of the balls. (*She divides the ball.*) *It is lighter than the sausage. Before the sausage was long, and now there are only little pieces.*

And the clay, is there as much, or less, or more? *Still the same thing. Yes, but it has simply been cut into pieces.*

You are going to make a pancake and tell me if there is still the same amount of clay or more or less. *Still the same amount. That doesn't change.*

And if the ball and the pancake are weighed on the scale? *Perhaps the same thing. (Hesitates): I am not very sure, I only thought. Because it is always the same clay it is just as heavy, but maybe it's even lighter. It is real thin.*

And when you make small pieces of it? *Oh, they are much lighter, the little pieces.*

(In the volume task she predicts immediately.) *The water rises because there will be something inside. I'll try it. (Shows that the rise in level is equal for the two balls.)*

Then the two balls are the same size, you see; they make the water rise the same amount. If instead of the ball the sausage were put in the water, how much would the water rise? (The water level is marked on the beaker with a rubber band.) *That rises higher; well I don't know.*

The ball and the sausage; do they take the same amount of space in the water, or does the sausage take more? What do you think? *The sausage takes more because it is longer.*

Could you make a ball again from the sausage? *Yes, that naturally will take up the same space in the water.*

And if you put all the little pieces in the water? *They will take up almost no space because they are so small.*

And if you make a ball again? *Then again the ball takes up as much space as the other.*

OBSERVATION 21—DOM., M, 11:4

His teacher requested that this young boy be examined. There was no indication of retardation from his physical appearance. Although he was repeating the third grade, Dom. still did not do satisfactory work. His record consisted of low grades, and the teacher complained of his inability in arithmetic and grammar. Dom. could scarcely add without the aid of his fingers or other objects, and he could not read a simple text.

Because his academic achievement had been fairly regular, it was important to be sure that this was a case of true retardation, and not underachievement. The case history tended to confirm the retardation; four brothers were mentally deficient, two sisters were of lowered vitality, and Dom.'s own development had been slow since early childhood. For these reasons an endogenous type of retardation was suggested. Investigation by the school doctor confirmed our hypothesis.

Tests other than those of operative reasoning revealed characteristics which indicated retardation. In Biäsch's test (1939) of general intelligence, the boy solved all of the problems at the seven-year level and found partially correct solutions for the eight-year level, but failed all questions at the nine-year level. General retardation was approximately three years.

Dom. showed an unexpected capacity in imitating drawings and in copying designs. He experienced considerable difficulty in concentration and attention, in spite of the interest he evidenced in his work. Representation of physical causality, as measured by Piaget's studies on children's conception of the world, was at an infantile level although development was above the level of egocentrism and corresponding realism.

Finally, it was noted that motor tests indicated retardation with major difficulties in physical coordination. Tests of operative reasoning, which were also administered, served to confirm the diagnosis of mental retardation.

Following the examination the child was removed from the regular class and placed in an institution. Not only did his general welfare improve but he continued to develop intellectually. At the end of two years, he was transferred from the dormitory into a special section of his new school. However, during the three ensuing years Dom. did not attain a normal level of intelligence, and he was not able to adapt to a regular school program.

Dom. understood the use of scales and closely observed the weighing process.

(*He forms two identical clay balls.*) *Both are the same size and weight.*

(*Carefully transforms one of the balls into a sausage.*) *This makes a long sausage.*

And if you put it on the scale? *The sausage would be much lighter.*

Why lighter? *Because it is the longest.*

Why is it lighter when it is longer? *Oh, you can tell real easy the ball is heavier. The other* [*the sausage*] *is rolled longer so it is lighter.*

Is there as much clay or more? *It is always the same amount of clay.*

Why the same amount? *Because if it were put together it makes a ball again, and now the ball is only rolled out.*

If the ball is made again will it be exactly the same as the other? The same size? *Yes, the same.*

We are going to cut the ball into small pieces. If they are weighed, what will the scales show? *Oh, they become lighter.*

Are you sure of that? *Of course, I believe it at least, because they are separated from each other, the little pieces, and each is a little ball. It is lighter. On the other hand, it is a big ball when it is all together and that makes it heavier.*

Is there as much clay in the ball as in the little pieces? (*Hesitates.*) *You could say there is more, because when you put all the little bits that makes a bigger ball; first you separated them and when you put together what had been separated that becomes bigger.*

And when you separate them, that makes less clay? *No, it is not even possible, because it is always the same ball. Only here it is separated, and there it is together. It is always the same amount of clay.*

Now we are going to make a pancake from this ball. (*He puts the pieces into a ball and then flattens it into a pancake.*)

How will the pancake be in comparison to the ball if both are put on the scale? (*First he takes them in his hand and weighs them.*) *The pancake is heavier because it is flattened and thick, and the ball is round, but we will see. We will weigh them.* Tell me first if you think there is as much clay or not. *Exactly the same amount of clay. The clay cannot change.*

OBSERVATION 22—ROS., F, 12:6

Ros. was in the second-year special class of an institution for retarded children. The case study furnished the following facts: illegitimate child, premature, mother psychopathic, language and walking first attempted at two years. At four years a pseudo-epileptic seizure was followed by appropriate treatment. Visual troubles (cataract) showed slight amelioration after operation. On the advice of the local school physicians Ros. was placed in a special class when she reached school age. Here her behavior was unstable, asocial, and agitated. The influence of the mother added to her disequilibrium. Therefore placement in an institution for abnormals was indicated. In the institution Ros. showed considerable difficulty in adaptation. At first she ran aimlessly in the new schoolroom and showed extreme irritability. Little by little, her behavior was stabilized. Periods of agitation (alternating with calmer periods) became more rare. When first seen by the examiner she appeared cooperative and was easily managed.

Because of difficulty in arithmetic, she participated in the arithmetic lessons of a lower grade. Although judged a very poor student at the beginning of her academic year, notable progress was made. Three years after the examiner first saw Ros. her teachers stated that she had experienced a maximum academic development; thus the previous prognosis was negated.

Results obtained from intelligence tests were contradictory. Three intelligence quotients were obtained. When the girl was between six and seven years of age an IQ of 60 was reported; the second of 86 was obtained at eight and one-half years (at the time transfer was made to the institution for the retarded), and finally a third of 35 was obtained at nine years and three months (this testing was not regarded as valid, however). The value of these quotients will not be discussed, but it is noted that the second quotient, like the third, was obtained by examiners who lacked experience in psychological diagnosis. Accompanying visual and emotional problems promoted errors in the estimation of intelligence.

Several tests complemented those of reasoning and confirmed the diagnosis of retardation. Learning was slow but constant (20th percentile) and the subject's drawing was comparable to that of normal children between seven and eight years of age. Operative reasoning in the task involving the transformation of clay balls furnished similar results.

Ros. made two little balls and demonstrated the correct use of the scales.

You can make a sausage out of this ball, and we will leave the other one just as it is. (*The task is done in a conscientious manner.*)

Now then, how will the sausage and the ball be on the scale? (*She says immediately*) *Not the same weight. The ball is heavier because it is round, and that [the sausage] is long.*

Could you make a ball again from the sausage? *Yes, it only has to be rolled up.*

Will the ball that is made from the sausage be like the other or heavier? *Just as heavy because it is the same size.*

And while it is a sausage? *The sausage is lighter.*

And how about the clay, is there as much of it or not? *That depends on how big it is* (*thinking*) *but, of course, there is as much clay. You see, it is much longer than that, but you can pick it up and make a ball again, so there is always the same amount of clay.*

Then there is as much in the sausage as there is in the ball? *Exactly the same.* (*The ball is remade, and Ros. declares with satisfaction the two are equal, but adds spontaneously*) *But it is still lighter.*

(The scales are used to show the equality of weight.) *Why is it the same weight? Because that balances. Because the scales make them equal.*

You thought of that before? *No.*

But why does it weigh the same? *I don't understand.*

And if you make little pieces from the ball and you weigh them again? (*She does it.*) *Oh, now it really isn't as heavy any more. It is so separated here, and there it is all together. There it is one piece; here it is torn apart.*

Where do you think it would be the heaviest? *There where it is all one piece.*

And the clay, is there more of it or always the same? *The same.*

Could a ball be made again from the little pieces? *Yes, but I don't know if it would be the same size. That depends on if I kneaded it well.*

Make a thin pancake from the ball. (*She does so immediately.*)

And when they are weighed together, what will happen? *This is thin, and that is thick: the pancake is much lighter than the ball.*

And the clay, is there as much of it, more, or less? (*Hesitates an instant.*) *As much, it is like the sausage, but much less lighter because it is not rolled up.*

OBSERVATION 23—ZWA., F, 13:4

The young girl was referred for examination because of arrested mental development. From the beginning of her school career she had been in a special class, but in her third year there was no academic progress, although she showed some capacity for manual work. Because the family situation was quite unstable (the father was being treated for alcoholism) decision was made to place the child in an institution for the mentally retarded where training could be given in household tasks as academic work continued.

Psychological testing, requested by school authorities, revealed mental retardation. Mental age as determined by the Stanford-Binet was nine years, and an IQ of 67 was obtained. Drawing also indicated retardation. All drawings of human figures were identical except for juxtaposed details. Learning by memory was relatively good, but slight perseveration in detail was observed. Associations were slow and of poor content. Verbs predominated in her speech. Lack of coordination was exhibited in small movements. A stereotyped laugh occurred at the presentation of each new test. Absence of a genuine interest in the problems, which was compensated by a need to be worthwhile, completed the picture of retarded intelligence.

Reasoning which was arrested at the second stage, and which contrasted with a free but misleading use of language, appeared to indicate her state of retardation. When seen two years after the first examination she appeared to have profited from the institutional environment. Although scholastic knowledge had increased very little, and she still lacked a sense of responsibility, skill had been acquired in household tasks.

(*Zwa. observes the equality of the two little balls and makes one of them into a sausage.*)

What will the scales show if the ball is put on one side and the sausage on the other? *The pan will go lower on the side of the sausage because the sausage is heavier. It is bigger, longer.*

Can a ball be made of it again? *Yes, then it is fat and thick again.*

Again the same size as before, or bigger or smaller? *Exactly the same size.*

The ball can also be divided into small pieces. *I am going to make small pieces out of it.*

And if you weigh them now with the ball, what will happen? *On the side where the ball is it lowers; the little pieces are so small, and there on the other side the ball is so fat; it is quite light here, and there it is heavy.*

Is there as much clay, or more, or less in the little pieces? (*Hesitates a moment.*) *Yes, there is as much, because all in all nothing has been taken away and when nothing is taken away there is always the same thing.*

And on the scales? *The ball is much heavier.*

(The little pieces and the ball are weighed.) *The same weight because there is as much clay, and then there are many more of the small pieces and a single fat one.*

Is there also as much clay or more or less in the pancake than in the ball? What do you think? *The same; it's like it was in the little pieces; nothing has been taken away.*

And about the weight? Is it also the same or not? *The ball is heavier. There, where the pancake is, the scale rises, and there it goes down.*

But why does the ball seem heavier? *Because the pancake is quite thin, and the ball is quite thick.*

The two are compared on the scales. (*Shows great astonishment.*) *Again the same. It is because there is as much clay; here it is only flattened, and there it's all gathered up.*

The following case illustrates retardation occurring between the first and second stages.

OBSERVATION 24—Bos., M, 10:0

Bos., a young boy of lowered vitality who suffered from chronic colds, had been placed in an institution for abnormal children upon the recommendation of the school physician. Past history indicated a gradual mental and physical deterioration resulting in a present retardation of approximately two years. For this reason he was considered mentally retarded. Intelligence testing done by the pediatrician and his assistants indicated inferiority in conceptual reasoning.

After several years of adapted instruction Bos.' performance in the class for retardates was outstanding. However, concentration on a task, objective interest in a problem, and continuity of work were prevented by his irritability, frequent fits of anger, and exaggerated self-esteem. Periods of nervousness were accompanied by feelings of inadequacy in factual knowledge which made the child feel obliged to learn everything over again.

An IQ of 88 indicated that he performed at or above a borderline level of retardation. Actually the case appeared to be one of slow mental development rather than retardation per se, and there were indications that his development would ultimately approach normal. Drawing, although not gravely deficient, was not at his age level, and his academic record indicated difficulties (40th percentile).

Operative reasoning, as noted above, was also retarded, but the mobility and performance evidenced during the interview periods was not indicative of mental retardation. The boy adapted to new experiences with a lively interest. Questions were asked and explanations demanded regarding material constructions. However, a need to be worthwhile was also apparent. At each failure the child became angry with himself and threatened not to continue.

When Bos. was seen three years later the prognosis was confirmed; although still slow in developing, his intellectual progress had enabled him to surpass his retarded classmates. Normal development was prevented by affective instability and lowered vitality, and his teacher questioned whether he was mentally retarded or merely a slow and difficult learner.

After experimenting with the scales Bos. declared: *They are just as heavy when the pans touch each other. One is heavier when it is lower, etc.*

He makes two equal balls and transforms one of them into a sausage.

If you weighed them again, what would the scales show? *It is the ball that is heavier because it is a little bit fatter and bigger.*

Is there the same amount of clay in both of them or not? *Not the same, no, because the sausage is longer. It has more clay.*

What were the two balls like in the beginning? *Exactly the same.*

And now if you wanted to make a ball again. *It would be exactly like the other.*

And when one is in a ball, and the other in a sausage? *I know; it is the same. You have only rolled one.*

You are going to divide the ball into little pieces. (*He does it, but says immediately*) *The ball is still heavier.*

And what about the clay; is it the same, or is there more or less on one side than on the other? *Just as much because it is only cut in pieces. If the other were cut in little pieces, there would be just as many little pieces.*

And how about the weight; is it also the same? *No, the ball is always heavier.*

(The child is asked to make a pancake and compare it with the ball.) *The pancake becomes lighter because it is thinner now.*

Why is it lighter when it is thinner? *When it is all thin and flat it does not weigh as much as a fat ball.*

Is there more clay, or as much, in the pancake? *I would say that there is more in the pancake. It is larger, larger than the other; no, it is still the same thing; it is not so fat.*

(Scales are used to compare the weight of the pancake and the ball.) *It is the same, I see, but it still weighs heavier when it is in a ball.*

Is it like you thought it would be? *No, but the pancake is very large. That makes it the same thing when it is so large.*

And now if the little pieces were weighed? *The little pieces are lighter, much lighter, than the ball.*

(Scales are again used for weight comparison.) (*Again the subject shows astonishment.*)

Can you explain to yourself why they weigh the same? *No, I don't know.*

Can you make a ball again from them? *Yes, if a ball is made again it is the same weight.*

A striking similarity exists between the retardates' reactions noted above and the known characteristics of reasoning found in normal children between seven and nine years of age. Two questions arise from these case studies of mentally retarded and slow-learning subjects: (1) do these subjects arrive at the notion of conservation through the same operative construction as normal children? and (2) are they simply obliged to follow automations which are foreign to logical processes?

The manner in which these retardates justified their answers will now be examined:

Observation 24, above, which was intermediate between Stages I and II, was instructive in this respect. The boy's capacity to utilize previous experience in thought construction was similar to that of normal children; only his late achievement of the notion of conservation would indicate retardation. Some of the characteristics typical of both the normal child and the retardate give evidence of the complete continuity that exists between both types of reasoning.

Bos., like the subjects in Stage I, started by saying that there was more substance in the ball than in the sausage—"because it is larger" —before realizing that "I know it is the same thing; it is just rolled up."

How does one explain the brusque conversion of propositions? Suggestions from the examiner's questions—"how were the two balls in the beginning?"; "Now, if you wanted to make a ball again," etc.— tended to provoke reflection on the reversible character of executed action. The reflection assured the invariance in quantity of matter: "It is just rolled up." The examiner's questions alone were not sufficient to bring about this change of perspective, because with other subjects performing at an inferior level the same questions were asked to no avail. Therefore, it was supposed that Bos. himself perceived the deformations of the ball under their operative aspect, *i.e.,* as reversible actions.

His reaction in relation to the little pieces tends to confirm this hypothesis. If there is "just as much [clay] in the little pieces," it is "because it is only cut in pieces," and "if the other is cut into little pieces, there would be just as many little pieces." The child became capable of mentally effecting the actions and of carrying them out as direct or inverse operations. At the same time he began to understand that there are compensations for largeness and bigness. As he compared the pancake to the ball he reasoned: "I would say there is more in the pancake; it is large, larger than the other [the ball] . . . no, it is still the same; it is not so fat." The dimensions were not considered as absolute any longer, but as relative sizes, and the enlargement and diminution changed without the quantity being altered.

Again the question is asked: does the retardate's idea of permanence of substance function as operative construction, or does it involve mechanisms that have nothing to do with intellectual development? The example just analyzed furnishes two indications in favor of the first hypothesis. First is the certitude with which the child suddenly confirmed the conservation of substance. The certitude is a logical certitude which has nothing in common with a proposition which is sometimes judged false or correct according to the reaction of the examiner. The second indication is that there is the possibility of effecting not only one isolated logical operation, but of effecting an ensemble or operative groupment. The subject accomplishes the direct operation, and is also capable of making the inverse operation; he even knows how to effect a composition of additive parts and of multiplying relations. If Bos. in the course of questioning arrives at a new concept it is due to a mental construction which the retardates cited in the first chapter were incapable of achieving.

Such an elaboration is possible only when the subject is near normal in development. Whether or not this elaboration can be accomplished by the more retarded subjects is undetermined. To this end, reference is made to the reasoning of mentally retarded children, ten and a half to thirteen and a half, cited above, who exhibited more obvious retardation because of their more advanced age.

The following excerpts show how certain children are aware of characteristics of operative transformations or of sectioning of substances and deduce from them the fact that the whole remains identical, and is independent of the arrangement of the parts:

Observation 19: *The same [substance]; it only has to be rolled into the ball, now it is just longer.*

Observation 20: *Still the same thing. Yes, but it has simply been cut into pieces.*

Observation 21: *It is always the same ball. Only here it is separated, and there it is together. It is always the same amount of clay.*

The following subject arrived at the idea of conservation by the compensation of diverse relations:

Observation 23: *There is as much clay; here it is only flattened, and there it's all gathered up.*

The following reasonings proceed from identification:

Observation 19: *You haven't taken anything away or added anything.*

Observation 21: *Exactly the same amount of clay. The clay cannot change.*

Observation 22: *There is as much clay. You see it is much longer than that, but you can pick it up and make a ball again, so there is always the same amount of clay.*

Finally, responses that show explicit reversibility are listed:

Observation 20: *The one you made the sausage of was just as big.*

Observation 21: *If it were put together it makes a ball again, and now the ball is only rolled out.*

Observation 22: *There is as much clay. You see, it is much longer than that, but you can pick it up and make a ball again, so there is always the same amount of clay.*

From these responses it is observed that subjects classified as retarded (but in whom certain ulterior development is possible) proceed by the same methods of reasoning as the normal youths of seven to nine years. The notion of conservation of substance was reached by logical reversibility and coordination of relations. Upper-level retardates then would not be incapable of logical operations. As discussed below, the possibility of attaining the concrete level of intellectual development distinguishes the retardate from the slow learner.

If consideration is given the fact that these retardates have developed beyond the prelogic stage and actually participate in the operatory processes of thought (which in the normal subjects tends toward a state of equilibrium), then do these same subjects have at their disposal sufficient intelligence for subsequent attainment of this equilibrium? The examiner finds this to be the central question in a diagnosis of retarded reasoning. If it is difficult to resolve the question of degree of intelligence in terms of mental development, and particularly if the unfolding of a pathological state cannot be predetermined with absolute certainty, one can proceed by relative approximations. The first approximation consists of establishing the actual level of reasoning.

Without speculating on the ulterior evolution of the above subjects, one sees immediately that, in spite of their entrance into operative construction, their reasoning remains limited and consequently in a state of disequilibrium. This is manifest particularly in the fact that the perceptive and intuitive data in relation to the estimation of weight or volume cannot be incorporated in their system of thought because this thought is too restrained and too rigid.

Illustrations of these limitations are listed, with responses in italics:

Observation 18: *The ball is heavier because it is round . . . be-*

cause the clay is rolled up. The pancake is considered lighter because flattened, and the little pieces weigh less, *because they are so small and thin and separated, and the other is together.*

Observation 19: *The ball is heavier because it is all round . . .* it *is still a big piece, still thick, and there it is quite thin.*

Observation 20: *It is lighter than the sausage. Before the sausage was long, and now there are only little pieces.*

Observation 21: *The sausage would be much lighter . . . because it is the . . . longest . . . you can tell real easy the ball is heavier. The other [the sausage] is rolled longer so it is lighter, etc.*

Observation 22: *The ball is heavier because it is round and that [the sausage] is long.* For the sectioning: *Oh, now it really isn't as heavy any more; it is so separated here, and there it is all together. There it is one piece; here it is torn apart.* For the pancake: *This is thin, and that is thick; the pancake is much lighter than the ball.*

Observation 23: *The sausage is heavier. It is bigger, longer . . . [the scale will lower] where the ball is . . . the little pieces are so small.* The pancake is estimated to be lighter, *Because the pancake is quite thin, and the ball is quite thick.*

It becomes evident that the mentally retarded children of the above group cling to their belief that a substance which remains permanent in its transformations can, nonetheless, change weight when it is elongated, flattened, or broken into pieces. If their reasoning has been found superior to that of the preceding group because it marks the birth of operative thought, it still remains limited because of its incapacity to surpass this degree and state of persistent disequilibrium.

Can such limited reasoning be assimilated to a disequilibrium which tends toward the progressive equilibrium characteristic in all mental growth, or do paranormal manifestations result in a branching which will be self-accentuated as the decalages of retarded development are compared to normal? This question merits examination. For the moment, let us focus (leaving it to be completed by more precise indices) on the banal observation that the interest of the retarded, attracted momentarily by the impromptu situation and the friendly atmosphere of free conversation, is more quickly influenced than that of normal subjects. When intellectual obstacles are present this is particularly evident.

And (19), questioned on the causes of displacement in the level of water, did not go beyond the frank declaration "because it just now rose." Str., without reflecting, simply repeated our question, "Yes, why?". . . I don't know"; still refusing to think, she later replied, "Well, I don't know." Likewise Ros. (22), when made aware of the fact that the weight remained constant, was led to the phenomenalistic explanation (characteristic of Stage I) "because the scales make them equal."

More than the words themselves, the tone with which they are pronounced, the look, the gestures that accompany them, and the psychomotor behavior can reveal the inertia behind which the less-gifted individual frequently retreats when the given problems surpass his immediate capacity of intellectual adaptation. The precise clinical value of such paranormal indications will be discussed later. Now attention is directed to the analysis of the various subjects' reactions concerning the dissolution of sugar and the composition of bars in relation to the second stage of reasoning.

Dissolution of Sugar

When passing from the test concerned with the transformation of clay balls to the test concerned with the dissolution of sugar analogous reactions are frequently observed in both situations. The same processes of adaptation of reasoning, which in the preceding experiment gave way to the notions of quantative conservation of substance, lead here to a continuation of substance, and this occurs in spite of its supposed disappearance, i.e., even when the physical processes develop outside the perceptual field. The subjects who confirm the quantitative conservation of substance in the test of the clay balls and who mentally reconstructed the piece of sugar in its totality did so because it was more difficult to dissociate the sugar from its quantitative measures (weight and volume) than to "retrieve" it without relying on weight and volume. There exists, nonetheless, a stage in which a certain number of retardates (as do normal children ages seven to nine years) suppose that the sugar cannot be annihilated and continues to exist, its invisible permanence being assured because of the presence in the water of "little grains of liquid" or of "vapor."

Some retardates in the second stage of reasoning deviate from the postulate that nothing is lost. Insofar as a subject looks for facts to show he is right in this, or, inversely, interprets the intuitive or experimental data (taste, visible remains in the solution, and constancy of level, etc.) in relation to their substantial permanence, these cases illustrate the beginning of logical and experimental construction. By these elementary inductive proceedings which rejoin operativity, the subjects whose interviews are listed below performed at a level in excess to that of Stage I (which is dominated by the impermeability to experimental givens and by subjective estimation).

Will reactions of the various subjects be sufficiently homogeneous to attain the same level of reasoning even though the number and quality of past experiences are variable from one case to the other? As shown below, the method of free conservation does not suppress the variety of personal memories and experimental observations, but it does disclose a manner of reasoning which is convergent in its structure with the second stage of the operative evolution of thought.

The interviews are preceded by excerpts from the case histories.

OBSERVATION 25—STI., M, 11:2

Because of scholastic insufficiency this boy had been placed in an institution for abnormal youths. According to the case history and the psychological diagnosis, mental deficiency was due to a combination of hereditary and environmental factors (retarded mother, illegitimate abandoned child, etc.). Even in the special class, where instruction was designed to meet individual needs, his performance was extremely irregular. As a result it was difficult to assign him to one specific level of mental development. Verbal and written expression were difficult for him. His spelling and writing were deplorable. By contrast, he had a lively interest in natural history. Arithmetic operations were comprehended and executed with ease. However, he did not know how to solve applied problems. Memory was frequently faulty, but this could not be attributed to true memory deficiency because general instability also had influenced his power of concentration.

There was disequilibrium in the realm of affectivity. He performed only when stimulated by thought of a reward, and quickly became discouraged when forced to work continuously and accurately. Sti. was a bad companion, a tease, and an aggressive troublemaker, but he did not want to admit his shortcomings. His lowered vitality (he was subject to tuberculosis) required special care, which the child exploited to gain privileges. Moreover, he suffered from enuresis.

During the clinical examination of reasoning, contact with the examiner stimulated the boy to maximum effort, and his attention focused on the experiment; in turn this permitted the determination of the operatory level. Because of its logical structure his level appeared to be analogous to that of normal children between eight and nine years of age.

What will happen if you put two pieces of sugar in the water? *That makes sugared water.*

The pieces remain like they are now? *They melt.*

Can you still see the sugar when it is melted? *No, you only see white water.*

White from what? *When it melts. You only know it is in the water, but it is melted.*

And how can you know that it is still inside? *Because the water is sugared when you drink it.*

The level of the water stays the same, or does it change when you put the pieces in? *The water rises because the sugar goes down.*

We will see (immerses the sugar). *You see, it rises because the sugar is heavy, and then it's necessary for it to have space.*

Because the sugar needs space in the water? *Yes, but not much; it melts. At first, yes, a little space, but after some time no more.*

When it is dissolved, where will the level of the water be? *Again at the rubber band* [*the place which marked the initial level*].

Why does the level go back down? *Because it doesn't need space any longer. It will all be melted.*

How will the sugar be now? (Stirs the sugar into the water.) *Very small, very fine.*

Is it still heavy, the sugar which dissolves? *Still a little, in any case heavier than pure water because there is more sugar inside.*

There is more inside? *Melted but . . .*

Something is left of the sugar? *Small particles.*

You have seen them? *Yes, something has stayed in the water. See the water is still up high.*

Why does it stay up high? *Because there is still a little sugar in the bottom of the glass.*

Is there enough in the bottom to make sugar of it again? *No, no only a bit.*

Do you see it? Look closely? *No, but there is still something.*

But why doesn't the level change? *Because there are still small particles. Small pieces that press the water up.*

Could the little particles be shaped again into a sugar cube? *No, half is melted.*

What does that mean, melted? Has it gone away? *No, it's still in the water.*

Any why can't it be seen any more? *I don't know.*

If you had good glasses, could you see? *No, you see nothing, you know because it is sugared.*

If the glass with the dissolved sugar were weighed and the glass with pure water and two pieces of sugar beside it were weighed, would they be the same thing or not? *It is heavier there where the pieces are still whole, and there one is completely melted and another almost.*

And when it is dissolved, it is no longer as heavy? *No.*

Why does the water level stay up? *Because that has made little bubbles, and the bubbles have risen; then the water has risen because it has made the bubbles.*

Where do these bubbles come from? *From the sugar.*

Are there bubbles in the sugar? *No, they come from the water.*

OBSERVATION 26—KEL., M, 13:3

The case study as transmitted by a children's clinic revealed retardation of an endogenous nature (the mother and several of her relatives were retarded). Psychomotor development had always been delayed. Walking and independent speech ocurred at two years. Physical rigidity was noted; although the boy's attitude was relaxed his steps were hesitant and heavy. Strabismus was also noted, and he was troubled with enuresis.

At school Kel. had a drowsy attitude, and had to be aroused from an apathetic daze. Language articulation was poor, but vocabulary was fairly adequate. In spite of his mournful and inexpressive air Kel. participated in all the pranks that occurred when the teacher's back was turned. Although untruthful and mean to his classmates, and a bad student in both spoken and written language, he was capable of making personal observations and reasoning coherently.

On first impression he appeared to be an imbecile, but his IQ of 69 indicated that he was an educable retardate. In his art, people were drawn first and then clothed without the lines of the body being erased. Academic achievement, although slow, was progressive. Finally, his quality of reasoning, which was at the threshold of the operative level, placed his retardation well above that of imbecility. In fact, Kel. was able to follow the special classes in an institution for retardates and to do elementary arithmetic.

What happens to the sugar when it is put in the water? *It melts, it is like snow when you put it in water—it melts too, and after it makes water.*
The sugar also makes water? *Yes, like water.*
But completely pure water? *Yes.*
It has no more taste? *Oh, of course it is sugared.*
Why does it have a sugared taste? *Because sugar comes from sugar beets and then that gives a sugared taste to the water.*
That happens just as it does when snow melts? *Only the snow is not sugared.*
You don't see anything any longer; it's as if it were water? *Still little specks.*
And when it is completely melted, do the little specks remain? *Yes, because there is still a bit of sugar inside.*
How do you know? *But I know the particles remain. There is still something inside.*
The level stays the same, or does it rise or go down when the sugar is put in? *The water rises because the sugar goes down.*
And about the weight; does something change when the sugar is put in? *A little bit heavier; oh, perhaps not. The sugar melts so it is quite light again. Ah, no, all in all it has to be a little bit heavier than the pure water because the sugar becomes water. That makes a bit more water, and that weighs a bit too, this water.*
As much as the water plus the piece of sugar beside it (it is placed on the scale)? *Ah, no, it's not either; it's still melted.*
Where is the level of the water when the sugar is melted? *The water goes down again because the sugar disappears. It's like it was bewitched; it has changed into water.* (Scales are used to show equality of weight.) *They are equally heavy, and too, the water has stayed up.*
Can you explain that? *Because the sugar has made water and you have more water now.*
But why does that weigh just the same as the two whole sugars? *Yes, just the same; I don't understand.*
Why don't you see any more sugar? *Because it has melted. It has become water. It is like the snow, but that still has some weight.*

OBSERVATION 27—PFE., F, 14:0

Prior to her entrance into an institution for retarded children, Pfe. was given a psychological examination. Born of a psychopatic father and a severely retarded mother Pfe. was the tenth of eleven children. Of these only three approached normalcy. Retardation was endogenous in nature.

At the beginning of her school career the child was in an institution for the severely retarded, but it was soon discovered that she was capable of progressing. A psychiatric examination established an IQ of 69.

Academic progress continued until she attained placement in the more advanced classes of special instruction without, however, being able to complete fourth-year arithmetic. When the young girl was seen later at the age of seventeen, she was assisting in the household tasks of a big institution. She could not perform tasks requiring a capacity for organization, but under supervision she could proceed on such practical jobs as dishwashing, washing, preparation of vegetables, errands, etc. Her work was satisfactory, and she was able to support herself through her own efforts. When examined at the age of fourteen she exhibited ability in drawing, and some academic skills, but as soon as problems requiring logical comprehension and experimental observation were encountered her intellectual inferiority was quickly perceived.

You are going to put the two pieces of sugar in the water and then we will see what happens. *I know, the sugar melts.*

What does that mean, it melts? *It goes to the bottom of the water and then it becomes very fine; it comes apart and spreads out.*

Can one still see it when it is in the water? *Yes, it is a little white.*

Does the water level stay where it is now, or does it move when you put the sugar in? *The water does rise because the sugar is quite light when it is melted.*

The glass, would it be equally as light as the other one which has only pure water, or still heavier? *That doesn't weigh any more at all.*

(The sugar is put in the water.) (*She shows astonishment when the water level rises.*) *The water rises, but when the sugar melts it won't stay as high.*

Look at the scales to see what happens when the sugar is put on it. *Now it is heavier.*

And when the sugar melts? *Again, the same thing as before.*

Then what happens to the sugar? *It is in the water at present.*

Why don't you see it any more when it is melted? *It is very fine; it is very fine sugar.*

Could you distinguish something with very good glasses? *You could see the very little, fine pieces.*

Is there still a taste, or nothing left at all? *It is sugared as there is some very fine sugar.*

Could you recover the sugar? *No, it's impossible.*

Why not? *Because at the present it is in the water, but melted into the water, and when it is melted it can't be recovered.*

Look at the water level; has it gone down like you had thought it would? *That has not completely lowered, I know, because there is still some sugar inside.*

And the sugar that is inside, does it still take up space? *Yes (hesitates), maybe.*

And the sugar, does it still weigh? *No, it doesn't weigh anything at all.*

But it is still inside? *Of course, it is in the water.*

But since you can't see it any more, how do you know that it is still in the water? *Because we put the sugar inside, we didn't take it out: it must still be inside.* (Scales are used to demonstrate the equality of weight.) *The glass is heavier than the other because it has sugar inside and the other one doesn't.*

OBSERVATION 28—ROH., M, 18:7

This young man was singled out for consultation by a relative, who, upon finding him abandoned and without a job, asked us to place him in vocational training. The psychological examination established his retardation. Test performances were at a nine-year level. Immediate memory and attention span were good, but there was difficulty in adapting to new situations. Roh., because of his ability to read and write, and because of his behavior in general (ability to travel alone and get about in a strange town), appeared to function at a level above that of imbeciles, although he was a retardate.

Review of his case history disclosed that Roh., after admittance into a primary school, had repeated some grade levels several times, and never passed beyond the fourth grade. Withdrawal from school occurred while he was in the fourth grade. Following this, a carpenter taught him to use tools, but Roh. lacked perseverance and preferred to spend his time prowling around train stations. Much time was spent observing locomotives, and his knowledge of them was surprising. However, in other areas his mental inferiority was evident. His walk and general appearance were those of a poorly coordinated person. Roh. had been rejected for military service, and the accompanying medical examination confirmed his deficiencies. The young man was subsequently placed in a workshop for retardates. Here, but not without difficulty, he learned to make objects of wood.

His reactions to the tests of the dissolution of sugar were most interesting. Throughout his rather nebulous explanations and numerous references to past unrelated experiences his reactions appeared to be centered at approximately the second stage of operatory throughout development.

Have you ever observed sugar as it melts? *When I have coffee it melts too.*

Then what happens? *It becomes fine and you don't see it any more.*

We are going to do it with pure water in order to see better. *You have to wait a little, and when you stir it good that makes sugared water.*

The level of the water is the same, or does it change when you put in the sugar cube? *When you put in the sugar, when you drop it, it splashes, but if you put it in slowly it doesn't splash; that makes something happen; I can't explain it very well.*

What does that cause? *Bubbles.*

And the level doesn't move? *No, but the oxygen raises the water.*

And if you put a stick in the water, would the level remain the same or would it rise? *As I have seen myself, the water stayed the same.*

We are going to do it now. You watch closely. *The water has risen, probably because the wood is heavier, and then it pushes the water.*

And when you put the sugar in? *Perhaps it rises a little. At my friend's house it didn't rise.*

(The sugar is put in the water.) (*Confirms the rise in level.*)

And when the sugar is melted? *It goes down, because the sugar is like lime when it melts it makes bubbles, very little bubbles.*

And after a while? *When you leave it for a little while you have a deposit on the bottom.*

And aside from the deposit is there anything in the water? *Yes, something remains of the sugar; I can't say exactly what.*

Does it still weigh; what remains of the sugar? *No, it's impossible, perhaps a little.*

And when you don't see anything more at all? *Oh, there has to be something left, but in any case it no longer weighs anything.*

And when you stir it well, until there isn't any deposit on the bottom? *It is like pure water, but there is something there.*

And how does the water taste? *Sweeter, more sugared than the other.*

Why sweet? *That comes from sugar which is melted inside. It changes into very small fine, threads.*

Could you make a whole piece of it again? *Impossible, it is such fine grains. If it's gone away, you can't gather it up; it is impossible to bring it back.*

But the sugar is no longer there? *No, there is definitely something that remains, but it can't be gathered up again.*

And what happens if snow melts? *There is water, but much less.*

If you put a snowball on the scales, when it melts does that move the scales, or do they remain still? *It becomes heavier; water is heavier than snow.*

Observation 29—Mul., F, 19:8

A psychiatric diagnosis revealed a congenital retardation. Although near normal physically, the young woman's mental development was disturbed, and shortly prior to the examination she had experienced a seizure. The Stanford-Binet indicated a mental age of twelve years, two months (complete success, however, was at the ten-year-level). The Vermeylen test indicated a mental development of seven years and nine months. Mul. experienced difficulty in transferring from one test situation to another, and tended to prolong the task of the moment. Attention span was short, as is noted in the test profile. In associative thinking, the specific and concrete dominated over the general.

In the different tests requiring operative reasoning a close study was made of her intellectual deficiency, which appeared to be above the level of imbecility. Imbeciles are not capable of logical reasoning and never pass beyond the first stage characterized by the negation of all the principles of material conservation (the transformation or the disappearance of substances removed from the perceptual field). Mul. was fixated at the second stage (conservation of substance with variation of weight). According to information obtained several years later, she had experienced no further mental development.

What happens if sugar is put in water? *The sugar melts; it dissolves. It becomes like powdered sugar.*

And in the end, does one still see some sugar or nothing more? *When I drink tea sometimes a little something is left on the bottom, but very little.*

Right now the two glasses have the same weight. (Scales are used to establish weight equivalence.) Two sugars are put in this glass, and then it is weighed again. *It is always the same; the sugars are so light.*

(Sugar is placed in one of the glasses.) *You can see on the scales that the sugars do weigh something.*

Does the level of the water remain the same or rise? (*Observes level.*) *It rises because the sugars take up a little space.*

And then when the sugar is dissolved? *The water comes down again a little; the sugars aren't as big now.*

And about the weight, how much will that weigh? *When the sugars are melted that weighs the same as the plain water.*

You are sure that it doesn't weigh any more when there is sugar in the water? (*She reflects.*) *Yes, it is just the same in the water. It must weigh a little.*

As much as the two whole sugars beside the glass? *No, not as heavy because here it is only sugared water.*

(Difference in water level is observed.) *The water stayed high, the sugar has melted.*

How was this possible? (*Mul. doesn't respond.*)

Why don't you see the sugar any more? *You want to know how it is when it is melted? There is a little on the bottom; it has become sugared water.*

Could you get the sugar back? *If you poured the water out you would find a little sugar on the bottom, but not very much.*

Enough to make a sugar cube? *No, it's like it evaporated in the water. Just some little particles are left.*

(The scales are used to demonstrate weight equality.) (*Long, astonished silence.*) *Because there in the beginning there were also two sugars.*

OBSERVATION 30—GIG., M, 36 YEARS

Gig. was examined at the request of the weaving supervisor in a workshop for the handicapped. He was incapable of learning the theoretical aspects of his job, even though he had worked in the establishment for two years. The skill he had acquired in pattern-cutting contrasted sharply with his marked intellectual inferiority. Although more advanced than most fellow workers (most of whom were imbeciles), he had difficulty in examining his product and correcting mistakes. The employer stated that Gig.'s character was excellent and that he was highly motivated, but the employer was unable to determine the reason for his lack of self-control. After excluding instability and unwillingness it was hypothesized that these difficulties were the manifestations of a more general intellectual deficiency. Gig. could continue at repetitive tasks, but was incapable of adjusting to new situations. As long as he continued to weave the same designs, all went relatively well, but when he was asked to work on more complicated and varied models he became disoriented. He was a retardate who was capable of good work if he could rely on acquired knowledge, but was incapable of making intellectual adaptations.

The subject's past history seemed to justify this hypothesis. Gig. had been in a special class throughout his school years. Many jobs with painters were terminated because of his intellectual insufficiency. Only in an institution, where life was adapted to the mental and physical deficiencies of the workers, was it possible for him to be gainfully employed.

As noted in the following interview, Gig. is not capable of reflection or of precise observation. The rigid patterns of experience deform the actual reasoning processes.

What will happen if two pieces of sugar are put in the water? *The sugar becomes liquid, it dissolves, the water becomes white and sugared.*

Can you still see the sugar when it is melted? *I watched once. You can't see anything in the water. But when it is melted you see something on the top of the water, something that shines like gelatin.*

The air that rises is seen also. But do you still see some of the sugar? *No, only little grains on the bottom of the glass.*

Is there still some sugar inside? *Oh, I didn't look, but there is still taste; it must come from the sugared substance which is in the water. And then there is always something left of the sugar, but you can't see it very good any more.*

Will the water level remain where it is when the two sugar lumps are put in? *The water lowers because the sugar sucks up the water.*

And does the weight change? (The glass of water is put on the scales.) *When the sugar is put in the water that makes it a little heavier of course, but it makes it less because the sugar sucks the water.*

(Sugar cubes are put in the glass of water.) (*Gig. is astonished as he examines it for an extended period.*) *The water rose because it is heavier on the bottom. That raises the water, but at my house when you put sugar in water you don't have as much water as before.*

And when the sugar melts, does the water stay up high or does the level go down? *The water becomes naturally blue. That changes color a little.*

But does the level stay high or not? *It goes down again because it is free on the bottom.*

We are going to stir in the sugar. *You will see if that goes down. Anyway, it has become heavier.*

Will the sugared water remain heavier than plain water, or does it become lighter again? *The weight has gone, but the sweetness stays.*

You are sure that it doesn't weigh anything any more? (*He watches attentively.*) *The water is transparent. Now, I didn't check at my house if it is heavy; anyway, the sugared stuff doesn't weigh as much as the whole piece any more.*

You see, the level has not gone down to the rubber band. *But it is still the same sugar as before the test. At my house I took a little glass like you have in laboratories. I tried it with a friend. We made sugared water, we saw that it becomes heavier as if it sucks the water, and that it lowers, then the water became completely clear and it went down several millimeters.*

Then you think it is heavier or like plain water? *Still heavier than plain water. You can't say the same weight. There is still something inside the sugared substance. Then that still makes a bit more weight. The sugar can't leave. It can't completely disappear, but you don't see it any more.*

You could get it back? *Oh, I don't even believe that because you can't see it any more, so it"s hard to catch it again.*

When the subjects in the first stage of reasoning witnessed the dissolution of sugar nearly all of them concluded it was completely destroyed, but another type of interpretation is presented now which prolongs the permanence of the substance beyond immediate perception, but without yet envisioning either the conservation of weight or of volume. Do such reactions give witness to a more evolved reasoning, or are they based on the fact that certain retardates have at their disposal either more precise past observations or a better capacity to analyze the experimental procedure? Or perhaps these two possibilities are really only one, and the experimental coordination and the operatory maturation develop synchronically in the mentally retarded as they do in the normal child. We must seek the answer in the analysis of responses involving reasoning processes.

Retardates of the second stage conceive of a substantial conservation of sugar in water not only because of deductive reasoning such as "because we put the sugar inside; we didn't take it out; it must still be inside" (Observation 27) or "The sugar can't leave. It can't completely disappear" (Observation 30) but equally as a result of intuitive and experimental facts. These same facts (taste, particles in the solution, level of water, etc.), to which the subjects of the first stage remained refractory, assume significance as indices of conservation.

Taste indicated the permanence of the substance:

Observation 25: And how do you know that it [the sugar] is still inside? *Because the water is sugared when you drink it.*

Observation 30: *But there is still taste. It must come from the sugared substance which is in the water.*

The remains or morsels show that sugar is dissolved in the water:

Observation 25: Can you still see the sugar when it is melted? *No . . . you only know it is in the water, but it is melted . . . there are still small particles.*

Observation 26: *But I know the particles remain. There is still something inside.*

Observation 27: *It becomes very fine: it comes apart and spreads out.* Why don't you see it any more when it is melted? *It is very fine; it is very fine sugar.*

Observation 28: *It changes into very small fine threads.*

Observation 29: *The sugar melts; it dissolves. It becomes like powdered sugar . . . it is like it evaporated in the water. Just some little particles are left.*

Observation 30: *You can't see anything in the water. But when it is melted you see something on the top of the water, something that shines . . . there is always something left of the sugar . . . the sweetness stays.*

Here is the same pattern of atomistic explanations that was noted in normal children, and at this developmental level it is only the prolongment of direct observation of the decomposition of sugar into particles, as in Bachelard's metaphysics of the dust (Bachelard 1932). Simultaneously the notion of liquidation as in melted snow is encountered:

Observation 26: Why don't you see any more sugar? *Because it has melted. It has become water.* In order to indicate that it does not disappear, leaving the remaining water pure, the child adds: *It's like it was bewitched; it has changed into water.*

Observation 30: The minute the question is asked of Gig. he said, *The sugar becomes liquid.*

It is noted that the subjects of the preceding stage did not even manage to conclude the permanence of substance from the constancy of level. However, at Stage II this fact is immediately interpreted as an indication of the continuation of a sugared substance in the solution:

Observation 25: *Something has stayed in the water. See, the water is still up high.*

Observation 27: *That has not completely lowered, I know, because there is still some sugar inside.*

The inverse is not necessarily the case; because for the subjects at this level the substance can perfectly conserve itself without occupying as much space as the whole piece. All the retardates whose interviews are analyzed above refused to believe in the disappearance of substance and confirmed that "something" of the sugar remains. As has been shown, certain subjects evoke more or less precise patterns of reasoning in order to explain the process of dissolution, while others are led to affirm: *Something remains of the sugar; I can't say exactly what* (Observation 28). In what way are such explanations superior to the mode of thought characteristic of the first stage? It is not so much the content of the notions and the invoked representations which seem to be the decisive sign of an evolution of thought as it is the coordination of perceptive and intuitive data which results from an objective system of interpretation and which completely distinguishes itself from the subjective assimilation of the preceding stage. The retardate at this level is capable of detaching himself from his own point of view and from immediate perception in order to adapt himself to the experimental method. Certainly, he has made only the first step in this decentration of the subjective ego and will be delayed in others because of the necessity to pass from problems of permanence of substance to those of weight and volume.

Although convinced of the permanence of the sugar's substance in the water, the individuals of this stage could not understand that the weight of the sugar was conserved. Responses which illustrate this fact follow:

Observation 28: Does it still weigh; what remains of the sugar? *No, it's impossible, perhaps a little . . . there has to be something left, but in any case it no longer weighs anything.*

Observation 29: *When the sugars are melted that weighs the same as the plain water.*

Observation 30: *The weight has gone, but the sweetness stays.* But at the end of the discussion: *Still heavier than plain water.* Without arriving at the idea of constancy of weight: *Anyway, the sugared stuff doesn't weigh as much as the whole piece any more.*

Likewise, all of these subjects foresaw the lowering of the water level:

Observation 25: Does the sugar need space in the water? *At first, yes, a little space, but after some time no more.* The level will be: *It rises because the sugar is heavy, and then it's necessary for it to have space . . . but not much; it melts.*

Observation 26: *The water goes down again because the sugar disappears . . . it has changed into water.*

Observation 27: *The water rises, but when the sugar melts it won't stay as high.*

Observation 28: *It goes down, because the sugar is like lime when it melts it makes bubbles, very little bubbles.*

Observation 29: *The water comes down again a little; the sugars aren't so big now.*

Observation 30: *It goes down again because it is free on the bottom . . . the sugar sucks up the water.*

Although the subjects cited above had completely surpassed the level of total egocentrism with its complete impermeability to the experimental method, they could not rid themselves of it entirely and thus remained only a half step away from the process of inductive elaboration. In the normal child, as previously established (Piaget and Inhelder 1941), the operatory development and the inductive coordination of the facts of experience are synchronized and correlated at each stage of mental development. Perhaps the reader is waiting to see what the discordance of these two aspects of thought does to the retarded to permit the inductive reasoning to be well in advance or behind the operation itself. Such foresight is the direct effect of the classical conception of logic, which at the outset separates true reasoning (reduced to the hypothetical-deductive method) from inductive methods (a return to a simple reading of facts).

If such a discordance were produced, we would be forced to establish a developmental diagnosis of reasoning; then, which of the two manifestations of thought would be the true criterion of intellectual development? In fact, we have never met a retardate capable of beginning operatory construction who at the same time did not know how to coordinate several experimental indices, nor, inversely, who was not capable of conceiving the permanence of substance without knowing how to reason by operations. This reciprocal correspondence of operatory and experimental reasoning seems to indicate again that the operation itself is not at all opposed to experiment, but that it is an action which is reversible, and by being reversible is rigorous. Emphasis is given the fact that this continuity and reciprocity of deduction and induction frequently observed in the normal child is also manifest in the thought of the retarded. Such observations throw new light on specific forms of pathological reasoning. Retardation does not signify lack of experience. On the contrary, to be retarded (at least at the Stage II level) is to participate in the general laws of construction of thought without attaining this level of maturation.

Because the structure of reasoning in these retardates is identical to that in the normal, which is known to be typical of a circumscribed stage of elaboration of the notions of conservation, it is possible to assign them a corresponding mental level and to determine the gap that separates them from the level which they normally would have attained. The wider the gap, the less chance the retardates have of catching up and attaining the equilibrium of adult thought. Is it possible, though, to define an approximate age beyond which the logical reasoning of the retardate will not progress? Is there a method of locating certain qualitative indices, which, joined with the gap in

normal development, would be symptomatic of a definitive arrestation? The previously noted clinical observations authorized the belief
that beyond thirteen to fifteen years the retardate as opposed to the
slow learner has a meager chance of acquiring new notions and logical
operations. The more accentuated the gap in development (in this
case the additional time required by the retardate to arrive at the level
of conservation of substance), the less mobile is the subject in his
adaptation to experience and the greater is his tendency to retreat behind past acquisitions. This is frequently marked by a lack of spontaneity in intellectual reactions. While the above enumerated phenomena were also observed by older retardates, these older subjects
tended to ask fewer questions and were willing to wait to be questioned before venturing their own solutions. However, this does not
mean that they talked less. To the contrary, certain were extremely
verbose. Observations or questions recalled a flood of memories,
which sometimes had to be curtailed in order to return to the essentials.

Two of the adult cases who participated in the test concerning the
dissolution of sugar may serve as examples. Rob. (28) spoke of the
lime which makes small bubbles, of oxygen which raises water, of
the stick which did not raise the water level at all, etc. Gig. (30) pre-
tended to have done the experiment himself: "I watched once. You
can't see anything in the water. But when it is melted you see something on the top of the water, something that shines like gelatin. But
at my house when you put sugar in water you don't have as much
water as before. . . . At my house I took a little glass like you have
in the laboratories. I tried it with a friend. We made sugared water;
we saw that it becomes heavier as if it sucks the water, and that it
lowers; then the water became completely clear and it went down
several millimeters." The curious part of these responses is that these
past observations are often badly assimilated or rely on false interpretations. Retardates, especially those more advanced in age, find it
difficult to be persuaded of their error; even when they correct a
previous unvoiced thought they maintain that at their house things
happen otherwise and thus impair the regularity of the results of
physical experience. They act as if they do not wish to learn anything
new and refuse to revise their past knowledge in relation to new facts.
They situate themselves in the past instead of reaching toward the
future.

Such an attitude is the very opposite of that of a normal child of approximately eight years who, if he does not suffer from affective or social inhibitions, is avid to learn, to throw himself into new hypotheses, and to profit from experience. When adequate, but narrowminded, mentality is revealed, as described above, one can be fairly certain this retardate is at the limit of his development. Many degrees exist between the attitude of a retardate who has reached his maximum and the attitude of a normal child. The upper limit is represented in the borderline type of retardation of Sti. (Observation 25), who, although retarded, was still developing.

Logico-Arithmetical Composition

It still remains to be determined if there exist in retardates intermediary levels of logical arithmetical composition corresponding to the notions and proceedings of reasoning arrested halfway between the egocentrism of the first stage and the equilibrium of the "group" or "groupment" characteristic of the achievement of logic in the normal child. The test of bars permits the revelation of a stage of composition both intuitive and operative, during which the retardate, like the normal individual, knows how to achieve the composition, A = C if A = B and B = C, provided the elements are homogeneous, *i.e.*, if they are the same shape and density and differ only in color. At this level of reasoning equivalence is established by an effective substitution of congruent elements (this substitution is difficult for the subject when he has to deal with heterogeneous objects or additive compositions). If more frequent affirmation of the equality of heterogeneous elements is given by the retarded than by the normal young child of the same level of reasoning it is because the retarded proceeds by perceptive regulations or by verbal mechanisms rather than by deduction. The tendency to replace operative reasoning by perceptive intuitive patterns seems to be a characteristic of retardation. If in the tests of conservation previous note had been made of paranormal deviations of the normal function of thought which are accentuated in the more severely retarded, it is in the same structure of reasoning that like phenomena will be presented.

The following examples are of interest because of the progress they indicate when compared to the primitive level (where no intuitive or logical composition was yet possible), and because of the tendency of the retardate to stop reasoning before coming to a conclusion. Subjects are cited for Stage I whose reactions are known in relation to notions of conservation.

OBSERVATION 31—BOS., M, 10:0
(*See Observation 24*)

GAME OF BARS OF THE SAME COLOR

You see these bars. We are going to weigh them. *Oh, that weighs quite a bit, that makes the scales go down.*

A-B (*weighs carefully and declares:*) *The same weight, they are as long, as large* (*compares them*) *and they are also the same size. They weigh the same.*

B-C (*declares:*) *Also the same size. They weigh the same.*

A and C? *Still the same weight: the bars are the same size.*

Red and blue? (*Is not sure beforehand: compares them and then weighs them.*) *The same.*

Blue and yellow? (*Uses scales to establish equality and then compares them.*)

Red and yellow (places at an angle). What are these two bars like? They haven't been weighed yet? (*Looks attentively at one, then the other, measures their equality by bringing them together and placing them parallel one beside the other.*)

But if you compare them as they are placed now on the table (at an angle)? *I see it just the same. I cannot say how, but they are the same.*

Red and bullet? (*Predicts:*) *The bullet is heavier.*

Why? *It is short, that makes it heavy on the scales.*

(Equivalence of weight is demonstrated.) *It weighs the same as the bar, the bullet.*

Blue and bullet? *The bullet is heavier. It is fatter, thicker; the blue is longer, thinner.*

(Another demonstration of weight equivalence.) (*Does not immediately believe the scales, and then after some time:*) *It is still the same.*

Bullet and yellow? *Just as heavy; no maybe not. It is heavier, or is it the same?*

Bullet + bar and two bars? *The same thing because here there are two and there there are two bars, that weighs the same, but the bullet is still heavier.*

Charcoal and blue? (*Demonstrates and then shows astonishment.*) *The same weight.*

Charcoal and bullet? *The charcoal is heavier because it is longer and bigger.*

The charcoal weighed the same as which bar? *The blue.*

And the bullet is as heavy as which bar? *The blue, ah, I understand. It is also as heavy.*

What do you understand? *They are always the same; they always weigh the same.*

Red + blue and charcoal + bullet? *Always the same.*

Look at them closely. *The two things* (*indicating the bullet and the charcoal*) *are heavy things; they are even heavier. Look how they lower the scales.*

(Compares the ball and the bullet; ball and charcoal, and states:) *Always the same.*

OBSERVATION 32—DOM., M, 11:4
(*See Observation 21*)

The testing situation is opened with the game of colored bars.

The red and the blue? *Just as heavy, just as big* (*demonstrates on the scales*).

Red and yellow. *Just as heavy.*

Yellow and blue (places at an angle), these two haven't been weighed yet. We are going to see how much they weigh. (*Compares them.*) *We can see they are just as big.*

Blue and bullet? *That has a heavy air, the bullet.*

(Demonstrates weight equality.) Red and the bullet? *That one there [the bar] is only longer, but it is still the same; it is also of iron, not really, the bullet is still heavier. I know that very well.*

The bullet weighed the same as which bar? *The same as the blue.* (*Then he takes the red and blue and compares them.*) *They are just the same size.*

Then what do you think? Are they the same weight or not (the red and the bullet)? *The same weight, just as heavy.*

How do you know? *That one is longer, and this one is thick.*

Two bars and one bar + the bullet? (*Hesitates.*) *I don't know. I think not the same because of the bullet.*

The bullet was equal to which bar? *The red.*

And the blue? *Also the red.*

The yellow equal to what? *The bullet.*

And the two sides of the scales? *I am not sure, perhaps the same, but heavier on the side of the bullet. We will weigh, then we will see.*

Red bar and bullet? (*Demonstrates weight equality again.*)

Red bar and charcoal? (*Demonstrates also the equality of weight.*)

Bullet and charcoal? *Oh, the bullet is heavier because it's lead.*

OBSERVATION 33—Ros., F, 12:6
(*See Observation 22*)

Red and blue? (*Demonstrates equality of weight.*)

Blue and yellow? (*Again demonstrates equality.*)

Yellow and red (placed at an angle)? *I think they are just as heavy because both are just as long.* (*Compares them.*)

Bullet and blue? (*Predicts:*) *The bullet is less. It is not as heavy. The bullet looks heavier.* (*Uses scales to demonstrate equality.*)

I repeat. The red weighs the same as the blue; the yellow the same as which? *Also the blue.*

The yellow and the red? *Also the same.*

How about the bullet and the red? *Also as heavy. No, no the bullet is still heavier. After all, it's lead.*

The bullet was the same as which bar? *As the blue.*

And the bullet with the red? *Still the same. It is also a bar.*

Bullet + red, and blue + yellow? *It is heavier, there where there are two, the same. On the other side there is one long and one short. It isn't as heavy.*

And the bullet was the same as what? *As a bar.*

Bar with charcoal? (*Uses scales to demonstrate equality.*)

Charcoal with bullet? *Oh, the bullet is heavier, because lead is heavier.*

OBSERVATION 34—Roh., M, 18:5
(*See Observation 28*)

Balances bars in his hands and then on the scales.

The red bar and the blue? *Just as heavy.*

The blue and the yellow? *The same.*

And if one tried the red and the yellow (placed at an angle)? *Also just as heavy.*

How do you know? *Because I already tried it on the scales.*

No, which ones do you weigh? (*Shows the red and the blue, and the blue and the yellow. Knows how to reconstruct the facts.*)

Good, then you haven't tried the red and the yellow together yet. *It is the same. They are just as long and just as thick.* (*Puts them parallel, one beside the other.*)

The bullet and the red bar? (*Demonstrates immediately on the scales.*) *The same weight.*

And if instead of weighing with the red bar you weighed with the blue bar? *It is the same because the bar is also of lead.*

It is like iron. It is not of lead. Look, you can see it very well. (*After a moment of observation:*) *The lead is still heavier.*

(Demonstrates equality of weight on scales.) (*Shows astonishment without looking for an explanation.*)

Two bars and one bar + the bullet? *It is heavier where the bullet is; that counts for something, the lead does.*

(Demonstrates equality of bar and charcoal.) *I would say that the charcoal is lighter.*

But can you see on the scales that it is the same? *Yes, I see.*

And the charcoal and the bullet? *The charcoal is heavier.*

Why is that? *It is larger and longer.*

OBSERVATION 35—GIG., M, 36 YEARS
(*See Observation 30*)

Demonstrates weight equality on the scales. *Blue and red = the same; blue and yellow = the same.*

And the yellow with the red? (Places them at an angle.) *Also the same because they are just as thin.* (*Compares them.*)

Yellow and the bullet. How do you think they will compare? (*Weighs them first in his hand.*) *The charcoal stick is lighter.*

And on the scales? *I think that the bullet is also heavier.* (*Demonstrates.*) *It is the same.*

Which is more correct, the scales or your hand? *It is the scales which are correct.*

The blue and the bullet? *Also the same on the scale. It is always the same on the scales.*

Are you sure of that? *One really would say that the bullet is heavier because it is lead. Me, I say it is the bullet which is heavier. I have already seen that the lead makes it heavier.*

(Demonstration of weight equality.) *The scales show they are equal. It's easy to see they are the same.*

But why? *I don't know, it's always the same.*

Two bars and a bar + a bullet? *Also the same? No, heavier there where there are two bars because here there are two and there only one bar and a bit of lead.*

You are sure they aren't the same? *Yes, absolutely sure, that can't be the same. Here two are the same, and there there is only one bar.*

Bar and charcoal? (*Demonstrates weight equality.*)

Bar and bullet? *The same, I've seen it.*

Charcoal and bullet? *Not the same. You think the charcoal is heavier because it is much bigger.*

A case follows which is intermediate between Stages I and II. Responses in relation to the dissolution of sugar indicated the boy performed at the upper limit of Stage I. After the experiment he visualized, and decided that the permanence of substance was possible. In the test of bars, as shown below, his reasoning was that of a person performing at Stage II.

OBSERVATION 36—RUE., M, 12:0
(*See Observation 10*)

The subject demonstrates the equality between the following bars: *The red = the yellow; the blue = the yellow.*

The red and blue (placed at an angle)? *The same weight, the same length and the same size.* (*He compares them.*)

The yellow and the piece of lead? (*Demonstrates their equality and observes for a long time without wanting to believe it, and then says:*) *Yes, the same weight.*

The red and the bullet? (*Hesitates.*) *Also the same weight because the red is heavy and the bullet is heavy.*

Exactly the same weight, or is one heavier than the other? *The bullet is heavier. The bullet is thicker.* (*Uses scales to demonstrate equality of weight.*)

Two bars and one bar + the bullet? *The same because the bullet is thicker and the other is longer.*

Then that makes the same thing? *I think that the bullet is heavier. After all, it is lead.*

A bar and the charcoal? (*Again uses scales to show weight equivalence.*)

Bullet and charcoal? (*In a persuasive tone.*) *But the bullet is heavier. You can feel it in your hand.*

And on the scales would that also be as heavy? *Of course.*

The bullet is equal to which bar? *The blue.*

And the charcoal, didn't it weigh the same as the blue? *Yes.*

Then if you weigh the bullet and the charcoal? *The bullet is heavier.*

The final case, which follows, appears to be characteristic of the first stage because of the individual's notions of conservation. At first glance he seems also to arrive at the second stage, because of his logico-arithmetical compositions. If Rue. was a case intermediate between two stages, Mug. is an example of reasoning typical of Stage I. The analysis shows that his affirmation of equality between bars does not result from true composition, but from mechanisms of regulation or of verbal habits.

OBSERVATION 37—MUG., M, 16:5

(*See Observation 11*)

The blue and the red? (*Predicts:*) *About the same, the same size.* (*Uses scales to demonstrate.*)

The yellow and the red (placed at angles)? *The same.*

How do you know it is the same? *The yellow is not as thick as the blue.*

But then why would they be as heavy? *We have to weigh them.* (*Demonstrates equality.*)

Bullet and the red? (*Says immediately without reflecting:*) *Also the same weight.* (*Then weighs them in his hand.*) *The bullet is heavier.*

We still have to show on the scales. (*Demonstrates equality.*)

Which is more correct, your hand or the scales? *The scales. It is the same.*

Then which bar did you weigh the bullet with? *The bullet and the red.*

And the red and the blue was how much? *The same.*

And if you compare the blue bar with the bullet? *The same, no, the bullet is even heavier.* (*Demonstrates on the scales.*) *The same.*

(Demonstrates that charcoal = red bar.)

Charcoal and bullet? *Bullet's heavier.*

The charcoal was the same weight as what? *A bar.*
And the charcoal and the lead? *The lead is heavier.*
Two bars and one bar + the lead? *Heavier there (indicates bar +
bullet).*
Why? *Because the bars are lighter and the lead is heavier.*

As opposed to the subjects grouped in Stage I, all these children
are capable of correcting the perceptive illusion that two bars placed
at angles seem to be of unequal length. Congruence is established by
a form of practical substitution, by placing one on top of the other.
Proceeding by such a method, which surpasses the perceptive level,
shows "intellectual" progress. All the same, these compositions barely
rise above the intuitive plane. This is clearly evidenced by the resistance these same children show when generalizing their composition
procedure to heterogeneous elements or to an additive composition.
Certain individuals manage to overcome this level, but only after
much groping and examiner's help. Others are led through it by
pseudo-reasonings, replacing intuitive or logical methods by verbal
automatisms or perceptive perseverances. However, all are equally
incapable of leaving the intuitive plane in order to pass resolutely on
to an operatory method, which alone permits deductive composition
of equalities.

The following show both the intellectual progress and the limits of
these types of composition:

Observation 31: Furnished at first with bars of the same color, Bos.
refrained from weighing them two by two—instead he placed them
beside each other, demonstrating their congruence. Having once used
this method of juxtaposition to affirm their equality, he foresaw (and
confirmed by the same method) that A = C. When bars of different
colors were used rather than identical ones, Bos. made lengthy observation of the obliquely placed bars; after this he rearranged them so
they would be parallel. He thus corrected the perceptive illusion by a
sort of intuitive reversibility without having recourse to a deductive
composition, which indicates the impossibility of his procedure being
logically motivated. When questioned about the way in which he had
just established the equality of weight, he could only give the following explanation: *I see it all the same* (that the bars are equal when
they are placed at angles). How do you see it? *I can't say, but they
are the same.* At this level, composition is evidently nothing more than

a substitution based on intuitive resemblance, but even the idea of substitution already indicates a true superiority over the procedures of the preceding level, where the retardate relied entirely on perceptive illusions instead of practical compositions.

Total failure in heterogeneous compositions proves that Bos. is incapable of reaching the operatory stage. The child easily saw that the lead was "bigger, thicker" and the bar "thinner, longer," but he did not try to coordinate these relations. Under the effect of the routine inherent in the experiment Bos. tried to find the correct solution by more convenient nonoperatory methods: It's still the same, simply dismissing the difference without abstracting it. In the same way, he supposed for additive composition that "it's the same," not through an analysis of partial equalities, but by passing it off with, "because there are two here and two there," only to contradict himself immediately thereafter, "but the bullet is heavier all the same."

Observation 32: Without preliminary pre-exercise, Dom. immediately superimposed A on C: *You can see the same size.* He even went further and tried to generalize this substitution procedure when one of the elements was of a different form. However, he managed it only with the examiner's help. He started with a false reasoning and wanted to explain why the lead equaled the red bar after having compared it to the blue: *This one [bar] is only longer, but it's still the same; it's iron, too.* Then he changed his mind immediately afterward, *No, not true, the lead is heavier after all, you know it easily.* For him, equality of weight had been based on illusory identity of substance (lead and iron) of which the two objects were made, and not at all on operatory reasoning. When this composition was analyzed with him step by step, he finally arrived at the correct solution: The lead weighed the same as what bar? *The same as the blue.* He compared the two bars, *just the same size,* and concluded that the lead also equaled the red bar. The structure of this substitution is nevertheless still close to that which is effected between homogeneous bars and remains linked to the perceptive condition that two bars can, in fact, be substituted one for the other. When the three elements were heterogeneous (bar, lead, and charcoal) Dom. remained under the illusion that the lead is *heavier, as it is lead.* He also met the same difficulties with the additive compositions: *I think it is not the same weight because of the lead.*

Observation 33: Ros. was less sure, but also compared the elements A and C: *I think they are just as heavy because both are just as long.* At first she was ready to affirm the equality of a composition with a heterogeneous element by a sort of automatism which was broken as soon as she thought again of the lead whose absolute quality was to be heavy. As in the preceding case, Ros. understood during the analysis that one bar can be substituted for another, even when one is not the same form: *Still the same, it's a bar too.* However, her reasoning, like that of the others, remained linked to the ability to substitute two elements of congruent form, and failed in additive compositions as well as in compositions with three heterogeneous elements.

Observation 34: From the beginning Roh. made errors concerning the equality of the bars; he thought all the equalities had already been established. When the facts were reviewed he maintained the idea of equality by explaining *just as long, and just as thick,* and placed the two bars in parallel position on the table. When it came to making compositions with lead, the regularity in the experiment with the lead seemed to lead him to predict equality. He thought that the bar was also made of lead, but after short observation he resorted to the tactile illusion: *The lead is still heavier.* When he used the scales to check weight equality between the bar and the lead, he could think of no explanation. This affords proof that he could not reason by deductive means. Likewise, he was incapable of constructing some equality between the lead and the charcoal, and of analyzing an additive composition.

Observation 35: Gig. also compared the homogeneous elements. In the composition with the lead he predicted equality, not through true reasoning, but because of having registered the regularity of the results: *It's always the same on the scales.* However, the question "Are you sure?" made him hesitate. *One really would say the bullet is heavier because it is lead, me I say it is the bullet which is heavier . . . I have already seen that lead makes it heavier.* That the idea previous to the equality of weight had little foundation in reason is shown in the reaction to the experimental check: *The scales show they are equal.* But why? *I don't know, it's always the same.* The same situation existed for additive compositions. He began by asking, *Also the same?,* then gave the answer himself, *No, heavier there where there are two bars because here there are two, and there only one bar and a piece of lead.* It was the same for the comparison between lead and charcoal (after having demonstrated that charcoal = one bar):

Not the same, you think the charcoal is heavier because it is much bigger.

Observation 36: Rue.'s reactions show a greater facility for the bar experiment than for the sugar experiment. While he believed (at least at the beginning of the experiment) that the substance ceased to exist at the time of the sugar's dissolution, he was capable of effecting semi-intuitive, semilogical compositions characteristic of the second level. By comparing the bars he established *just as heavy, just as long, and just as wide.* When questioned about their equality when compared with the lead, he hesitated, *Just as heavy too, because the red is heavy and the lead is heavy,* then contradicted himself: *The lead is heavier, the lead is thicker,* etc.

The problem is how to interpret such a decalage—that is, the difference in the reactions in different experiments. Are not the same operations involved? Or is the child unstable and inconsistent in his reactions? Or, perhaps, is he an example of an intermediate level of reasoning? Rue.'s behavior tends to confirm the third possibility, as is shown in the following observations. After denying the sugar's conservation, the child was capable of interpreting the conservation of weight because of the permanence of substance, thus showing his performance to be at the upper limits of Stage I. Moreover, his manner of procedure in the bar experiment (where he shows the absence of any operatory composition) proves that for these compositions he is at the threshold of Stage II. At the time of the examination Rue. was at an intermediate level and could substitute one bar for the other more easily than he could conceive of the conservation of the sugar (substance) in the solution. The perceptive illusion of the sugar's disappearance was stronger than that produced by the oblique placement of the two bars.

In certain cases, however, similar reactions can assume markedly different diagnostic significance. It is necessary to distinguish carefully between the rare cases of slight decalages, such as Rue., and those which show only the apparent superiority of one result over another, as is found in Mug.'s case (Observation 37). His ideas of conservation place him at Stage I, but the bar experiment seems at first glance to elevate him to Stage II.

Like the other subjects at this level, he began by affirming that A and C were "the same." When asked to justify his affirmation, he denied it. There is no certainty that he understood his contradiction. He stated that "the yellow is not as thick as the blue," and then, when asked why they would be "just as heavy," he replied, "We need to weigh them." Such a proposal indicates absence of reasoning rather than an intuitive or operatory composition.

Why did Mug. at one time affirm their equality as if he had just established a real mental construction? The reason seems to be that he perseverated, and in certain cases this perseveration recalls the mechanisms of perceptive regulation. The child shows a sort of anticipatory attitude which causes him to predict equality. Perhaps he can see it or feel it, while comparing the objects, more easily than the normal child, since certain illusions are less accentuated in the mentally retarded. Thus, if he manages to annul the illusion, it is not necessarily by a conquest of reasoning, but by the play of independent factors of thought.

The bar experiment referred to above permits the description of a stage of semi-intuitive, semi-operatory reasoning where equal compositions are possible; however, they are still related to one condition, *i.e.,* congruency of the elements. When this condition is destroyed, and objects of heterogeneous form and density are used, the retardates fail in these equality constructions and stray in pseudo-reasonings.

Progress in the first stage (which is analogous in normal children and in the mentally retarded) is manifest in the possibility of referring to a common measure by the substitution of one bar for another, most often through superposition. By placing in a parallel position the bars which were presented to him in an oblique position, and then by measuring their size, the child of this second stage rises above the perceptive order and corrects the illusion under which the subjects of the first level remain.

Why don't these same retarded children make one more step and generalize this method of reasoning for all the elements, such as the piece of lead or the charcoal? Why are they inept at additive compositions? The reason is twofold:

First—as was emphasized in *Le Développement des quantités physiques* (Piaget and Inhelder 1941)—it is necessary in heterogeneous compositions to effect a differentiation between substance and weight by disregarding the former in order to reason only on the latter. However, at the second level of reasoning this differentiation is still difficult. The same subjects when confronted with the clay balls and sugar always reasoned with relation to a global substance and not in relation to weight as such.

The second reason, although complementary, resides more in the intuitive than in the operatory character of these compositions. Certainly there is more than one simple reconciliation of perceptions, more than one method of simple visual measure. A measure of some kind is implicit because in displacing the bars the child makes some sort of action which is the inverse of that made in putting them in the oblique position. However, this action (which could be called reversible) still lacks the logical precision by which the child (or the retardate) on a higher level predicts equality without having recourse to actual measures. As long as homogeneous elements are used, the distinction between a practical or empirical reversibility and logical operations is difficult. Progress from one to the other can be unperceived and is noticed only in the increasing certitude which accompanies the child's reasoning or in his rapidity of judgment. The distinction becomes more and more evident as the experiment pertains more and more to heterogeneous elements and to additive compositions, *i.e.,* when substitutions by manipulation become impossible.

The progress as well as the limits of this level of reasoning are common to retardates and to normal children. However—and this fact is of great interest to the study of clinical signs of retarded reasoning —the normal child can be led to overcome, little by little, the intuitive method; if not, he remains openly opposed to the equalization of heterogeneous elements. The retardate differs in that he willingly avails himself of a pseudo-reasoning. This may lead to answers which are correct, but which do not necessarily result from a logical procedure. On one hand, the regularity of the experiment has more influence on thought which is less spontaneous and tends to perseveration anyway. On the other hand, perceptive illusions, which are weaker in the retarded than in the normal child, are less opposed to equalization. If at times the retardate gives responses which appear superior to his true level of operatory reasoning, it is because factors exterior to reasoning support and facilitate or even substitute for reasoning.

Analysis of the reactions to the conservation and composition experiments just cited present a new stage of reasoning. All the subjects arrived at conclusions unknown to subjects at the first level. They affirmed the quantitative conservation of the substance (during the transformations of the clay ball), or they conceived the notion of a continuation of substance (in spite of the apparent disappearance of the dissolved sugar), or they corrected a perceptive illusion by substitution (two bars of the same length appear unequal when placed at an angle).

These results are of interest because they clearly oppose those of the preceding level. The retardate at this second stage has not only enriched his knowledge, or enlarged his methods of thought, or perfected his reasoning, but a true reversal of viewpoint also has occurred in him. Conservation, which was rejected by the individuals classified in the first stage, is affirmed anew with certitude and justified by a logical motivation and a coordination of experimental facts. In the same way, the perceptive illusion which influenced the first stage gives way here to actual measure of bars by comparing them. The same facts (taste, sugar particles still visible in the solution, and constancy of level or of weight), interpreted at first in relation to the substance's disappearance, are now assimilated as indices of the permanence of substance. In summary, in precise problems of substance conservation and in homogeneous bar composition, the above cited results are the antithesis of the reactions characteristic of the first level.

The observation of such a conversion of reasoning in terms of the same experimental matter seems more revealing of mental level than the single comparison of results obtained by means of tests that are graduated but heterogeneous in relation one to the other (in that they do not always measure the same thing). Operatory experiments afford closer contact with the internal processes of genetic evolution than do tests which judge the superiority of one reaction in relation to another in terms of the average success age in the normal child. *This comparison of the notions and methods of reasoning (which, in the same situation, show qualitative changes in different groups of subjects) reveals the mechanism of transformation.*

As has been shown, this mechanism is characterized at this level by the advent of operatory thought, which becomes progressively detached from intuitive methods and in certain respects freed from its initial egocentrism. If Stage II subjects affirm that as much clay will be found after the transformations or sectionings of the clay ball as in the initial state, they do this by one of four ways: (1) they rely on inverse operation (the possibility of returning to the departure point without altering the parts); (2) they postulate the identity of everything independent of the parts' displacement; (3) they comprehend the compensation of all the relations (coordination of length, width, and height); or (4) they identify each part with itself during the transformation. In these four distinct but interdependent cases, it is through a system of operations that the subjects reach a notion of conservation unknown to Stage I. In other words, it is always in relation to a "groupment," *i.e.*, a system of logical or "physical" (material) operations from which the retardate, like the normal six- to eight-year-old, constructs ideas characteristic of this second stage. The sugar dissolution experiment best shows the true and continuous construction that takes place, rather than just juxtaposition of new notions, or a logic born *ex nihile* and simply added to the egocentrism of the first stage.

Nothing is more instructive than to observe the way in which the subjects coordinate and interpret experimental facts in relation to the central idea of the conservation of sugar substance in the solution. Whether the idea of a necessary conservation causes the retardate to seek experimental proofs to support it, or inversely, whether relating different indices gives rise to a conservation of substance hypothesis, there is always reciprocal penetration between operatory coordination and experimental induction. At the first stage neither deduction nor experimentation was possible, and at the third stage deduction seems to dominate induction, but in the intermediary Stage II, the interaction of the two aspects of reasoning is clear. An analogous fact is observed for the bar compositions; in this instance, reasoning depends still more closely on intuitive method. In order to state that A = C, having observed that A = B, and B = C, the subjects proceed to measure by congruency. Intuition alone is not sufficient; equality is not perceived without comparison. They compare one element to another in order to verify an equality hypothesis. This hypothesis appears to precede experimentation without being purely deductive, and thereby lacks logical precision.

The progress common to these different reactions typical of the second stage consists then in the dominance of logical reversibility over the irreversibility of immediate perception. In other words, there is the birth of operatory thought which is progressively disengaged from the perceptive and intuitive assimilation belonging to the preceding stage.

Does this logical and genetic superiority of operatory reasoning correspond to a more general intellectual progress? Do the subjects who are on the threshold of the operatory level for notions of conservation or of equal composition behave in an adequate manner in other situations? These questions arise when recognition of a clinical index of general significance is sought.

It is instructive to note that at the second stage of the conservation notions, all the retardates were equally capable of carrying out fundamental arithmetic operations, either by practical manipulations, or by resorting to an intuitive content. On the other hand, those of the first stage either completely failed, due to ignorance of the significance of the same operations, or they brought into play simple verbal automatisms. Such a correlation between "physical" reasoning, whose logical and psychological mechanism has just been analyzed, and arithmetic comprehension relies on the profound unity of thought, that is, on the synchronism of the formation of the first "groupments"—both logico-arithmetic (classes and relations) and "physical" (partition and displacement). A child or adult retardate may seem to have greater facility in one or the other domain, but analysis will show that this advancement or retardation results from extra-intellectual factors (memory, attention, learning techniques, a slowing down of intellectual activity caused by the child's emotional state, etc.) and not from a real difference of reasoning level. According to the observations, this is revealed as perfectly coherent from one experiment to another, or shows only insignificant decalages, which are discussed in the following.

It is possible to go further and draw conclusions from this sign of reasoning level which are applicable to the whole of intelligence, or even for general behavior of the individual? Such a generalization is impossible a priori. What would be the crucial experiment of intelligence or of behavior? Should reference be made to the IQ, to scholastic performance, to adaptation in practical life or perhaps to a particular process such as educability? Doesn't the difficulty of deciding on a fact general and precise enough to express the intellectual quality or the degree of mental development show that there is no perfectly homogeneous level of mental organization? Without becoming involved in this question, which is outside the framework of this research, it can be noted that each time there is concern over the establishment of a mental diagnosis, it is necessary to find the relation between operatory reasoning and all the other functions and facts in play. The particular type of retardation present in each of the subjects is determined by the integration of operatory reasoning into the ensemble of a clinical picture.

Once it is known that certain retardates reach a beginning of operatory construction, and thus of logical reasoning, it is astonishing to realize that they are arrested there (for example, adults who are fixed at the second level) or that some spend more time than normal people in attaining Level III (as in the development of slow learners).

Why is it that the mental retardate who has risen above the pre-logical level will not be able, sooner or later, to attain maturation of reasoning? (Which in the problems analyzed in this work means to construct the "groupment" of the conservation of volume.) In more general terms, why does retarded intelligence remain deficient? This fundamental problem of the psychopathology of oligophrenia cannot be resolved on psychological grounds, much less on operatory reasoning alone. However, it can be interesting to determine, within the limits of thought itself, the concomitant factors causing the arrest or abnormal slowing down of mental development.

If the reasoning relative to substance conservation cannot be generalized by weight, or if the equal compositions remain strictly limited to bars of equal form and congruent dimensions, it is because the operation in play is not detached from the intuition and perceptive methods which still play a part in the subject's reasoning. These methods can in certain cases assist reasoning. For example, when several transformations were effected, there was an empirical return to the initial ball. It is time to recall the intuitive and experimental facts in support of the permanence of sugar substance in solution, or the regularity in the equal compositions, or the possibility of proceeding by actual measures. While it is a matter of reasoning with substance (as opposed to weight or volume) from which there is direct intuition of the dimensions, reasoning will always be helped by perceptive methods. However, these perceptive methods are not enough to suppress the optical illusions which cause belief in the augmentation or the diminution of tranformed or dissolved substance, or of the displaced bar. These beliefs are due to reasoning, and can only be more or less facilitated by perceptive or intuitive factors. These same factors, while supporting reasoning, can equally restrain its free un-folding; this is true in most retardates of this level. Although they sometimes lead to results apparently analogous to those of operatory reasoning, methods involving substitution are more obvious in the bar experiment than in the experiments involving the clay balls or the sugar; in the last two the result of the operation is more obvious than the experiment with the bars. In these last cases observation is manifest only in the justifications which may be incomplete, while in the bar experiment the equality composition $A = C$ (if $A = B$ and $B = C$) represents the operation itself. At the second stage the operation detaches itself slowly from intuitive procedures (substitution by comparison of congruent elements) and easily becomes simple perceptive regulation and verbal persistence.

In conclusion, *reasoning of the retardates at the second stage is characterized by a beginning of operatory construction* and is completely different from the reactions of the preceding level. However, this construction remains unfinished because the retardates do not leave these methods of substitution behind (perceptive or intuitive regulations, verbal patterns, etc.), or if they do, it is done too slowly. Thus, a state of *psuedo-equilibrium* is created (as opposed to the equilibrium characteristic of the completion of operatory construction), which remains subordinate to more abstract or complex evaluations. The psuedo-equilibrium is also distinguished from the transitory equilibrium of the normal young child. This open and mobile equilibrium enlarges and consolidates itself by assimilating new facts. Between this mobile equilibrium and the typical retardate's psuedo-equilibrium, all the transitions are possible.

It has been noted, but not discussed, that the older the retardate, the more he relies on the substitution procedures mentioned, as though to spare himself the effort of personal construction by applying ready-made schemes. This phenomenon, which could be called paranormal, is full of information for the prognosis of reasoning, and should be carefully noted in connection with the construction of tardiness in relation to the subject's age.

Second Section: Stage III

Some mental retardates during the course of Stage II arrive at the beginning of operatory construction, a beginning which leads normal people to substance conservation. However, even in the retarded cases where operatory character was almost complete, it seemed that at the second level the operation was still relying on intuitive and empirical elements of varying degrees. The problem is: can a stage be found in retardates which is superior to the second and which is characterized by an advance of the operations over the perceptive facts which support reasoning? In normal evolution a third stage exists, which is characterized by the conservation of weight, a notion that is always preceded by substance conservation. Interestingly enough, this stage can be shown to exist in retardates, and it is characterized by an operatory advance.

Why are these examples considered as characteristic of a third stage? In the normal person succession of stages corresponds to chronological order, but this order has no significance in retardates as examined at various ages unless there is detailed knowledge of their previous individual development.

Here operatory criteria become significant. If weight conservation constitutes a stage superior to that of substance conservation, then the retarded subjects who arrive at conservation of weight must also possess substance conservation, without the reverse being true. The first section was devoted to subjects who affirmed substance conservation without discovering that of weight. Below, a group of retardates are analyzed who understand weight conservation and who demonstrate that they also know that of substance. First, some reactions will be cited relative to the transformation of the clay ball.

OBSERVATION 38—EUG., M, 14:10

The boy was questioned at the end of his school career. Eug. had been in the upper section of a special class in an institution for the mentally retarded. His medical case history stated that slow progress was complicated by disturbances of psychic and social equilibrium. Eug. was an illegitimate child whose father was retarded and delinquent. He was underdeveloped physically, had rickets, and had not walked until he was two and one-half years old. His poor academic achievement probably was a result of his physical inferiority as well as his mental development. The teachers noted that he became easily fatigued. Psychiatric examination at the age of eleven placed his IQ at 83. Hysterical reactions of revolt and of depression, accompanied by threats of suicide, were noted.

When first placed in the school (immediately following the psychiatric examination) Eug. was difficult to control. Teaching efforts were resisted; temper tantrums followed by depression resulted when any constraint was encountered. Lacking in self-confidence, Eug. had continually to be stimulated to work. He was at the bottom of his special class, and was jealous of the success of his classmates.

Suprisingly, at the end of two years, his behavior changed. Apparently Eug. had attained a degree of emotional stability. His self-esteem did not become so easily challenged. He evidenced interest in his work and tried zealously to fill in his scholastic gaps. Nonetheless, his intellectual capacities remained limited, not surpassing those of an upper-level retardate, although he made good observations and was interested in natural history and geography. When concrete methods were used he achieved comprehension of arithmetic operations. However, all formal reasoning remained inaccessible to him. Later, during on-the-job training, Eug. could not follow the theory courses which were indispensable if a diploma was to be obtained. However, his practical work was entirely satisfactory, and he appeared to be capable of self-sustenance.

Eug. found the reasoning experiments even more intriguing than drawing, arithmetic, and job-training tests. His latent anxiety disappeared and he completed his tasks.

The problem was quickly understood and Eug. made two identical balls. Then he complied with the request to change one into a sausage.

If you put the sausage back on the scales, will it weigh as much, or be heavier or lighter? *The same weight, because nothing was taken away.*

Are you sure? *Yes, it must weigh exactly the same.*

We are going to divide the sausage into little pieces, and reweigh them on the scales. *It is still the same because nothing was taken away.*

And if you put a very thin pancake in place of the small pieces? *That doesn't change the weight. The thinner it is, the more spread out it is, so it comes to the same thing.*

Is there as much modeling clay in both, or not? *Of course, that can't change, because nothing is taken away!*

Not for the divided pieces either? *Of course not.*

Now we will leave the weighing and see how much room a pancake takes up in water. See, we'll mark the level of the water when nothing is inside. (*He does so very carefully.*)

And if I put the ball inside, what will happen? (*Points to a higher level.*) *The water rises, because something has been put into it.*

And why does the water rise when something is put into it? *It takes up room.*

(The ball is put in and the displaced water level is marked.)

And if instead of the ball, I put in the little pieces, where would the level rise to? *Still higher because it is cut up.*

Why higher when it is cut up? *Because there are so many little pieces.*

And if instead of the little pieces, you put the sausage? (*Long moment of reflection.*) *All in all it rises the same as the ball, because nothing is taken away. But the little pieces aren't together, they aren't in one piece, not something solid . . . I have trouble explaining it, and they weigh the same. Only with the sausage, it chases water from both sides, and with the ball it presses directly down.* (*Makes a movement from top to bottom.*) *No, all the same it rises more with the ball.*

Show me where you think the water rises for the small pieces, where for the ball, and where for the sausage? (*He points highest for the ball.*) *For the sausage a little bit less, because it presses less downward than sideways.*

And do a ball and a sausage take up the same space? *The sausage takes more space.*

But then the water would have to rise more? *Not necessarily. It's in a different position in the water, so the water rises less.*

And the little pieces? *Oh, the little pieces take up still more room because there are so many.*

(Experimental check.)

What do you see? *Oh, no, the water rises the same in all of them.*

How do you explain that? *Because they weigh the same.*

As before, in Stages I and II, it is interesting to review the cases of several persons who had had seizures. Different mental functions often develop in a disharmonious manner; therefore, knowledge of this type of logical reasoning may be of value.

OBSERVATION 39—EM., F, 14:5

Em.'s medical case history indicated that her developmental difficulties might have resulted from birth injury, and her intellectual development was comparable, at certain points, to that of retarded children.

The girl was of cheerful disposition, related well to her classmates, and did not show the irritability frequently found in persons who have seizures. Her teacher noted her ability for observation and personal reflection. However, Em. was easily distracted, made many mistakes, and often had difficulty in expressing herself. She was retarded two years in her academic work.

A psychological examination resulted in an IQ of 94; successful test performance ended at the ten-year level. Mental test scores indicated that she could reason with concrete facts but was completely unable to do so at the abstract level. This fact was substantiated in the operatory analysis.

Em. understood the operatory experiments rather quickly. She observed carefully, expressed her thought coherently, and was capable of concrete operations, but she could not engage in reasoning at the formal level. Instead, the girl relied entirely on concrete intuitions.

She made the two balls, demonstrated their equivalence, and then transformed one into a sausage.

If you put them back on the scales now? *It is surely still just as heavy because I took nothing away. There is still as much clay.*

We will divide the sausage into little pieces, then compare the ball with the little pieces. *It is just as heavy too.*

But other children told me it weighed less when the clay was divided. *No, it's all the same if I have it all in one piece or if I separate it into many pieces.*

What happens to the water level if I put the ball into the glass of water? *The water rises.*

Why? *If I put in something heavy, it has to rise.*

Why does it have to rise when it is heavy? *It's the pressure that counts. When the ball goes down, that presses the water up.*

Here is a small lead ball and a big clay ball. Which is lighter? Which do you think will make the water rise more? *The lead, because it is heavier.*

(Experimental check.) *Oh! The ball makes it rise more. It is bigger and takes up more room.*

(Demonstration shows that each ball makes the water rise the same because they are equal in size, *i.e.,* they occupy the same amount of space.)

If you put the little pieces in the water instead of the whole ball, will it rise the same or not? *With the little pieces a little bit less, because they are smaller than the big ball. They are cut up in pieces, and, when cut, they take up less room.*

And if you put in the sausage instead of the little pieces? *The sausage isn't as high as the ball, it isn't as large, and it needs less room.*

And the pancake and the ball? *With the pancake the water rises more. It takes up more room. It is much larger and bigger.*

Could you make the ball again from the pancake? *Yes.*

And how would this second ball be in relation to the first? *Again the same, because it is the amount of clay here as there.*

But as for the pancake, do you think it will take up more room in the water? *Yes, more.*

(Experimental check.) *Yes, the same, I don't understand. It is still larger. I can't understand.*

And if you check it for the little pieces? *Oh, that makes it less high, because they are divided.*

OBSERVATION 40—WEH., F, 23 YEARS

Weh. was referred for consultation for two reasons: although she had been enrolled for two courses at a housekeeping school, she remained unable to perform her job as kitchen helper without close supervision. In addition, she had difficulty adapting to new situations which required either initiative or cooperation with the housekeeper. At these times she either pouted or made insolent remarks. Failure to make friends at school kept her an isolate.

Because she had been raised by understanding parents, her difficult behavior and her insufficient performance could not be attributed to environmental causes, but they did suggest possible mental deficiency. Weh. had been in the lower grades of a school for normal children. When she reached the upper grades she first repeated a class, and finally was transferred to a special section (development class). She showed marked retardation in arithmetic and grammar, and had continued difficulty in written composition. Her blank expression, heavy walk, lack of intellectual interests and slow physical reactions suggested mental retardation. An IQ of 79 was noted; learning was slow and irregular. Infantile modes of graphic expression and gaps in arithmetic comprehension were found. Her operatory reasoning, illustrated below, was characterized by fixation at the third stage. As soon as she was presented with problems beyond her capacity for immediate assimilation she became irritated and refused to try to think them through.

She made two identical balls and transformed one into a sausage.

If you weighed the ball with the sausage? *They would be exactly the same weight. There is always as much clay. Nothing has been taken away.*

And if you cut the ball into small pieces and weighed them with the sausage? *Still just as heavy.*

Why? *Because it is still the same weight. It doesn't matter if it is separated because if you make a ball again, you would have the same ball.*

What will happen if you put one of the two equal balls into each of the beakers? *The water rises.*

Why? *Always when you put something in, it goes to the bottom and the water rises.*

The same or not? *The same for the balls.*

And if you put the ball in one glass and put the little pieces in the other? *It rises less because between the little pieces there is water, and that doesn't rise, and for the ball there isn't any water in between.*

And for the sausage, where does the water rise? *In any case, not less. I think the same. We weighed in the beginning and it is the same weight.*

(The ball is compared with a metal bearing heavier than the ball.) Which of these two objects would make the water rise most? *With the metal, it is very heavy: it goes down more to the bottom and then the water rises more.*

(An experimental check is made.) *It is not as big. I understand; it makes the water rise less.*

And the sausage and the ball? *The sausage makes it rise more. It takes up more room in the water.*

Could you make a ball from it again? *Yes.*

Would it be like the other one again? *The same size.*

Is there as much clay? *Always, it doesn't change.*

And does it take up more room in the water? *Yes, it is longer.*

And the little pieces, where do they make the water rise to? *I think still higher than the ball, there are so many of them.*

And the pancake? (*The young girl makes one.*) *It will rise less; it is too thin.*

And the weight? *Always the same, nothing was taken away.*

OBSERVATION 41—EBE., F, 24 YEARS

The young woman whose interview follows had been engaged in farm work for several years, but has enrolled in a professional course to learn sewing. Her performance in this class suggested possible retardation, and resulted in referral for diagnosis.

Her physical appearance as well as her motor and intellectual behavior indicated possible cretinism. Ebe. was hard of hearing, and had thyriod trouble. Her physical reactions were slow, and insufficient muscular control produced defective speech. Medical examinations confirmed these observations. An IQ of 77 served to classify her as a borderline retardate. In spite of immediate appearances, the deficiency was not grave, but was characterized by slow development and early fixation. She experienced difficulty in following the regular classes of a small, rural school, but she had learned the fundamental concepts of reading, writing, and arithmetic (had she been in a larger town she undoubtedly would have been placed in a special class). Because of her slowness in learning, Ebe. was not admitted to the sewing course, but was placed in a sewing shop for retarded girls. Besides the sewing instruction, she followed courses in speech and gymnastics. Since she was highly motivated, there was a real possibility that she could develop into a good worker and be placed in a sewing factory.

An analysis of her reasoning succeeded better than verbal or academic tests in confirming her state of borderline retardation, but revealed at the same time unsuspected capacities for personal thought and mental construction.

(She compared the balls and divided one into small pieces.)

If you weighed the ball with the small pieces, would it still be the same weight or not? *The weight can't change. It is the same together or separated.*

We are going to put a ball into each of the glasses and watch the level of the water. *(Demonstrates.) It rises just the same. The balls are just the same.*

And if instead of the second ball you put the little pieces? *It would also rise the same because it is as heavy.*

A clay ball and a small metal bearing caused the water to rise the same, and the bearing weighs more on the scales. *You will see it rise more with the bearing because it is heavier. (She demonstrates). It rises less for the bearing.*

Do you understand why? *No, it's funny. It is so heavy.*

It is the size which makes it rise more; it does not depend on the weight. The ball takes up room in the water so the water has to rise higher. We have seen that the two balls occupy the same space because they are the same size. Now the ball and the small pieces— will they take up space too? *The small pieces more because they are separated.*

Why do they take up more room when they are separated? *Because when they are in a simple pieces it is smaller and rises less.*

Could you make a ball again from the small pieces? *Yes.*

The same size as the other or bigger? *The same size, no clay was taken away.*

And the little pieces occupy more space or less? *No, more, because they are separated.*

And if instead of the small pieces you put in a sausage? *Oh, that takes up less space than the ball. It is thin.*

OBSERVATION 42—HIL., M, 14:11

At the time of the interview Hil. was a student in an institution for the mentally retarded. After spending most of his school years in a normal class, his lack of sexual discipline, often followed by attempts to run away, required that he be placed in an institution for observation. Summary of a psychiatric examination, administered when he was thirteen years of age, found him approximately four years retarded intellectually and affectively; tendencies toward lying, stealing, and sexual perversion were also disclosed. Both parents appeared to be incapable of providing their children with proper supervision, and it became necessary to place Hil. under the care of a guardian. The boy probably suffered from both an inherited pathology and moral abandonment.

During the two years Hil. was in special class, some intellectual progress was made. Arithmetical understanding included addition, subtraction, multiplication and fractions, and he could solve problems which required these operations, problems which frequently are difficult for true retardates. Likewise, as a baker's apprentice he showed he was capable of following the complementary theory courses. From a strictly intellectual point of view it appeared that he was not a true retardate but functioned at a retarded level because of emotional problems. These emotional problems were so severe that he could not profit from education.

At school any work requiring sustained effort, such as writing and drawing, showed marked indiscipline. His performance on learning tests was distinguished from that of true retardates by his rapidity of comprehension and intellectual resources, but he did display fixations and a short attention span. His social behavior revealed feelings of instability. After leaving the institution for abnormal children he was placed as an apprentice, but his vagrant ways led to his arrest as a delinquent.

Hil.'s case is interesting because a clinical examination of operatory mechanisms shows clearly the distinction between slow though not retarded reasoning and the other factors which impede his general development, factors which have to be analyzed by other methods.

(*He made two identical balls, weighed them, and transformed one into a sausage.*)

How much does that weigh now? *The same.*

Are you sure it's the same? *Yes, because now it is only long, because I made a sausage from the ball and because I took the same clay, and so it is as much clay.*

Now is there as much clay as before in the ball? (*He compares.*) *Yes, the same.*

And when you divide it into small pieces? *It is still as much clay. We took the same clay and we weighed it in the beginning. It is always the same weight.*

We are going to make a pancake to see if it is the same, or if, perhaps, it changes weight. *Oh, no, impossible, because it's the same clay!*

What will happen if I put the clay in this glass of water? *The water rises. When you put something in, it weighs on the water and presses it up, and when the ball is on the bottom there is no water in the ball's place.*

Then you could say that the ball takes up room. You see that the two balls occupy just the same places (points to the level marked by the rubber band). Show me where the water will rise with the ball and where with the pancake. *The pancake takes up more room.* (*He points to a higher level.*)

Do the little pieces make the water rise? *It only rises one half as much because it doesn't take up as much room* (starts to laugh). *But it also comes from the ball. Can I try? It must make the water rise the same amount.*

And if you compare the ball and the sausage, where does the water rise with the sausage? *It still rises the same because it is as heavy and because the size is the same.*

Several of the above reactions, given as samples of patterns of the third operatory stage accessible to certain retardates, are striking because of their similarity to those of normal nine or ten-year-olds. Two criteria determine the third level. One is the progress that it shows over the preceding level; the other is its limits in relation to the invariance of weight and the variability of volume as shown in the transformations of the clay ball.

These subject affirm weight conservation by relying on exactly the same operatory mechanisms as for the notion of substance. During the preceding stage, by contrast, weight conservation is an unknown notion, and the child does not permit himself even to consider it as a possibility.

The invariance notion of conservation of weight, revealed by retardates at the third stage, is due also to conscious understanding of the reversible character of the actions of transformation, of sectioning, and of the coordination of relations. The following examples justify this statement:

Observation 38: *That doesn't change the weight. The thinner it is, the more spread out it is, so it all comes to the same thing.*

Observation 39: *No, it's all the same, if I have it all in one piece or if I separate it into pieces.*

Observation 40: *It doesn't matter if it is separated because if you make a ball again you would have the same ball.*

Observation 41: *The weight can't change. It is the same together or separated.*

Observation 42: *The same weight because now it is only long.*

The difference between the reactions of Stage II and Stage III is not manifest in the actual operatory structure (as was the case between Stage I and II), but in the differentiated contents upon which these same structures operate. It can be asked why the retardate as well as the normal child, once he has attained the operatory stage, has more difficulties in establishing the invariance of weight than that of substance? This "horizontal decalage" in the elaboration of the notions of substance and of weight is explained by psychological and logical reasons. To postulate the invariance of substance the child simply had to "rediscover" it during its displacements, while to ascertain conservation of weight it was necessary also to weigh it in his hand. The action of hand-weighing provokes consideration of a new factor, a tactile-kinesthetic illusion. (The ball weighed in the hand seems heavier or lighter following its transformations.) In freeing himself from these illusions the subject makes a remarkable effort at decentration; he renounces his subjective evaluations in order to use measuring instruments such as scales. Progressive differentiation and logical implication of the notions of substance and of weight correspond to this increasing liberation from initial egocentrism. In reality, all subjects who achieve the notion of weight conservation also affirm substance conservation (it was seen that the reciprocal was not true for Stage II subjects), and most of them referred to it in their discussions.

Observation 38: *Of course, that can't change, because nothing is taken away.*

Observation 39: *It is surely still just as heavy because I took nothing away. There is still as much clay.*

Observation 40: *They would be exactly the same weight. There is always as much clay. Nothing has been taken away.*

Observation 42: *Also as much clay. I took the same clay . . .* Perhaps it changes weight? *Oh, no, impossible, because it's the same clay.*

Observation 41: Also affirms, *No clay was taken away.*

The logical implication of notions of substance and weight conservation (which at first are not differentiated from volume, then became progressively differentiated in the same order as their invariance) indicates, therefore, a system of psychological integration. This act of integration of past knowledge into a new elaboration, which accompanies a renewed accommodation to the experimental facts, seems to assure continuity and coherence of operatory construction. Although the progress of reasoning from Stage II to Stage III may be noticeable only in its results, it nonetheless denotes a logical and psychological process of construction and represents another advantage of operatory groupment over methods of subjective assimilation. Only at Stage III does the operation appear to be entirely liberated from substitution methods, on which it was dependent at Stage II. The rapidity with which subjects at this level conclude the conservation of weight without having recourse to an experimental check is noted. Their exclamations show this: "Of course," "That can't change," "Oh! no, impossible," etc.

However, an operation minus intuitive methods still meets obstacles at this level. This is evident when one passes on to problems relative to conservation of volume. All subjects, except Hil., who had already made the transition to Stage IV, predicted volume alteration and gave reasons similar to those used at lower levels to justify substance and weight variation. As volume can be evaluated only by displacement of water level, the subjects predicated either a higher water level or lower water level for the immersion of the sausage, the pancake, and the divided clay than for the ball and gave the following justifications:

(The reflections referring to the transformed ball are grouped together.)

Observation 38: *Only with the sausage it chases water from both sides, and with the ball it presses directly down;* and then thinks: *No, all the same it rises more with the ball,* and then, *the sausage takes more space;* in order to explain the contradiction: *It's different in the water.*

Observation 39: *The sausage isn't as high as the ball, it isn't as large, and it needs less room. . . . With the pancake the water rises more. It takes up more room, it is much larger and bigger.*

Observation 40: *The sausage makes it rise more. It takes up more room in the water,* and the pancake, *Less it is too thin.*

Observation 41: The sausage: *Oh, that takes up less space than the ball. It is thin.*

Observation 42: (transition case) Believes in the beginning, *The pancake takes up more room.*

This is obviously not a question of systematic illusions; the successive transformations of the ball are either over- or underestimated. The trait common to these reactions is the absence of coordination of the relations of length, width, and height which, by their compensation, would assure conservation of volume. Due to the lack of this multiplication of relations, the third-stage retardate retains confused notions of volume and weight which "chases the water" higher or lower according to the object's length or diameter. This confusion is even more evident in the division of the clay into pieces:

Observation 38: *Still higher because it is cut up. . . . Because there are so many little pieces. . . . But the little pieces aren't together, they aren't in one piece, not something solid. . . . Oh, the little pieces take up still more room because there are so many.*

Observation 39: *The little pieces make the level rise a little bit less because they are smaller than the big ball. They are cut up in pieces and when cut take up less room.*

Observation 40: *It rises less because between the little pieces there is water, and that doesn't rise, and for the ball there isn't any water in between;* and then contradicts himself, *I think still higher than the ball, there are so many of them* [*the little pieces*].

Observation 41: *The small pieces more because they are separated . . . because when they are in a simple piece it is smaller and rises less.*

Observation 42: For division he first thinks, *It only rises one-half as much because it doesn't take up as much room.*

These subjects were perfectly capable of understanding that everything remains constant in spite of the displacement of the parts as long as the question concerned the clay ball's substance or weight, but then refused to extend this same operation to volume. In what way is an operation bearing on an object's volume more delicate than the preceding operations, and will it remain inaccessible to the mentally retarded?

A problem involving third-stage operations is now undertaken. Reactions similiar to those found in the retardates listed below are also found in normal children below eleven or twelve. Both groups stumble over the perceptive and intuitive resistances, and at the outset they do not manage operatory coordinations of all relations. The difficulty common to this level of reasoning seems related to the fact that no direct intuition of volume quantity is possible. Evaluation is made by an abstract coordination of relations. Now, it is quite possible that a subject (normal or retarded of any age) should know how to reason about the quantity of matter and weight, since he has firsthand experience of these (even if this experience is influenced by illusions), but he still does not manage to "group" abstract relations. This seems to be the case in Stage II subjects, who are perfectly capable of concrete operations, but who are incapable of passing on to the plane of formal operations, where there is no recourse to perceptive intuitions. Is this double character of a nonformal operatory reasoning, which was just described in relation to the reactions to the clay ball's tranformations, general enough to be considered as a sign of this level of reasoning? Consideration will be given the question, as dialogues are analyzed which demonstrate how the retardates who were superior to Stage II envisage sugar dissolution and bar and volume composition.

The reactions of several subjects in relation to sugar dissolution will be listed. In attributing a permanent weight to the substance that is invisible in the water, these subjects show a reasoning capacity similar to that just described.

OBSERVATION 43—MOR., M, 15:7

Mor., a retarded child who walked alone and uttered his first words at approximately two and a quarter years, was referred by a school doctor to a special class for primary instruction. The intelligence test administered upon admission established an IQ of 89. Mor.'s teacher considered him a slow learner with performance below normal in all areas. Conscientious and docile, the boy acquired, during his eight years of special instruction, basic learning in the various academic areas. Gardening and carpentry were especially enjoyed, and he became skilled in these areas, but there was continuing difficulty in arithmetic. As long as the task was measuring, dividing, or adding concrete quantities, his performance was adequate, but when reasoning on abstract or fictional facts was required, Mor. became frustrated and was quickly lost. He never solved any riddle.

At the end of his schooling, when it became necessary to locate employment for him, consultation was sought. A psychological examination confirmed the diagnosis of learning difficulty. Mor. reacted slowly but precisely to all practical tests, but adaptation to new situations was slow, and he lacked personal initiative. His attitude was that of a docile child who needed to be directed.

As Mor. was intellectually incapable of following a professional course he was placed in a carpenter's shop, where, under the supervision of an understanding master, he learned to be an assistant and was soon able to contribute toward his expenses.

What happens when you put the sugar cubes in the water? *The water will rise.*

Why? *It's the weight of the sugar.*

Why does the weight make the water rise? *It raises the water. I can't explain it very well.*

And if you put the metal bearing in instead of the sugar? (The metal bearing is compared to the sugar. The child states the metal bearing is heavier.) Which would make the water level rise higher? *The bearing, naturally, because it is heavy. It weighs more.*

(This is verified.) *It's the sugar after all that makes it rise higher.*

Why is it the sugar? *It takes up room in the water.*

What will happen to the sugar? *It melts.*

What does that mean? *It turns into powder, then it disappears from our sight. I mean to say that it can't be seen anymore.*

Where will the water level be once the sugar is melted? *It stays up high. The sugar contains something. It's hard to explain. That is to say, no, it goes down again. It doesn't take up as much room any longer.*

But which do you think is more correct, that it stays up high or that it goes down? *It is more correct to say that it stays up high because there is always equal weight. The weight stays the same. The melted sugar hasn't been taken out, it is still in there.*

Why can't you see it anymore? *It becomes a kind of liquid. It mixes with water.*

But why do you think that this liquid weighs the same as a piece of sugar? *It is in liquid instead of being in a piece, but it is the same quantity of sugar.*

And what do you think now about the water level? Does it stay up high or not? *It must go down just the same because in the beginning it is the sugar which makes the water rise, but then it melts.*

But you say that it still weighs as much. *Of course, but it doesn't take up any more room at all. It is still heavy, but, how do you say it, it doesn't weigh as much any more. It is no longer like the bearing which pressed on the water.*

Observation 44—Wal., M, 15:11

Wal. was a twin. He had congenital defects, rickets, and was in poor health. Physical and mental development had always been slow (his first words were spoken between two and one-half and three years). Incapable of following normal instruction, he was placed from his sixth year on in an institution for abnormal youth. An intelligence test given at the time of his admittance established an IQ of 85, which indicated he was a slow learner.

The following notes were extracted from his case history:

Wal. observes closely and enjoys collecting animals and plants. He likes to draw. Anything which pertains to practical intelligence interests him, but his judgment and reasoning with "formal" facts are extremely weak. Class standing in arithmetic and grammar is quite low. Several years after leaving school he still refuses to write a letter for fear of making too many spelling mistakes.

Beneath his attitude of self-assurance he hides an inferiority complex. He is emotionally unstable and needs to be stimulated in areas requiring intellectual effort. If difficulties are anticipated, he quickly refuses to cooperate and offers passive resistance.

Because of their experimental aspects, the conservation tests captivated Wal.'s interest. It was amazing to see him, in spite of his failures
in arithmetic, adapt so easily to operatory problems and arrive at a
true logical construction. However, as illustrated below, difficulties
were encountered when the test proceeded to reactions relative to
weight and volume, *i.e.,* when formal operations were involved.

We are going to put this sugar in the water, and you tell me what
will happen. *The sugar melts.*
What does that mean, it melts? *It dissolves. It becomes very fine. It
turns into water. It's like snow; it becomes water.*
And then there is nothing more? *Sweet water.*
Could you get the sugar back? *No, yes, that is, you have to heat it
and then the water boils. The water goes away and only the sugar will
be left.*
You have already done this? *We tried it at school with salt. It's
about the same thing.*
What would the sugar be like that you find when you heat the
water? *Like a thin sheet.*
Could you put it back in the shape of a cube again? *Maybe if you
got it all back. All in all, yes; the sugar cannot be lost except a little
of it stays in the dish.*
Where is the water level now? (The level is marked.) And when
you add the sugar? *The level rises a little.*
When? Now when you put them in, or when they melt? *Now when
you put them in, because they need room and that makes the water
move.*
And when the sugar melts? *When it begins to dissolve it mixes with
the water and then it doesn't need as much room.*
We are going to put the two glasses on the scales and see if it
changes the weight when we add two pieces of sugar and they melt.
First it becomes heavier, not much, the sugars are not very heavy.
(*Demonstrates.*)
And when they are dissolved? *It is always heavier than plain water,
but* (*asks himself*) *is it always the same as the whole sugar? After all,
the air leaves.*
Does the air weigh too? *Yes.*
And why do you think that it is still heavier than plain water?
When it mixes with the water it makes a new water. There is always

something of the sugar in the water. It is like a kind of juice, and then there are little particles, very small.

How can the sugar become juice? *I don't know, but when you drink the water you have the sugar again.*

And if you put a glass with two pieces of sugar on one side of the scales, and one with juice on the other, which would be heavier? *That has to be exactly the same, after all, the sugar is completely in the water.*

And will the level remain up high or go down as you predicted? *It weighs the same, but it doesn't necessarily take up the same room. When it is in liquid, in juice I don't know. It may make more or less. Usually sugar sucks up water; I think that it lowers all the same.*

We will try it first on the scales. *No need, it's bound to be the same. (Demonstrates equality with the glass which holds the two sugar cubes.)*

And then the level? *Oh, I would say that it doesn't go down. I understand; because the sugar melts, but that doesn't matter. It's still inside. It keeps the same size. It's only mixed with the water.*

OBSERVATION 45—SAM., M, 15:3

Sam.'s slow development was considered congenital by the examining psychiatrist, and he also had a history of seizures. The Vermeylen Test indicated he was four and one-half years retarded in mental development, but the Stanford-Binet assigned him an IQ of 104. His reaction time was very slow. Sam. had always been docile and friendly, but was never either overjoyed or extremely depressed. His attitude was unchildlike. All work was conscientiously done, and nothing was forgotten, but it was impossible for him to speed up his tempo of activity. He had been in special classes, and had attained seventh-grade level in all subjects except arithmetic, which he performed at a sixth-grade level. His teachers stated that his ability to comprehend exceeded his ability to communicate. His vocabulary was poor, and his sentence structure was rigid and monotonous.

No emotion was shown during the psychological examination. Sam. was very precise in his drawings. The learning test was not difficult for him, and he concentrated on the task at hand. At first he showed astonishment at the sugar dissolution experiment but when he became familiar with the task Sam. showed coherent reasoning, although he did not surpass Stage III.

What happens if you put two pieces of sugar in the water? *The sugar melts. It dissolves.*

And what does that do? *It becomes soft and fine.*

Does the level stay where it is? *No, the water rises because there is sugar inside, and the sugar needs room and then there is more water inside.*

Where does this water come from that there is more of? *From the sugar. It makes a kind of sugared water.*

Can you still see something of the sugar when it is melted? *You can't see it very well any more. In the end, not at all.*

Why don't you see anything more? *Because it is melted.*

But what does that mean? To melt? *It's similar to the snow.*

What happens to snow when it melts? *It makes water.*

Is it the same for sugar? *It also makes a kind of water, but it still keeps its taste: it is a liquid sugar.*

(The equality of the two glasses is demonstrated.)

Now we put in the sugar, will that change the weight or not? *Then the glass becomes a little heavier.* (Verifies this fact.)

And when the sugar melts? *It's the same whether the sugar is beside it or inside.*

Does it weigh the same when it is melted? *Yes, because it makes a liquid.*

We haven't checked the level yet. Where will it be now? *The water rises still higher because there is more of the liquid. The sugar becomes a juice and now there is the extra juice in the water. That makes still more.*

(An experimental check is made.) *It stayed about the same; when I do it it makes more.*

Observation 46—Hol., M, 22 years

This young man spent most of his school years in the special instruction section of an institution for difficult children. Retardation prevented him from following the job-training courses, and his instability prevented him from following work regulations and a fixed schedule. Because he liked adventure and disliked supervision he ran away from the institution and worked at a variety of jobs. Finally he was arrested for begging without a license, and was sent by the police to a vocational guidance office. Following this, Hol. was placed in a weaving shop for the retarded or handicapped. However, as was predicted, Hol. did not work consistently. At times he showed progress and was trusted with complicated patterns, but a period of sub-standard work always followed. He was opinionated and failed to relate well with fellow employees.

His psychological examination indicated Hol. had difficulty in re-tention and concentration. Even when a problem interested him, as the conservation and composition experiments did, he initially struggled with a flood of confused thoughts, as was evidenced in his frequent exclamation, "Wait, I have to think." Surprisingly, he maintained a coherent core of reasoning, at least for the moment, as can be seen in the following interview:

What will happen to the sugar when you put it in the glass of water? *Sugared water.*

But does the sugar stay in a piece? *Ah! There is a sugar crystal which comes from a country far away and then there is another sugar that is found here. There are carrots and we make pieces of sugar from them, and then there are other sugared substances made from wood. And then there are plants which have a kind of flower that comes up in the spring, and when you pick it and suck it is sugary.*

But these pieces you have in front of you, do they stay the same in the water or do they change? *The sugar melts and when it is melted it becomes white; it becomes very tiny, but big crystals, when you put them in cold water they don't melt like tiny crystals, but in hot water they do.*

And when they are completely melted? *There is nothing left. Well, there is still the sugar, but you can't see it. It isn't in a lump; it's still sugared of course.*

It's not just the taste that stays? *No, from sugar you just can't drink the taste.*

Does the water level stay in the same place, or does it move when you add the sugar? *Obviously the water rises when you add weight to it.*

And when the sugar is melted? *It lowers a bit.*

Down to the rubber band again (indicates the mark for the lower level)? *No, not completely, but almost.*

We are going to put the two glasses on the scales. You see when they have only plain water they are the same weight, and when you have one glass with melted sugar and the other with plain water what will the scales show? *Heavier there, where the melted sugar is, of course.*

And if you put a piece of sugar beside the glass on the scale? *Wait, I have to think. You would say that it's lighter when the sugar is liquid and that depends naturally on the weight of the piece of sugar. But if in the beginning both sugars were the same weight it doesn't matter if that one is melted, it's still a sugar. It weighs just the same amount.*

But the level will lower all the same? *Oh, that, that's another matter. When you don't see it any more it doesn't take up any more room, and then it is a liquid. It's no longer a piece. It no longer presses on the water.*

We are going to do the experiment and watch exactly what happens (adds the sugar). *You see, I was right. It rises. Now you will see that it goes down.*

(Both glasses are put on the scales.) (*Demonstrates weight inequality of the sugar water and the plain water.*) *A sugar lump is still heavy enough.*

What happens to the sugar itself when it melts? *It becomes soft: then you see little parts that separate: then you see nothing more, just a bit of whiteness.*

But when you see nothing more can there be something all the same? *Of course, I don't know exactly, but it is so fine that you can't see it. There is still powder in the water.*

Could you recover the sugar? *Oh, I don't think so, after all just think, you can't see it, or you would have to have a very fine strainer.*

And you still think that the level goes down? *Yes, melted sugar takes up a little bit of room, but never as much as a piece.*

Check for yourself. Did it go down? *That's funny, I would say that it stayed. In any case it hasn't lowered much.*

Can you find an explanation? *But did you use good sugar? Because usually when you put sugar in and it melts, the water goes down. I don't understand.*

OBSERVATION 47—KAR., M, 14:5

Kar.'s case is similar to that of Hil. (Observation 42), who is in the transitional stage between Stages III and IV of operatory reasoning. The case history seemed to indicate that this was not a question of true mental retardation, but of retarded development due to health problems and environmental deprivation. Kar. was threatened with tuberculosis and spent several years in a preventorium. When he regained his health his schooling had been so neglected, and his parents were so incapable of assisting in his academic progress, that decision was made to place him in an institution. Scholastic work accomplished in the institutional setting showed two characteristics:

1. Progress was astonishing. Kar. was avid to learn, was proud and thought well of himself; he quickly became the most advanced student in the special class. Intellectually, he was normal, not retarded.

2. He was very negative and resisted any form of educative discipline. The boy adopted a domineering attitude toward his classmates, organized pranks, and planned to play truant. His sexual behavior caused concern, and he was closely watched. However, efforts of the staff to educate him failed and he was discharged.

Kar. was happy to cooperate in the experiments. During the examination of his learning capacities, he made intelligent hypotheses, and compensated for memory difficulties by his verbal fixation. He enjoyed discussions, and the free conversation, which was part of the concrete experiments, pleased him.

You are going to tell me what happens when I put the sugar in the water. *It dissolves and then there is more water.*

Why does it make more water? *Because there is something in the sugar. The sugar makes juice and then that makes juice again in the water.*

The sugar is still inside when it is dissolved? *It's inside but not in one piece. When you drink it you know it's sugared.*

Could you get it back? *No, inside is inside. You can't take it out.*

And if you could dry up the water? (*He thinks a minute.*) *Then you find a sugar deposit on the bottom, and maybe if you could pour out the water you would also find it again.*

Enough to make another piece of sugar? *If you were very careful, maybe, but I can't imagine it.*

What will happen to the water level when you put two pieces of sugar in the water? *First the water goes down because the sugar absorbs the water. Then when the sugar is melted the water comes back to its former place.*

And the weight in relation to plain water? *It is naturally heavier there where the sugar is inside.*

And when the sugar cubes are completely melted? *It's still the same weight.*

The same weight as it would be if I had a glass with two pieces of sugar beside it? *It has to be the same weight because there are two sugar cubes in both. It comes out the same.*

And the level? You see that it rises when you add sugar. *Yes, first it rises, but then the water goes into the sugar. The sugar absorbs the water, and in the end the water is free again. (He looks at it.) No, it can't change, because it still has the sugar inside!*

But why can't you see it any more? *It is so fine. It's like powder.*

Although all subjects in the second stage were persuaded that the sugar could not cease to exist in the solution, they refused to attribute a constant weight to it. Progress in the third stage, then, consists of postulating conservation of weight. The interviews previously cited confirm the results established in relation to the transformation of the clay balls. The sugar experiment is better suited than the transformation of the clay balls to permitting an understanding of the reasoning process which leads to the notion of constant weight. In mentally reconstructing the piece of sugar in spite of its disappearance from the perceptual field, it is impossible to think solely about questions of substance, weight, and volume. To affirm the conservation of weight, we assume that the subject uses the notion of conservation of substance to support his arguments and that he imagines this conservation of substance fairly precisely. It is also assumed that weight is considered as a composable quantity (as opposed to the dynamic intuition of weight).

The following are extracts from interviews which show how subjects who predicted the conservation of weight represented the invisible permanence of sugar. (Subjects' remarks are in italics.)

Observation 43: *It is more correct to say that it stays up high because there is always equal weight. The weight stays the same. The melted sugar hasn't been taken out, it's still inside.* The subject easily realized that the sugar *disappears from our sight,* and describes it as *a kind of liquid. It mixes with the water.*

Observation 44: Wal. became certain of conservation during the course of the interview. *That has to be exactly the same, after all, the sugar is completely inside.* He even refused to check it: *No need, it's bound to be the same.* However, conservation as a complete scheme did not seem to him inevitable because at first he asked himself the question: *And when you add the sugar does the level rise a little?*, and when he thought of *the air which leaves,* he even predicted a slight diminution because he believed the air also weighed something. Wal. made a spontaneous comparison between sugar dissolution and snow: *It becomes very fine; it turns into water. It's like snow; it becomes water.*

Observation 45: Sam. was persuaded from the start: *It's the same whether the sugar is beside it or inside,* and relied on the representation of a sugar transformation: *It makes a kind of sugared water. . . . It's similar to the snow. . . . It also makes a kind of water, but it still keeps its taste; it is a liquid sugar.*

Observation 46: Hol. also finished by discovering: *But if in the beginning both sugars were the same weight it doesn't matter that one is melted, it's still sugar. It weighs just the same amount.* But to arrive at this reasoning he had to first separate it from his belief that the sugar is lighter in a liquid state: *You would say that it's lighter when the sugar is liquid.* He explained the invisible permanence of sugar in the solution by a kind of atomism. When nothing more is seen could there still be something? *Of course, I don't know exactly, but it is so fine that you can't see it. There is still powder in the water,* prolonging thus the dissolution process beyond the limits of perception; he described the processes in the following terms: *It becomes soft; then you see little parts that separate; then you see nothing more, just a bit of whiteness.*

Observation 47: Kar., who was slow but not retarded, predicted at the outset: *It has to be the same weight because there are two sugar cubes in both. It comes out the same.* Dissolution for him is a kind of inverse process of sugar crystalization: *The sugar makes juice and then that makes juice again in the water.* Why can't you see them any more (the pieces)? *It is so fine. It's like powder.*

A clearer representation of the dissolution process, as described in the above statement, is provided by the progress of operatory reasoning that leads to conservation of weight. At the second level, it is true, the retardates already knew how to interpret the taste, the sugar particles, or the level of constancy as signs that an invisible substance was present. Most of them, however, did not worry about *how* the substance was conserved. On the other hand, at the third stage, they tended to seek an explanation that would ascertain the continuity

between the two successive stages of dissolution. Intuitions of liquifi-
cation or of pulverization are the same at all levels. The manner in
which the retardate refers to them, and the coordination that he
establishes between these empirical facts and the logical necessity of
the conservation of quantities (which is weight in the present case),
seems to show a better correspondence between the methods of experimental deduction and induction, and to indicate a better adaptation to the experiment.

Experimental observation makes it possible to distinguish the
quantitative aspect of weight, which, prior to this level, is not differentiated from volume, and (as Stage II reactions prove) is subject
to variations.

Mor. (Observation 43) established the distinction between the two
interpretations of weight: *It is still heavy, but, how do you say it, it
doesn't weigh as much any more. It is no longer like the bearing which
pressed on the water.*

If the illusion of weight, due to the effort required to discipline or
remove an object, is corrected at this stage by reasoning, the illusions
relative to volume still resist the mental operation which quantifies it
(or measures it objectively). It has already been observed that none
of the retarded subjects could predict the conservation of the volume
of a clay ball during its transformation. This was true, also, for a
sugar cube. All of these retardates refused to believe in the conservation of the volume of sugar when it was dissolved in the water; all
predicted that the water level would come back down to its initial
level, or at least lower appreciably. The following reasons were used:
The melted sugar hasn't been taken out, it is still inside (Observation 43); *When you don't see it any more it doesn't take up any more
room* (Observation 46); *When it begins to dissolve it mixes with the
water and then it doesn't need as much room* (Observation 44).

Several relied on the observation that sugar absorbs water: *Usually
sugar sucks up water; I think that it lowers all the same* (Observation
44). Or they predicted that the level goes down first and then goes
up again: *First the water goes down because the sugar absorbs the
water. Then when the sugar is melted the water comes back to its
former place* (Observation 47). On the other hand, others assumed a
rise in level: *The water rises still higher because there is more of the
liquid. The sugar becomes juice and now there is the extra juice in the
water. That makes still more* (Observation 45). Some thought about

the "pressure" which is no longer the same when the sugar is dispersed or liquified: *It is a liquid instead of being in a piece . . . it is no longer like the bearing which pressed on the water* (Observation 43).

Some subjects consider that the separate grains of sugar occupy less space than a sugar cube or even that they have lost all volume. Others think that these grains exert more "pressure." The result is the same: the level, which rose when the sugar was immersed, seems to lower during the dissolution. Another prediction is also possible. The product of the solution (juice or liquid) is simply added to the former level. In predicting thus the variability of volume, the retarded person willingly refers to past or present experience—*the sugar absorbs the water*—but retains only a particular or superficial aspect of this. In order to affirm the conservation of volume (*i.e.,* that the sum of the volumes of each grain remains unchanged in spite of their displacements), it is necessary to admit that each particle remains identical to itself, and that all can be returned to their original state. The notion of conservation of volume relies, then, on an operatory groupment. Only, this no longer deals with concrete facts but with invisible particles which can be composed only by an effort of imagination. This operatory construction, concerning abstract or mentally represented facts, is precisely what retardates are incapable of achieving.

The progress of operatory reasoning leading to the notion of weight conservation corresponds to a more evolved logico-arithmetical composition, as will presently be shown. While the subjects of the preceding stage advanced slowly beyond the intuitive level, and in doing so relied continually on practical substitutions, all the retardates just cited as having arrived at the third stage of conservation of notions effected with no difficulty all the compositions of weight equality, and were no longer worried by the heterogeneity of form and density.

The procedure of reasoning and the form it takes are practically identical from one subject to another. This is not surprising, since, in contrast to conservation problems (where each subject draws more or less consciously on personal experiences), the bar test frees the logical structure of the retardate from intuitive facts and reduces these to a few well-determined perceptive illusions. Moreover, if at the preceding level several intuitive methods could be used to decide on the equivalence between different objects, at the strictly operatory level, a single procedure is imposed, namely the mental composition of relations. For the sake of brevity only a few characteristic reactions will be cited.

OBSERVATION 48A—HIN., M, 14:10

(*See Observation 37*)

(*He compares the red bar with the blue.*) *Same weight.*
Then the blue with the yellow. *Same weight.*
And if you weighed the red with the yellow? (The two are placed at an angle on the table.) *Oh, it's the same weight because both were the same as the blue.*
We are going to compare the red bar with the lead one. (*Weighs in his hand.*) *The lead is heavier, I think.*
We are going to see on the scales. *No, it's the same weight. I would have said that it's heavier.*
The lead with the blue bar? *Also the same weight.*
Why? *Because the blue bar is equal to the red bar, so the lead is equal to the blue too.*
(The red bar plus the lead, and the yellow bar plus the blue are compared.) *The same, the lead equals the blue, the lead equals the yellow, and the bars are all equal, and we saw that the lead was just the same as a bar.*
The bar and a piece of charcoal? *We have to see on the scales. I would say that the charcoal is lighter.* (*Checks on the scales.*) *Ah, no it is just the same.*
And if the charcoal were compared with the lead, what would the scales show? *Oh, wait* (*laughs*) *the same too, of course, because the charcoal is equal to a bar and the lead too. They are all the same.*

OBSERVATION 49A—WAL., M, 15:11

(*See Observation 44*)

(*He makes the following demonstrations.*) *Red and blue the same, red and yellow the same.*
Blue and yellow? *The same weight too because both weighed the same as the red.*
Blue and the lead? (*With astonishment:*) *It's the same weight too. I wouldn't have said so.*
Red and the lead? *The same weight.*
Why? *Because I saw it with the blue.*

But in your hand you would say that the lead is heavier? *Yes, but I know [that it is the same] because it was that way with the other bar and all the bars are just as thick and just as heavy as each other.*

The bar plus the lead and the two bars? *They are all equal because the piece of lead and the bars are always the same weight. They are equal.*

Blue and charcoal? *Can I see? Oh, it's the same weight too.*

Lead and charcoal? *(Laughs.) That's the same weight too, I know.*

How do you know? *I saw the lead with the bar and then the charcoal with the bar and it's always the same. They are equal. The lead equals the charcoal.*

OBSERVATION 50A—HOL., M, 22 YEARS
(*See Observation 46*)

(He demonstrates the weight equality of the following bars:) The red as heavy as the blue, the blue as heavy as the yellow too.

Red and blue (placed at an angle)? *The same. It was compared with that (points to the blue).*

Red and the lead? *(Hesitates.) The same? No, in my hand it seems heavier. (Demonstrates the equality on the scales.)*

Blue and the lead? *The same weight too, because we saw that it was the same as the red bar, and the two bars, the red and the blue, were just as heavy.*

Bar plus lead and two bars? *The same weight because the lead equals the red, and because all the bars are just as heavy as the lead.*

Blue and charcoal? *It's funny. I think it's lighter. Let's see! (Demonstrates equality.)*

Charcoal and lead? *I would say that the lead is heavier when I see it like that. (Lifts it.) But it's the same of course because I compared it with the bar.*

Charcoal plus bar and lead plus bar? *It is exactly the same weight because the charcoal and the lead weighs the same, and each equals a bar.*

These four interviewees resolved all the problems of compositions of equivalences of weight. A rapid one-by-one analysis will show the operatory character:

The reactions to the simple composition of homogeneous elements (differentiated only by color) are first.

Observation 48A: *Oh, it's the same weight as both were the same as the blue.*

Observation 49A: *The same weight too because both weighed the same as the red.*

Observation 50A: *The same. It was compared with that [points to the blue].*

Although this kind of composition was already known at the second stage, progress is shown by the interiorization of the operation. It is no longer by the process of comparing the bars that the subjects of this stage manage to substitute one for another, but by mentally referring to the common element of the two equalities. Moreover, the substitution does not remain limited to objects; it is generalized to relations. Being capable of abstracting qualitative differences, the retardates just cited know how to retain the relation of quantitative equivalence. This was observed when, in the experiment of homogeneous bars, a heterogeneous element in the form of a piece of lead was introduced.

Observation 48: *Because the blue bar is equal to the red bar, so the lead is equal to the blue too.*

Observation 49: *The same weight. . . . Because I saw it with the blue.*

Observation 50: *The same weight too, because we saw that it was the same as the red bar, and the two bars, the red and the blue, were just as heavy.*

These last reactions show a complete operatory capacity, but alone they cannot prove that reasoning is really freed from the intuitive methods of the preceding stage. When two elements of the composition are homogeneous the operation can still be held up by a sort of interiorized experiment which consists of a mental comparison of the bars. Several borderline cases of the second stage were capable of this. Subjects of the third stage go a step further and compose equalities made up of three or more heterogeneous elements, all with the same ease.

When they were asked to compare the lead and the charcoal (which each subject had found to be equal to a bar) they reasoned as follows:

Observation 48: *Oh, wait [laughs], but the same too, of course, because the charcoal is equal to a bar and the lead too. They are all the same.*

Observation 49: [*Laughs.*] *That's the same weight too, I know . . . I saw the lead with the bar and then the charcoal with the bar and it's always the same. They are equal. The lead equals the charcoal.*

Observation 50: *I would say that the lead is heavier when I see it like that [lifts it], but it's the same of course, because I compared it with the bar.*

They reasoned the same way in additive situations:

Observation 48: *The same, the lead equals the blue, the lead equals the yellow, and the bars are all equal, and we saw that the lead was just the same as a bar.*

Observation 49: *They are equal because the piece of lead and the bars are always the same weight. They are equal.*

Observation 50: *The same weight because the lead equals the red, and because all the bars are just as heavy as the lead. . . . It's exactly the same weight because the charcoal and the lead weigh the same and each equals a bar.*

The conversations cited above appear to dispel doubts concerning the operatory nature of these reasons. If one is accustomed to questioning the capacities for logic in the mentally retarded, one is surprised when certain retardates manage to formulate real deductions, particularly since their reasoning is in a form analogous to that of syllogism, which has long been the prototype of logic.

The elaboration of the notions of conservation (in particular that of weight) and the logico-arithmetical compositions just revealed require exactly the same operatory mechanism. If, in the test of conservation, the structure of reasoning was revealed only in analysis of the compositions of equalities, this structure is directly given by the subject's responses. The possibility of logical thought in retardates at the third stage cannot be denied.

However, to attribute an operatory capacity raises a diagnostic problem: would the structure of reasoning of retardates at the third stage be, from the outset, comparable to that of a normal individual over eleven to twelve years whose logical development has reached a certain stage of equilibrium? If this is so, how can the difficulty, which the same subjects show in imagining the conservation of volume, be explained? Would this difficulty be due to chance conditions of the experiment rather than to resistances inherent to reasoning? If one is restricted to the bar test, this problem remains insoluble. When the bars are replaced by the problem of volume, exactly the same obstacles can be seen to limit the complete generalization of operatory mechanisms.

The following experiment is used for this purpose; it has previously been analyzed from a developmental standpoint. The subject is presented with a set of aluminum cylinders that are identical in form and height. A second experiment is composed of objects of homogeneous form, but of different weights, and then a third experiment is composed of objects of different forms, but all of equal volume. This volume, as in the conservation experiments, cannot be measured directly, but is easily estimated by the displacement of water when the objects are immersed in two glass beakers. The principle is the same as in the preceding experiment except that it is a question of composing volumes, and two beakers filled with water rather than scales afford comparison. Subjects at the first stage show an incapacity to imagine any composition of volume; at the second stage, the composition of volumes of homogeneous weight is too difficult, and at the third stage—the one we are presently considering—subjects fail to see cylinders of heterogeneous weight are equal in volume (differentiation of weight and of volume is discovered inductively). What is still lacking at this level is discovered only at the fourth stage; this is the composition of heterogeneous forms or of volumes which are simply displaced.

The following shows how the subjects, whose reactions to notions of conservation and compositions of equality of weight are already known, reason when confronted with this new situation.

Observation 48B

Hin. demonstrates displacement of water for the following volumes:
Red and black? *Just the same.*

Black and orange? *Exactly the same.*

Red and orange (both standing)? *Both are the same weight; the water will rise the same amount.*

Red standing and orange lying down? *Where it is lying down it takes up even more room. The water will rise higher.*

Red and lead cylinder? *The cylinder will make the water rise higher.*

Why? *It is heavier.*

We will see. (Demonstrates equality.) *Oh, it's the same. (Takes them out and places them one beside the other.) They are just the same size.*

The lead cylinder and the orange? *The same.*

It doesn't matter that the lead cylinder is heavier? *No, I saw it's the size that counts.*

A long cylinder (three times the volume of a bearing) and the piece of lead? *The water rises more for the lead. It's the lead which is heavy after all.*

What does the rise in the water depend on? *Oh, yes it's so long! (Demonstrates that the level rises much higher for the cylinder.) This is so big, and the other is little, it's the big one which makes it rise more.*

The long cylinder and two bearings? *It rises more for the big one, [i.e., the cylinder] because the water rises higher. It is long, it pushes the water very high.*

Three bearings and the cylinder? *It could be just the same. (He compares the three bearings and demonstrates a size equal to the cylinder.)*

The big cylinder on one side, and the three bearings, but laid down? *With the cylinder the water rises higher. The bearings are placed so that they are wide.*

But there are three of them just the same? *Yes, but the cylinder is higher.*

(The bearings are placed vertically in the water.) *Like that the water rises the same amount.*

(Two vertical bearings and a horizontal one are compared with the big cylinder.) *It rises higher with the big cylinder.*

OBSERVATION 49B

Wal. compares the following cylinders:

The red and the black? *It rises the same.*

The black and the orange? *It rises the same too.*

The red and the orange (orange standing and the red lying down)? *(Hesitates a minute.) Perhaps it makes the water rise the same? No, it doesn't, because the red is lying down. The water rises more with the red.*

Why does the water rise more with the red? *It takes up more room in the water when it is lying down.*

Show me which of the small cylinders make the water rise the same. (*He points.*) *The red and the black, the black and the orange.*

And if all are standing in the water? *Oh, then the same, but when one is lying down it takes up more room.* (*Demonstrates equality.*)

The lead cylinder and the black: they make the water rise the same or does one rise more than the other? *I think the lead more. It is heavy.* (*Weighs it in his hand; but demonstrates equality.*)

Cylinder and the red? *The same.*

Why the same? *It's not the weight that counts. It's the size, see.* (*Compares them.*)

Lead cylinder standing and the red lying down? *The water rises more where it's lying down.*

(Compares the equality of level for a small cylinder and a wax sausage.) Two small cylinders on one side and a cylinder plus a sausage on the other? *To the red, oh, yes, it was the same.*

Two small cylinders lying down and one standing plus the sausage? *Higher there where the cylinders are lying down, it is larger when they are lying down. They make the water rise higher.*

OBSERVATION 50B

Hol. observes the equality of level for the red and black cylinders; then for the red and orange.

Where will the water rise to for the black plus the orange (orange lying down, black standing up)? *More for the orange; when it is lying down it is larger. It makes the water rise some more.* (*Demonstrates equality.*)

The red cylinder and lead cylinder? *Oh, it rises more for the lead. It is heavier.* (*Demonstrates equality.*) *But why? That's another matter.*

But why does it make the water rise the same? *One is heavier. The other is lighter; because both are the same size, yes the same size. If one were small it would take up less space.*

The lead and the black cylinder? *It rises the same too, because they are the same size.*

It doesn't matter if that one is heavier? *No.*

Why doesn't it matter? *Because both are just as high and they are both as big around.*

Black cylinder standing and the lead lying down? *Higher when it is lying down. It takes up more room. It is longer.*

When you have two brass cylinders standing in one glass, and one brass cylinder and one lead in the other? *The same height.*

Why? (*Reflects at length.*) *Because they are all the same height.*

Even if one is lead it doesn't matter? *No, because it is the same distance around.*

Two cylinders placed together vertically and two placed together horizontally? *Those lying down need more room.*

Why do they need more room when they are lying down? *Because they are longer.*

(Two identical balls are made, A and B, and the equality of level is demonstrated. One is transformed into a pancake and again the equality of level for the ball and the pancake is demonstrated.

Where does the water rise to for the ball and where for the pancake? *The pancake needs more room, the ball less.*

Ball and sausage? *The ball needs more room: the sausage cuts the water more.* (*Demonstrates equality.*)

Pancake and sausage? *The pancake makes the water rise higher. It is larger.*

Two phenomena are noteworthy because they are characteristic of this stage. One is the fact that subjects of this stage do not possess at the outset the notion of volume (as differentiated from weight); they manage to elaborate it only inductively during the experiment. The second is the insurmountable difficulty of composing volumes made up of elements which are different in shape or position.

In fact, all the retardates of this level predict that a lead cylinder makes the level of the water rise more than a brass cylinder although their form is entirely the same. It is only after immersion in water that they discover the law of displacement of level in relation to volume:

Observation 48B: *No, I saw it's the size that counts.*

Observation 49B: *It's not the weight that counts. It's the size, see!*

Observation 50B: *One is heavier. The other is lighter; because both are the same size, yes, the same size. . . . It rises the same too, because they are the same size. . . . Because both are just as high and they are both as big around.*

At the beginning of the interview the height of the water level was still predicted in relation to weight, or, more exactly, in relation to a poorly differentiated weight + volume notion. This obvious lack of differentiation permits better understanding of the difficulties that the interviewed retardates found in the conservation of volume at the time of its displacements in water (transformation, sectioning, or dissolution). Due to inductive procedures, the law according to which the water level is displaced in relation to the volume of an immersed body is discovered by contact with the facts. This is further proof that the mental retardate of this level can profit from the experiment and, on certain points, can forget his own viewpoint when it is in disagreement with experimental facts.

The role of such an experimental attitude, in the elaboration of notions of conservation and of atomism, has already been noted. Thus, the experiment of the composition of volumes confirms and elucidates the previous observations.

As no retardate was able to conceive of the conservation of volume by himself (just as none knew how to deduce from two equalities of volume a third, or how to make an additive composition when the objects were placed differently in the water or were heterogeneous in shape), they often predict:

There where it is lying down it takes up even more room. The water will rise higher (Observation 48B); *There where the cylinders are lying down, it is larger when they are lying down* (Observation 49B); *Those lying down need more room* (Observation 50B).

Even when it has been demonstrated that the big cylinder is equivalent in volume to three small ones, as soon as one or the other is displaced, the equivalence seems destroyed:

Observation 48B: *With the cylinder the water rises higher. But there are three of them just the same? Yes, but the cylinder is higher.*

Finally, when an experiment involves objects of heterogeneous forms, each of which has been compared to a cylinder, the retardates refused to admit equality of volume: *More where the sausage is, it's so long* (Observation 49B); *The ball needs more room; the sausage cuts the water more* (Observation 50B).

In order to know how to achieve equivalences of volume, it is necessary to be able to postulate their invariance during displacement. This postulate, as has been shown, relies on an operatory groupment. One can proceed either by the inverse operation—mentally moving the cylinder from a horizontal to a vertical position—or by coordination of relations—comparing the dimensions of length, width, and height.

Such operations, all of which succeed in relation to weight, cannot be generalized at once to volume. The above facts confirm this. Nothing could demonstrate more clearly that operatory mechanism is in fact indissociable from content on which it works. To know how to carry out operations in relation only to weight does not necessarily have the same significance as being able to effect them when volume is involved (the notion of volume implies that of weight). Although composition of volumes, and the idea of their conservation, correspond to the achievement of logical construction in the normal child, the impossibility of attaining the last stage seems to be an extremely characteristic sign of mental retardation.

In the first section of this chapter, the existence of the beginning of operatory construction in certain mental retardates was shown. Their reasoning is arrested at a stage of pseudo-equilibrium because it still relies on intuitive facts, which in one sense support the operation but in another hold it back. The analysis of the reactions characteristic of Stage III reveals an analogous situation, although on a different level. The notion of conservation of weight, and the corresponding compositions, require a groupment which is more detached from its intuitive supports than the notion of the conservation of substance. However, this groupment cannot in turn be generalized to volume. If the common character of the similar reasonings at the second and third levels is to be found in the incomplete operatory construction, the later reasonings show, nonetheless, a very clear superiority over the earlier ones.

The quantification of weight is more difficult to achieve than that of substance. Passage from the second to the third stage is essentially a progress of: (1) differentiation, and (2) logical implication. In differentiation, the conservation of weight has to be viewed in the abstract as distinct from matter in order to compose objects of diverse densities. By implication, the conservation of weight always and necessarily indicates that of substance also. An integration which ascertains the continuity of operatory development corresponds to the widening of the field of notions. In the young retardate, this integration is always contemporary with (and dependent on) progress of causal explanation and of inductive reasoning. Proof of this is the attempted atomistic explanation of the process of dissolution and the elaboration of the law governing the rise of the water level in relation to the volume of an immersed body. The progress of reasoning characteristic of the third stage, in relation to the preceding stage, is manifest not only in a few isolated reactions, but also in a homogeneous system of thought.

The outstanding feature of each of these individual cases is that this progress of reasoning corresponds to a more evolved level of development. The case histories of the subjects at the third stage show that they are all capable of reaching the higher grade of special instruction, and are capable of practical work, but not of profiting from job training that includes theory courses (such as those customarily given in the Canton of St. Gallen to future carpenters, gardeners, tailors, shoemakers). In the special classes of their schools, these retardates present some common characteristics. They are often remarkable because they are very observant, and sometimes because of their ability in factual subjects such as natural history, and practical work (carpentry, gardening). They understand elementary arithmetic if it is applied to practical situations.

A more pertinent question would be why their operatory reasoning (as in the experiment of composition of weight of heterogeneous objects) includes systematic, but abnormal aspects. In fact, the results pertaining to the conservation of the quantification of weight are acquired at a much later age than is found in normal subjects. Above all, these results are not surpassed in the retardate, whereas in normal subjects they are superseded by conservation and quantification of volume. What is there in questions of volume that is not in the questions concerning weight, and why is the retardate unable to solve them?

As Piaget has established in *Le Développement des quantités physiques* (Piaget and Inhelder 1941), the conservation of weight involves concrete operations, whereas that of volume requires formal operations. Weight is a perceptible fact; it requires structuration and quantification, using concrete relations and logico-arithmetical conservation. Volume, on the contrary, is a system of relations, and it is further removed from simple perception. To handle the relations of volume requires formal reasoning, and it could be asked if retardates are not arrested in their development just at the level of formal thought, even though they are capable of concrete operations.

Therefore, the lack of conservation of volume can be considered a clinical sign because it implies the absence of formal reasoning. In the normal child there is continuous passage from the conservation of weight to that of volume. These two discoveries occur in close succession (between ten and eleven years of age). In the normal child, the conservation of volume indicates that logical development has been achieved; the notion of conservation of volume integrates all preceding notions through a unique process in which each transitional phase is distinct. If, on the contrary, the retardate does not reach the final phase, this failure in itself is indicative of an arrestation, and is of clinical importance. No subject classified as retarded has attained conservation of volume, and the few cases who did enter the fourth stage were not true retardates, but slow learners.

If future research confirms this finding, it would be extremely instructive in the interpretation of the intellectual mechanism of the retarded. Thus, the absence of the notion of conservation of volume would correspond to a more general deficiency—the absence of formal reasoning. Without additional experimentation it can be verified by the grades in the school records that the subjects all show difficulties with hypothetical-deductive problems (*i.e.,* "1" is to "2" as "2" is to "4," etc.) and with fractions. On the other hand, each time a verification is attempted by a test of formal reasoning based on logical propositions (operations of implications such as the test of three colors by Burt,* or the same but in terms of weight, or the absurd sentences of Binet) the same difficulties were encountered. The problem will be discussed again in Chapter 5 where the paranormal aspects of reasoning in retardates are examined.

* Edith is blonder than Suzanne, but she is darker than Lili. Who is the darkest of the three? (See J. Piaget, 1923.)

4. Abnormal Intellectual Oscillations

In the last two chapters, consideration was given to certain types of retarded reasoning which can be placed at well-defined levels of mental evolution. Can this correspondence between fixations and arrestations in the retardates be generalized to stages in normal children without further proof, or should consideration also be given to deviations and alterations of thought shown in certain integrations which do not obey the same laws of construction? Furthermore, would the method of relatively free conversation (which was found practical in this research because it reveals the individuality of reasoning) reveal a variety of intellectual reactions unrelated to the central operatory mechanism? In other words, do the reflections of retardates during physical experiments constitute abnormal phenomena as well as simple arrestations at certain levels of development?

Contrary to what was expected, no process of reasoning has been observed thus far (most of the subjects in the research were younger retardates) that has escaped the evolutionary structures of operatory groupment (Piaget and Inhelder 1941). Even the way of formulating judgments and the intellectual behavior in the test situation duplicated reactions observed in normal children. The rational and experimental construction, therefore, would be identical. However, all cases do not have simple fixations at specific levels, and certain phenomena do not belong in the rational framework just mentioned. What is interesting in these irregularities is that they do not constitute deviations termed "para" in contrast to cases termed "hypo," but seem to "oscillate" (using oscillation, as Pierre Janet did, to mean oscillation of tension or of psychological level) among several levels, each of which constitutes one of the characteristic stages of normal evolution. These oscillating reasonings are discussed in this chapter.

The group characterized by oscillations comprises only 10 percent of the subjects tested; 90 percent were either tentatively or definitely fixated at precise levels of mental evolution. After examining the significance of the fixations, there remains an analysis of the psychological nature of oscillations of reasoning. Different types of oscillations are distinguished: (1) reasoning showing progress during the experimental situation, (2) simple oscillations between two levels, and (3) retrogressive reasoning, or reasoning which drops to a lower level during the interview. After having examined the three types of oscillations, abnormal decalages are studied; these raise a problem analogous to that raised by the preceding cases.

1. Progressive Reasoning

A child starts by affirming spontaneously a group of propositions whose logical structure would place him at a given stage of thought. He later leaves this stage behind, either during conversation with the examiner or upon confrontation of his predictions with experimental facts. Once the initial level is left behind, he is able to consolidate his notions and logical operations in a groupment characteristic of a level superior to the initial stage.

In such cases, the complex problem of developmental diagnosis is posed. To determine their level of reasoning, should consideration be given to the starting point or the finishing point? Or (as in certain tests of mental level), is it advisable to establish an average among all the obtained answers? It appears impossible to decide this question a priori. Each of the processes of progressive reasoning demands a psychological analysis of the factors involved.

Progress during a testing situation is not pathological in itself. In a previous work (Piaget and Inhelder 1941), numerous examples of this were given. What is observed in certain retardates is only an exaggeration of a normal phenomenon, and it is this that will be clarified now.

Progress during the interview is observed in slow learners only. Therefore, the reasoning progress is of value as a clinical index. A problem arises however: why do some children show themselves capable of logical notions and surpass their original level during the test situation, yet deny or ignore these notions at the beginning of the examination period? The following hypothesis can be made: their thought is blocked, frequently by a group of complex factors which are both interindividual and intraindividual (social and affective). The influence of these factors on intellectual activity must be determined.

Examples are given of retardates who, after seeing the demonstration carried out by the examiner, become capable of going beyond their initial level, but who on their own initiative are incapable of assimilating the group relations which are discovered. They also show difficulty in analyzing by themselves a new problem, although they can reason step by step once an introduction is provided. That this initial difficulty is based on an intellectual deficiency and expresses an evident (although slight) mental retardation is proved by the fact that their reasoning does not correspond to that expected of their chronological age.

The first case is one of a near-normal subject, and it recalls a phenomenon often seen in reactions which are midway between two levels of reasoning. To facilitate comparison, only one experiment, the transformation of clay balls, is used.

OBSERVATION 51—REG., F, 11:7

The child equalizes the two clay balls and verifies their equality on the scales.

You see that the two balls are the same size and the same weight. Make one of the balls into a sausage. (*She transforms it and says spontaneously:*) *The ball is heavier because it's like that in a ball.*

Could you make a ball out of it again? *Yes, it would be exactly like the other ball afterward.*

Is there more clay in the ball or in the sausage? *In the two it's the the same amount of clay. You didn't take off anything.*

(The sausage is broken into little pieces.)

How much does the ball weigh in comparison to the small pieces? *The ball is heavier because it's a whole ball.*

Is there the same amount of clay, more, or less? *Always the same because it was a ball in the beginning.*

And why do you think it has become heavier? *Oh, no, it's the same thing, just as heavy because in the beginning it was as heavy.*

Why do you think it is just as heavy although it's in small pieces here? *You didn't take any away.*

But what did you think when you made the ball into a sausage? *That the ball was heavier, but that's not right because you could make the ball again.*

And if you made the little bits into a thin pancake? *It would be the same weight because you could make the ball thin too, and it would be exactly the same thing.*

(It is explained that the two balls require the same space in the water, and the child marks the equal levels.) Where do you think the water would rise to if instead of a ball I put a pancake in the glass? (*Indicates a higher level.*) *With the pancake it goes up higher because it's wider.*

And with the little bits? *The water doesn't go up as much; this [the pancake] is much wider and the little bits are so small.*

And the amount of clay, is there the same or less? *There is as much because it's just as heavy.*

And why do you think it is just as heavy? *Because they were weighed as balls, and nothing was taken off afterward.*

Where does the water go up to with the ball, and where with the little pieces? *Higher with the ball. It is bigger.*

The child starts by denying the conservation of weight after transformation into a sausage and after it is broken into pieces: *The ball is heavier because it's like that, in a ball . . . because it's a whole ball,* without giving more explicit reasons, while at the same time she affirms that the substance is always the same because *you didn't take away anything,* or because *it was a ball in the beginning.* Like normal children under nine years, Reg. was not surprised at this contradiction. For the time being, she does not understand that the conservation of substance necessarily implies that of weight. As has been previously seen, it is easier to effect a reversible operation when this concerns an extended substance than when it is a question of quantifying the weights. The conception of weight is influenced longer by subjective evaluation.

A simple question which does not contain any direct suggestion causes the child to revise her first affirmation and correct it:

Why do you think it has become heavier? *Oh, no, it's the same thing, just as heavy because in the beginning it was as heavy.*

It could be supposed that Reg., suspecting that her first response did not satisfy the examiner, repeated by simple verbal analogy what she had just affirmed in relation to conservation of substance. However, this was not the case, and the manner in which the child was motivated to make the prediction proves it was a question of true conversion of thought toward the operatory groupment. *Because you could make it like a ball again . . . you didn't take any away,* concerning relation to the comparison between the ball and the pancake: *It would be the same weight because you could also make that [the ball] thin, and then it would be exactly the same thing.*

Although the child was not very eloquent, the phrases quoted above indicate that during the interview she made real progress. While incapable at the beginning of envisioning weight as a constant quantity, in the end she understood the logical necessity of its invariance. Nevertheless, this thought progress remained limited. The questions which promoted the idea of conservation of weight were not effective when used in relation to conservation of volume: *With the pancake it goes up higher because it's wider;* and when questioned on the pieces of clay: *The water does not go up as much because [the pancake] is much wider and the little bits are so small.*

How should such a development of thought be interpreted, and which diagnosis should be proposed? It is noted, first, that the child could not go beyond the third stage in the notions of conservation, and, at the age of eleven years and seven months, as noted in Chapter 3, this indicated a slight retardation. Is it necessary to go further, and situate Reg.'s reasoning according to her reactions at the beginning of the interview at the second stage? To do so attributes to her a more profound retardation.

In answering these questions it is useful to distinguish two things: diagnosis of the actual level of thought, and determination of its equilibrium. This information permits insight into the prognosis. As far as the diagnosis of mental level is concerned, the child's reasoning is situated halfway between the second and third operatory stages. Equilibrium of thought is characterized by its mobility and its consolidation in relation to experience. The child showed herself capable of making progress in a determined situation, whose genetic and functional significance is previously known. Consideration of this fact permits the formulation of the hypothesis that Reg., although slightly retarded, could make future progress in reasoning.

These predictions were confirmed. Because of her retardation the child was removed from her normal class and placed in a special class. Because the diagnosis of slight retardation led to this placement, the prognosis deduced from the interview and cited above was probably more favorable than results obtained from other types of mental tests. Subsequent scholarly performance confirmed the diagnosis of slight retardation. Once placed in a scholastic atmosphere that took her difficulties into account and stimulated her efforts through specialized instruction, the child made real progress and was able to follow the development program planned for her in the special class. Therefore, it is supposed that at the beginning of the interview, just as in her normal class, the child did not achieve maximum performance, and the factor of social inadaptation was added to her difficulties created by her slight retardation. From analysis of this "progressive" reasoning, a plausible hypothesis can be formulated: the intellectual exchange between the individual and his environment can retard or accelerate (according to the case) the development of thought. The following example is particularly interesting:

OBSERVATION 52—BEAT., F, 12:0

Beat. understood the use of the scales. The two equal clay balls were made with her assistance; she then transformed one into a sausage.

Do they both still have the same weight now? *The ball is heavier because it is round and all the clay is together.*

Is there as much clay when it is all together as when it is stretched into a sausage? *There is more clay in the ball because there is more of something inside. You see, it isn't the same. (She points to the circumference of the sausage.)*

You can transform the sausage into small divided pieces. *(Says spontaneously:) There is still less clay because there it is all together [indicates the ball] and there it's all separated. (the divided pieces.)*

Could you make a ball again from the little pieces? *Of course.*

This new ball, what would it be like in relation to the first? *Exactly the same.*

Why exactly the same? *Because you put it back together and squeeze hard.*

Would it have the same weight too? *I don't really think so.*

(The child does the experiment and demonstrates the equality of size and of weight.)

Now you are going to make a pancake from one of the balls. *(She carefully transforms the ball.)*

And if you weighed the ball and the pancake together now? *The ball would be heavier all the same.*

Why heavier? *Because the ball is one piece. It's squeezed and the pancake is spread out.*

And about the clay, is there as much or more in the pancake or maybe less? *Oh! There is just as much.*

Are you sure? *Yes, nothing was taken away.*

But now that you've made a pancake, what would the ball weigh in relation to the pancake? *I think it's the same too because it's the same clay and nothing was taken away; so it weighs the same.*

And now if you weighed the pancake with the small pieces, what would the scales show? *Lower on this side [where the pancake is] because when it is separated it doesn't weigh as much as when it is all together.*

But is there as much clay or less when it is lighter? *No, there is as much clay, but wait, I have to think. Suppose it weighed as much after all? I would say so, because it is still the same clay.*

And when you make the sausage? *In the sausage it is lighter. It's thin, but I'm not sure, nothing was taken away here either. It would have to weigh the same. In any case there is as much clay.*

(It was explained to the child that the ball displaces water. She marked the elevated water levels on both glasses.)

And if you put the sausage in the water instead of the ball? *It wouldn't be the same, just think! The ball is bigger. First of all, it is heavy, and it is round. It takes up much more room and the sausage is thin; that doesn't do much to the water.*

This reasoning process, similar in structure to the preceding (Observation 51), is, however, more astonishing because of the progress shown during the interview. The subject starts with the idea of absence of conservation and concludes by affirming with logical certitude the invariance of substance, and even of weight. Indication of this is found in her first phrases: *There is more clay in the ball because there is more of something inside,* a statement which contrasts with the frank affirmation at the time of the transformation into the pancake: *Oh, there is just as much . . . I think it's the same too because it's the same clay and nothing was taken away so it weighs the same.*

This new conviction, arising from a particular transformation (the transformation into a pancake) is generalized afterward to all the transformations of the balls. The child thus shows herself capable of correcting her previous predictions dictated by egocentric judgments. She even ventures, although with hesitation, to predict the constancy of weight. When questioned about the pancake she says: *I think it's the same too, because it's the same clay and nothing was taken away, so it weighs the same.*

When making a comparison with the divided clay she first believes: *When it is separated it doesn't weigh as much as when it is all together,* but then she changes: *But wait, I have to think. Suppose it weighed as much after all? One would think so, because it is still the same clay.*

However, this reasoning progress is limited. When the clay is transformed into a sausage she again predicts the variation of weight, adding with hesitation: *But I am not sure, nothing was taken away here either. It would have to weigh the same.*

If she views the conservation of weight as a possibility, and even a probability, she does not postulate it with certitude a priori, and completely denies that of volume.

Two traits appear to characterize this reasoning: progress during the experiment, and the limits of its operatory construction. The difficulty in crossing the threshold of the third and fourth stages of conservation at an age where, normally speaking, quantitative conservation is achieved is a sign found in all retarded thought, and has been discussed previously. The operatory progress witnessed during the discussion with the child will be analyzed. Beat., questioned under the same conditions as the other retardates, passed from the level of the first genetic stage to a level situated halfway between the second and third stages (the process of reasoning repeating exactly the same genesis of operatory construction as has been studied in the normal child).

When such a development of thought is witnessed, the question arises as to why the child did not attain it in the first place. In other words, if one hypothesizes that the final reactions mark the real capacity for effecting logical operations, what factors could have contributed to the inferior performance which was evidenced in the initial responses? The observed initial inhibition seemed to be progressively lifted by conversing with the child. However, retardation alone does not lead to such a disequilibrium, and there is reason to believe that such inhibitions arise, at least partially, from environmental deprivation.

Indications have been found which confirm these suppositions. Beat. appeared retarded and showed herself incapable of profiting from normal class instruction. Both teachers and the school physician advised transfer into a special class. Her mother, who was strongly opposed to the transfer, was a mentally retarded divorcée who alone was responsible for the child's education. In order to avoid social stigma she changed addresses continually and attempted to hide the child at home. Beat. no longer attended school. Moreover, the discrepancy between her chronological age, her physical appearance, and her capacities became more marked from year to year, separating her from her friends, and leaving her alone with her mother.

Under such conditions it is not surprising that the child did not immediately know how to manage in a new situation. She could not use logical mechanisms, which require intellectual exchange as well as internal maturation. Is it not also surprising that the child, having overcome the first difficulties of adaptation, should make the progress observed in the conversation quoted above? While admitting that the subject is retarded, the progress shown above seems to indicate a mobility of thought which guarantees possible future development. However, this evolution depends largely on the intellectual stimulation offered by the social environment. Measures had been taken to place the child, not in a boardinghouse for retardates, but in an instutition primarily for slow learners. Unfortunately, just prior to placement the mother escaped the scholastic regulations by disappearing from the Canton of St. Gallen with Beat. The case is of interest because of the disequilibrium which was revealed in social relations, and it is regretted that follow-up was impossible.

In contrast, the interview with a child whose intellectual development could be followed closely for several years is cited below.

OBSERVATION 53—PHIL., M, 13:9

Phil. made two balls of equal weight. After transforming one of them into a sausage he was asked:

Do they still have the same weight or has this one changed? *The sausage is lighter because it is thinner than the ball.*

Is there as much clay in both or more or less on one side than on the other? *Just as much clay because in the beginning I made a ball with that* [*he points to a sausage*].

And now is there still as much clay? *Yes, just as much.*

But without weighing the same? *It's lighter [the sausage] like I said.*

You are going to divide the sausage into small pieces and then tell me how much the ball and pieces will weigh on the scales. *They are much lighter because they are such small pieces.*

And why are they lighter? *Because they are so small.*

Is there as much clay or less when it is divided? *Still the same because in the beginning it was all one ball.*

Could you make a ball again? *Of course, it would be just the same ball as before.*

And now the little pieces are lighter; are you sure? *Yes, the little pieces can't weigh as much. (He checks on the scales and demonstrates equality of weight.)*

Why are they equally heavy on the scales? *Maybe you didn't look carefully.*

Look carefully and see. *It's true, it's the same. That's because in the beginning it was in one ball, and it was the same weight.*

But you thought when it was in little pieces they became lighter because they were so small? *But after all, it can't change.*

Make the ball again and change it into a very thin pancake, you know, pancakes like they make at the carnival? *Oh, I know, it's still the same weight.*

But why isn't it lighter when it's so thin and flat? *It was a ball before too.*

You are sure that it doesn't change? *Yes. (Then in a hesitating tone:) Maybe a little bit lighter. After all, it's so thin.*

What do you think is correct. *The same weight, no, I was right. It was the same ball before, and there is as much clay.*

(The child observes as the two balls are put in water.)

What happens to the water level? Look closely! *The water rises higher now because there is more inside, and when there is more, the water rises and does not go down.*

And if I put the pancake in the water instead of the ball? *The water would rise less, but if you made a ball again the water rises like in the other glass.*

And if you put the little pieces in the water? *The water will rise too because there is more inside than before. It would even rise up to where we marked it with the rubber band because the little pieces weigh as much as the bail.*

But when they are just as heavy, do they necessarily take up the same space in the water too? *No, not as much room.*

And if it takes up less space, can the water rise up to the rubber band? *No, only halfway. It only rises a little, but not to the higher rubber band.*

And now if you put the sausage in the water? *It's just as heavy. It rises a little.*

(A small cylinder is put in the water and the displaced water level is marked; then a ball of clay is put in and the water level is again marked.)

Which makes the water rise higher, the cylinder or the ball? *The ball.*

What does the water rise depend on, the weight or something else? *It is because the ball is bigger.*

Now you are going to mark the level for this ball and the level for the sausage that you make from the other ball. (*He hesitates.*) *It doesn't rise as much with the sausage. It takes up less room.* (*Reflects.*) *Oh! no, it's the same after all because it's the same weight. Oh, I understand—it's as big too, because, you see, you would have the same size again if you made the sausage into a ball, so now too it's the same size and the same amount of clay.*

This reasoning is interesting because the child is capable of constructing new notions in relation to experimental observations; the fact of the identity of weight before and after the transformation of a clay ball into a sausage not only makes him understand weight conservation but triggers the generalization of the explanatory scheme to include all the transformations of the clay ball. Progressive elaboration of the principle of the conservation of volume is also shown.

The progressive elaboration which develops during the interview will be shown step by step. Phil. started by affirming conservation of substance, but he strongly denied that of weight:

Just as much clay because in the beginning I made a ball with that. . . . They are much lighter because they are small pieces . . . the little pieces can't weigh as much.

He was not immediately persuaded by the experimental check showing the constancy of weight:

Maybe you didn't look carefully.

In contrast to cases at inferior or fixated levels which remain unchanged, Phil. corrected himself immediately:

It's true; it's the same. That's because in the beginning it was in one ball and it was the same weight. When reasons were sought for this new statement—but you thought when it was in little pieces they became lighter because they were so small?—he showed a deductive capacity and justified his idea with admirable assurance: *But after all, it can't change.*

His momentary hesitation shows that the generalization of reasoning when the ball was transformed into a pancake was not due to a verbal formula, but resulted from a new operatory construction: *Maybe a little lighter, after all it's so thin.* This idea was immediately rejected: *The same weight. No, I was right. It was the same ball before, and there is as much clay.*

After this change of reasoning due to the experiment, the elaboration of the notion of conservation continued and the progressive dissociation of notions of dynamic weight and of geometric volume (which were confused at first in the child's spontaneous thought) were shown.

In comparing the ball to the pancake he at first thought: *The water would rise less;* but for the pieces he predicted the constancy of level and explained it: *Because the little pieces weigh as much as the ball.*

However, this constancy still relied on lack of differentiation between weight and volume. Once this distinction was understood, he again doubted the invariance of volume, then finally explained: *Oh, I understand; it's as big too, because you see, you would have the same size again if you made the sausage into a ball, so now too it's the same size and the same amount of clay.*

Thus, it is operatory reversibility which dominates the perceptive illusions in the end, coordinating the intuitive relations into a coherent groupment.

As was seen, this work was laborious. As the child ended by having the idea of complete conservation, it is surprising that the last groupment, which implies all the preceding ones, did not seem obvious to him from the beginning. Retardation alone was not sufficient to explain the initial difficulties. It is probable that other factors, due to environment rather than to mental organization, reinforced his difficulties in adaptation.

The boy had just been placed in a special education class, but it is not in the discrepancy between his thought capacities and schoolwork that the reason for the apparent disequilibrium in his reasoning should be sought, nor can this discrepancy explain his intellectual inhibitions when confronted with the experiments. However, it is possible that habits previously acquired in an environment which neglected or even slowed his full development influenced his performance.

This hypothesis (which was established before Phil.'s case history was known) was confirmed. Phil. was the illegitimate child of a retarded mother, and he had not had adequate schooling. At the time of placement in an institution for abnormal children, his language and his emotional responses were infantile, and his physical and mental development was well below normal. Since his previous education had been neglected it was not surprising that the child performed below his true level. Because the environment had offered no stimulation, his faculties had been incorrectly assessed, and he had long been considered more retarded than he was. Thus, this restraining influence had exerted continuous effect on Phil.'s mental habits and character. The psychological report indicated infantilism and lack of intellectual vitality, but there was a capacity for combinatory thought. School reports also indicated the child was initially very timid, but he overcame this bit by bit and made good progress. Two years after the examination it was learned that Phil., at his own slow pace, had successfully completed a special class program. His capability for solving mathematical problems almost equaled that of normal children. Here is an example of mobility, and of the possibilities of developing a power of reasoning which could be defined as "progressive" during the clinical examination.

The next case is of interest because it shows both a progress in reasoning and a tendency to remain caught up by illusions. Such a tendency is intermediate between the "progressive" type of reasoning and the true "oscillating" type.

OBSERVATION 54—TRU., F, 12 YEARS

This child was not very talkative, but her facial expression was animated and showed concentration. She carefully made two equal balls. When asked to transform one of the balls into a sausage she immediately said without being asked: *The sausage is lighter because that is long [the sausage], and that is round.*

Why is it light when it is stretched out? *It is heavier where it is packed together.*

Is there as much clay or not in the ball as there is in the sausage? *Yes, there is as much clay, it's only long, but the amount of clay stays the same because nothing is taken away.*

Will you divide the sausage into small pieces and tell me how much they will weigh in relation to the ball? *The same weight again, it is like the ball because I made it into pieces, in spite of that, everything is still there.*

Why do you think it is lighter when it is in a sausage? *Because it is stretched out.*

And now you are going to weigh the ball and the pancake that you made. (*She reflects at length.*) *The pancake will be heavier because it is stretched and it weighs all over the scales.*

Is there as much clay, or more, or less, in the pancake? *Still as much because nothing was taken away.*

Could you make a ball again from the pancake? *Yes, and it would weigh exactly the same as before.*

(The examiner puts each of the two balls in two glasses and the subject states:) *The water rises because the ball needs room in the water.*

If you put the pancake instead of the ball? (One of the balls is made into a pancake while the child watches.) *The pancake needs room too.*

As much as the ball or more or less? *Less.*

Why less? *Because it is thinner.*

(One of the balls is divided into little pieces again.) Where will the water rise to this time? *It rises as much as with the ball because each of the pieces needs room.*

Are you sure? *Yes, because you could put them back together.*

And how about the ball and the pancake? Doesn't it need as much room? *No, much less.*

And the sausage? *With the sausage it would rise just as much as with the ball. The sausage needs as much room as the ball.*

Why as much? How do you know? *It needs more room in length and the ball needs more in roundness, it all comes out the same.*

And what is the weight of the ball if you compare it to the sausage? *It's still the same weight. You only changed its shape.*

And for the pancake, is it the same or is it different? *Oh, the pancake is so thin it makes the water rise less.*

And if you weighed the pancake with the ball? *But I told you, the pancake weighs all over the scales: It's heavier.*

Tru. started therefore by stating the conservation of substance and denying that of weight, and ended the interview by imagining the conservation of weight and volume when the ball was divided, although she was unable to generalize this principle to all the transformations of the clay ball. The following step-by-step study of her reasoning reveals the clarity of her justifications.

Is there as much clay or not? *Yes, there is as much clay it's only long, but the amount of clay stays the same because nothing it taken away.*

This shows the child's awareness of the operations necessary to conclude quantitative conservation. When the topic changes from conservation of substance to that of weight her line of reasoning is just as clear, although she makes opposite conclusions: *It is heavier there where it is packed together.*

By taking into account only these two statements and their justifications it could appear that this case is an example of Stage II. However, when the experiment progresses to the division into small pieces, the child's reasoning shows a different structure: *The same weight again; it is like the ball I made it into pieces, but in spite of that, everything is still there.*

The child understands, then, that the whole is equal to the sum of the parts, and her conception of the quantity of substance supports her idea of weight. Do these logico-physical operations show a true change of reasoning in the direction of progress in thought? The following statements prove that if in certain situations there is an operatory structuration of intuitive facts, in other situations this structuration remains incomplete. In spite of the repeated experimentation, the subject maintains the idea that the sausage changes weight because *it is stretched out.* As for the pancake, *it is stretched and it weighs all over the scales.* Two simultaneous and contradictory conceptions are present: either weight is imagined as a composable quantum or as a variable quality. The coexistence of two contradictory notions is not exceptional; it even characterizes a level of thought transition and can be observed frequently in the normal child of eight to ten years. The paranormal aspect of this child's reasoning is the fact that, in all parts of the experiment, sectioning seems to have a special place: *The water rises as much as with the ball because each of the pieces needs room.*

Are you sure? *Yes, because you could put them back together.*

From there the child ventures to conceive that volume is conserved when the ball is transformed into a sausage: *It needs more in length and the ball needs more in roundness, it all comes out the same.*

While admitting at this time the constancy of weight: *It's still the same weight, you only changed its shape.*

It is curious that when the subject was questioned about the pancake she remained firmly attached to the subjective impression that the pancake displaced less water, being "so thin," but weighed more because "it is stretched out." Two things should be mentioned: (1) this reasoning, as in preceding cases, is a "progressive" type—at the end of the interview the child gave evidence of a logic entirely superior to the reflections at the beginning; (2) this progress is not homogeneous—the operatory reasoning continually encounters certain perceptive obstacles and approaches found in cases of "true oscillations." The problem is to know why the progressive adaptation shown in the experiment is not a complete adaptation, and why there is a tendency to hesitate on questions about the small pieces. If the child is just incapable of imagining conservation of volume, she could be viewed as intellectually retarded. The heterogeneous responses seem to indicate a more complex disequilibrium and reveal the interactions of the subject's affectivity with her intellectual maturation.

In an attempt to analyze these indices of character, which could be related to this particular intellectual behavior, the following observations were collected. According to the psychiatric examination, Tru. had only slight intellectual retardation, but her difficulties in social adaptation were serious. She seemed to be fearful of being underestimated and not being accorded her true value. She was asocial, a bad student, and a liar who could not admit her mistakes. In the preceding cases, the inhibitions of reasoning sprang mainly from a disequilibrium between the child's true capacity and the lack of intellectual stimulation from the social enviroment; in Tru.'s case the same oscillations of intellectual behavior were influenced by organic difficulties. A history of epileptic seizures had led to her placement in a clinic. The irritability which accompanies this pathological state and the resulting disequilibrium are well known. The child's periodic states of inferiority and the accompanying tension influenced her intellectual behavior; aspects of this syndrome were noted in the interviews.

From the analysis of "progressive" reasonings in the diagnosis of the equilibrium of thought, there is indication that factors inhibiting intellectual exchange combine with the retardation of mental development. Once these obstacles are removed, future development becomes possible.

2. The True Oscillations

While the progressive oscillations, found in several of the examples, are encountered only in slightly retarded children, true oscillations, *i.e.,* constant fluctuations between two levels, can be observed in all degrees of mental retardation. Most often the closing phase of the interview does not show marked progress or decline in relation to the opening phase. A diagram of the thought processes would take the form of an undulating movement. True oscillations generally show accentuated troubles of intellectual equilibrium.

If oscillation is the trait common to this group of reasonings, a close analysis will distinguish several types of dominant factors. Three of these are anxiety, suggestibility, and hesitation, and all three are manifest in the undulatory fluctuation of the reasoning processes (these traits can appear singly or combined in the same individual).

Young retardates whose reasoning is influenced by anxiety move constantly from one explanatory system to another, but these fluctuations cannot be attributed to pressure either from experimental facts or from the examiner. As soon as the child proposes a solution he retracts it and almost contradicts himself because of fear of being wrong. The suggestible subjects, as the adjective indicates, submit to any proposal and try to adapt themselves to persons rather than to objective facts. The hesitant subjects give endless consideration to a variety of possible opinions; they can't decide on a solution, but they do not verbalize this indecision because of fear of appearing wrong in the presence of the examiner. Examples are presented of each of the three forms of oscillations and the problems they pose for the diagnosis of reasoning.

a. Effect of Anxiety on Operatory Reasoning

OBSERVATION 55—WAL., M, 10:5

Wal. could explain operation of the scales. *When that [he points to one of the pans] is down, it is heavier; it weighs more; it weighs on it, then it has to go down, and when they weigh the same they balance, you can see it.*

(He carefully makes two equal balls, takes a long time to verify equality of weight on the scales, and is not easily satisfied.)

You can make a sausage with one of the balls, and we will leave the other as it is. (*Shouts spontaneously:*) *Only a sausage, I could make a carrot too.* (*He transforms the ball and asks all the time if he is right.*)

If you weighed both on the scales, what would the two pans show? Point to it. (*He reflects for a long time.*) *Both are the same weight because if you roll that up again, it's just as heavy as before.*

And in the sausage, is it the same weight? (*Startled:*) *Wasn't I right?* (*Weighs them in his hand.*) *The ball is heavier after all.*

Then, which is right, what you thought at first or what you say now? *The sausage is heavier because it's rolled up like that. It takes up both sides of the pan, and that is heavy.*

Is there the same amount of clay, or more on one side? *The same amount of clay, but it is lighter because the sausage would have to be thicker, then it would be heavier.*

Could you make a ball from it again? *Can I try it?*

But think first. What would it be like in relation to the other? (*A long, tense period of reflection.*) *There is less clay when you roll and squeeze it again. You will see, if I make a ball again, that is less. Say, are you going to show what I said to the teacher? Why are you writing all that down? Promise you won't tell it to anybody, for sure, promise me!*

(The child is asked to divide the ball into small pieces.) How much would the little pieces weigh? *The ball is heavier because there it is separated and it doesn't weigh so heavily.*

Is there as much clay on both sides? What do you think? *A little bit more in the ball, because these [he points to the small pieces] if you put them together again, there wouldn't be as much. Am I saying something wrong? Now I want to see how it is on the scales.*

(He does a check on the scales and is not satisfied. He puts the small pieces right in the middle of the pan.) Why are you piling them up like that? *So it will balance better.*

And if they are spread out, isn't that the same thing? *It's lighter, Oh, I see, it's the same. I was wrong. You won't tell the director! But wait, I want to see when the scales stop.*

(The examiner touches the scales to stop their movement.) *It's not right if you hold it.*

(*He watches attentively until the scales are balanced, then in a disappointed tone:*) *The same weight.*

Why does it weigh the same? *Because each of these corners is a little heavy.*

Now you are going to gather up the little pieces and make a pancake of them. (*He takes pleasure in the activity and relaxes.*)

Show me how the scales would be if you weighed the ball with the thin pancake. *I have to think.* (*After a long pause:*) *There is as much clay, only it's spread out, but it's just as heavy, only spread out. It all comes to the same.*

Are you sure that what you said is right? *Yes, if you put it back in a ball again it makes a ball the same size.*

(Then they go on to the problem of volume. He sees that the level rises the same for both identical balls.) Where would the water rise to for the sausage? *Higher, because the sausage is long.*

And for the pancake? *Even higher. It completely fills the bottom, then the water has to rise.*

And for the little pieces? *Almost not at all. They are so small.*

In contrast to the children who adapt slowly, Wal. easily takes part in the experiment. All of his manipulations are accompanied by a lively interest. Absorbed in his activity, he begins with a bit of reasoning which has surprising astuteness: *Both are the same weight, because if you roll that up again, it's just as heavy as before.*

Normal thought development shows a reversible construction; however, the asking of the question, "And in the sausage is it as heavy, too?" shakes the child's conviction. He is afraid he has made a wrong judgment. His logical certitude collapses and does not resist subjective impression. Weighing the ball and the sausage in his hand, he finds: *The ball is heavier after all.*

As the coexistence of two contradictory ideas in the child is possible, an attempt is made to determine which predominates: *Then, which is right, what you thought at first or what you say now?*

Then he clearly decides: *The sausage is heavier because it's rolled up like that. It takes up both sides of the pan, and that is heavy.*

How can this momentary collapse of a reasoning, which seems to be based on an operatory groupment, be explained? Is it due to a simple problem of memory, as can be observed in certain types of grave instability? No, it is nothing of the kind. The child knows exactly how to repeat the two propositions. The hesitation between the two conceptions, and more particularly the collapse of the objective system of formal operations in favor of egocentrism, clearly reveals the fragility of his logical thought. The child can't achieve the ensemble of logico-physical operations characteristic of the third level of conservation notions.

However, he is far from being fixed at the second stage, as is shown in his justifications relative to the conservation of substance. He begins by affirming: *The same amount of clay.*

It is curious that the questions "Could you make a ball from it again? What would it be like in relation to the other?" which suggest the reversibility on which he based his idea of weight conservation, confused the child this time, causing him to think: *There is less clay when you roll and squeeze it again. You will see, if I make a ball again, that is less.*

In the same way he predicts the inequality of weight and substance in the sectioning of the clay: *A little bit more in the ball, because these, if you put them together again [the little pieces], there wouldn't be as much.*

Everything appears to indicate that the child has denied once and for all the idea of conservation and that his answer is an example of retrogressive reasoning, a type of reasoning which makes use of verbally acquired notions without being capable of personal elaboration. However, this was not true of Wal., and his reactions to the experimental verification clearly showed his intellectual and personal comprehension of the problems posed. Not only did he explain the equality of weight by an operation which at least implied colligation —*Because each of these corners is a little heavy*—but faced with the experiment of the transformation of the clay into a pancake, he correctly predicted: *There is as much clay, only it's spread out, but it's just as heavy, only it's spread out. It all comes to the same . . . if you put it back in a ball again, it makes a ball the same size.*

The child caught up again, and at the end of the interview he returned to his initial level.

What happened in between, and how can this momentary collapse followed by a consolidation of thought be explained? It was due in part to a slight intellectual deficiency, because in none of the intellectually normal children examined had such a regression been observed. This seemed to indicate therefore a fragility of the higher-level notions. However, intellectual deficiency alone could not explain such oscillations of thought, and it is interesting to analyze the child's affective behavior as manifest during the conservation. Also noted was the child's emotional tension. Only for brief instants did the objective interest for the problem itself predominate over his latent fear of being inadequate. In the moments when he was absorbed by his activity, Wal. performed at his maximum potential, but these short instances were immediately followed by lapses into emotional egocentrism. Several times he asked if his results were to be sent to his classroom teacher, the director, and others. He also refused to accept that his prediction was wrong, and he became depressed and in some way ceased to reason. However, emotional contact with the examiner was good, and when intellectual interest was awakened, Wal. became motivated.

An attempt was made to see if these fragmentary observations corresponded to permanent traits of the child's intelligence and affectivity. Wal., an illegitimate and abandoned child, was considered by his teachers to be asocial, ambitious, boisterous, quick-tempered, and subject to depression. His achievement was below his intellectual capacities. Once he was in an understanding atmosphere, there was intellectual progress. An examination of the child two years after these investigations found him better integrated, but still highly retarded. It is concluded that his social problems influenced his poor intellectual performance. In this particular case, lack of confidence in himself and others (anxiety over appearing inadequate) disturbed the operatory construction itself.

b. Indices of Suggestibility in Reasoning

Before engaging in an analysis of the reasoning of highly suggestible subjects, a question of method will be considered. It could be supposed that the reasoning obtained in conversation with retardates was the result of leading questions. Isn't it easy to obtain whatever is wanted from these subjects? The case report of retardates at clearly defined levels proves that this is not true. The retardates who tended to remain at the lower level of operatory thought furnished, in their unchanging attitude, an astonishing demonstration of nonsuggestibility. But the retardates of Stages II and III, in spite of experimental stimulation, did not totally rid themselves of their egocentric points of view. An ensemble of reasonings, although provoked by the questions and experiments, showed original intellectual reactions in the subjects examined. Findings might be different if, instead of morons and slow learners, true imbeciles were used whose "no matter whatism" (Binet 1909: 137) is a characteristic trait. As the experiment was limited to morons and slow learners, suggestibility in operatory reasoning did not occur with greater frequency than in normal children. It is necessary—and it is evidently a condition of all reasearch of this type —to present questions which do not suggest responses; the examiner should not be confined to registering verbal formulas without placing them in the operatory context of thought. If, nonetheless, suggestibility is such that it is impossible to attain an original operation of thought, this seems to be an index of disequilibrium of reasoning whose structure requires description.

OBSERVATION 56—GER., F, 10:2

The child prepared two balls and determined their equality on the scales. Then she transformed one of the balls into a sausage.

If you put them back on the scales, would they weigh the same or would one be heavier than the other? *The same weight.*

Why the same weight? *Because they both weighed the same in the very beginning.*

But now one is in a sausage; is that all the same? *Oh, no, then it's no longer the same weight.*

One would be lighter? *Yes, the sausage.*

Why? *Because you rolled the ball, then it became lighter. The sausage is lighter than the ball.*

Is there as much clay in the ball as in the sausage? *As much; that's why I had the idea that it was the same weight.*

Why do you think so now? *Because before it was the same weight.*

Is there as much clay or not? *The same.*

Now you are going to check if it's right, if you figured it out well. (*Before doing the checking:*) *No, no, it's not the same weight.*

Which would be heavier, according to you? *The sausage.* (*She looks at the examiner. Not seeing any affirmation:*) *No, the ball is heavier.*

We are going to try something else. How much will the little pieces weigh? (The sausage had been divided into little pieces.) *They are lighter.*

Why lighter? *Because they are cut into pieces.*

Is there more clay in the little pieces or as much? *As much clay. They are the same weight.*

Is there the same amount of clay or more on one side than the other? *In one pan there is more clay; it's cut into pieces, and because before I made such a long sausage from it.*

Then if you put them on the scales, what would happen? *The little pieces are heavier, or after all the same? The same weight; after all, it's still the same clay.*

Do you want to make a pancake from one of the balls? (*Says immediately:*) *It's the same weight.*

Why? *One is longer and the other larger. It all comes to the same.* (*As nothing is said immediately:*) *I think it's a little bit heavier.*

Where is it heavier, on which side? *The ball is heavy. The cake does not weigh so much.*

What will happen if I put each of the balls in a glass of water? *The water does not stay where it is. It rises a little higher.*

Why does it rise? *Because there is clay in the water and that makes it rise a little.*

But why does the clay make it rise? *The water rises a little, because that [pointing to the ball] goes down.*

(It is shown that the level rises exactly the same for both balls.)

You see each ball takes up room in the water; then that makes the level rise. If you put the pancake in instead of the ball, would that take up as much room? *The pancake goes to the bottom too. That makes the water rise.*

And where will the water rise to? (*Indicates a level similar to that of the ball.*)

But before you said there was more clay in the pancake. Why does that make the water rise the same? Why would it take up as much room? *Yes, the pancake takes up a little more room.*

Why more room? *No, the same. It is the same weight.*

How do you know that the ball and the pancake take up the same amount of room? *The ball is high. That makes the same thing as the pancake does in width.*

And if you put the ball in one glass and the sausage in another, would the water rise in each glass? *It rises the same amount because the clay [of the sausage] goes to the bottom of the water too and pushes the water still higher.*

What do you think, will the ball and the sausage take up as much room or not? *No, the sausage takes up more room.*
Then, where will the water rise to? (*She indicates a much higher level.*) *It rises much more.*
And now if you weighed the ball and the sausage, what would the scales show? *The sausage is heavier because it makes the water rise higher.*
(Experimental check.) *Oh, it's the same. Yes, it weighs the same.* (*She clearly shows a lack of interest.*)

In "progressive" cases a continuous thought process is shown. In Wal. (Observation 55) a search for the truth is observed which is momentarily thwarted by his emotional egocentrism. In Ger., however, whose interview is cited above, fluctuations were so frequent that it was no longer a true development of thought, but only oscillations between contradictory affirmations. The child started by affirming the conservation of weight *because they both weighed the same in the very beginning.* A question intended to provoke more precise reasoning—But now one is in a sausage; is that all the same?—was sufficient to influence her thinking: *Oh, no, then it's no longer the same weight,* and to make her give as her reasons for weight variation: *Because you rolled the ball, then it became lighter. The sausage is lighter than the ball.*

But when she was questioned about conservation of substance she reverted to her first idea: *That's why I had the idea that it was the same weight.* As soon as the child was asked to use the scales to check her prediction she regressed again: *No, no, it's not the same weight.*

Her indecision proved that her statements reflected a desire for immediate satisfaction rather than a true intellectual operation: Which would be heavier according to you? *The sausage,* and, not seeing any affirmation: *No, the ball is heavier.*

When the clay was divided into small pieces there was the same situation: at first: *They are lighter. . . . Because they are cut into pieces,* and then later: Is there more clay in the little pieces or as much? *As much clay. They are the same weight.*

These oscillations are not limited to the problem of weight (which could still be considered as a phenomenon of thought development which is characteristic of intermediate cases); they are also manifest when it is a matter of making a statement on the conservation of substance: the same amount of clay or more on one side than the other? *In one pan there is more clay; it's like that cut into pieces . . .*

and the next minute: The little pieces are heavier, or after all the same? *The same weight.*

Contradictions continued during discussion of volume. In comparing the ball to the pancake she said: *The water rises a little, because that goes down.* In indicating the same level as for the ball: *The pancake takes up a little more room.* Why more room? *No, the same. It is the same weight;* or, *The ball is high. That makes the same thing as the pancake does in width.*

When the comparison is between the ball and the sausage, contradiction is still more noticeable because in the same sentence she says: *It rises the same amount because the clay [of the sausage] goes to the bottom of the water too, and pushes the water still higher [than for the ball].*

In this type of reasoning, it is hardly a question of adaptation to the problem nor of method of thought. The child is looking for emotional and social satisfaction, but not an intellectual one. Finality of thought is troubled. Her intellectual means being insufficient to procure the desired approval, she turns difficulties aside, thus avoiding all effort of personal reflection. As she attempted a solution to the problem, Ger. was uncritically open to any suggestion from the examiner. No matter what the question, it could change her preceding affirmations. She is easily influenced throughout the interview, since she lacks self-control and does not dominate the situation.

An interesting aspect of this behavior is that the absence of self-control is not limited to intellectual questions but is equally manifest in her emotional life (lying, stealing, etc.). These character defects were the cause of Ger.'s placement in an observation class.

In oscillations of reasoning due to suggestibility, the diagnosis goes beyond the logical domain to examination of the emotional and social deficiencies. The suggestibility can influence thought finality to the point of disturbing the operatory equilibrium itself. Suggestibility of reasoning, therefore, is only a particular sign which will take on its full significance when considered with other factors in the total clinical picture.

c. Hesitant Reasoning

Although similar in appearance to the preceding types, hesitant reasoning reveals a distinct mental functioning. Somehow, oscillations are interiorized. When the subject is confronted with a problem which slightly surpasses his intellectual level, he does not dare to formulate a precise judgment nor decide between two ideas. The same type of hesitation can be encountered in an exaggerated form in the hesitancy of certain neurotics who are endowed with normal intelligence. Hesitation of subjects in the present study is manifest on an intellectually defective plane, and the hesitation is partly conditioned by this deficiency.

OBSERVATION 57—EDI., M, 13:5

The child demonstrates the equality of the balls, and when asked to transform one into a sausage he observes: *Look how long it becomes.*

And now if you weighed both of them again? *It would be almost the same weight, only longer.*

How do you know that it is almost the same? *Oh, because I weighed it before.*

And now when you weigh it again, is it still the same? *No, it's lighter. It's lighter than before all the same. (He weighs it in his hand.) It's become longer and also lighter; I think. (All this is said in a hesitant tone without conviction.)*

Is there as much clay or not? *In the sausage there is almost a little more because it is bigger.*

(Upon request the child divides the clay into little pieces, and as he becomes interested in his manipulations he says:) *The little pieces are certainly lighter because I made them so small. They've been crumbled up.*

Is there still as much clay, or more or less? *(He hesitates.) I don't know.*

Could you make a whole ball again from the little pieces, a ball as big as the other [the control ball]? *It would be bigger than the first, but it would be bumpy with lots of little corners. You could see that it was little pieces before.*

And about the weight? *The same weight again. No, a little heavier, no, I don't know. No, a little heavier after all because it would be a little bigger [the one that had been transformed].*

We will check it on the scales. *(Astonished:) Yes, it's the same weight, I see.*

Why does the ball weigh as much as the little pieces? *Because I separated them, because I made it into little pieces. (After a long moment of reflection:) Well, because I see it on the scales, and before I didn't see it.*

(The ball is transformed into a pancake.)

And what weight will the pancake have in relation to the ball? *The ball doesn't have the same weight, the pancake is lighter. (He says it again with conviction.)*

Are you completely sure? *Yes, because the ball is heavier.*

But the clay, is there as much or not? *I don't know. I have to think about it. I think as much, because it's the same size: the other is only flatter.*

Could you make a ball from it again too? *Yes, but would it be the same size? [He asks himself]. Yes, maybe.*

You think so, but you aren't sure. *I don't know, I think so, but maybe it would be bigger after all.*

Would both balls have the same weight again or not? *If they are both the same size, then yes, I think they would have the same weight.*

Or do you think one differs in weight from the other? *No, both balls are just the same weight after all, because they are the same size.*

But you are still hesitating? *To say they are the same weight is more correct because they are just as wide, and round, and big.*

And when one is in a pancake? *Then it is larger and not as high. Then it isn't quite the same after all.*

(Another check on the scales.) *Now I know why you know it's always the same weight, because in the beginning you made them the same weight on purpose and then you checked on the scales.*

And then you divided it into little pieces. *Then it isn't as heavy any more.*

A transcription of the conversation with the child does not sufficiently illustrate the distinction between different types of oscillation. Also, the attitude toward the experiment varies from one case to another. While Wal. (Observation 55) advanced his affirmations with conviction, but lost sight of his previous reasoning, Ger. (Observation 56) said what she thought would win approval, and Edi. (Observation 57) did not like to take the initiative; this was shown in his opening remarks.

When comparing the ball and the sausage, he reflected for several moments and then replied: *It would be almost the same weight, only longer.*

But when the question is pressed he "folds up" and changes his mind: *No, it is lighter; it is lighter than before.*

And the same situation recurs for the conservation of substances: *In the sausage there is almost a little more because it is bigger.*

Note the frequent use of the word "almost," which seems to show better than anything else the indecision and fear of compromise, a rare phenomenon in young children as well as in retardates who usually are not concerned with the correctness of their statements. Edi.'s hesitant reasoning tended to appear when questions and experimental problems surpassed his intellectual level. Each time he made a spontaneous observation from perceptive facts without thoughtful correction of them, he expressed himself with a kind of vivacity, or at least showed much less inhibition. For example, as soon as he made the little pieces of clay he said: *The little pieces are certainly lighter because I made them so small. They've been crumbled up.*

When asked: Is there still as much clay, more, or less?, he hesitated a long time and could not decide one way or the other, finally giving up: *I don't know.*

Later, when the question of weight was asked again, the wavering and indecision between two possible solutions reappeared: *The same weight again. No, a little heavier. No, I don't know. No, a little heavier after all because it would be a little bigger* [*the one that had been transformed*].

The same tendency is noted in discussion concerning the pancake: *I don't know; I have to think about it. I think. . . .*

When asked: Are you completely sure? . . . But the clay, is there as much or not?, he replied: *I don't know. I have to think about it. I think as much, because it's the same size; the other is only flatter.*

The impression is given that the child talks more to himself than to the examiner: *To say they are just as heavy is more correct because they are just as wide, and round, and big;* but he adds, *Then it is larger and not as high. Then it isn't quite the same after all.*

The disinterest that was revealed by the preceding subject did not reappear in Edi.'s case; instead, the child had genuine difficulty in verbalizing his ideas and his reasoning, and in coordinating them in relation to questions and objections coming either from the examiner or from the experimental facts. Also, he was unable to profit from the experimental check; here his explanation was of a purely phenomenalistic nature:

Now I know why you know it's always the same weight. Because in the beginning you made them the same weight on purpose and then you checked on the scales.

After twenty minutes of discussion the child was still less sure of the conservation of weight and substance. His statements affirming conservation of either substance or weight were superior to his level of operatory reasoning, and because of this they seemed unrelated to the real functioning of his thought. In this way, Edi. stood halfway between cases of oscillation and clear cases of regression, which are discussed later. While subjects of "retrogressive" reasoning make verbal formulations which are not based on fact, Edi. worries about verification. However, being unable to establish agreement among the few notions of conservation which he acquired through interpretation of perceptive facts, he wavered between two possible solutions and was unable to make a clear decision one way or the other. These hesitations appear due partly to a retardation of operatory mechanisms— in other words, to an intellectual deficiency.

Are the hesitations reinforced by a permanent attitude of the child which expresses a grave emotional disequilibrium? It could be that the child finds it difficult to make a decision in any situation which requires an intellectual adaptation. In order to orient clinical research in this field it is indispensable not only to observe the child's behavior in all possible situations, but to study the antecedents of his emotional relations with his social environment.

In this particular case the child's father was in prison. His mother and grandmother were retarded and also had schizophrenic tendencies. Unfavorable scholastic experiences also contributed to the child's emotional and intellectual disequilibrium. His mutism at the time of entrance into the institution for abnormal children indicated some emotional involvement. He was hostile, and hid under the school benches. Little by little this resistance was overcome, but a general inhibition broken by aggressive explosions persisted. His teacher said that each time Edi. was not immediately successful in solving a problem, he became "nervous," refused to go on, and tried to escape the difficulty by pseudo-afflictions (slight palsy, paralysis of the right arm).

When the child was seen two years later his scholastic performance had improved and his method of thought was more consolidated. It seemed that an adapted instruction, together with suitable educational environment, had promoted self-assurance, which made possible a true communication and served to increase his intellectual development. Because the subject is a true retardate he will not reach the level of adult thought; but the environment in which rational mechanisms are acquired will always have an influence, either by stimulation or by inhibition, which will lead to equilibrium or disaggregation of reasoning.

True oscillations between two operatory levels are not themselves a sign of retardation, but, if combined with retardation, seem to reveal a momentary or constant disequilibrium of thought. In contrast to "progressive" cases, these true oscillations occur at all levels of retardation. However, a prognosis cannot be based on oscillations alone, but depends essentially on the interaction of constitutional and social factors. When the psychiatric examination does not reveal any pathological problem of mental disequilibrium, there is chance for a remediation of social and emotional conditions which will permit a reestablishment of equilibrium.

3. Retrogressive Reasoning

Regressions during interview were due to a progressive deterioration of acquired notions and are amplifications of those previously encountered in oscillations. There is disagreement between the workings which are exterior to the subjects' logic and the internal maturation of thought methods, methods which are normally interdependent. Reasoning which deteriorates poses problems inverse to those encountered in "progressive" reasoning. Why does the child who made a certain number of affirmations at the beginning of the interview end by questioning them and abandoning them afterward? The explanation seems to be that the notions formulated in the beginning do not correspond to the child's true intellectual level. They result from a sort of learned logic, and not from personal interpretation. The deteriorations of this more or less artificial superstructure are found especially in severe retardates over fourteen or fifteen years of age.

In view of these phenomena of regression, another hypothesis could be formulated relating this deterioration not to an intellectual deficiency, but to a loss of attention after a momentary tiring of the task. Normal and retarded children exist who regress after concentrated reflection; although the regression could be due to emotional reasons, present consideration is given to intellectual factors involved.

Two examples of retrogressive reasoning follow. The first is a fourteen-year-old boy (Observation 58); the second is a twenty-year-old man (Observation 59) who at the time of the examination was following a job training course for abnormal persons.

OBSERVATION 58—HER., M, 14:0

He operated the scales and made two identical balls while constantly speaking of something else.

You saw that both balls are the same. Now you are going to transform one into a sausage and then you will tell me if it still weighs the same or if it has changed. *The ball is heavier.*

Why do you think it is heavier? *Because it is bigger and thicker.*

Is there as much clay or not in the ball and the sausage? *As much clay because both were balls at first.*

Could you make a ball again? *Yes, wait, I will do it quickly, and then it will be just as heavy again.*

And when it's in a sausage it isn't as heavy? *On the ball's side it weighs down; it pulls the scales down.*

And now you are going to make small pieces. (*While he divides the clay he says:*) *That doesn't weigh; that doesn't pull it down, but the other does* [*the ball*].

Why don't the little pieces weigh? *Because they are lighter.*

And why do you think they are lighter? *Because they are only little pieces. They aren't heavy.*

Is there as much clay or not? *As much.*

How do you know that? *Because you can make two balls again.*

We will see if you were right about the weight. [Checks on scales.] *I don't think that is right.* (*He checks it a long time.*) *Both the same weight!*

How do you explain this? *I see, because the points* [*of the scales*] *touch.*

But you thought it would be different. *Yes, because there is more clay when you stretch it and when you tear it up.*

More clay than in the ball? *Yes, more.*

And if you make a ball again would it be the same size or would it be bigger? *The same size.*

And why do you say there is more clay when it is in a ball than when it is in small pieces or in a sausage? *Because when you make a ball again it shrinks after all; you squeeze and that makes less.*

(Two balls are made again and he demonstrates their equality.)

Do you want to make a pancake with one of the balls? (*Without hesitation he starts to work.*)

What will the scales do when you put the ball on the other side? *It's heavier where the ball is.*

Why? *Because the pancake is thin, I know: I've already weighed things.*

Is there as much clay or not? *More in the pancake. It's all flat.*

We are going to put each of the two balls in a glass and you are going to show me how much the water will rise. (*He marks the levels.*)

You see it rises exactly the same. If you put a pancake instead of the ball, how much will the water rise? *The water rises all the way up.* (*He points to a level much higher than for the ball.*)

Why higher when it's the pancake? *Because the pancake is so light.*

And why does the water rise high when it's light? *I think it takes up much more room than the ball.*

And how much will it rise with the little pieces? *It only rises a very little bit because the pancake is much bigger than the little pieces.*

Her. begins by completely affirming conservation of substance: *As much clay because both were balls at first,* while denying that of weight and volume: *That doesn't weigh* [*the little pieces*]; or, *Because it is bigger and thicker* [*the ball at the time one is transformed into a sausage*].

Briefly, his judgments seem to show reasoning characteristic of Stage III. However, the curious and revealing thing in his poorly formulated statements is that the experimental observation of conservation of weight does not make him aware of the necessity of conservation, but causes the collapse of the structures of logical mechanisms which are unattached to the functioning of his thought.

He tries to question equality of weight and ends by observing it in a phenomenalistic way. How do you explain this [inequality of weight]? *I see, because the points* [*of the scales*] *touch.* When he is asked to justify his previous reasoning—but you thought it would be different—he bases his reasoning on substance: *Because there is more clay when you stretch it and when you tear it up.* He even says: *Because when you make a ball again it shrinks after all; you squeeze and that makes less.*

Likewise in the transformation to a pancake he not only acts as though he had not observed the conservation of weight on the scales, but he even affirms in a tranquil manner: *More in the pancake. It's all flat,* without worrying about making his present statement agree with those he affirmed a minute before.

From the outset it is seen that there is a grave deficiency of thought. After a deterioration in the inverse direction of operatory construction, he finishes by completely and clearly denying all conservation. Even the suggested empirical return to the initial stage has no effect. He believes it is, after as before, "the same size," but between times "it shrinks." The child is unable to profit from any of the indications given by the experiment. This proves that the operatory mechanisms of thought, refractory to experimental facts, remain fixed at the pre-logical level.

Still more astonishing is the fact that the subject's first responses indicated conservation of substance. Two facts must be distinguished: (1) a formal mechanism of thought was due to scholastic or social formation, or even to personal acquisitions so recent that the child applied them indiscriminately, or (2) the ordinary level of his intellectual operations remained in a state of relative incoordination. The apparent surface logic would result from instruction. Although hardly capable of constructive thought, the child would have acquired during his school years a more or less precise method of calculation or reasoning which would reflect on the present problems. It is observed that certain abnormal children have acquired skill in multiplication and division without understanding the reciprocity of these operations. This analogy is discussed later.

It is important not to be duped by words, and necessary to search for the true thought level. In Her.'s case, determination of level was relatively easy. His years of special instruction had furnished him with reasoning patterns which he adapted to the experimental situation. However, when he was made to reflect on concrete facts which contradicted his predictions, he became totally confused and the indecision which followed signified his low mentality. Conversation with the child managed in some way to reestablish his equilibrium of thought. His reasoning, although elevated at first by the acquisition of certain badly assimilated notions, was classified as that of a fourteen-year-old who had hardly surpassed the logical level of a five- or six-year-old.

His level of reasoning was that of an imbecile, and the phenomenon of regression, which showed intellectual passivity, indicated a grave deficiency. Prognosis for future thought development was poor. While progressive reasoning in these subjects showed thought in formation, retrogressive reasoning showed either a definitive fixation at the true level or indicated possible future decline.

Her., for example, made no scholastic progress for several years, in spite of the teacher's efforts. After several years of excellent special instruction he remained at the second-grade level. Arithmetic comprehension did not surpass numerical notions of 1 to 10. Fundamental operations were learned mechanically, but without any real comprehension. However, the boy did some types of manual labor, such as basket weaving, satisfactorily, but apart from this training, his mental development remained stationary.

The contrast between a recently acquired logical mechanism, and real operatory functioning of thought is more noticeable when applied to older subjects. If this study were not limited in principle to the diagnosis of reasoning of young retardates, it would be possible to devote a special chapter to the thought transformations which are produced at the moment the retardate's intellectual development has stopped, although these persons continue to acquire certain social and practical techniques in relation to their activities. One typical case is cited below. Zwe. (Observation 59) is twenty years of age, but has not yet passed the first stages of reasoning. However, he dexterously manages to hide his profound ignorance.

OBSERVATION 59—ZWE., M, 20 YEARS

Zwe. made two equal balls, and upon transforming one into a sausage said spontaneously: *The ball is heavier [hesitates] or the same weight after all. Nothing was taken away and nothing added, but on the other hand I think that the ball is heavier because it was left alone.*

Is there as much clay or more in the ball? *As much, because I weighed it in the beginning.*

And when you transformed one into a sausage? *Still as much. (Hesitates.) No, I don't think so, it shrank because it's long.*

You can make two balls again and divide one into small pieces. (*Manipulates with pleasure.*)

What will the scales show with the ball on one side and the little pieces on the other? *The ball is heavier. The little pieces aren't heavy at all now.*

Could you make a ball again from all these little pieces? *Of course.*
And what weight would this new ball have in relation to the other?
The same weight again, but when you make it into little pieces it be-
comes lighter because they are little pieces.

About the clay, how much is here in the little pieces? *Oh, not the*
same, there is more in the little pieces. (Reflects:) *No, it's the same;*
when you weighed it it was the same, so in the same way I suppose
that when you make little pieces, it doesn't matter.

Is it the same weight too, or heavier or lighter? *It has become*
lighter, but there is as much clay. There is the same amount of clay.

It doesn't matter that the pieces are separated? *When I look at it*
like that I see there is more in all those little pieces. There is more clay
after all.

What will it be like for the pancake? You can make one and compare. *It is the same thing only round. Nothing was taken away; it*
weighs the same too.

Could you make a ball again from the pancake? *Yes, but wait,*
there is more clay in the pancake after all. So I don't know if that
makes the same thing again.

But you said that it weighs the same as the ball. *Yes, I said so, but*
when I think about it I see that it is thinner. I think it is lighter. (Ex-
perimental check with the scales.) *Oh, it's what I said before after all.*
That is more correct.

(The displacement of water by the immersion of the balls is explained to him. Zwe. marks the level of the displaced water.) *And*
if you put a small metal cylinder instead of the ball? *It would rise*
higher with the lead. It is heavy.

(Experimental check.) *Oh, the ball is bigger; it takes up more room.*

(The two balls are immersed.) *It rises the same for both. The balls*
take up the same room.

And if you put a ball and a pancake in each of the glasses? *It rises*
higher with the pancake because it is larger.

And where will the water rise with the little pieces? *The water rises*
very little. (He points to a slightly elevated level.)

Why so little? *The ball takes more. It is heavier.*

But you remember the lead "took up less" although it was heavier?
There is more inside the ball.

And more as in the little pieces, or the same? *Much more.*

More what? *Clay.*

And if you compare the sausage and the ball, do they take up as much room in the water or not? *The water rises higher with the sausage because it is larger.*

(Experimental check.) (*States simply:*) *It doesn't rise higher with the sausage. The sausage isn't as long as I thought.*

It is not only the wavering formal thought which is characteristic of his mentality, but also the dexterous procedures he employs to keep from compromising himself that distinguish Zwe.'s performance from the hesitant performance found in certain young retardates such as Edi.

Thus, Zwe. began by simultaneously affirming two contradictory things: *The ball is heavier . . . or the same weight . . . nothing was taken away and nothing added, but on the other hand I think that the ball is heavier because it was left alone.*

Contradiction is again observed in answer to questions relative to the conservation of substance: *Still as much . . . no, I don't think so, it shrank. . . .*

The following two ideas were found to coexist in relation to sectioning: *The same weight again, but when you make it into little pieces it becomes lighter,* and *there is more in the little pieces.*

The affirmation—*No, it's the same; when you weighed it, it was the same. So in the same way I suppose that when you make little pieces it doesn't matter*—seems to show operatory construction, *i.e.,* a coordination of spatial relations, leaving weight and substance invariant, but the simple question "Could you make a ball again from the pancake?" collapses this conviction like a house of cards: *Yes, but wait, there is more clay in the pancake after all. So I don't know if that makes the same thing again . . . when I think about it I see that it is thinner.*

Later, in relation to the problem of volume, the subject has to reengage his thinking, and it is easily seen how his notions of conservation rely on superficial formalism and not on a maturation of thought: *Oh, the ball is bigger; it takes up more room . . . there is more inside the ball.*

Zwe. also starts by using the notion of volume as well as occupied space: *The balls take up the same room,* but falls into the lower notion where weight and volume are undifferentiated: *The ball takes more; it is heavier.*

Although Zwe. at first knows how to formulate conclusions which show conservation of weight and substance, and although his reasoning repeats exactly the corresponding operatory mechanism, he cannot maintain and defend his ideas. He abandons them during the interview when he is confronted with experimental facts. Thus, he seems to reveal his incapacity to think logically. This revelation indicates that care should be taken in evaluating all formalism which is detached from the lively functioning of thought, and nothing could show more clearly the necessity of proceeding clinically, *i.e.,* testing mental processes, and observing development without being limited to a simple registering of results.

Zwe.'s case, although analogous to that of the preceding subject (Observation 58) in structure and level of reasoning, is nonetheless distinguished from him by his efforts to hide his real incapacity for constructive thought. His general physical appearance also served to hide his mental incapacity. Like many subjects of his kind, he gained a false assurance because people continually overestimated his mental capacity. When this happens to a retardate, he struggles to maintain this façade, and flees from clear decisions which would risk compromission. It is only in the moments when there are no possible detours or loopholes, as during a forced discussion, that he gives up and no longer makes a personal effort, realizing somehow that the game is lost.

As in Her., the prognosis is relatively poor. Because of Zwe.'s advanced age, there is little chance that he will change the habits which give rise to his misleading assurance and become capable of learning from experience. Zwe. upon leaving school was placed several times in jobs which involved working with peasants. His superficial work and his lack of job perseverance caused dissatisfaction; therefore, the only recourse was to place the young man in a community institution.

A case such as Zwe.'s must not be confused with the mental instability, encountered for example in certain epileptics; in these cases previous acquisitions are maintained in spite of a progressive deterioration of the intellectual processes. Cases exhibiting this type of malfunctioning are not included in the present study; therefore they will not be discussed. In the mentally ill there appears to be a continuous process of regression—not those declines which are repeatedly followed by a return to a level which is stable in itself.

4. Abnormal Decalages

Before diagnosing the different oscillations of reasoning noted during the interview, a final category of disequilibrium of thought, which also escapes classification by fixation at genetic stages, must be examined. This category includes phenomena which Piaget termed "decalages" (Piaget 1941b) and which are illustrated in the following example: a child observing the transformation of the clay balls appears to reason as though he believed in the conservation of weight, or even of volume, but when he is confronted with sugar dissolved in water, he hardly surpasses the level of conservation of substance; or he might appear superior in purely formal problems, but inferior when reasoning involves experimental facts.

When confronted with such phenomena, it is necessary to distinguish carefully the three particular types of decalages. First, it is an accepted fact that certain children have greater difficulty in reasoning on one perceptive ensemble than on another. For example, it is easier to believe in conservation of substance when simple transformation of a solid object is involved than when the substance is dissolved in water and disappears from view. In the same way it is easier to understand that the sum of the parts equals the whole when the clay is divided in only three pieces rather than a dozen. Such "horizontal" decalages (termed horizontal because they happen on the same operatory level) constitute in fact only a slight modification of the general synchronism in the elaboration of logical groupment.

As this gap between notions and operations widens and surpasses the normal variation because of large or small perceptive resistances, two other explanations must be envisaged. Either this decalage is only apparent (*i.e.,* it is due to a verbal mechanism and has no relation to the functioning of thought, and is thus confused with "retrogressive reasonings" mentioned above) or it comes from a blocking of social exchange which shows an exaggeration of the phenomena of true oscillation.

Examples of apparent decalages would be pointless. It is simply noted that certain retarded children who have verbal facility apparently succeed better in formal tests (for example, those of bar or volume composition) than they do in conservation experiments. However, in each of these cases, if the child is closely questioned, the true operatory level finally appears through the verbal and schematic façade. The true operatory level corresponds to the notions of conservation which these children possess.

By contrast, if, in spite of precautions in interrogation and in the detailed analysis of the child's responses, a real decalage exists between the reasonings as they relate to different experiments, this decalage poses an interesting diagnostic problem. Only one subject showed clear oscillations from one test to another. Without knowing the ensemble of factors which could have conditioned such behavior the oscillations are noted in the following discussion concerning the dissolution of sugar.

OBSERVATION 60A—HOP., M, 14:10

What happens if you put the sugar in the water, and what becomes of water? *It gets wet: there are little bubbles that rise.*

Does the water level stay where it is [it is marked with a rubber band] or does it move when you add the sugar? *The water rises because the sugar is heavy.*

Why does it rise when the sugar is heavy, and what does it do? *The sugar goes down, and as much as it goes down the water rises.*

And if you put a clay ball in the water instead of the sugar, does it do the same thing? *The ball is big and heavy and that makes it rise more.*

What happens to the sugar which was once in the water? *It melts. Bubbles rise. The sugar is on the bottom of the glass and the water becomes sweet.*

Could you get the sugar back when it is melted? *No, if you pour the water out and you didn't stir then you might still find some sugar, but if you stirred it's impossible. You will find nothing more, it's no longer there.*

The water level remains elevated or not? *Evidently the water goes down because the sugar is no longer heavy, because there is nothing more in the bottom of the glass.*

(Experimentation starts. Hop. states in the beginning that the two glasses of water are the same weight.) What will the weight be when the sugar is added? *It becomes a bit heavier because of the sugar.*

(The sugar is added to the water and the increase in weight is demonstrated.) And when it will be melted? *Then it is no longer at all heavy.*

Not at all? Why? *I mean not as heavy as when it is in pieces because, after all, there is still some of the sugar in there, because the water is still sweet. Well, no, the sugar is no longer in there after all.*

And how did you imagine that the water could be sweet? *Because the sugar was melted by the water. It became damp and then it disappeared, and now it's exactly the same again as plain water.*

(Scales are used to demonstrate that the sugared water weighs more than the plain water.) *It's heavier than plain water after all. The sugar isn't completely melted after all.*

What do you think about the water level? Will it go down again like you said? *Oh, the water stays the same because the sugar is still in there and that counts for something.*

But is the melted sugar still as big, does it still take up room? *No, you can't see it any more. It's melted.*

Would you still see it if you looked at it with a magnifying glass? *Yes, something, but not much.*

What would you see? *Oh, when the sugar is completely melted you wouldn't see anything more.*

But where did you get the idea that if you had added sugar it weighs more than plain water? *There is more water now in the glass.*

Where does this water come from? *It must come from the sugar.*

But how does that happen? *It is transformed, but I don't see how exactly.*

From these reflections the central idea appears that the child believes in the conservation of substance at one moment and that he doubts it at others. In any case he cannot conceive of the conservation of weight nor that of volume. Everything happens as if he remained at a level intermediate between the first and second stage of the notions of conservation. Several characteristic statements are singled out:

Could you get the sugar back when it is melted?

At one time he reflects: *It's impossible. You will find nothing more; it's no longer there.*

But at another he admits: *There is still some of the sugar in there, because the water is still sweet.*

Then he reverts to the former: *No, the sugar is no longer in there after all.*

And later, when he is asked to explain the sweet taste of the water: *Because the sugar was melted by the water. It became damp and then it disappeared, and now it's exactly the same again as plain water.*

It is seen that Hop. is capable of discussion and weighing the value of his arguments without being able at the outset to make a logical postulate that nothing of the substance is lost. Dominated by the appearance of things, he, like normal young children, tries to explain sweetness of the water by what happens to the sugar which finally disappears.

As for its weight, soon after the dissolution of sugar the child predicts: *Then it is no longer at all heavy.*

Then he immediately corrects himself: *I mean, not as heavy as when it is in pieces.*

But when he observes the constancy of weight, this does not lead him to conceive of a particular mode of conservation of substance, but only gives rise to the idea that *the sugar isn't completely melted after all.*

Curiously enough, after this experimental observation he predicts the constancy of level because: *The water stays the same because the sugar is still in there, and that counts for something . . . there is more water now in the glass . . . it must come from the sugar . . . it is transformed, but I don't see how exactly.*

In the following such reasoning, one perceives that it is not a question of homogeneous fixation at a lower level, but that Hop. struggles with the facts without being able to liberate himself from perceptive illusions in order to dominate them by the operatory groupment of superior levels. There seems to be a particular blocking whose nature must be determined.

The first impression is reinforced by the contrast observed between the reactions just listed and those which were manifest in relation to the experiment involving the transformation of the clay balls, reactions which show clearly a superior level of reasoning.

OBSERVATION 60B

(Makes two identical balls with care.) *Oh, I saw immediately by the size that they weren't the same weight, but now it's exact.*

You are going to transform one of the balls into a sausage and then you will tell me how much the sausage weighs. *Just the same because I didn't take any clay away or add any.*

Then there is as much clay too, or maybe more or less when it's in a sausage? *The same, of course.*

And if you put the ball and the sausage each in a glass of water [the glass is in front of the subject] where would the water rise for the ball and where for the sausage? *I'm not sure. I would like to see first. There is as much clay so maybe it would take up as much space.*

And if you divided the sausage into little pieces and put them in the water where would the level rise? *They are smaller. They take up less space. No, it rises the same too because even though they are pieces they weigh the same.*

But does it depend on the weight for the water to rise the same? You see this little stone and the ball? They weigh just the same. Which of the two will make the water rise higher? *The ball because it is bigger and with the little pieces I know now. All of them together take up room so it rises the same amount.*

And if you tried it with the ball and the pancake? *(After a long hesitation:) That and that are two things, both have the same weight of course, and because they have the same weight the water rises the same amount.*

Why does the water rise? *Because of the weight.*

But remember the experiment with the stone and the ball? *Yes, it's the size that counts, I understand. See, for the clay and the pancake one isn't bigger than the other: it only has another form.*

Could you make a ball from it again? *Yes, and it would be exactly the same size if you took nothing and lost nothing in rolling it up.*

When the reflections about the sugar are known it is truly astonishing to see that the child knows how to reflect with perfect coherence, and that he manages (after several hesitations which show a true adaptation of thought and a structuration of perceptive facts) to dominate quite well all the problems of conservation.

His reasoning concerning substance is: *I didn't take any clay away or add any.*

For weight: *Because even though they are in pieces they weigh the same.*

After several wrong assumptions in volume he finally understands: *With the little pieces I know now. All of them together take up room so it rises the same amount,* or *both have the same weight of course, and because they have the same weight the water rises the same amount.*

Why does a child who knows a normal structure of reasoning which is only slightly retarded in relation to his real age fail to give proof of a similar intellectual maturity when he reflects on sugar dissolution? That is a question which cannot be answered by operatory analysis. Discussion of Hop.'s behavior may reveal several indices which will help explain this bizarre discordance.

No other subject refused so tenaciously to establish contact with the examiner. After spending fifteen minutes in complete silence he began to make little grunts and said, *This is childish; I'm not going to take part in such stupid things. Am I at the police station?* and similar remarks. For this reason his teacher had never been able to have a psychological examination carried out.

During his first weeks at school, Hop. did not take part in classroom activities. Each time he was spoken to, he hid his face in his arms as though it were a defensive gesture. Hop. had spent many years in an institution for the very severely retarded and his future development was considered hopeless. Because of this experience he had developed a deep mistrust, and lived in complete emotional and intellectual isolation.

From all the experiments offered to Hop., only one interested him: the transformation of the clay balls. Manipulation of the clay immediately and completely captivated him, so much so that he forgot that he was being examined. The clay reminded him of previous work with pottery and of his desire to become perfect in this skill. He worked carefully and replied with pleasure to any technical questions in relation to the transformation of the clay. His remarks became spontaneous.

That the normal functioning of reasoning requires interest in the questions asked is undeniable. Poor scholarly results can be due to the fact that the method of presentation does not correspond to the intellectual or emotional needs of the students. The new "special schools" are inspired by knowledge of the needs or functional interests of the child. In Hop., however, the problem was more serious. His lack of interest was not limited to specific problems or methods of instruction but was part of a more general attitude. He was completely negative to any question which he could not understand at once. This mental attitude prevented him from approaching problems calmly and objectively and from performing at his maximum. However, when interest areas were touched on (in his case this was anything that could be manipulated) the barrier fell and he reflected and responded almost in spite of himself.

"Regression in reasoning" (which can be manifest in the form of decalages, or rather, in "false" decalages, since only momentary superiority is apparent) always indicates a particularly marked mental retardation. When true decalages are encountered (*i.e.,* a retardation conditioned by emotional blocking), it can be asked if this does not imply a pseudo-retardation of a subject who has been somehow "held" below his true intellectual level for a long period. No doubt this is what happened to Hop.

It would be superficial to try to relate all abnormal intellectual oscillation to deficiencies in social environment and to neglect constitutional factors. On the contrary, it is believed that the oscillations described in this chapter will always be signs of a deficient mental condition. Whether this deficiency conditions the problems of communication or whether these problems are added to the deficiency—in either case—the oscillations are the product of both factors. If mental organization is intact, problems of a social nature have no really lasting effect on intellectual development. (All the so-called "difficult" children of normal intelligence examined by the same method furnish proof of this.) If there is intellectual deficiency without problems of communication, it is the result of more or less homogeneous fixations, such as those described in Chapters 2 and 3. When there is interaction between mental deficiencies and emotional and social problems, the operatory equilibrium is affected to some extent. What is this interest factor (as opposed to the interindividual factor) of operatory disequilibrium? What does it consist of in the case of oscillations when they are coupled with problems of intellectual communication with the enviroment? A discussion of this follows.

Diagnosis of reasoning in young retardates, even if limited to the genetic aspect, is in no way reduced to a simple determination of levels. It is necessary both to examine the state of the equilibrium of thought at the level in question, and to study the possible signs of disequilibrium or of disentegration. If the groupment expresses a certain equilibrium of thought, disequilibriums are then the sign of special problems.

The reasonings set forth in this chapter all show a lesser or greater alternation of equilibrium and are thus different from cases of homogeneous fixation to any level of development. As has been demonstrated, these disequilibriums are manifest, without exception, in the form of oscillations between the ordinary levels of development. The low incidence of such cases is again noted.

After analyzing each case of oscillation used as an example of a different type of reasoning in which disequilibrium is encountered, two points will be discussed:

A. The diagnosis of oscillatory reasoning.

B. Disequilibriums and laws of development.

a. The Diagnosis of Oscillatory Reasonings

Although the individual context of each form of reasoning poses particular problems for mental diagnosis, a brief schematic discussion of the diagnosis suggested by each of the three groups of oscillations can be undertaken. The diagnosis (and therefore the implied prognosis) seems to be conditioned by two essential factors: the levels between which oscillations are effected, and the particular form of disequilibrium manifested by them. While determination of levels is easily made by analysis of the notions and operations, as referred to in the preceding chapters, the study of disequilibrium requires a more subtle examination of the thought processes that characterize them. Consideration is now given to the factors which make up this disequilibrium in each of the types of oscillations.

(1) PROGRESSIVE REASONINGS

The most general trait of progressive reasoning is the contrast observed between the level of notion and operations spontaneously effected by a subject and the real capacity for groupment and of adaptation to a precise situation. Here disequilibrium is nothing but a step in the consolidation of higher equilibrium. This consolidation is not always accomplished without either the intervention of an examiner, or the influence of intuitive or experimental relations, or simply the progressive familiarization with the new situation. Whatever the particular reasons which contribute to initial blockage, an interesting fact is that the child overcomes this blockage, thus proving that his reasoning is still in the process of development. If it is a question of a rupture in the equilibrium, it tends toward a superior equilibrium. Thought is still in formation, in this case, and it is thus distinct from cases of definitive retardation.

Such a declaration permits more favorable diagnosis than is possible in clear-cut cases of arrestation. The mobility of the mental processes is noteworthy, because the more acute forms of mental retardation are characterized precisely by the rigidity of their schemes. Mobility reveals therefore the constructive aspect of reasoning.

Will children capable of modifying their judgment and of developing their reasoning in a situation like that of the interview be equally capable of future development? Can they be judged superior to children classed as clearly retarded? Yes, provided two types of development are distinguished from each other: (1) the simple intermediate cases which, like normal children (but retarded in relation to them), are found in progression between two levels; in this case diagnosis is confused with determination of the genetic level, and (2) those whose progress is greater and who are apparently functioning beneath their real level. In both cases it is a question of children on the border between retardation and normal intelligence. One could hypothesize a more optimistic prognosis for progressives than for those who, though at the same level, are fixated. The reason is that any system of operations, as noted in Chapters 2 and 3, is not merely a system of interior norms, but is also a system of communication. Conditions of social exchange can be such that the child remains fixated at a point below his true level. These can be subjects who do not think for themselves and who by manipulation can be stimulated to reflection; they can also be subjects suffering from emotional inhibitions who do not immediately perform at their maximum because of inferiority feelings, fear of failure, etc.

Each of these progressive cases poses a purely intellectual problem and raises a host of questions concerning the relation of the level of logical reasoning with the ensemble of mental organization, and the exchanges of this organization with the social environment. These questions cannot be resolved by analysis of reasoning alone, but require its integration in an ensemble of diagnostic procedures.

(2) REGRESSIVE REASONINGS AND DECALAGES

Declines in levels of reasoning during the interview present an inverse problem. In "progressive" cases, a consolidation of an equilibrium of thought in formation could be observed, but here its disaggregation is present. A sort of involution corresponds to the evolutive process of the elaboration of the notions of conservation. Disequilibrium is manifest by a marked dissociation between the logical mechanism shown by the children's first responses and the real functioning of thought which appears in proportion to the collapse of the first thought processes. Frequently children and retarded adults momentarily affirm and even justify principles of conservation or of logical composition which surpass their capacity for rational and experimental elaboration. The first interventions of the examiner and encounters with perceptive obstacles often lead to deterioration and then to a series of judgments contradictory to the initial affirmations, which the examiner questions and which are progressively denied by the subjects. After having formulated operations showing an apparent equilibrium of thought, these retardates then revert to a natural incoherence of reasoning which unites all the characteristics of the egocentrism of infantile thought.

Once this increasing disequilibrium of thought is demonstrated, what are the conclusions to be drawn from it for the diagnosis of reasoning? It must be noted immediately that these are all cases of relatively grave intellectual deficiency and any attempt to place them on a developmental scale must take into account their final level of reasoning.

What permits such a diagnosis, and why are the higher responses not taken into account, since they alone seem to be perfectly coherent, at least at first? It can be supposed that when a subject seeks to answer questions only for his own justification, his responses correspond more closely to acquired logic than to personal elaboration. From the instruction that the subjects followed, as well as from their social environment, thought patterns have been formed which they try to apply in response to questions posed by the examiner.

It is known that the formal mechanisms assuring conservation— *e.g.*, when a collection of beads or a liquid is transferred from one container into another (Piaget and Szeminska 1952)—are linked by all the intermediate schemes to sensory-motor patterns which permit recovery of a disappeared object. A child of one or two years already knows that if two beads are transferred from one box into another they can be recovered from the second. Later he will realize the same is true for three or four beads. It is only the numerous or more complicated ensembles which will result in the idea of nonconservation. These intuitive notions of conservation at the time of a displacement or a transfer can yield to training education. For example when, in beginning arithmetic, these subjects learn to recover six tokens through counting, or to equalize two collections of dissimilar appearance but composed of the same number of elements, it is clear that they are trained to a sort of composition which leads them to handle certain schemes of conservation. It would then be these acquired modes of reasoning which would dictate their initial responses during the interview, while those that follow indicate their true level. In other words, in the beginning they would simply give an illusion of operatory thought, while prolonged conversation shows they are incapable of it.

To explain this type of thought an example is given of a retardate who was trained in a special class, and knew how to repeat $3 \times 2 = 6$, $3 \times 3 = 9$, $3 \times 4 = 12$, etc. From the point of view of knowledge, he seems superior to a six-year-old who does not know these formulae. If he has to compare four groups of three objects to three groups of four objects, it is quite possible that, after having admitted equality because of his learned operatory schematization, he then doubts real equivalence to the degree that he refuses to believe that twelve objects are still equivalent to twelve others, whether spread or put in a pile. Real thought would then be on a lower level than acquired thought.

In order to illustrate this point better, scholastically trained retardates are compared to mentally ill persons who change during the clinical examination, but whose real deterioration becomes evident when they are engaged in a more precise discussion. Just as these mentally ill have a residue of socially acquired habits, these retardates from fourteen to sixteen years, without being mentally ill, wear a sort of intellectual or scholastic mask which falls when they are examined through conversation.

These would be the reasons for the first affirmations encountered in the interview, and which seem, at first glance, to be at a level superior to these subject's real level.

Although the subjects' elaboration of these initial notions remains minimal, it is these elaborations which immediately show the deterioration. It is interesting to observe that exchange with another, such as occurs during the conversation, exerts an effect contrary to that produced in "progressive" cases. If in these last the examiner's questions and the articulation of experimental facts has helped to mobilize and to detach reasoning, this same procedure has an opposite effect in the "regressive" cases. As soon as the child is obliged to adapt his schematization to the precise and varied experimental facts, the schematization crumbles and gives place to a profound disadaptation. It is true that the more dexterous subjects try to withdraw from the examining situation by proposing all the possible solutions in order to avoid compromise, but it is easy to show their real incapacity for all the operatory coordination, and thus to grasp the true character of their reasoning.

Having witnessed such a deterioration of thought it is necessary to guard against results which, on the surface, are remarkable for their astuteness. Diagnosis of reasoning will often be less favorable than the estimations which might be based on certain tests, particularly on formal and verbal tests.

Moreover, as these types of retardates learn to practice automatic mechanisms which are applicable to all situations, and which spare them any real effort of adaptation, there is risk, particularly in older retardates, that they will maintain this practice. Prognosis for their reasoning is poor because fixation or even a future regression is possible.

(3)   TRUE OSCILLATORY REASONINGS

An analysis of progressive and regressive oscillations showed that both were dominated by a disequilibrium between a real capacity to execute the operations and the apparent result of reasoning. During the examination the subjects showing "progressive" oscillations were found to be superior to the level presumed on first impression, and those who were "retrogressive" were inferior. To explain the internal inconsistency of operatory reasoning with performance in the examination, it can be supposed that the operatory mechanism is influenced in various ways by the subject's intellectual exchange with his environment. Operatory thought is both individual and interindividual; consequently, all groupment implies an intellectual exchange with the environment. In retardates whose operatory mechanism is abnormal the system of exchange can be impaired; therefore it can be assumed that subjects showing progressive reasoning were inhibited by the intellectual environment. During the examining period, their thought inhibitions disappeared. On the other hand, the subjects who exhibited regressive reasoning may appear in other social situations to perform at a higher level than is found to exist in the examining situation. The "clinical" method of relatively free conversation would reestablish the equilibrium of reasoning. The conversation, which is in itself a form of intellectual exchange, would oblige the retardate to become aware of ideas and to accomplish logical operations which correspond to the maturity of his thought.

Clinical conversation was not able to eliminate the disequilibrium of reasoning in subjects presenting true oscillations. It would seem that the disappearance of inhibitions observed in progressive reasoning and the effect of disintegration observed in regressive reasoning compensated for each other in these cases. An explanation of the phenomenon of true oscillations in retardates follows.

Two groups of factors must first be distinguished:

(1) instability, a complex syndrome, which is based on organic conditioning
(2) intellectual and affective deficiencies resulting from environmental conditions

Study of abnormal oscillations emphasizes three types of deficient reasoning: anxiety, suggestibility, and hesitation. These deficiencies themselves do not denote retardation, but they influence thought processes.

The anxiety of not meeting the situation adequately or of being misjudged, whether observed in normal subjects or in those revealing a pathological disequilibrium, always results from difficulty in communicating intellectually and affectively with the environment. The anxious child who wrongly estimates his ability, either by feelings of inferiority or superiority, is unaware of his actual value. Self-evaluation depends on how a subject is judged by those around him, and on the value which he attaches to these people (his judges). The deficiencies of self-evaluation cause the disequilibrium of these exchanges.

The underestimation or overestimation by those who surround him can result in a mixture of insecurity or superiority which, in Wal.'s case (Observation 55), overshadowed his objective interests and impaired his mechanisms of reflection.

The disequilibrium of thought in suggestible retardates is conditioned by difficulties in interpersonal relations. Instead of objective adaptation to intellectual problems posed in the examining situation, the suggestible children related these problems to their emotional ones. Interest in the problems or the objective exchange with the examiner did not promote a search for solution; the search was for approval to satisfy his self-esteem. The method of clinical conversation does not meet this need because it abstains from agreeing or disagreeing with the child's answers. In the end the child states all possible solutions. Thus, the suggestible retardate demonstrates no more personal belief in one idea than in another, or at least his beliefs remain very broken down or changeable.

In subjects with hesitant reasoning, the same need for approval is so incorporated in their way of thinking that they cannot decide on any solution. To attribute this trouble to reasoning does not explain it. It isn't sufficient to analyze the intellectual development of the subject; it is also necessary to analyze his affective relationships, and to try to determine their cause. Both the progressive construction of the operatory mechanism and the development of satisfactory interpersonal relations comprises a totality whose factors are interdependent. If the intellectual aspect has been dissociated from the totality in order to permit a more complete analysis of it, the results lead to an acknowledgment of the interdependence of intellectual and affective aspects of behavior. This conception of action as a totality prevails in contemporary psychology.

(For Janet, "primary" action = intelligence and "secondary" action = affectivity; for Claparède, "techniques" and "affective finality"; and for Gestaltists, the "perceptive field" and the "total field," etc.)

b. Oscillations and the Concept of Operation

To explain abnormal oscillations of reasoning, consideration was given the intellectual exchange with the environment, but is this within the framework of the operation? Does the hypothesis of social influence contradict the central idea that reasoning evolves as a result of the maturation of the operatory mechanism of thought? Thus, the second question simply extends the first.

The development of operation includes an individual internal equilibrium, and a social aspect. Of what does the latter consist? Logical operations, as opposed to perceptions and representations, are means of exchange between the individual and the group. Operatory rules result from discussions with others and become norms which are imposed by social life. Thus, success or failure in communicating intellectually with the environment could increase or inhibit the individual capacity of the subject. Furthermore, the environment could provide the individual with ready-made schemes and indoctrinate him with certain thought habits. The greater the individual's capacity for personal expression the more he will resist environmental influence or will assimilate it in a personal way, so that environmental acquisitions become an integral part of his method of reasoning. On the other hand, the less personal his assimilation, the more the schemes and habits will be learned without alteration, and they will remain on the surface of individual thought.

However, if the environment has had deformative results on the individual, intellectual exchange by discussion with others and verification of individual perspectives are corrective factors of thought. In freeing himself from the egocentrism which dominates his action and intuition, the individual becomes capable of organizing and consolidating systems of actions and representations in the totality of operatory relations which make up the "group" or groupment. The formation of an equilibrium of interior norms and the exchange of these with others are closely related and depend on the process of intellectual maturation of the individual.

In normal subjects and in most retardates the two aspects of thought (interior coordination and social influence) are so interrelated that it is impossible to distinguish them at first glance, but a discordance is noted in those who oscillate. Intellectual exchange can inhibit certain subjects, thus falsifying or delaying their methods of reflection (in progressive cases). It can stimulate other individuals and give them false assurance by furnishing them with ready-made mechanisms (in regressive cases). It can also provoke a constant need for contact and for approval (cases of true oscillation), which has an emotional consequence on reasoning. Social environment can have a deforming influence on these subjects which can only complicate the primary trouble of deficiency.

Because of the discordance between internal coordination and environment, it is even more surprising when cases of disequilibrium manifest themselves in real oscillations between levels of normal development and not as phenomena which could no longer be considered within the framework of normal development.

As seen in Chapter 3, stages of fixation in retardates correspond to levels of reasoning which obey genetic laws. The analysis of oscillations confirms this law. In these cases of disequilibrium of reasoning, one expects to find exceptions and deviations in the operatory mechanism and in the law governing integration of notions. Why, even in subjects who oscillate, is it impossible to find the notion of conservation of weight without that of substance, that of volume before that of weight, etc.? It is because there is remarkable constancy in genetic succession.

In the discussion of the preceding diagnosis, reasoning was considered from the viewpoint of its genetic level and its operatory equilibrium. It was noted that difficulties of social exchange could combine with retardation in the development of logic. If the study is not limited to the diagnosis of reasoning (*i.e.*, to purely intellectual deficiencies), it becomes necessary to enumerate all possible intervening factors as well as those just discussed. Certainly the mechanisms of fixation, of attention, of reaction, of mental alertness, and others, are constantly present in the reasoning of the retardate, but these factors neither add to nor interfere with the intellectual construction. They are constantly present and inherent in the construction itself.

Until psychology achieves a detailed analysis of mental mechanisms, it is advantageous to describe them either from an intellectual point of view, or an affective point of view, or an organic point of view. Each description encompasses all factors, but each from its own viewpoint. These diverse, but complete, descriptions are parallel to one another because of the mental totality referred to above.

Whatever the relative importance of the operatory mechanism, it is a necessary factor which must be known both as an internal equilibrium and as a social exchange. If difficulties in communicating are either directly or indirectly the cause of oscillations (because social contact and rapidity of development are influenced by affective and constitutional factors), it is not a problem that can be solved today. All factors are interdependent, and the sector chosen for study is extricated from this totality, a sector which can be said to be determined by one's point of view (or interest). The obtained results can be integrated into the complete diagnosis. The integration of partial factors into a clinical picture of retardation will permit a more precise description of the symptoms.

5. Conclusions

A factual analysis of the experiments has been presented in Chapters 2 to 4. General questions raised in Chapter 1 will be reconsidered now, and facts which provide answers will be presented. Three problems in particular will be discussed in terms of the obtained results: the genetic diagnosis of reasoning, the clinical indices of mental retardation, and, finally, the contributions of the psychology of pathological reasoning to the theory of mental development.

1. The Genetic Diagnosis of Reasoning

For the first problem, the genetic diagnosis of reasoning, the method of operatory analysis makes possible a conception of logical operations which are in opposition to a certain number of current ideas which frequently are admitted without discussion. These concern the nature of reasoning and its function in everyday mental life. The usual conception that has distorted most tests of reasoning has two characteristics: (1) it considers logical reasoning as a special aptitude, as a sort of particular faculty or a subfaculty of intelligence; (2) the conception is atomistic. According to the opposite conception, the operations constitute the organs or general instruments of mental equilibrium considered as a whole. These operations are interdependent.

The classical conception, which is presently opposed, is the result of prejudices of logic against which psychology has taken a stand. It is also the result of inverse prejudices which the psychology of action has admitted, believing that in doing so it was becoming free of the first set of prejudices.

As everyone knows, the logic of Aristotle is largely a matter of grammar, *i.e.,* essentially, the creator of logic analyzed the forms of speech, giving a limiting and clear direction to the multisecular works of the logician. This tradition of verbal logic has led to the neglect of the study of operations as such. Attention has been directed exclusively to a classification and a description of the results, both of which necessarily took on an atomistic form. Even logistics, or the algebra of logic (which renovated the Aristotelian style) studied classes, relations, and propositions, separately, as though it were a question of independent unities and not of total operatory systems (groupments).

When psychologists sought to formulate a psychology of intelligence based on experiments and concrete observation, and no longer limited themselves to repeating what the manuals of logic said about the concept, about judgment, and about the syllogism, they adopted an opposite position. They sought to show in thought a prolongation or an interiorization of action, and in reasoning a "mental experiment" or an empirical search for solutions which have become an interior production of hypotheses. Logic, from the psychological point of view, was reduced to a modest position; it became nothing but a small part of intelligent activities, *i.e.,* that which insures the control and the well-regulated formulation of notions. Instead of realizing that this function of equilibrium concerned the whole of intelligence, and that the operation touches on every action potentially reversible, psychologists continued to believe that this was the only logic possible. They restricted as far as possible the role of verbal logic and limited themselves in their diagnosis of reasoning to the use of tests of definitions, syllogisms, and verbal reasonings of every kind, but without definite links with each other. Their model was the grammatical atomism of the logicians.

The writer concurs with Piaget in thinking that if intelligence is a mental adaptation to new situations (according to the definition of Claparède), and if all the transitions insure the continuity from action to thought (habit, sensory-motor intelligence, and conceptual intelligence), then the domain of the operation is the whole field of intelligence in the widest sense of the word. In fact, the operation is contained as a seed in sensory-motor intelligence, and therefore in perception and habit themselves, and mental or interiorized operation is only a finishing point of the action of intelligence in general. A logical operation is only an action which has become reversible. Reasoning, or the coordination of operations, is the form of a balance to which the whole of intelligence is oriented.

It follows that if the logicians where wrong in identifying reason with verbal thought by exaggerating the importance of the latter, the psychologists were wrong when, in reducing verbal thought to its correct proportions, they continued to identify logic with this verbal thought, and therefore limited further the part played by reasoning. Moreover, if operatory reasoning is the form of equilibrium that governs all mental coordinations—and Piaget's work tends to verify this theory—then logical operations do not appear to be suitably separable from each other for study in an isolated or atomistic state. Operations constitute wholes, or groupments, whose formation must be followed from the sensory-motor action to abstract thought. It is also necessary to study this formation as a system of totalities. For this reason, the experiments used in this study start with action, but end with formal systematization.

If operatory reasoning does govern mental coordinations, the different experiments used in this present study of reasoning, while unlinked to each other in the form in which they are presented, can serve as a point of departure for an operatory analysis of the groupments they are related to respectively. Definition tests, for example, refer in reality to groupments of addition or multiplication of classes. The absurd sentences refer to many kinds of groupments of relationships, and the tests of deduction, using the model of the syllogism, are related to "nested" classes, etc.

To illustrate this, a review will be made of some well-known tests, the purpose of which is the diagnosis of reasoning.

a. The Definitions

These have become an integral part of most tests of reasoning and occur also in certain tests designed to evaluate the global level. Binet attributed a diagnostic value to them when he asked young children questions such as "What is a fork, a table, a mother?" or older children, "What is charity or justice?" or even when he asked adults to define abstract notions such as "laziness and idleness." In the same way, comparisons between remembered objects—for example, between "a fly" and "a bee," or the distinctions between "a king" and "the president of the Republic"—imply at any rate, some form of definition (Stern 1928).

It is interesting to study certain definitions in relation to the diagnosis of reasoning, on condition that they are used only as a point of departure for a genetic analysis of the operations they require. The definitions were studied above all from the viewpoint of a conceptual and verbal determination, *i.e.*, from that of the psychological mode of reasoning which they embrace. They remain, however, unrelated and atomistic.

Proceeding in an empirical fashion, Binet and Stern, with Gregor and Roloff among others, drew up lists of words seriated according to the correct definitions obtained at various age levels. It was noticed that abstract notions were understood only fairly late. Before eleven years of age the child usually can define only concrete words; when he is twelve or thirteen semiabstract notions of a political or social nature, such as "law," "order," "money," are accessible to him. It is only from thirteen or fourteen years on that logical or ethical concepts are correctly defined.

How should this picture be interpreted? Can the incapacity to define abstract words before the age of eleven or twelve indicate without doubt the level of comprehension of the notions? Let us suppose that a boy of ten finds it difficult to define the notions "courage" or laziness"; should we therefore refuse to admit that he has a precise and lively idea of these notions, or should we admit that he cannot describe them logically? In this case, should we consider him intellectually inferior to another child who at the same age gives a schematic definition of these notions? It is evident that the identification of a conceptual and verbal formalism with the level and quality of intelligence is fortuitous. Even at the levels where children try to give abstract definitions, Stern had observed as many individuals giving a concrete type of definition for an illustration as those giving an abstract definition, without being able to attribute a definite superiority to one or the other of these types. It would appear that if a person limits himself to verbal definitions, without studying the psychological mechanism of which they are the result, it is difficult to distinguish the reasoning behind all the automatisms which embrace it.

Apart from the seriation of correct definitions according to age, the evolution of their psychological structure has also been studied. There

is a current observation whose clinical importance was first emphasized by Binet (1903): the child begins by giving definitions based on
use and then on descriptions, before he is capable of formal definitions.
In other words, an object is first linked by the subject to his egocentric activity before being classed among things and before being
characterized by a system of concepts. This order of succession of
the three types of definitions indicates without doubt an aspect of
the evolution of thought. Can one go further and consider these
general stages in each particular case as levels of reasoning? Can a
type of definition independent of its content be used as a point of
reference for mental diagnosis? This is certainly the underlying idea
in the tests of definition. Such a generalization seems to encounter a
real difficulty, that of time lag. In fact, according to the content of the
definitions, it is possible for the same child to define, for example, a
mother as "a woman who has children," giving thus a generic term,
but in defining a bee he will say "it makes honey," remaining thus in
the definition-by-use stage. In the same way one finds adults perfectly
capable of logically defining a familiar object, but who encounter,
without exception, difficulties when they are asked to define a zoo-
logical species in any other way than by simple description, or even
to define an organ (an eye "is for seeing") in any way other than by
usage. Therefore, a type of definition has significance only in its precise
context, and all these notions do not lend themselves equally to an
analysis of reasoning.

However, certain notions can provide us with interesting indications
on the functioning of childish logic, because they rest on an operatory
construction. The notions of "brother," or "left," and "right," of
which Piaget has made a genetic analysis, are recalled (Piaget 1928a).
The definition of the notion of brother is first confused with that of
boy, then later placed in a relationship with the family, and finally
around nine years is defined as a reciprocal relationship. In the same
way, the notions of left and right are freed from the egocentric point
of view the moment the child is capable of accomplishing a converse
operation. Now, to follow closely in a clinical conversation the elaboration of inverse operations on which these two notions depend, and
to show the difficulties which the children encounter makes it possible
to analyze the mechanism of thought in action, and thus to better the
simple graduation of statistical results. Rather than have him reason

on acquired notions, it would perhaps be perferable to make the child conscious of, and to systematize, the concrete operations which can be detected in the experimentation and observation as such.

b. Problems of Syllogisms and of Mathematical Reasoning

If in the tests of verbal definition the difficulty of dissociating the role of language from that of reasoning exists, it might be expected that logical or mathematical problems which require effort in deduction arise more directly from the functioning of thought. Examined closely, these tests often constitute either thorny problems of logic, constructed on the model of the syllogism, or problems of arithmetic contained by a more or less artificial context.

Here, for example, is a sample of the problems of reasoning drawn from the tests of Burt (1919), whose strange formulation is mentioned by Stern (1928): "In hot climates, one finds aloes and rubber; heather and herbs only grow in cold countries; herbs and aloes need a dry soil; on the Amazon it is hot and wet; which of these plants does one find growing there?" It would be difficult to find a better way of confusing the child. If he is not able to solve such a problem, how is it possible to dissociate the operatory difficulties arising out of the manipulation of the addition of classes, from the surprise he feels when confronted with such a strange problem?

The creators of these tests, in their search for precision, appear to have lost from view the functional aspects which they rightly demanded in their criticism of the traditional school. Even if one admits that, in certain cases, the child might be interested in such mental gymnastics and might make a real adaptive effort, however, being able to solve the problem, what does this reveal? That he is incapable of deduction? Evidently not, since he is perhaps capable of composing equalities on the basis of $A = B$, $B = C$, therefore $A = C$ when it is a case of reasoning in the presence of concrete objects (as shown in the experiment with the bars), and that it is accomplished more easily if physical manipulation is possible. His failure does not prove anything more than his incapacity to construct logical composition on certain fictitious givens. Now, such a difficulty can be interesting after the level of eleven to twelve years of age (age of formal reasoning), but it is of no significance before this. Even after eleven or twelve years it is still necessary to dissociate reasoning as such from the artifices particular to its verbal formulation.

Here again is an example of a false operatory problem: everyone knows Terman's famous test for practical intelligence: the "pail test" (Terman 1919). It is presented as a test for superior adults and depends on a system in which the parts are incorporated into each other and into the whole accompanied by an elementary system of measurement. The solution to this problem, which is easy for a subject who has some scholastic training, is difficult without this training, but for reasons which have nothing to do with the operatory mechanism of intelligence. The author met a professor of higher mathematics who encountered difficulty for some moments when these questions were put to him. As far as the child is concerned, a problem like this one deserves all the objections which the psychologists made to a certain conception of scholastic work when it is not functional, but proceeds by verbal automatisms. If, instead of presenting these pails by speech, actual pails and liquids are presented to the child (Piaget and Szeminska 1952), the development of an entire operatory mechanism (which is a reminder of the construction of the different notions of conservation) is observed. It is only in relation to the knowledge of such a genetic development, and by situating it in a context of experimentation and true deduction, that the pail test acquires a diagnostic significance.

c. Absurd Sentences

To think logically is to obey the principle of noncontradiction. The absurd phrases, which Binet, Pieron, Ballard, and Claparède (Claparède and Schuler 1917) have developed as diagnostic tests, show contradictions between propositions.

The contradictions can be of different kinds. The absurd sentences used by E. Claparède and Mme. A. Leuzinger-Schuler (1917) are based either on material impossibilities or false estimations, or else on contradictions in terms, erroneous deductions, or errors of reasoning. They are graduated according to achievement by age. Claparède emphasizes that these achievements are based on an empirical classification which should be verified by genetic analysis.

Research conducted in collaboration with Rennes at l'Institute de la Science de l'Education on the clinical analysis of absurd sentences disclosed that they did not correspond to a simple and clearly determined operation, but to all sorts of factors which varied a great deal according to the propositions involved. First of all, consciousness of material impossibilities is not always comparable to consciousness of logical contradictions. Ignorance of physical laws which prevent the subject from perceiving the inherent contradiction has not necessarily the same clinical significance as the discovery present in deduction which is formal thought. It is indispensable to analyze in advance all the notions on which the absurdity is based.

To perceive the incompatibility of the notions involved requires a capacity for formal and purely logical deduction on the part of the child. Below the level at which this is possible (eleven to twelve years) a child seeks to verify empirically each particular judgment of which the absurdity is composed, because he is unable to compare imaginary facts and to reason with hypotheses. If one wishes to use a complex test such as the absurd sentences as a diagnosis of reasoning, it is well to undertake a psychological analysis not only of the facts implied, but also of the different forms of logical reasoning, to distinguish carefully two kinds of factors (the contents of the notions and the formal structure of reasoning).

The following absurd sentence is given as an example of the first type: "This road is steeper when you go up it than when you came down." Far from appearing to children of all ages as a formal contradiction independent of its contents, such a proposition necessitates a precise understanding of the reversibility of the displacements on an inclined plane, and this understanding rests on a previous entire operatory construction. To evaluate the different answers given to the absurd sentence at different levels of mental development, it becomes necessary to understand the construction of the ideas of geometry which the child might possess; so far, this is an area which has been little explored.

As an example of the second type, the following famous sentence of Binet is given (Binet and Simon 1917): "I have three brothers, Paul, Ernest, and me." The answers given to this sentence are difficult to evaluate. Descoeudres (1917) has assembled judgments by different people on the ambiguous response, "a brother is missing." Half of these people were of the opinion that this answer was correct; the other half judged it false. The analysis of the logic of symmetrical relations has shown to what extent these answers depend on a progressive construction (Piaget 1928a).

d. Seriation Tests

By contrast, interesting tests have been developed which require real operatory construction on the part of the child. However, they do not take account of the character of this logical groupment and are used simply as question of perception. Binet's test of the ordering of five weights, which requires the intelligence of a ten-year-old, is cited as an illustration. In his commentary in *La Mesure du développement de l'intelligence* (1917) he states "in fact the weighing method used by the child must not affect our conclusions. Only the result of this weighing is important, the estimation of the differences (Binet and Simon 1917: 21). Such an ordering requires the use of the operations of asymmetrical relationships. Other work (Piaget and Inhelder 1941) has shown (and the results coincide with the ages given by Binet) that the operatory seriation of the five weights is only the end of a development whose first stage is characterized by the absence of composition. This is due to a lack of any judgment of relationships. The second stage is characterized by an empirical seriation and by unrelated pairing. Therefore, the child below nine or ten is incapable of correctly seriating several weights. It is not through a lack of perceptive discrimination, but it is because the child is younger or retarded in his mental development and cannot construct the groupment of asymmetrical relationships because of his insufficiency in operatory logic.

The diagnosis of reasoning based on formal tests of the kind described above appears to have made two opposite types of errors: either too much attention has been given to a particular or peripheral trait of thought, as though reasoning could be dissociated from all its experimental contents, or else highly complex problems have been used with the intention of drawing from them unequivocal indices concerning the level and functioning of reasoning. Generally, the authors of these tests imagined reasoning as a pure faculty, a structure emptied of its content, a mold into which anything could be poured. In tests of this type, when a child is asked to define concepts, to combine them in a deductive fashion or to extricate their internal contradictions, previously completed concepts are shown, but the interplay of operations required to build them is not revealed. Verbal formalism is examined while the active elaboration of the instruments of logic escapes analysis.

Of course, such a static and nonfunctional conception of reason is not current in the psychology of reasoning. It is paradoxical, however, that it reappears each time measure and estimation of thought is required, *i.e.,* every time it is more important to apply measure than to understand thought. It is noteworthy that in these authors a large gap remains between the finesse of their theory of the psychology of intelligence and the clumsiness of their methods of measurement. They saw its insufficiency in thought and accepted the fact that it was defective in practice.

e. Clinical Experiments of Operatory Logic

The few experiments discussed in this work as samples of an instrument for the analysis of the diagnosis of reasoning appear as extensions of a previous genetic analysis of mental operations. As mentioned in the beginning of this chapter, these experiments arise from a very different conception of reasoning, whose differential characteristics will be discussed. There is opposition between the logic of propositions and that of operations; while the first is only a general form and applies to any content, the second consists of the elaboration of a specific content. The logic of propositions insures formal coherence, but only in accordance with the rules of implication and incompatibility. It assumes that these notions already have been constructed and the operations achieved, *i.e.,* they have to be there before they can be used. By contrast, operatory logic works directly on the givens of perception and intuition; it articulates or coordinates all these relations in a closed system as it extends or elaborates them. At all times the operatory logic is under the influence of the particular experiment itself. To advance the logic of propositions as the prototype of all logic means to erect a watertight barrier between the functioning of gnostic intelligence and its development (such as in the intuitive and sensory-motor elaborations). In a word, it is a barrier between reasoning and experience. If one does not respect this functional continuity of intelligence with the integration of successive structures, it is difficult, from the point of view of diagnosis, to attribute a psychological and clinical significance to a failure or a success in problems of formal logic.

To establish clinical signs of abnormal reasoning it must be possible to grasp not only a complete structure of thought but also its functioning. To penetrate to this functioning of thought means to follow the norms of its construction in their elaboration. The operation is the most general element in this construction, and is defined by an action which has become reversible. The operation is the active element of thought whose roots lie in the coordination of practical schemes. For example, between the act of assembling the elements in a pile and that of uniting them in thought into a totality, there is no opposition, but continuity on successive levels. The logical operation does not differ from the sensory-motor operation in anything but its greater mobility and its reversibility, *i.e.*, in the possibility of coordinating successive actions through reflection into a single network. Operatory logic, which has been taken as the model of reasoning against which the abnormal phenomena of retardation will be measured, constitutes, therefore, a stage or rather a period (divided into several stages). It is a particularly important period in intellectual development because it is linked by all kinds of transitions to inferior as well as to superior levels, to sensory-motor operations as well as to the level of formal reasoning.

When one wants to provoke such an operatory construction in the subject's minds in order to determine the level of his reasoning and to discern the paranormal difficulties particular to retardation, two methodological conditions must be observed: (1) the test must be functional, *i.e.*, it must awaken a real need for adaptation in the subject, and must raise a problem whose solution requires a whole groupment, and (2) a clinical method must be used, as it is the only method which permits an "on-the-spot" analysis of the unfolding of logical processes.

(1) The choice of experiments. Although every problem of reasoning can lead to an operatory analysis of thought, it is advantageous to bypass the study of verbal notions and engage the child in actual experimentation, to give him concrete materials, to make him act or reflect on his actions, and thus to incite the construction of these notions as much by experimental observations as by appropriate questions. The notions that seem most suitable for operatory analysis of reasoning are the principles of conservation, because they are always based on groupments of logical operations or on mathematical groups. In fact, the physical world, as it appears, is nothing but a flood of irreversible changes. In order for thought to orient in space and in time it needs points of reference, *i.e.,* permanent systems. These systems, which sooner or later impose, with a feeling of necessity, some principles of conservation on the subject's mind—as discussed in relation to material quantities (Piaget and Inhelder 1941)—are constructed progressively by the interaction of deduction and experience. This elaboration occurs between the child's fourth and twelfth years. There are several notions of mathematical and physical conservation which the child elaborates: for example, the notions of "number," "time," and "space." Among these, the development of material quantities appears to give a particularly precise picture of the stage of development. Each operatory level is made upon new groupments, while the notions of conservation of substance, weight, and volume are integrated following an order of genetic construction. The experiment of the deformations of the clay ball makes it possible for the examiner to follow this elaboration of successive groupments. The experiment concerning the dissolution of sugar also shows the interdependence of deductive reasoning and the experimental interpretation of intuitive facts. Finally, the composition of the bars as a control reveals the logical mechanism of these same groupments.

(2) The clinical method. For such tests to be of functional value, as Claparède used the term, it is necessary to present them clinically. Our experiments have nothing in common with tests, but tend to be an exchange of views, a relatively unstructured conversation about experiments of elementary physics which arouse the child's curiosity. In most tests the child, once given the instructions, finds himself in front of problems to be solved. In our method the examiner is in some way part of the experiment. When it is a question of behavior and particularly of practical intelligence, the observation of different phases of the coordination of sensory-motor schemes, in relation to certain material, can be sufficient to show certain interesting clinical indices. As soon as one goes from the level of action to that of reflective intelligence, the subject's contact with the facts of the experiment must be accompanied by interindividual exchange. The elaboration of the rational notions necessitates a discussion which, at this level of development, cannot be entirely interiorized. Questions, objections, and encouragements that stimulate experimental observation and control are used to make the child conscious of the notions and of the mental attitudes which often remain implicit. The need he has to motivate and to formulate his ideas and beliefs tends to make his system of thought coherent. If, however, difficulties and failures of deduction persist, these will often be the indices of an incapacity for operatory logic.

The clinical method requires careful practice, and the examiner must not suggest to the child a direction of thought which is not his own, nor naïvely attribute the same value to all he says.

To proceed clinically means to rid oneself of any realistic attitude, and to interpret the facts as relative signs. It is necessary to know how to organize an experiment, how to pose the problem and conduct the conversation in such a way as to be able to decide between hypotheses. It is equally necessary to observe any fact which might depart from or contradict preconceived patterns of behavior. Finally, the examiner must adapt himself to each case in order to stimulate the child, follow the lines of his thought, and at the same time, direct it toward crucial points. The techniques of clinical conversation cannot be learned overnight; long preparation is required. This is perhaps the principal obstacle to using these experiments for operatory diagnosis. While everyone admits that a doctor needs several years of theoretical and clinical preparation before he is ready to examine a patient, one frequently considers superfluous an equivalent preparation in applied psychology, as if it were easier to determine the functioning and the structures of mental organization than to examine a physical organism.

2. Clincial Indices of Mental Deficiency

Having discussed the conception of logic on which these examinations are based, as well as the principles of the clinical method, which permits an operatory analysis of thought, it is now fitting to discuss what contribution to the interpretation of reasoning the facts as set forth in Chapters 2 to 4 can make to the area of mental deficiency.

There has been no effort to systematize the signs of mental deficiency nor to establish a complete clinical picture of deficient thought. To do this would require a multidimensional description of mental functions, a study of the effects of deficiency on each one of these functions, and the establishment of the laws governing their network in order to systematize their exact symptoms by progressive cross sections. If it is hoped that the studies of pathological psychology will make it possible to provide a precise syndrome of mental deficiency, and thus to improve on the usual description of the phenomena of oligophrenia based on the simple absence or insufficiency of normal capacities, it is suitable at this point to begin by a clinical analysis of each one of these different mental functions and of their particular structures.

Such an analysis requires a comparison with normal processes—in other words, identification and differentiation with a developmental model. It is for this reason that this work approached first a clearly defined problem, namely, in the paranormal manifestations of deficient reasoning, does an operatory kernel survive which is common to all thought? If this is the case, can the operatory mechanisms be compared to stages of reasoning as they have been described in previous genetic studies? Finally, does the fact of situating a deficient child at a given level of reasoning imply a certain prognosis concerning his ulterior development or his continued arrestation at the observed level?

If, for certain psychologists who usually describe deficiency as a simple and global retardation of mental development, to raise such a problem is a truism, for others, the comparison of a pathological (and therefore irreducible) mental state with that of a normal child during development seems rash. Now, operatory analysis of reasoning in young retardates appears to be suitable ground for examining whatever is correct in each of the two interpretations. How do the processes of reasoning studied in the previous chapters join the steps of operatory construction, and in what respect do their crystallizations, which take place either before this is complete or in a paranormal way, differ from this operatory construction? Discussion of this serves as a conclusion to this work.

Three groups of facts are relevant:

1. The striking and quasi-total analogy between the reasoning of a group of subjects (who differed markedly from each other in most of their other reactions) and the egocentric mentality of young children.

2. The parallelism in the process of construction and of the integration of the notions of conservation in the normal and the abnormal child, and the fixations which occur midway and prevent the final equilibration of thought.

3. The paranormal oscillations between different levels of construction and the effect of social exchange on the fragility of intellectual operations in the mentally deficient.

In discussing the first point, a type of reasoning perfectly homogeneous and identical to that of young normal children at a prelogical stage was found in certain retardates (some were slightly retarded, and some functioned at the upper limits of imbecility). They differed from each other in age, academic achievement, practical training and general behavior. The convergence of their beliefs in the variation of the quantity of substance when a deformation or a division of the clay ball was executed will be remembered, as will their unusual idea of the way in which dissolved sugar ceased to exist, and their refusal to consider the brass bar as identical to itself in the course of composition.

Not only the content of their thought, but the structure of their reasoning corresponds exactly to that which characterizes childish egocentrism. If the abnormal children who were classified in the first stage are unable to attribute a quantitative permanence to substance and therefore to weight and volume, all these subjects—and their motivations and justifications clearly prove this—are incapable of logical operations (or in this particular case of "physical" operations) which constitute the groupment necessary for the construction of this first invariant.

Finally, the assimilation of intuitive and experimental facts typical of these retardates is governed by what has been noticed previously as a dominant trait of the method of induction in normal children below seven years of age. Instead of submitting to experimental observations, the retardate of this level, just like the young child, deforms reality through the use of previously established schemes of prediction, and remains thus impermeable to what it can teach him.

The similarity of the different traits discussed leaves no room for doubt as to the structural identity of the intellectual reactions between the retardates and the young normal children from four to seven years whose performances during these experiments were studied previously. Therefore it appears legitimate to attribute to both a common mentality as far as their operatory reasoning is concerned. Such a conclusion appears interesting because it renovates the interpretation of debility. Instead of describing the reasoning of these oligophrenics in an entirely negative way, it is possible to attribute to them a mentality or system of thought whose function, in the evolution of mental life, is recognized in a "positive" way. When the retardate, like the normal child, is unable to reason by operations, his thought is not necessarily chaotic. In the absence of a groupment, mental activity does not disintegrate, but is centralized around an "antagonistic" pole, which is that of individual activity, to the extent to which this opposes itself to the activity of reason. The child's mentality is characterized by the predominance of perception over intellectual elaboration, or of the subjective over the objective; in a word, it is exactly the mentality which Piaget called the egocentrism of childish reasoning.

One objection arises immediately: does the fact of attributing to these abnormal persons, between ten and twenty or more years of age, a reasoning similar to that of the young preschool child mean that their mental organization is reduced to a level which hardly surpasses that of a six- or seven-year-old? Is this saying that all their psychic functions are similar to those of small children and thus overlooking their past and future development? Evidently not, and if the interpretation of deficiency as a retardation or arrestation at an inferior level of development is correct, insofar as it corresponds to the normal development of a particular function such as operatory reasoning, the clinical observation of the behavior of the same abnormal children shows how such a simple reduction is made difficult by the surprising variety of the paranormal manifestations. The few notes in each case history give only a limited and incomplete idea of the variety of subjects examined. The discovery of the same egocentric mentality and impermeability to operations in certain retardates and young children does not mean that varying types of paranormal phenomena, which are constantly present, are not noticed. These phenomena strongly influenced the general behavior of our subjects, and to some extent their behavior in the experimental situation. Some were interested in the test from the beginning, while others needed to be stimulated to reflection; some were verbose while others expressed themselves in monosyllables; some had fluctuations of attitude and attention, while others perseverated. If it is possible, in spite of this diversity of behavior, to describe a common method of reasoning it is because the choice of the tests and the method permit the discovery of a functional kernel of thought among other mental manifestations. The problems of conservation activate the functioning of intelligence, independently of the contingencies due to verbal and memory acquisitions, and in particular to training at school. The method of exchange by conversation stimulates and provokes the interest of the subject and encourages him to expend his maximum intellectual ability. However, if the analogy between the mentality of certain retardates and that of a child at the prelogical stage is a striking one, it is still more striking when there is a beginning of operatory construction followed by an arrestation before its completion! A discussion of this follows.

It is false to pretend that all retardates, as one might have expected, remain permanently at a stage inferior to the notions of conservation (*i.e.,* absence of conservation). On the contrary, it has been seen that the majority of subjects examined surpass this level and arrive at the conservation of substance or even that of weight, without achieving that of volume, which implies achievement of all the others, and without being able to generalize the compositions of equivalence to any intuitive content. These partial constructions—and they are of interest for the diagnosis as well as for the theory of development on which they are based—far from taking the form of uncoordinated judgments, become crystallized into clearly defined stages, each one being characterized by a definite groupment of the relations of substance or of weight. If the retardates are unable to arrive at Stage IV (construction of volume), it is because their reasoning processes are still at the second stage and impregnated with intuitive elements which tend to take the place of reasoning. The retardates arrive at concrete operations during the third stage, but do not attain formal operations (Stage IV).

Two questions must be discussed in this context:

1. To what extent is it legitimate to believe that the retardate who affirms the conservation of substance is using a real operatory construction, and is not simply influenced by unconscious suggestions?

2. By what right is intellectual superiority attributed to the subjects who achieve the conservation of weight over those who achieve only that of substance?

Because of the docility and suggestibility of certain retardates, it could be asked whether the subjects performing at the second and third stages fail to achieve the notions of conservation because they are more influenced by intellectual exchange and by the facts of the experiment, or whether they are more suggestible than others who remain impermeable to this clinical method for reasons other than intellectual superiority? Does our method of relatively unstructured conversation risk imposing on the subjects, who lack personal opinions, an idea which they would not have discovered alone? Do not the correct answers bear witness to a need for approval rather than an operatory elaboration? The clinician must be aware of these objections at all times. When it is a question of problems whose solutions require certain knowledge and memory, it is often difficult to dissociate the part played by suggestibility, and that of the personal activity of the subject. If one studies the operatory problems, for example conservation, there is a clinical sign which is most capable of revealing a sui generis construction: the feeling of logical evidence and interior certitude with which the subject affirms conservation. This certitude often manifests itself by the profound surprise shown by the subject when he is asked to justify his affirmation. Moreover, the very fact that this certitude remains limited to a partial construction and cannot be generalized to any intuitive contents appears to confirm the hypothesis that there exists in certain retardates a rational, but partial and unachieved, elaboration.

The second question has yet to be answered; how can it be proved, for example, that a retardate who knows that the weight of any substance remains constant has acquired an intellectual maturity superior to the child who believes only in conservation of substance, after the substance has been submitted to one or more transformations? It must first be remembered that the normal child has been observed throughout a perfectly regular genetic succession during which he arrives at the conservation of substance before that of weight, and conservation of weight before that of volume. This takes place according to a law of progressive differentiation of these notions. It would be reasonable to expect to find exceptions, i.e., inversions in the order of acquisition in the case of retardates, as it is often possible to find coexisting in their thought, notions which belong to very different levels. As shown throughout Chapter 3, the normal genetic progression of the principles of conservation continues to take place in the slow development of a retardate. There is a cardinal reason for this: the principles of conservation do not follow each other by superposition alone, but integrate themselves psychologically by logical implication with the others. To affirm the conservation of weight always implies belief in the constant quantity of substance because the weight presupposes the material substratum which is the substance-quantity.

The constant order of such an integration appears to make possible a comparison between the reasonings of our subjects and a developmental scale, and the admission that, within the limits of deficiency, intermediate levels of intellectual construction exist. These levels correspond to the operatory stages of normal development. One can conclude that the retardate follows the same evolutive process as the normal child, but does it slowly and with precocious fixations, and without ever achieving final equilibrium. His reasoning is coherent to the extent to which it is still mobile and progressing, but is, nonetheless, in a state of unstable equilibrium because it is arrested sooner or later at an intermediate level, a level which does not allow him to enlarge and generalize the operatory construction beyond concrete facts.

If in the majority of cases mental deficiency manifests itself as a fixation at intermediate levels of operatory construction, some subjects (see Chapter 4) have intellectual reactions which make it possible to situate them at a definite level, because they oscillate between successive systems of thought. Although these oscillations obey the same laws of operatory construction and integration as the notions involved, they differ distinctly from the fixations or arrestations by the fragility of their thought mechanism. Three sorts of oscillations may be distinguished (progressive, retrogressive, and true oscillations), each of which raises particular problems for diagnosis and prognosis, as well as for the determining of operatory equilibrium. The first type (who work below their maximum operatory efficiency at the beginning of the examination, and consolidate their system of thought during conversation) give some promise for future development. The second type, who are reduced by clinical analysis to their real level, which is often well below what verbal appearances first suggest, seem to have very little chance of progressing further. Those children who really oscillate cannot be situated at a definite level, and show by this fact that their thought is disequilibrated in a more complex way. In order to formulate a prognosis of their reasoning it is necessary to study the influence of the extra-intellectual factors which break down the operatory system itself.

Subjects who present oscillations in their reasoning have shown that, apart from the internal and individual aspect of thought (which consists in the groupment of the operations), it is well to consider an aspect of equilibrium which is interindividual and interoperational. The relations which an individual has with his environment can disturb his system of thought. These relationships can cause a loss of self-esteem, and reduce the subject's performance to a level below his real potential. Alternatively, they can give him an exaggerated idea of the importance of his opinions, and render his intellectual processes imprecise. Although the clinical interrogation (as seen in Chapter 4) manages, in a certain number of cases, to reestablish, at least momentarily, intellectual equilibrium and thus situate the reasoning of the retardate at a corresponding genetic level, there are extra-intellectual factors which can influence the operatory mechanisms to the point of destroying their internal coherence.

This fact raises an interesting problem in the study of the efficiency of reasoning. Why do emotional factors, social constraints, and all kinds of constitutional instabilities (*e.g.,* fluctuations in mental and motor tonus) have such a striking repercussion on the operatory equilibrium of certain retardates? Because they are momentary, these same factors have hardly any effect on a normally developed logical structure. The oscillations are not entirely irreducible phenomena, but are the exaggeration of the fluctuations met with in certain normal subjects. For example, the proportion here is the same as between amnesia and simple distraction. Although the child with normal intelligence may be able to consolidate his thought quickly when faced with a purely intellectual problem and to put aside factors which would otherwise disturb his behavior, the retardate cannot react in the same way. He lacks both the stability and the mobility of thought. His mental level, which reflects very slow maturation, remains fragile.

The normal child, who goes through several successive stages in the course of a few years, detaches himself easily from each preceding level, but the retardate goes through the same development at a much slower rate. Even when he has attained a superior level, his thought bears the imprint of a system of reasoning he has just outgrown. If he happens to be troubled in his intellectual adaptation, he runs a much greater risk than the normal child of hesitating between two systems of thought, which therefore coexist. This hesitation shows itself by the oscillations between the two operatory levels. However, these oscillations are still within the framework of the normal development of operatory construction. This observation concurs with what has been noticed thus far concerning the dominant traits of deficiency. In the normal child, these three integrated levels are generally separated by intervals which are characterized by a diminishing tempo. Between the conservation of weight and that of substance the time lag is very small (the average is two years), while the time lag between the acquisition of the conservation of substance and that of the notion of the object in general is about six years. Moreover, there is less time between the discovery of the conservation of volume and of weight (approximately one year) than between the conservation of weight and the conservation of substance.

The normal child's passage from one level of equilibrium to the following one is more and more rapid (on the average, six, two, and one years respectively). This is explained by the increasing mobility of operatory thought. On the contrary, in retardates there is a gradual slowing down, or in some cases a permanent state of stagnation.

These notions of the speed of development, of tempo, or of mobility in the language suggested by operatory analysis appear to be able to replace the static notion of intellectual quotient suggested by the test method. In fact, the entire question of prognosis, which will be discussed later, is based on a sort of extrapolation of the curve of speed of this development.

From a theoretical point of view, there is a way of interpreting through these notions the general intellectual equilibrium of the retardate (that is, as opposed to the momentary or partial equilibrium referred to so far). Normal equilibrium is in fact ever-widening because it includes an ever-increasing number of notions. It is also increasingly mobile. By contrast, the mentally deficient child reaches the first levels of this construction but remains fixed there for several years. If one wished to express this situation in the language of physics, one would speak of "false" equilibrium. It is known in fact that a physicochemical system is in a state of false equilibrium when its modifications are annulled, or slowed by friction or viscosity, without the internal forces of the system being themselves in equilibrium. In the same way, the retardate who has reached the elementary forms of operatory organization is capable of remaining at this level for years. It is as though he lacked the interest, the curiosity, and the general activity which, in the normal child lead the subject to ask new questions and to find the solutions, both of which lead him to superior levels. There is therefore in the retardate a sort of "false equilibrium." If the term "mental viscosity" did not already have a precise psychiatric meaning, one could speak of "genetic viscosity" to characterize this state. This false equilibrium naturally explains the considerable differences in age which often separate one stage and the next. In spite of the apparent contradictions it also explains the oscillations between two levels which have been just discussed. In the normal child, evolution is more rapid, and there is direct passage from one level to the next. In the retarded (provided one admits this sort of "viscosity" which is necessarily linked to the achievement of a given level) traces of the previous level will persist much longer than in the normal child, when the subject is in a transitory stage from one level to the next. It is possible to be simultaneously confronted with two heterogeneous systems in the same individual. At this point, the emotional and social factors add their influence to this situation. According to the degree of confidence or distrust which the child feels for the examiner, it is possible to make him advance or regress between these two coexisting states which make up the "false equilibrium." Lack of interior mobility is the cause (thus the oscillation does not result from a greater mobility than that found in the normal child, but it does show the existence of these "viscosities").

The analysis of the causes and the factors of this false equilibrium that is peculiar to mental deficiency could, without doubt, lead to broader questions of interest, *i.e.,* affectivity, psychomotor activity, etc. Although their discussion is not within the scope of this book, these notions are indispensable for the practical application of our research, particularly concerning the question of diagnosis and prognosis.

The conclusion to which this study leads, therefore, is that *mental deficiency could be defined as an unfinished operatory construction,* and this by opposition to imbecility and idiocy, where there is no operatory construction, and to normalcy, in which operatory construction is completed sooner or later by formal operations. However, in the mentally deficient child these formal operations are never achieved, hence his operatory construction is unfinished.

It is worthwhile to underline this definition of mental deficiency. When authors of the usual criteria of mental deficients (as opposed to imbeciles and slow learners) are consulted, the imprecision of their notions of mental deficiency is striking. For example, Terman (1919) defines the mentally deficient child as one with an IQ of 40 to 70; Lutz (*Lehrbuch,* 1938) limits mental deficiency to an IQ between 70 and 90; Tramer (1942) to one between 70 to 85; Meili (1937) uses the limits of 70 to 80 for slight deficiency and below 70 for true deficiency. The intellectual ages indicated by Binet are of interest. Idiocy is a mental age of from zero to two years, imbecility from two to seven years, and retardation from seven to twelve years. For Simon, retardation is defined by a mental age of seven to ten years (or seven to eleven years) and slow learners from eleven years up. It will be seen that these ages correspond to the criterion proposed in this work. Other authors link their definitions to output: the idiot cannot speak; the imbecile communicates by speech, but not by writing, while the retardate can write, but is incapable of higher-level learning.

The notion of the incomplete construction of operativity, as just defined, permits proposal of the following definitions. However, prior note is made of the fact that from the dynamic point of view, when the speed of construction is greater than average there is the equivalent of an IQ above 100, and when the speed is less than average it results in slight forms of deficiency. Among these inadequacies *mental deficiency begins when the subject will never be able to make up his retardation of operatory construction.* From a static point of view (*i.e.,* a final equilibrium, or the false equilibrium which is never outgrown), it is possible to say that:

1. the idiot never outgrows the sensory-motor compositions (previous to language);

2. the imbecile is capable of intuitive thought (egocentrism, irreversibility, but no operations);

3. the retardate is capable of operatory construction which he is incapable of completing, *i.e.,* "concrete operations" as opposed to formal operations;

4. the slow learner is capable of achieving formal operations and thus in time of reaching the full development of a normal child.

What is this incapacity in the retardates to achieve the compositions of volume? It has been seen that in the normal child the notion of the conservation of substance is acquired between the seventh and eighth year, and that of weight between the ninth and tenth year. (Thus this verifies the age limits given by Binet; the imbecile is below the mental age of seven, and incapable of the substantial conservation of volume.) The great difference between conservation of volume, *i.e.,* the completion of the physical operations studied thus far, and the conservation of substance, and of weight, is that the notion of volume is not based on direct intuition as in the case of substance (action of rediscovery) or of weight (action of lifting), but on a system of abstract relations. (Volume is not identical with perceived voluminousness, but implies the coordination of three dimensions.) The physical operations relative to volume are therefore much closer to formal operations, which are usually acquired between the eleventh and twelfth year. Therefore, the retardate could not attain the level of formal thought. To be retarded means, therefore: *to be able to think by concrete operations, but not by formal operations.* The retardate is thus different from the imbecile because of this beginning of operatory construction. He also differs from the normal individual or the slow learner by inability to complete this operatory construction by formal or hypothetico-deductive reasonings.

This definition of retardation as a construction which is incomplete because it is not formal, and which is necessarily related to the notion of the speed of development, makes it possible to discuss several observations concerning prognosis. When one is asked to diagnose adult reasoning disability, it is necessary to establish that the subject is capable of some operatory construction, and also that he is fixed at a level which would be only transitory for the normal individual, *i.e.,* that he is in a state of false equilibrium. According to whether he has reached the level of substance or the level of weight (the second or third stages of the corresponding groupments) his degree of deficiency is judged by the final stage of his operatory development. Since he is adult, the speed of his mental and particularly his operatory growth must be nil; the prognosis is that of a final arrestation or of mental stagnation.

The problem of prognosis becomes highly complicated when, instead of adults, children are examined, because the criterion of deficiency (possible, but incomplete construction) is not sufficient. For example, a child of ten years who has not yet acquired the notion of the conservation of substance cannot be considered immediately as an imbecile or even as an idiot. It is quite possible that during the following years he will yet attain Stage II (without ever outgrowing it). According to the above definition, then, he is classified as a retardate. Although the final state of logical and mental evolution can determine with certitude the degree of mental retardation, the clinical psychologist is, nonetheless, obliged to give his opinion on the probability of the future development of the subject, and to fix, at least hypothetically, his future level of achievement. To do this, knowledge of two facts is indispensable: first, the speed of the subject's development, and second, the accelerations, whether they be positive, negative or nil, which can intervene during this development. As an example, a constant speed of development is supposed in a child of eleven years who has attained the level of the conservation of substance. He will, therefore, have taken eleven years to accomplish the evolution which is accomplished by the normal child in seven or eight years. Around the age of fourteen or fifteen, when logical development can be considered as complete or arrested, he will be at the level of a nine- or ten-year-old, *i.e.*, at the level of the conservation of weight, but probably unable to attain that of volume. Thus, he is to be regarded as slightly retarded. By contrast, if at the age of eleven, he has no notion of conservation and reasons with the same egocentric schemes as those employed by a child of five or six, and if one continues to admit the constancy of the speed of development, he will just attain at puberty the level of the conservation of substance (level of approximately seven years). It is therefore a case of a retardate on the edge of imbecility.

The only drawback is that such prognoses are based on a purely fictitious given—that of the constancy of speed of operatory development. Even if the IQ remains constant with age, nothing proves that the speed of development is uniform. What is more, nothing is known in advance about the general tendency of the curve of mental growth for the retardates examined.

Research by Vermeylen (1922) shows that different types of retardates can be characterized by developmental curves. A priori, and admitting hypothetically that the normal curve is an exponential, three possible types of curves can be distinguished. These are set forth in Table IV.

Such curves remain schematic and are based only on gross clinical observations. However, they are rendered more precise by establishing fairly exact points of comparison with normal development, and thereby become valuable for diagnosis and prognosis. This necessitates, first, that the dynamic or cinematic curve of normal development be established and, second, that the same processes be analyzed in the retardate to determine the deviation of these processes from the normal curve. Present knowledge of mental development and of reasoning is either too general or too particular; the gross operatory development of the principal logico-mathematical and physical groupments is known, but it is necessary to analyze in more detail the horizontal and vertical decalages. It is particularly necessary to study the intuitive compositions which make up the transition between the first sensory-motor groupments and operatory logic, *i.e.*, the practical compositions which are contemporary to egocentrism. When the conditions

TABLE IV

Developmental Curves Characteristic of Various Types of Retardates

1. The type which begin normally, but which get further and further from the normal curve with a level of arrestation followed by progressive regression (as in the case of certain retardates possessed of demented evolution or epilepsy).

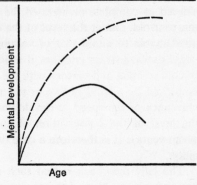

2. A curve of development similar to that of the normal child, but which exhibits slight retardation and convergence from a certain point onward (these subjects are pseudo-retardates).

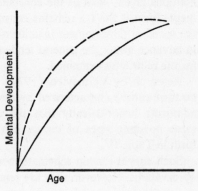

3. A curve which departs more and more from the normal curve, but does not show regression; there is deceleration and arrestation at an inferior level (this model probably characterizes the educable retardate).

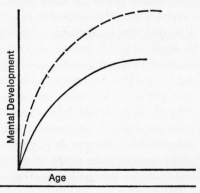

of equilibrium peculiar to each level, from sensory-motor action to hypothetico-deductive thought, are known, points of reference can be used which are both rigorous and delicate, and which can situate the abnormal phenomena of mental deficiency. In the meantime, and by contrast, observation and operatory analysis of the manifestations of deficient thought can be of great value for the theory of development itself. A concluding discussion of this follows.

3. Deficiencies in Reasoning and the Theory of Development

The point of departure and guiding line of this research has been Piaget's developmental theory. According to this theory, the development of reasoning is envisaged on the model of the progressive organization of an operatory mechanism. It was shown in the first chapter how such a conception is a continuation of the classical theory of the stages of development while it opposes the theory of progressive accumulation of acquired results, and the linear and cumulative succession of structures. Piaget's theory presents the double advantage of being both general (by saying that logical operations derive from practical, firsthand experience) and precise (by saying that operatory equilibriums are manifest as groupments or groups, *i.e.,* well-defined systems). The present research attempted to use this theory in a method which diagnosed reasoning in the mentally deficient. Strict application of the genetic hypothesis was observed, as were the rules of scientific verification. The current desire for simplifications which facilitate the application of diagnostic tests did not influence this research. The results obtained from these assessments of the reasoning of young retardates seem to contribute precision to the theory of development upon which the research was based. These results affirm this theory and enrich it in a new way. The possible interactions between the theory of development and the results of its application to diagnosis will be emphasized now.

According to the writer's working hypothesis, the analysis of certain rational notions (for example, the notions of physical conservation) permit the detection of certain precise operatory structures (groupments) which could be considered as markers in the normal and pathological development of reasoning. This hypothesis has been confirmed. The conclusion was that the assessments based on groupments provided unequivocal signs of levels of development. For example, the inability to construct the groupment inherent in the notion of conservation of weight or of volume can be interpreted as a sign of mental deficiency, provided this occurs after thirteen or fourteen years of age (the age at which the development of logic is normally complete). Such mental deficiency would be characterized by a state of "false equilibrium" (capacity for some logical constructions, but inability to complete them), while normally developed intelligence is recognized by its ability to attain the equilibrium which is assured by the groupment of all the perceptive and intuitive facts involved.

Do these facts confirm our initial hypothesis, or is there risk of this being a circular definition, the groupment being by definition the specific act of intelligence, and the operatory stages being levels of development, since the levels attributed to retardates are operatory stages? It is, after all, their incapacity for a total groupment which reveals their intellectual deficiency. If the observed facts really reveal such a circle, it is not based on the artifices of the definitions, but on the interdependence of two parallel and synchronic evolutionary series. These two series are the construction of logical norms in general and the mental growth of each individual. The analysis of pathological reasoning, and in particular of mental retardation, appears particularly suitable for showing the interdependence of these two processes.

When one studies normal thought development in order to determine the conditions necessary for knowledge in general, and to show its structures (as Piaget is now doing for the notions of number, quantity, space, time, and speed), one discovers that the logical construction of notions and of operations always accompanies mental development according to age—that is, it accompanies general psychological evolution. Although a progressive groupment of relations for each notion has been discovered which corresponds approximately to a progression with age, the decalages and the fact that the groups of children concerned are not perfectly homogeneous intellectually make it difficult to determine in detail the interferences of logical and psychological development.

There is temptation, using statistical methods, to extend the research on development to include a great number of subjects in the hopes of obtaining a more precise idea of the average mental ages which correspond to the successive acquisition of rational notions. However, this approach involves risk of attenuating individual differences in the developmental unfolding of operations (differences in the speed of development, etc.) without being able to say if the possibility or the existence of a given groupment is really a precise sign of intellectual maturity. It is possible that the appearance of any mechanism of reasoning or any notion could be due to school influence or to other extra-intellectual factors which have nothing to do with the operatory quality of intelligence.

By contrast, when a method which could be termed "negative correlation" is used, it is possible to grasp more precisely the interdependence and profound unity of operatory and mental development. The method is used to seek signs which indicate normal intelligence through the study of relative failures and insufficiencies in cases where individuals have been diagnosed by other methods as being abnormal and slightly deficient. The fact that there is found in these subjects, who suffer from intellectual and behavioral problems, the existence of a common operatory construction which obeys the same laws of integration illustrates the profound unity between the logical and the psychological. This construction, which can never attain its final equilibrium in the retardate, appears to show that the completion of the groupments is synonymous with the intellectual equilibrium peculiar to the mental age of twelve or thirteen years. The retardate thus would participate, although in an incomplete manner, in the processes common to all rational elaboration. That which is most general in the development of knowledge is the elaboration of logical norms, and that which differentiates it most clearly is the development of each individual in relation to his group. The two factors join in operatory development.

If the study of pathological reasoning can contribute thus to the verification of the hypothesis of the parallelism between logical and psychological evolution, can it go further and say that "the normal child can be discovered in the pathological child"? When consideration is given to stages, Wallon's observations in clinical studies of psychomotor activity are remembered. In the abnormal child, whose functions have all reached approximately the same point, it could be possible to date the appearance of these functions. If such a conception can be verified in the case of elementary levels of mental life, in which the stages follow each other quickly and are at all times dependent on the integration of concomitant nervous centers, then this theory encounters serious difficulties in the domain of the superior levels of mental life and in reasoning in particular. How would it be possible to affirm in this domain that all the functions of the abnormal child have ceased to develop at approximately the same point, and to attribute the character of an evolutive stage to this generalized state, if it is done by reference to a normal mental development in which the coexistence of different functions or structures had been previously observed? For example, to say that the memory of a retardate is at the same level as his language and his reasoning is possible only in relation to a hypothesis which is based on evaluation of normal development. Otherwise (and in the absence of concomitant neurological signs) the consideration of the arrestation of various functions at a deficient level, as proof of an exact synchronism between the stages attained by these functions, is simply to beg the question.

Although it is impossible to determine the stages entirely through observation of the pathological, there is, in the domain of the logico-psychological stages, a striking fact which supports the preceding conception. All who have used the clinical method, and have sought to determine the stages of the development of notions and operations in the normal child, know how difficult it can be to limit these stages to a particular age period. In reality, a continuous flood of transformations of thought is observed, and it is only by partially artificial separations that stages can be defined. These stages are only markers which are necessary for comparison between logical structures. It is difficult to assign a particular age to each stage. Even though the order of the stages remains the same, the speed of evolution can vary from one child to the next, depending as it does on the influences of the environment which can stimulate or inhibit the maturation of the subject.

Stages, therefore, are in no way static levels, or unlinked successive steps in a discontinuous evolutionary movement. The best proof of this lies in the intermediate cases; these are the subjects who construct their notions during the experiment itself. Certain children are recalled who were particularly intelligent, and who progressed during the conversation in an astonishing manner, thus outstripping the performance of their contemporaries. Now, when a retardate is examined, the picture is clearer, as the intermediate cases who progress from one operatory level to another are rare. When they do occur (as shown in Chapter 4) they are those cases who resemble the normal child most closely. Apart from the cases of oscillations who represent a bare tenth of all subjects examined so far, and show special difficulties of operatory equilibrium, the manifestations of reasoning in the retarded child are usually more homogeneous than in the normal child. They are in the same way crystallized around a common kernel which is characterized either by egocentrism or by partial groupments. This fact makes the operatory stages appear to be a natural psychological fact. (This observation is not necessarily applicable to domains other than that of reasoning.)

The greater homogeneity noticed in the stages of reasoning reached by the retardate may be explained by the deficient child's slower speed of development, and by the final or premature fixations which can occur as he develops. As his speed of development is slower, he stays longer at any given level, which means that examination of this child is more likely to reveal arrested structures of reasoning than periods of transition. Moreover, the normal child, interested by the experiment, tries to resolve and assimilate the facts using new hypotheses, while the retardate readily confines himself to the knowledge he has acquired previously. His thought is less mobile than that of a normal child, his interest is not as quick, his need to know is strongly reduced or directed toward practical ends, and he profits less from the stimulation of the experiment and the clinical conversation. The more the child's reasoning ability differs from his chronological age, the stronger the fixation to the level achieved. This fixation can thus take on an increasing significance as a psychological level.

Such facts show the advantage to be gained in studying the psychopathology of reasoning in order to understand more clearly the stages of the normal child. Moreover, when one seeks to decide that such a stage is superior or inferior to another, one can no longer refer simply to an empirical succession of stages based on the statistics of the average ages. Such a decision is possible only when it is based on a real integration of stages, the knowledge of which will be useful to the psychology of normal development. Two conditions are necessary for a psychologist to be sure he is dealing with the psychological manifestation of a certain stage. It is necessary: (1) that the appearance of this new stage be conditioned by the preceding one, and (2) that the manifestations of the preceding stage be found again in the new stage (in other words, the new implies the old). There must be no doubt concerning the reality of this integration.

At the present moment, such integrations are known in only two domains—that of physiology and that of logical intelligence. In other domains of mental evolution the mechanisms have not yet been perceived or described. For example, it will be admitted that the conditioned reflex (like the well-known salivary reflex linked to the sound of a bell) implies more simple reflex mechanisms, *i.e.,* the absolute reflexes which have been absorbed and generalized. In the same way, it is understandable that the notion of fractions implies a previous understanding of whole numbers, *i.e.,* a derived operation implies the elementary operations which it has developed and integrated (logical implication).

Between these two poles of mental life—the integration of reflexes on one hand and the unfolding of operatory logic on the other—it is difficult to determine how a superior stage derives from the preceding one. Until it becomes possible to describe mental evolution more precisely, it is necessary to keep in mind the general laws, such as progressive submission to experience, and the gradually increasing parts played by relativity and reversibility. This is, in fact, the tendency to reach a natural and unavoidable equilibrium defined by the term groupment, and the norms of these groupments which appear to direct mental development.

Even in the special domain of reasoning, however, where logical implication mixes with psychological implication, and where a real correspondence between operatory stages and mental levels is observed, certain problems subsist. These are the difficulties of speaking of operatory stages in terms of mental levels, and of fixing a definite age at which the achievement of any given operatory groupment is normal. These difficulties are caused mainly by what Piaget has termed decalages, whose existence has been discussed previously in this work. It is possible to find subjects who show their ability to effect a certain logical construction in a given situation (which means that the corresponding level of mental age would be attributed to him), but it is not possible to be sure that these subjects are reasoning in precisely the same way when faced with other problems, which either differ from the first in their perceptive or intuitive content, or are logically "analogous" to them. It is hardly possible to tell whether the subjects feel the same ease or difficulty in structuring logically all such situations. This impossibility of generalizing the operatory structure a priori to any intuitive content is often disconcerting when an effort is being made to establish general stages of reasoning.

However, in the domain of mental diagnosis, the situation is a little clearer. The psychologist needs to be aware of the existence of these decalages; moreover, he must never confine his observations to one experiment only, and he should be careful not to give too absolute a value to the results.

Within the limits of the present research (with the three experiments: clay balls, sugar, and bars) these decalages were the exception, while very similar reactions in different experiments were the general rule. The subject Hop. (Observation 60) was the sole illustration of an important decalage. This subject, who had progressively built up the notions of conservation in the case of the clay balls, remained fixed to an intermediate level in the experiment with the dissolution of sugar. The same subject, however, presented many serious disturbances of emotional and intellectual equilibrium which made it possible to question the diagnosis of retardation. The decalage in this case seems to confirm, as the exception, the rule of homogeneous levels of reasoning of retardates. There were no other cases who seemed to be clearly more advanced in one experiment than in another.

By contrast, each time there is such a decalage, it renders the diagnosis more difficult because it does not fit this rule, and requires a more subtle analysis of quality. It is to be remembered that the experiment with the bars must be practiced and interpreted carefully. The retardate often seems to solve this problem more easily as it is a question of logical composition, because he is, by definition, more inclined to perseverate and is less sensitive to the illusions of weight. For him, therefore, it is more difficult to reason in the presence of more complex experimental facts (clay balls, sugar, etc.). Once these nonoperatory factors of the child's thought have been discerned, the homogeneity of the reactions of the retardates is striking. The rare decalages give evidence of the relative discontinuity of the processes of development in these retarded subjects, and thus facilitate the detection of stages as the natural steps in the operatory and mental construction. In the normal child these stages are more difficult to discern, as in his case the many decalages are proof of the continuity of his development. In this connection, the phenomenon of "false equilibrium" can be of real use in the study of the successive states of equilibrium which are characteristic of normal development.

If these stages thus constitute in the retarded child a less continuous succession of levels than in the normal child, they also show a lesser operatory mobility, and a new problem can be raised now and discussed as the final part of this study. The question is to know whether the incomplete (or "false") equilibrium, which is typical of the thought of the retardate, is not a sign of an intermediate situation between operatory reversibility and the "regulations" which characterize perception and intuitive thought. Piaget considers these regulations to be characteristic of perceptive and intuitive equilibrium, and in opposition to the reversibility peculiar to the strictly operatory equilibrium. The regulations are shown by *compensations* between opposing forces (Piaget 1943). They often give a misleading impression of reversibility, as in the questions of "good shape," etc. (Gestalt). It is possible that in the incomplete or false equilibriums peculiar to retardates, a factor intervenes which explains precisely why the operation, not yet being pure, is both supported and limited by the perceptive elements in question. These elements would help understanding and therefore the operation, but only in part. In another way they would hold back its development, and play the part of friction, or "developmental viscosity," as we have termed it above.

Three examples supporting this hypothesis of an intermediate state between perceptive or intuitive regulation and operatory reversibility can be cited. First, it often happens, during questioning, that a retardate will notice and state conservation once or twice, and then will reflect less on the questions that are likely to follow. He applies the scheme of conservation as a sort of perceptive or representative shape. Second, the experiment with the bars is certainly more difficult to use with retardates because these subjects generalize the equality more quickly than the normal child. This is not due to superior logic but, on the contrary, to verbal or perceptive tendencies to perseverate. These first two examples are obviously similar to the regulations which intervene in the phenomena of predisposition in the domain of perception and intuition.

Third, the explanation for the oscillations themselves can be found in this hypothesis. The link between the oscillations and the state of false equilibrium will be remembered. From the present point of view, these oscillations could be compared to the fluctuations of perception in the cases of reciprocal images (examples: staircase in relief, cube seen in perspective, etc.). In these cases, the eye oscillates ceaselessly between two equally stable systems without ever making the final decision to chose one or the other of them.

Afterword*

It was not without some hesitation that we yielded to the kind proposal of our publisher to reprint this long unavailable book. One seldom takes pleasure in reediting a book of one's youth, but is tempted instead to write it over again, in an attempt to synthesize one's subsequent work, the work of students on whom one has had some influence, and valuable controls that were suggested by the original work. It required the friendly insistence of our colleagues and students to persuade us that there was perhaps some purpose to be served by holding to the original text, such as it has been cited, since it is now difficult to find, while completing it with a new introduction which would imply the continuous progress which has taken place since its publication.

It is in fact rather encouraging to note the development, since 1943, of certain ideas on psychological diagnosis, ideas which we attempted to defend in our first edition, and which are now better substantiated by the totality of the psychogenetic work issuing from the Geneva current.

First, there is a clearly experienced need for diagnostic instruments with which to analyze the psychological processes themselves, not just the output and the performances which result from them. The insufficiency of methods founded exclusively on the use of tests has be-

* At the suggestion of the translator, Bärbel Inhelder's Introduction to the Second Edition has been placed at the end of the book as an Afterword. It was felt that the information contained in it may prove more beneficial after the reader has become conversant with the experiments and techniques that have discussed in the main body of the book.

come increasingly apparent: even though these methods furnish a precise measurement, it is not nearly as easy to know just what they have measured. To declare that a subject is capable of answering a a certain question is one thing, but to understand how he arrived at his answer is another. If we wish to know what he is capable of drawing from his success, *i.e.,* whether he is able to generalize from it, or even to utilize it appropriately, it is the process of construction that interests us, and not the result alone. Such a diagnosis cannot be reduced to a simple screening process: we have to make a qualitative analysis in depth rather than to count on techniques of measurement alone, measurement which loses all significance without deeper analysis.

Second, it follows that we cannot dissociate diagnostic instruments from the theory which frames them. All too often, pragmatic application is divorced from psychological or psychopathological theory. If he wants to avoid a restrictive and above all uncontrollable empiricism, the practitioner needs to base his procedures on a general interpretation, for this is the only way he can confer significance to the innumerable behavioral specifics of the child he is examining. Purely metrical and empirical methods run the risk of losing sight of the essential.

There is no question that statistical procedures are indispensable, but as our third point we must stress the remarkable suppleness that has entered psychological measurement during the last few decades. For example, the analysis of variance and the use of ordinal scales permit causal and hierarchical analysis far beyond that of classical methods and lend themselves to precisely this union of theoretical interpretation and practical utilization which has so often been lacking in ordinary diagnostic procedures.

Fourth and finally, the comprehensive perspective which satisfies these various demands for diagnostic methods can be only a genetic interpretation. We are not implying facile procedures, like replacing the IQ with stages of development to which subjects can be assigned, nor simply identifying a certain pathological manifestation with a fixation at a certain level or stage. More fundamentally, a genetic approach is characterized by seeing all behavior as relative to a mode of elaboration, and consequently interpreting any reaction as a function of the constructive process from which it results. That the work of Geneva is currently in favor in a good many countries is not simply a question of fashion: an analysis which is both qualitative and genetic, bearing on the process of construction of intellectual operations, is today considered indispensable in giving meaning to what empirical and statistical inventories simply describe without being able to interpret.

This is the context for our efforts to perfect diagnostic procedures, which are founded on an operational and genetic analysis of cognitive behavior. Twenty years ago, this method seemed long and costly beside the expeditious procedures of tests and quantitative statements of output. Today, however, we know that this method has established itself as more valuable and effective. In this regard, we should like particularly to thank J. de Ajuriaguerra for his continued interest in this point of view, as shown in the work he directs at the Clinique Psychiatrique de Bel-Air and at the Centre Médico-Pédagogique de Genève. He has consistently taken genetic construction into account in his interpretations of pathological phenomena, and he has also been able to integrate in his daily practice those methods which might seem to be inapplicable on a larger scale, and to generalize from them.

In the first part of this introduction we shall indicate how it is now possible to establish a hierarchical scale of operations, based on developmental research carried out since the publication of the first edition. The second part will point out possible uses of these diagnostic processes, not only in the mentally deficient but also in other areas of pathological thought.

I. Establishment of an Operational Scale to Serve in the Diagnosis of Reasoning

In the first edition of this work, we discussed the reasons why a metric scale of the Binet-Simon-Terman type seemed to us insufficient for diagnosing reasoning, and we emphasized the necessity for qualitative analysis of the processes and structures of intellectual operations, but without yet having at our disposal a sufficiently large collection of tests or sufficiently refined statistical methods to establish a true operational scale. Since then, a series of new genetic experiments, some of which could be transformed into diagnostic tests (along with some of the older ones), make it possible for us to develop such a scale.

After the publication of *Le Développement des quantités physiques chez l'enfant* (Piaget and Inhelder 1941) the studies conducted by Piaget and myself were extended to other aspects of children's knowledge, specifically, notions of space, geometry, speed, time, and chance, the formation of elementary logic of classes, and finally the transition from the concrete operations of childhood to the formal operations of adolescence. More recently, we have undertaken with Piaget and our collaborators at the Institute a body of research on the formation of symbolic imagery in its relationships with the development of operations.

The extension of these studies has given us a wider and, above all, a more coherent view of the manner in which children of our society progressively construct their representation of the world and of the instruments of thought which are indispensable to this construction. This research, originally oriented toward genetic epistemology and an analysis of logical structures, has in turn furnished us a rather complete picture of the genesis of the operations which the child elaborates in the course of his development. Moreover, it was possible for us to establish a "synchronic" study, not just a "diachronic" one, as it had been until then, of the steps in the development, showing both the unity and the differences in these many different developmental processes. This synchronic picture permits us, henceforth, to locate normal and pathological phenomena with respect to the genetic construction in its entirety.

The experiments that revealed the most about the development of operativity were then set up as tests, standardized and statistically evaluated by Vinh-Bang. Discussion of this work appears later. Such an ensemble of tests constitutes a diagnostic instrument in the form of a genetic scale which reveals both the hierarchical and the synchronic succession of operations. While awaiting the publication of this scale—on which our colleague Vinh-Bang has been working for about ten years—we would already like to point out the great significance for the operational diagnosis of mental deficiency and of other phenomena of child psychopathology of this system based on the genetic analysis of operational mechanisms.

A. THE OPERATIONAL TESTS

The tests termed "operational" are distinguished from performance tests by this characteristic: they permit us to examine the stages in the development of certain operations which the child uses to solve a group

of problems of the same type or structure, such as classifying or ordering objects, understanding invariance or quantitative variations during
figural transformation, or imagining a combinatorial system corresponding to a network of formal operations.

In Piaget's conception, an operation is an action capable of unfolding inwardly, and its fundamental characteristic is its reversibility. The
child's cognitive activity becomes operational when it acquires a
sufficient degree of mobility to permit an action of his own (classification, addition, etc.) or a perceived transformation in the physical
world (of a ball of clay, a volume of liquid, etc.) to be annulled in
thought by thinking of an inverse or reciprocal action. If such are the
characteristics of a concrete operation, the formal operations can be
considered as second-power operations. For example, formal operations constitute a combinatorial system of classes, or a group of relations which unite the systems of concrete operations in a new totality.

We would like to mention briefly, by way of example, a few of the
experiments relating to the formation of concrete operations, and to
outline others which shed light on the transition to formal operations.
By generalizing from these experiments it would be possible now to
establish diagnostic methods of the type described in this volume.

1. *Tests Relating to Concrete Operations*

We shall limit our choice to three groups of experiments, some of
which have already become standardized tests. They are (a) conservation, (b) classification, and (c) symbolic imagery.

a. Tests of Conservation

The experimental situations which permit us to understand most
clearly the stages in the formation of concrete operations in normal
children—as well as in the mentally deficient—are those where the
subject, confronted with changes in the configuration of clay, water, or
discrete objects, must understand that the total quantity remains the
same although their appearance or arrangement has been transferred.
In order to be certain that the quantity does not vary, and to justify
this certainty by logical arguments, the reasoning has to be supported
by a mobile system of operations which imply the attainment of a certain degree of reversibility without which any articulation of the
reasoning remains very unstable.

Encouraged by the diagnostic value of tests of physical conservation
in the study of the mentally deficient, we are now extending our scale

to other tests of the same type. These include the conservation of numerical equivalences established by one-to-one correspondence, and the conservation of continuous or discontinuous quantities while beads or liquids are poured from a short wide glass to a tall thin glass, as these tests are described in *The Child's Conception of Number* (Piaget and Szeminska 1952). They also include tests of conservation of spatial quantities such as the invariance of length, studied in *The Child's Conception of Geometry* (Piaget, Inhelder, and Szeminska, French 1948, English 1960).

The combination of these tests of conservation lead to the establishment of a finely articulated scale, since several different perceived or perceptible contents are structured progressively and in a constant order by the same operational mechanism.

b. Tests of Elementary Logic: Classification

The role of tests of classification in the evaluation of the degree of mobility or rigidity in the categorization function has long been recognized, particularly in cases of aphasia or schizophrenia. It was brilliantly demonstrated in the case of aphasics by Goldstein and Scheerer, and in the case of schizophrenics by Hanfmann and Kasanin, starting from the work of Ach and Vygotsky. More recently, Oléron, Vincent, and others have established classification tests in order to determine the level of abstraction in deaf-mute children. The progressive matrices of Raven have been used (although their use is questionable) in the determination of a G factor.

Notwithstanding the variety of classification tests available to clinicians, we believe it useful to include in our operational scale certain tests taken from the research contained in *The Early Growth of Logic* (French 1959, English 1963). This was done because they appear more effective in analyzing the role of operational activity in the gradual structurization of logical systems of classification.

Thus, we have recourse to a group of tests of spontaneous or provoked classification, of geometric forms as well as of objects with some real-world significance. The objects or pictures can be classified successively or simultaneously according to several criteria or hierarchical structures based on inclusion rules.

The origins of classification are found in sensory-motor activity, joining and separating objects according to functional criteria. The child at the preoperational level of activity tends to form a "figural collection," a sort of "complex object," as Vygotsky has already re-marked. These figural collections appear to express a lack of differenti-ation between the figural and the conceptual aspects of a group of elements. At the beginning of the operational level, the child shows himself capable of putting elements in a class according to some common characteristic which distinguishes them from all the other elements, which in turn constitute a complementary class. The child progressively discovers the possibility of establishing additive (hier-archical) and multiplicative (double entry tables) class relationships. These discoveries imply an anticipatory and retroactive mobility of the operational activity, consisting of looking at the same elements from several different points of view at once.

The diagnostic value of such tests, compared with conservation tests, seems to us to reside in the fact that they reveal the degree of mobility of the operational activity and unmask its obstacles not by verbal arguments alone, but also and essentially by the effective pro-cedures which the child uses. The agreement or disagreement between these processes, in classifying elements either according to their figural characteristics (squares, circles, etc.) or according to their conceptual characteristics (animals, persons, etc.) is sometimes sufficient to enable us to differentiate between a general operational deficiency and a specific difficulty in the formation or use of symbols.

c. Tests Bearing on the Relations between Operativity
    and Symbolic Imagery

Struck by the frequent discordances between operativity and repre-sentative imagery in certain children whose scholastic performance was clearly insufficient, we felt the need to distinguish between the pri-mary and secondary factors in their deficiencies. It might be that difficulty in symbolic expression stemmed from a primary deficiency, such as would be the case in a child of limited intellectual resources; but on the other hand it might be that specific difficulties in symbolic representation hindered the learning of written or oral language (as is manifest in dyslexia) to such an extent that these disturbances pro-duce certain phenomena of pseudo-retardation. It is therefore im-portant to study carefully these two aspects of cognitive development, operativity and symbolic representation, and their interrelations.

The observations made by Piaget on the origins of the symbolic function in his own children and all the experimental research carried out under his direction in Geneva on the development of mental imagery now permits a better understanding of certain difficulties in symbolic imagery in terms of the normal genetic construction.

The symbolic function starts to appear in the child's second year and is characterized by the progressive differentiation of the signifier (label) from the signified (object). Signifiers can be not only verbal signs such as words, but also mimed symbols and recalled or even anticipated images.

We have carried out but not yet published a body of experimental research on the formation of image signifiers which constitute figurative symbols of thought. To date, the investigations have been limited to spatial images, but it would be interesting to study the formation of auditory images, in connection with the development of language.

Symbolic imagery can never be studied directly, but only through the gestures and drawings of the children, or by giving them pictures to choose from, or by their verbal comments. Thus, our experiments are concerned with the child's anticipation of changes in geometric figures or of the paths of moving objects. Included in the experiments were (1) displacements or rotations of one square in relation to another, (2) the respective paths of three beads on a stick when the stick is rotated 180 degrees, and (3) the transformation of arcs into straight lines.

Psychophysiological findings, along with behavioral observations of young children, suggest the hypothesis that symbolic images are not perceptual residues, but that they grow out of imitation. The child's first imitation consists of making an approximate copy of a model which is present before him. Later on he succeeds in evolving models which he can no longer perceive directly (deferred imitation), and still later his behavior suggests that he seeks to sketch out internally his imitative acts.

We can observe children exploring a shape visually or through gestures, which amounts to imitating the contours of the shape, and then seeking to reconstitute the shape as a mental image. These images are approximative, taking into account certain features while neglecting others, and the approximations become qualitatively different during the course of development.

At first, mental representation is essentially static. At the preoperational level, the young child can evoke and reproduce certain figures and movements that he perceives (distorting them, of course, according to his motor and imitative repertory), but he cannot yet anticipate the changes of position of one figure in relation to another, for example, nor represent the successive modifications in the transformation of a figure or the successive steps of a movement.

With the development of operativity, and under its influence, the representations gain in mobility. At the operational level the child starts progressively to anticipate successive states of a figure which moves in relation to a fixed frame of reference.

Symbolic imagery never attains the dynamism of operativity itself. But it does normally become sufficiently mobile to fulfill a function in the evocation and elaboration of spatial relations which is complementary to that of language in the formation of conceptual relations.

2. *Tests Bearing on Formal Operations*

If we define mental deficiency as the incapacity to achieve the level of formal thought, which in our society characterizes the thinking of adolescents, we must examine with care each twelve- to fifteen-year-old subject who is regarded as deficient, and determine the possibilities and the limits of his making the transition from concrete operations to formal operations.

The research we have devoted to this transition in preadolescents and adolescents (Inhelder and Piaget 1958) is very useful when it comes to determining whether a preadolescent subject with major scholastic difficulties has a normal operational potential, or is limited pathologically, or is, perhaps, disturbed.

Our experiments, some of which are in the process of being adapted for diagnostic purposes, permit the analysis of the processes underlying formal thought without depending uniquely on verbal behavior, as do tests which conceive of formal thought in terms of prepositional logic. The experiments attempt to get at the strategies and methods by which children and adolescents organize the exploration of a physical or chemical phenomenon as they try to discover laws and to prove them. Now, as Piaget has been able to show, the development of these strategies is isomorphic to the development of the structures underlying formal logic, specifically, the lattice structure and the "group of four transformations" (INRC group).*

Thus, through studying the children's experimental strategies, we

---

* Identity, inverse or negation, reciprocal, correlative.

can follow the development of more and more rigorous and systematic forms of complex intellectual organization, which turn out to be isomorphic to logical structures. If the hypothesis of certain neurophysiologists and cyberneticians is true, that these structures correspond to potential cerebral connections, it would be interesting to look closely at deficiencies or pathological deviations of this formal thought in action.

The experiments are suitable even for young children and the mentally deficient, for they consist essentially in actively trying to solve a problem. One test, for example, requires the subject to reproduce a color by making the proper mixture of five colorless liquids. Three of the liquids combine to produce the color, a fourth is neutral, and the fifth prevents the color. Children at the preoperational level mix the liquids haphazardly, thinking that pouring the same liquid over and over again, or mixing all of them at once will sooner or later produce the color. Their belief, still penetrated by animism or magic, is impervious to experience. Children at the level of concrete operations make a succession of combinations of two liquids at a time, but do not yet envisage a combinatory system. Preadolescents and adolescents gradually come to use a complete combinatory system. Without expanding on all the other possible examples, let us simply note that psychologically the transition to this last strategy depends on a transition from thinking in terms of the actual to thinking in terms of the possible, a capacity to anticipate a total array of possible cases, and then to choose revealing combinations. This mental organization of all the possibilities requires operational structures whose logistic analysis, carried out by Piaget, reveals the isomorphism with a lattice system or INRC group.

B. THE PROCEDURES OF STANDARDIZATION AND OF STATISTICAL EVALUATION

The need for widely applicable diagnostic instruments and the need to make the instruments available led us to undertake, with Vinh-Bang, the attempt to standardize the interrogation procedures and to evaluate the results by statistical methods capable of constituting a tableau of developmental results which could be translated into an operational scale. While awaiting publication of this scale, we would like to outline briefly the steps which have enabled us to pass from developmental research to diagnostic applications and to underline the utility of complementing the qualitative description of the genesis of operations with a hierarchical scale.

1. *The Standardization of the Procedures of Investigation*

a. Exploratory Method

The method employed for our original developmental research consisted of exploring the processes of thought. It was based in part on the clinical interview used by Piaget in his first investigations and in part on more carefully controlled experimentation. In this "operational" research, whose aim was to determine the mechanisms rather than the content of thought, questioning the child never takes place in a vacuum, but starts from concrete experiences. The child himself, through his observations and manipulations, seeks solutions to the problems, with the experimenter encouraging him to respond.

Certain aspects of the exploratory method are described in the appendix of the first edition, but it is important to stress more than we do there the active participation of the experimenter in the exchange with the child. Not only must he establish rapport with the child but he must constantly be thinking of the possible significance of the child's responses and behavior, in order to direct the discussion toward crucial points, while still following the meanderings of the child's own thought.

Twenty years of experience have confirmed our first impression that this method of exploration is the best-suited for approaching a new domain of children's thinking. Each time we have tried to standardize the questions ahead of time and to decide on the succession of interventions by the experimenter, we have lost valuable information and occasionally even bypassed the essential (Fraisse and Piaget 1963: *1*).*

b. Standardized Method

Standardizing the procedure is profitable, then, only when we already have an inventory of all the types of response to the problem at hand and can establish among the responses a natural order in terms of the increasing complexity of the implied operational mechanisms.

* Fraisse correctly notes that in the Geneva work the question at first is concerned with clearing little-known ground, and only through this is one able to arrive at systematic controls.

Standardization becomes necessary when we attempt to validate the qualitative findings by statistical analysis.

While our method of standardization approaches that of the experimental method, it is distinguished by its greater flexibility. Elsewhere in this work we have stressed the insufficiency of the test method and its rigidity in the diagnosis of reasoning processes, so that we need not discuss that again here. Also, our collaborator E. Schmid-Kitsikis is at present preparing a study on the advantages of developmental and operational methods over various quantitative methods.

Nevertheless, if we think it legitimate now to introduce a certain rigor in the examining procedure it is because this procedure was not established a priori but on the basis of our preliminary experiments. Knowledge of developmental data permits us to develop a strategy in interrogation which, while keeping in mind the essential, anticipates the various possible modes of reaction and prepares in advance a series of interventions which enable us to interpret these reactions. In this strategy, the examiner plays a more neutral role, perhaps, than in the original investigations, in that he is an organizer rather than an explorer. Because of its more formal examining procedure, this strategy makes it possible to gather a collection of objective data which can be treated statistically and transmitted to other people.*

2. *Statistical Evaluation*

a. Classification of Behavior

The preliminary step in quantitative evaluation consists in determining the qualitative criteria for classification of behavior. This step is important, because the significance of subsequent statistical validation may depend on the often difficult choice of criteria. In contrast to certain statistical methods, which start from null hypotheses, this choice of criteria is warranted in the case of our operational scale because the previous studies have already established classes of behavior which are clearly defined and are developmentally significant. Each is based on a collection of indices bearing on the level and the dynamics of the operativity involved.

The degree of refinement or approximation of classificatory schema utilized by the psychologist are then relative to the end pursued. For

* The work in progress with Vinh-Bang describes the standardized procedures.

example, in the tests of conservation contained in this work, a classification into preoperational, intermediate, and operational behavior appears sufficient to permit us to distinguish different levels of accomplishment. But this framework is not sufficient for diagnostic applications because it is also necessary to take into account all types of nuances which can be brought out only through a rather thorough longitudinal study. In this context let us note research which we carried out with G. Noelting with groups of children between four and fifteen years of age, following their evolution at regular intervals during a period of five years. These observations permitted us to distinguish a succession of transitory behavior within each of the behavior classes, and to understand the developmental relationships among them (Piaget and Inhelder 1941; 2d ed. 1961). This qualitative hierarchy and the relative speed of the transition processes are indispensable aids in the diagnosis and, above all, the prognosis of operational possibilities in the development of both normal and pathological children.

b. The Relative Frequencies of Classes of Behavior.

Once the classes of behavior are clearly defined, we must establish their respective frequencies and see whether these frequencies correspond to chronological development.

TABLE V

The Acquisition of Notions of Conservation of Substance, Weight, and Volume in the Transformation of a Ball of Clay (Percentage of Correct Solutions for 25 Subjects of Each Age)

	Ages:	5	6	7	8	9	10	11
Substance	Nonconservation	84	68	64	24	12	–	–
	Intermediate	0	16	4	4	4	–	–
	Conservation	16	16	32	72	84	–	–
Weight	Nonconservation	100	84	76	40	16	16	0
	Intermediate	0	4	0	8	12	8	4
	Conservation	0	12	24	25	72	76	96
Volume	Nonconservation	100	100	88	44	56	24	16
	Intermediate	0	0	0	28	12	20	4
	Conservation	0	0	12	28	32	56	80
Explanation in terms of volume (Percent included in the preceding percentages)			0	16	16	28	56

At the present time we are not able to put at the disposal of clinical psychologists a complete repertory of tests with standardized procedures of interrogation, correction procedures, and statistical evaluations. Instead we will limit ourselves to extracting as examples some tables of frequencies relative to the results contained in this work, taking care to point out the approximate character of the frequencies.*

TABLE VI

The Acquisition of the Notions of Conservation of Substance, Weight, and Volume in the Dissolution of Sugar in Water (Percentage of Entirely Correct Solutions, without Taking Account of Learning in the Course of the Experiment; a Total of 134 Subjects)

Ages:	8	9	10	11	12
Substance	57	57	83	73	90
Weight	22	40	50	78	80
Volume	7	37	33	53	57

TABLE VII

The Acquisition of the Notion of Volume in the Rise of Water Level When Cylinders Are Immersed (Percentage of Correct Solutions for Predictions, and Postfacto Explanations; 27 Subjects of Each Age)*

	Ages:	8	9	10	11	12
Phase I	Postfacto explanation	7	4	15	37	48
Phase II	Prediction	11	15	26	63	63
	Postfacto explanation	15	26	59	70	81
Phase III	Prediction	15	19	40	70	85
	Postfacto explanation	15	19	44	78	92

* A "correct solution" means a prediction of equal rise in water level for equal volumes, or an explanation in terms of volume alone when confronted with the equal rise.

The comparison of the results of various tests of conservation described in 1 of Part I of this introduction is set forth in the following table:

* Temporary indications of raw results are presented while awaiting the publication of more complete statistical analysis.

TABLE VIII

Acquisition of Different Notions of Conservation (Percentage of Successes for 25 Subjects of Each Age for Each of the Tests)

Ages:	4	5	6	7	8	9	10	11
One-to-one Correspondence (a)†	8	50	75	80				
Exchange of One for One (b)	4	46	64	84				
Pouring Beads (c)	–	22	54	96				
Pouring Liquids (d)	–	4	18	74				
Conservation of Substance (e)	–	16	16	32	72	84		
Conservation of Weight (f)	–	0	12	24	52	72	76	96
Conservation of Length (g)	–	8	4	20	68	96	–	–
Conservation of Volume (h)	–	0	0	12	28	32	56	80
(Including explanations in terms of weight: See Table I)								

† a, b = Piaget and Szeminska 152: chap. 3.
  c, d = idem. chaps. 2 and 1.
  a, b = idem. chapts. 2 and 1.
  e, f, h = Piaget and Inhelder 1941: chapts. 1, 21, and 3.
  g = Piaget, Inhelder, and Szeminska 1960: chap. 4.

Such tables permit detailed interpretation of the different pathological troubles in relation to the framework of normal evolution. Examination based on several tests of conservation whose relative degrees of complexity we know makes possible a subtle articulation of the steps of development, and above all it enables us to place the varying degrees of pathological homogeneity and heterogeneity in relation to normal developmental gaps.

C. THE BEHAVIORAL HIERARCHY

Although the tables setting forth the frequency of various behaviors have undeniable pragmatic value for a preliminary diagnosis, they are not sufficient to validate the idea of a hierarchy of successive stages of operational construction. In fact, and as Vinh-Bang (1959) shrewdly observed, developmental curves based on the frequencies of success in terms of age, even if they undergo correlational statistics, do not enable us to say whether the order of appearance of the various notions and operations is constant, nor, above all, whether the order corresponds to a hierarchy such that achieving a superior operation supposes the existence of a lower one without the reciprocal being true.

In order to use statistics to determine whether the developmental succession of certain behaviors does follow such a hierarchical process, or whether it is simply a question of fortuitous temporal succession, it is necessary to resort to procedures of hierarchical analysis such as Guttman introduced into social psychology. We owe a debt to L. J. Cronbach for having suggested that we use ordinal methods as far back as 1954. Vinh-Bang can be credited with showing that in most instances the stages of formation of operations that we had previously established by means of qualitative analysis are in fact hierarchical. But he went further, and found that the indices of reproducibility for the solutions furnished for various tests are not the same for all ages. This is of great interest: first of all, because it promotes understanding of the dynamics inherent in the normal evolutionary processes, in that it implies that the diverse types of operational behavior do not always follow the same speed of development; and second, because it empowers us to compare the accelerations and decelerations of pathological development, particularly those of the deficient, with those which characterize the diverse processes in the evolution of reasoning in the normal child.

Such hierarchical analysis appears to open some new perspectives on the theoretical and practical implications of confrontations between the qualitative developmental data and their statistical evaluations. In fact, the ideas of hierarchization and of relative speeds of development, which these quantitative methods bring to light, are strikingly close to the concerns of genetic analysis and, consequently, of its practical applications.

In this perspective, let us note the interesting endeavor of M. Nassefat (1963), who, starting from the hierarchial analysis, proceeded to establish indices of homogeneity. Correlational statistics enabled him to find, in the transition from concrete operations to formal operations, successive periods of homogeneity, transitory heterogeneity, and final homogeneity, thus giving statistical status to the qualitative notion of stages.

II. Contribution of Genetic Psychology to the Study of Certain Pathological Phenomena

The interest aroused in certain psychological and psychiatric circles by a diagnostic method based on intellectual operations and the convergent results obtained by our colleagues and students has encouraged us to continue the application of developmental studies to pathological phenomena, integrating new data as it comes, and refining our instruments for the diagnosis of psychopathological cases.

We shall limit ourselves here to a brief outline of the direction of some of the clinical work done since the first edition of this work. In the area of deficient reasoning, recent investigations and those now in progress put us in a better position to define its special characteristics, so that we can make diagnoses and even prognoses of subsequent evolution with a higher degree of probability. In another area, the procedures of operational diagnosis have been used to study the disintegration of cognitive functions in senile dementia, leading to comparisons between the processes of disintegration of operativity and the mode of construction of this operativity in the child. Abnormalities in the reasoning of so-called "prepsychotic" children appeared at first to escape all cognitive analysis, and to derive solely from affective problems. However, it now seems that in these cases the dysfunction of the adaptation to reality is also manifest within the operativity of these children. Finally, a body of research on aphasia currently under way in Geneva helps us to isolate those language troubles which arise from deficiency of mental potential, and to detect certain impediments in the development of the symbolic function. We shall review rapidly what seem to be the contributions of this method in each of these areas.

A. THE DEVELOPMENT OF REASONING IN
THE MENTALLY DEFICIENT

Our early work provoked research which extended and enlarged upon the same idea.

1. A systematic study published by J. Ranson (1950) led to some remarkable results. Dissatisfied with the diagnostic results obtained by the usual intelligence tests, she submitted 30 educable mental retardates to our tests of physical conservation. Of these 30 children, 17 produced results in accord with those obtained previously by the Binet-Simon tests. In 11 cases, the operational diagnosis appeared to be nearer the psychological reality as judged by observations of the behavior of these children over a considerable period of time than the results obtained from traditional tests. In one instance, the operational examination even permitted a valuable correction of a previous

incorrect diagnosis. In another case, an exceedingly disturbed child was not able to function to the maximum of his potential, so the analysis seems to have added nothing of significance.

Ranson supported our conception of mental retardation as a pathological fixation of operativity at some incomplete level of development. Moreover, she confirmed our hypothesis about the significance of exaggerated oscillations between two levels of development, namely, that they attest to the interference between a deficient intellectual structure on one hand, and troubles of affective and social exchange on the other.

"These tests," she told us, "allow us to determine the child's stage of intellectual development independently of school learning, while at the same time providing prognostic indications pertinent to this school learning. . . . The tests also serve to some degree to indicate ineffectual social relations."

2. Our colleague and friend René Zazzo, with a remarkable team of collaborators, has devoted the last several years to a multidimensional investigation of the mentally deficient (Zazzo 1960a). The working hypothesis is that there exists "heterochronic" development, which is peculiar to the mentally deficient; cognitive evolution does not follow the same rhythm as somatic development, and the result is a singular form of disequilibrium. This is manifested, for example, in the superspeed of the retarded in such tests as crossing out each instance of a specific symbol in a long list of symbols (Zazzo 1960b: 257-60). Zazzo suggests that true debility corresponds to a selective deficiency of cerebral potential.

He supports our conception that there is a characteristic form of dynamism in the evolution of deficient reasoning. His observations in Paris, along with new investigations in Geneva, appear to confirm the existence of functional peculiarities, which we noted as resulting from differences in speed (acceleration or retardation) between abnormal and normal intellectual development. After a period of oscillation, the normal child passes at a relatively rapid pace through several successive stages, disengaging himself from earlier forms of reasoning. The mentally deficient child pursues this same development at a slower pace; moreover, when he attains his upper limits, the reasoning often retains marks of preceding levels. One could even say that the transitions from one level to the next, up to the end of adolescence, become more and more rapid for the normal child, because of the increasing mobility of operational thought. However, in the mentally deficient child, we observe a gradual decrease of development, ending in a state of stagnation. While normal thought evolves in the direction of progressive equilibration of operations, defined by increasing mobility and stability of reasoning, the thought of the mentally deficient person appears to end in a false equilibrium characterized by a certain viscosity of reasoning.

Zazzo, too, mentions this "genetic viscosity" which, according to his theory, agrees well with the weakness of intellectual dynamism pointed out by his collaborator M. Hurtig (1960). According to this Parisian group, the mentally deficient have greater difficulty adapting to truly new situations because conditioning takes first place and impedes operational thinking. "This explains, at least in part," remarks Zazzo, "the oligophrenic inertia described by Luria as well as the genetic viscosity analyzed by Bärbel Inhelder. The mentally deficient regresses more frequently than the normal child to earlier long practiced modes of thought. He falls back into very deep ruts."

3. Research at Marseille confirms the fact that the operational construction of the mentally deficient follows the same path as that of the normal child, but remains incomplete. In addition, in a verbal communication to the author, Cahier stated that after the end of their schooling, the disintegration of these structures occurs more rapidly in mentally retarded than in normal subjects. If this phenomenon is found more generally, it will have considerable theoretical significance in showing the importance of the integration of inferior structures in superior structures for the stability of thought.

4. In Geneva, research is in progress in the psychiatric clinic on the different manifestations of deficiencies in children of the same mental level but of diverse chronological ages and etiologies. The research utilizes our test in an effort to understand the multitude of dynamic aspects of reasoning in subjects who remain fixated at the same stage of operatory structures.

5. During the testing of children in various Geneva schools, we have had occasion to analyze the thought processes of preadolescents with various scholastic difficulties. It was important to ascertain the developmental potentials of each subject and to determine if the limitation of these potentials resulted from a true debility, so we took special interest in the upper and lower limits among the mentally deficient. Since we have today a battery of tests which define the

different levels of concrete and formal thought, we tried to determine to what degree the reasoning attained by retardates performing at the upper limits was or was not characterized by a homogeneity of forms of thought, for each class of tests.

If operativity were essentially determined by the contents on which it acts, formed by daily experience, by sociolinguistic relations and particularly by school, we would expect thirteen- to fourteen-year-old retardates who have had seven or eight years of special school to show a wide variety of solutions, depending on the problem posed. By contrast, if operativity were not principally determined by the assimilated contents, but developed more fundamentally from the subject's own constructive activity, then we ought to find a coherence similar to that of the normal child.

In fact our pilot study seems to indicate that for severely retarded who were classified at the upper limit of imbecility, a striking homogeneity exists between the different modes of reasoning, such that we can assign the operational structures to a precise level of genetic evolution. This homogeneity appears to be even greater in the profoundly retarded than in normal young children in the course of their evolution.

Thus, certain thirteen-year-old subjects who were subjected to approximately twenty operational tests stood, according to the hierarchical scale established with Vinh-Bang, at a level characteristic of normal children of six years of age. It goes without saying that the manner of approaching the problems, the interest, the use of information, and the satisfaction drawn from the experimental confrontation are very different from the intellectual dynamics met in younger normal children. Nonetheless it is striking to see how closely the structures of reasoning and the modes of justification correspond to those present in young children when they start the transition from preoperational thought to the most elementary manifestations of operativity. These indications support the hypothesis that operational construction, while certainly not independent of the behavior on which it is built, is elaborated, nevertheless, according to its own laws.

Still more interesting are cases of the same chronological age (approximately thirteen or fourteen years of age) who perform at the upper limits of mental retardation, which we characterized in the first edition of this work by a fixation at the level of concrete operativity. These more recently examined subjects confirm our previous results and fit into the previously defined category, but they furnish new data as well. We found in these subjects a quasi-homogeneous terminal of concrete operations, not only in the limited sector of conservation but also in all other sectors—classification, notions of chance, geometric constructions, etc. However, not the slightest beginning of formal operations was seen in any of the cases. When these subjects were presented with problems whose solution required a formal type of organization, for example the anticipation of a combinatory system, they behaved, not like normal adolescents at the threshold of formal thought, nor even like children at the temporary equilibrium level of concrete operations, but rather like young children of six or seven years of age in the process of elaborating the most elementary concrete operations. As soon as the problems become more complex and cannot be solved step by step, it is as if the retardates give up any attempt to organize and simply repeat the same actions over and over again, hoping somehow that the accumulation of the same actions will produce, sooner or later, the desired effect. They react to their failures with magic-phenomenalistic explanations.

In brief, we see that analyzing operativity in all these situations allows for finer methods of individual diagnosis and prognosis which go far beyond assigning the retardate to a given stage of development.

B. The Disintegration of Reasoning in the Case of Senile Dementia

Even if only heuristic value is given today to Jackson's hypothesis on the "hierarchic dissolution," and we no longer expect to find in the degenerative processes the exact reverse of the developmental mechanisms, it is still interesting to compare the degeneration of certain aspects of thought, and in particular its operativity, with the child's development, and with the development of the mentally deficient.

1. This comparison is now possible, due to the work of J. de Ajuriaguerra and his collaborators, R. Tissot and M. Rey-Bellet, at the psychiatric clinic in Geneva (in press). In their vast neuro-psychiatric study on senile degeneration, they have attempted to make use of some of our operational tests. The results clearly show that elderly people affected by senile dementia reason in a manner analogous to that of children of various age levels, and the more advanced the disintegration the more it is marked by a collapse of

operational structures. Those who were only slightly deteriorated still solved problems which required the higher concrete operations, but appeared to be incapable of elementary formal operations. Among other things, they could comprehend and justify the notion of the conservation of weight, but on problems of conservation of volume there was great instability.

In other old people, where neurological signs and tests of performance and behavior revealed an advanced deterioration and the case histories showed no indication of previous debility, the reasoning was frankly preoperational (characterized among other things by the loss of elementary notions of conservation of matter). Finally, some cases who were observed longitudinally offered an interesting picture of the progressive collapse of operativity.

True, the disintegration does not affect the operativity in a uniform and homogeneous manner. The operations bearing on spatial relations appear to deteriorate more rapidly than logico-arithmetical operations. On the other hand, traces of one level of reasoning in the midst of another level are even more marked than in the mentally retarded, and occasionally one observes some residue of higher types of reasoning in lower levels of thought.

2. Research now in progress by our collaborator H. Sinclair on the relations between language and thought in senile dementia clearly shows that the disintegration of language does not correspond entirely to the involution of thought. In particular, the functional use of language by the aged differs from that of the child of the same operational level. The aged lose the ability to comprehend and carry out verbal commands before they lose the normal automatic use of words. In our experiments they seem to lose numerical relations before they lose the ability to make quantity and size comparisons. By contrast, in young children numerical comparisons and the conservation of countable collections of objects appear earliest, both in language and in operativity. In language development, comprehension of instructions comes early, while the functional use of words appears to develop in close correlation with the operational development. In spite of these differences, there exists a certain parallelism between deterioration processes of the instruments of communication and those of operational mechanisms.

These few indications show us that the disintegration of operativity, much more than of the instruments of social communication, appears to follow, at least approximately, the reverse of developmental construction. This offers indirect proof that the operational structures are not uniquely a cultural product, elaborated on the basis of social interrelations, and that the laws of operational development, whose inverse we see in senile dementia, seem to be dependent on the laws of cortical integration.

C. Operative Troubles of Children Termed Prepsychotic

It may be of interest to use our operational tests to examine some children whose behavior gives evidence of a poor adaptation to reality. These children, who have difficulty primarily in relating to others, manifested in the course of these examinations a distorted assimilation of reality. Not only is their representation of the world often perturbed but the operational nucleus of thought itself also appears to be affected. Without yet being able to systematize the symptoms of this dysfunctioning, we were aware of striking discordance within operational activities. Solutions at the operatory level, although often fragmentary, were obtained in certain situations, but the reasoning often retained arguments which were frankly preoperational. These forms of preoperational thought appeared chiefly in problems of conservation, which imply certain invariances in the thought processes.

These preoperational forms of thought differ from those that are observed in mentally deficient children in their incoherence and in the nature of the proofs and explanations. The explanations of these children often reveal a lack of differentiation between the self and the exterior world, as well as magico-animistic types of representations.

These disturbances are also very different from those that are sometimes observed in neurotic children, where, in the course of otherwise normal reasoning, we find exaggerated oscillations between two successive types of reasoning. These may be considered as symptoms on anxiety, indecision, or fear of making mistakes, but the representation of reality is not distorted. The affective troubles do not appear able to disturb the operative nucleus or the adaptive activity as such.

By contrast, the children termed prepsychotic appear to remain in a sort of emotional dualism between the ego and the outside world. They seem to have developed an ensemble of withdrawal behaviors to escape a confrontation either with others or with physical reality. They tend to assimilate information in an autistic and egocentric fashion, altering it according to their needs and fears, by a more or less permanent indifferentiation between the affective and cognitive processes.

These few observations, which do not profess to be generalizations, appear to indicate that the elaboration of operativity depends not on maturation alone, but that it requires both cognitive and affective functioning oriented toward the adaptation to reality and confrontation with the environment.

D. Operativity and Problems with Symbolic Imagery in Dysphasic Children

In cases of language deficiency, in which semantics and syntax are fragmentary or distorted, it is helpful to know whether these troubles are grafted onto a normal or a pathological intellectual development. It goes without saying that the intellectual development of a child with language difficulties never corresponds exactly to that of a child communicating normally with others. However, language inadequacies have different diagnostic and prognostic significance: (1) if they are combined with a normal intellectual potential which permits some compensations and some substitutions, or (2) if they are part of a limited potential, as is the case in the mentally deficient, or (3) if they participate in a dysfunctioning in adaptation to reality, such as is observed in children termed prepsychotic.

Each time that we can establish a normal development potential, such as by determining a normal operational level with a certain degree of mobility in the intellectual functioning, it is important to know up to what point the language difficulties are associated with deficiencies in symbolic function. Such deficiencies may be manifested by difficulties in recalling or anticipating visual images.

In normal children, we have been able to establish a relationship of synchronous evolution between the development of operativity and that of symbolic images. The slow development of retarded children appears to affect simultaneously the operative and figurative aspects of thought. By contrast, in children who have language difficulties but who are not regarded as mentally deficient or prepsychotic, these two aspects of cognitive functioning are often at different levels of development. While the development of operativity usually proves to be nearly normal, that of figurative symbolism often corresponds to earlier stages. This discordance and these retardations in the construction of image symbols lead to the supposition of a specific deficit of the symbolic function, of which language troubles could be one manifestation.

In studying any child with a language problem, we must look not only at the deficiencies in his figurative representation but also at his operational resources. These resources could permit him to compensate for and give some direction to his inadequate figurative symbolism.

III. Conclusions

The import of these remarks is to show the benefit of comparing pathological manifestations of cognitive development with normal development. While the pathological phenomena of thought profit from analysis in a developmental perspective, the analysis of pathological aspects enriches and helps refine operational theory itself. This was noted in the first edition of this work, but now many additional facts and controls are available.

We have just seen that when there is discordance between the operative and figurative aspects of thought, the phenomenon of the discordance itself gives some weight to the hypothesis of a relative independence of operational construction with respect to its symbolic support. Indeed, the operativity orients the development of symbolism and even permits compensations when symbolism is disturbed. As we have found in a large body of research with normal children, the transition from static images to anticipatory images in general is due to operations. While for its part imagery assists in the functioning of the operations, it does not modify their structures, so there is not complete reciprocity between these two aspects of cognitive mechanisms.

The disturbing effects that social difficulties have on the operativity of prepsychotic children indicates, on the other hand, how much the formation of intellectual structures is linked to the adaptive functioning of thought; here again, psychopathological study is useful in determining the role of social factors in the development of intelligence and the close connections which link affective and intellectual evolution.

Evidence that the disintegration of cognitive operations follows developmental laws in reverse appears to confirm the conception that operativity constitutes an integrative process.

Finally, further studies of retardation itself enables us to go beyond the analysis of levels of operational construction, and to furnish some hypotheses about laws of normal and pathological equilibration, as manifested in the flexibility of the structures in normally developing children contrasted with the tightly closed structures of the retarded.

The above-mentioned results of tests carried out on both seriously and slightly affected mental deficients are of some importance from the viewpoint of the genetic theory of operations. We have been aware for some time that since the development of the normal child is rapid and complex, the study of pathological troubles which exclude certain modes of activity is of interest in permitting us to dissociate different factors and to arrive at some relatively homogeneous, stable stages. In this regard, mental debility can be of exceptional interest because of the fixation at certain stages of development with a minimum of paranormal deviations (insofar as it is possible to distinguish "hypo" from "para" phenomena, as explained in Chapter 1).

In the mentally retarded, there seems to be a different sort of closure of an operational system from that in normal children. In normal children, part of what it means to achieve a lower level is opening the way to the next level. It seems important to distinguish this type of closure from a "ceiling" phenomenon in the operational structures of the mentally deficient. In a normal child, a system can be called closed when each element has become tied to each other element, so that the system is totally coordinated. But by this very fact, the system becomes integrateable into a more extended system, so that its closure constitutes at the same time an opening in the sense of a possibility for continued evolution. In the deficient, the achievement of a certain structure appears final, without the possibility of subsequent progress. Thus it is necessary in this case to speak of a ceiling rather than of closure in the operational sense.

These facts appear fundamental from the viewpoint of equilibrium theory. From our point of view, the equilibrium is mobile in two senses. In one sense it is mobile because it implies an activity of the subject in order to maintain structural invariance by compensating for external disturbances. In the other sense, this equilibrium is mobile and dynamic in that it is responsible for the progress, mentioned above, which occurs every time a structure proves insufficient to resolve a given problem, and a new and broader structure must be developed in which the previous equilibrated systems can be integrated.

In the retarded, the ceiling form of equilibrium is not mobile in either of these senses: it is a passive and in some sense perseverative stability. That is why reference is made in this work to pseudo-equilibrium, in the sense that physicists use this term to refer to states which attain apparent stability, but only because of a factor of viscosity.

BÄRBEL INHELDER

Geneva, Switzerland
August 1963

Appendix A

A List of the Cases Examined

The following table sets forth descriptive data on the 159 subjects examined in the present study. Uniform information was not available on all subjects because of the diversity of schools, institutions, and medical opinions. The intelligence quotients (Stanford-Binet, Terman, Vermeylen, Biasch, etc.) for the subjects were obtained by persons with diverse training and background, and this lack of consistency is noted. The term "deficient" as used in Chapter 2 denoted retardation or oligophrenia; in this table the use is the more restricted one proposed in the conclusions (and is used in contrast to imbecile or slow learner).

ABBREVIATIONS

No.: the numbers in the first column correspond to the observations as cited in the text.
Sex: M = Masculine, F = Feminine
Level: The figures in parentheses indicate either the highest level attained by the subject or the level partially attained during the interrogation.

Form of Equilibrium:

Fixat. Fixation
Inter. Intermediate between two stages
Progr. Progressive
Retro. Retrogressive
Oscil. True oscillations
Decal. Decalage

Class Assignment:

N. Normal class
R.C. Repeated class
Dev. Development or slow-learner class
Sp. Special class
Prep. Preparatory class for special instruction
Obs. Observation class
Tut. Tutoring
R. Sch. Released from compulsory schooling
Rem. Remedial school
Diffic. Difficult
Dist. Boisterous, disturbing influence
Unstab. Unstable
A.Mind Absent-minded
Li. Lies, Falsehoods
Lang. Ret. Language retardation
Lang. Def. Language Deficiency
Undisc. Undisciplined
Schol. Schooling
Thi. Thief
Vagabond Vagabond, vagrant
Mil. Serv. Military service

Medical Information:

Defect. Defective
N. Sp. Nothing special
Hered. Hereditary
Dev. Development
Endoc. Trouble Endocrine trouble
Ric. Rickets
Instab. Instability
Epilep. Epilepsy
Vis. Vision
Ret. Retardation
Cong. Congenital
Alcoh. Alcoholic, Alcoholism
Musc. Atroph. Muscular atrophy
Microcephal. Microcephalic
Infant. Paral. Infantile paralysis
Psychop. Psychopathic
I. Imbecile, Imbecility

Hystr. Hysteria
Traum. Traumatic
T.B. Tuberculosis
Susp. Suspect, Suspected of
Schiz. Schizophrenia
Sl. Slight
Cretin. Cretinism
Disequil. Disequilibrium
Environ. Environment

SUBJECTS INCLUDED IN STUDY

No.	Age	Sex	Level	Form of Equilib- rium	Class Assignment When Examined	Medical Information	Class Assign- ment Two Years After Examination	IQ	Reasoning
1.	7:6	M	II	Fixat.	1 N. Dist.	Nervous	3 Obs.	90	Normal
2.	7:10	F	(I)/II	Progr.	2 N. Diffic.	Defect. Environ.	3 N.	84	Normal
3.	7:11	F	I	Fixat.	1 Sp. Slow	Retarded	3 Sp.	77	Indication of Retardation
4.	8:2	M	II	Fixat.	2 N. Unstab.	Enuresis, Nervous	4 Obs.	72	Normal
5.	8:3	F	I	Fixat.	2 Dev. Diffic.	N. Sp.	4 Sp.	70	Indication of Retardation
6.	8:4	M	III	Fixat.	2 Stutters	N. Sp.	4 N.	94	Normal
7.	8:5	M	I/II	Inter.	1 N. 1 R.C.	Hered. Alcoh.	2 N. 3 R.C.	77	Retarded
8.	8:5	F	II	Fixat.	2 Obs. Undisc.	Defect. Environ.	4 Dev.	78	Normal
9.	8:6	F	II	Fixat.	2 Dev. Unstab.	Defect. Environ.	4 Dev.	90	Normal
10.	8:6	F	I/II	Inter.	2 Dev. Slow	N. Sp.	4 Dev.	79	Retarded
11.	8:6	F	I/II	Fixat.	2 N. Diffic.	N. Sp.	3 Sp.	71	Indication of Retardation
12.	8:7	M	I/II	Inter.	1 Sp. Diffic.	Ric.	3 Sp.	77	Retarded
13.	8:8	M	I	Fixat.	1 Sp. Diffic.	Retardation	3 Sp.	75	Retardation Indicated
14.	8:8	M	I	Fixat.	2 Sp. Diffic.	Retardation	4 Sp.	76	Retardation Indicated
15.	8:9	M	I/II	Inter.	1 N. 1 R.C.	N. Sp.	3 N. 1 R.C.	88	Retarded
16.	8:11	F	I	Fixat.	2 Dev.	Retardation	4 Sp.	86	Retardation Indicated
17.	8:11	M	I/II	Inter.	1 Dev. Diffic.	Retarded Develop- ment	3 Dev.	95	Retarded
18.	9:0	F	I	Fixat.	2 Dev. Diffic.	Retardation	4 Sp.	77	Slow Learner
19.	9:1	F	III	Fixat.	2 Obs. Slow	Endoc. Trouble	4 N.	88	Normal
20.	9:1	M	I/II	Inter.	2 Sp. Unstab.	N. Sp.	4 Dev.	80	Retarded
21.	9:2	M	I	Fixat.	2 N. 1 R.C.	Retarded Develop- ment	Rem.	74	Slow Learner
22.	9:2	F	II	Fixat.	2 Dev. Diffic.	Defect. Environ.	4 N.	85	Retarded
23.	9:2	F	III	Fixat.	2 Dev. Slow	N. Sp.	4 N.	90	Normal
24.	9:3	M	I	Fixat.	2 Sp. Diffic.	Slow Learner	4 Sp.	81	Slow Learner

25.	9:3	M	II	Fixat.	2 N. 1 R.C.	Rickets, Unstab.	4 Obs.	80	Slightly Retarded
26.	9:4	M	II	Fixat.	2 N. Diffic.	N.P.	Rem.	79	Slightly Retarded
27.(7)	9:5	F	I	Fixat.	1 Dev. Diffic.	Retardation	4 Dev.	72	Retarded
28.	9:5	F	I	Fixat.	2 N. 2 R.C.	Retardation	3 N.	73	Retarded
29.	9:6	F	I/II/I	Oscil.	2 Obs.	Nervous	4 Obs.	80	Slow Learner, Unstab.
30.	9:8	M	I	Fixat.	2 N. 1 R.C.	N. Sp.	4 Sp.	61	Retarded
31.	9:8	M	III	Fixat.	3 N. Thl.	N. Sp.	Rem.	95	Normal
32.	9:10	F	I	Fixat.	Sp. Prep.	Epilep. Ret.	—	69	Retarded
33.	9:11	F	I/II	Inter.	2 Dev. Slow	N. Sp.	4 Dev.	80	Retardation Indicated
34.(24)	10:0	M	I/II	Inter.	2 Sp. Diffic.	Ret. Vis. Defect	4 Dev.	88	Retardation Indicated
35.	10:0	M	III	Fixat.	3 N. Diffic.	Defect. Environ.	Rem.	95	Normal
36.(56)	10:2	F	III/I	Oscil.	2 Dev. Thl.	N. Sp.	4 Dev.	78	Retardation Indicated
37.	10:2	M	(IV)III	Fixat.	3 N. Diffic.	Nervous	5 N. Tut.	90	Normal
38.	10:2	F	III	Fixat.	3 N. Ll.	N. Sp.	Rem.	87	Retardation Indicated
39.	10:2	F	II	Fixat.	2 N. 1 R.C.	Lordosis	4 Sp.	70	Retarded (I.)
40.(8)	10:5	F	I		1 Sp. Diffic.	Cong. Ret.	3 Sp.	69 / 82	Retardation Indicated (I)
41.(55)	10:5	M	III/I/	Oscil.	2 Sp. Dist.	Social Ret.	5 Sp.	85	Slow Learner
42.	10:6	M	II	Fixat.	3 Sp.	Backward	5 Sp.	68	Retarded
43.	10:6	F	I	Fixat.	1 Sp. Diffic.	Hered. Alcoh.	2 Sp. 1 R.C.	66	Retardation Indicated (I)
44.	10:7	F	II/III	Inter.	3 N. Lang. Ret.	Defect. Environ.	5 N. Tut.	82	Retarded
45.(5)	10:7	M	I	Fixat.	2 N. 3 R.C.	Cong. Ret.	4 N.	65	I. Indicated
46.	10:7	F	II	Fixat.	2 Sp.	Ret.	4 Sp.	62	I. Indicated
47.	10:7	M	II	Fixat.	3 Sp. Slow	Ret. Dev.	5 Sp.	70	Slow Learner
48.	10:8	M	II/III	Inter.	4 Dev. Distr.	Trouble Endoc.	Obs.	78	Retardation Indicated
49.	10:9	M	I	Fixat.	2 N. 2 R.C.	Backward	4 Sp.	60	I. Indicated
50.(2)	10:9	M	I		3 Sp. Obs.	Ret. Epilep.	Obs.	72 / 88	I. Indicated
51.(19)	10:10	F	II	Fixat.	2 Sp.	Backward	4 Sp.	67	Retarded
52.	10:11	M	I	Fixat.	2 N. 2 R.C.	Backward	4 Sp.	66	I. Indicated

SUBJECTS INCLUDED IN STUDY (Cont'd)

No.	Age	Sex	Level	Form of Equilibrium	Class Assignment When Examined	Medical Information	Class Assignment Two Years After Examination	IQ	Reasoning
53.	11:0	M	II	Fixat.	3 Sp.	Backward	5 Sp.	71	Retarded
54.	11:0	F	II	Fixat.	3 N. 2 R.C.	N. Sp.	4 Sp.	73	Retarded
55.(20)	11:0	F	I	Fixat.	2 Sp. Diffic.	Slow Epilep.	3 Sp.	92	Slow Learner
56.	11:1	M	I	Fixat.	1 Sp.	Backward	3 Sp.	68	I. Indicated
57.	11:1	M	I	Fixat.	1 Sp. Distr.	Backward	4 Sp.	70	I. Indicated
58.	11:1	M	III	Fixat.	4 N. Diffic.	Meningitis at 7	6 N. Tut.	81	Retardation Indicated
59.	11:2	M	I	Fixat.	2 Sp.	Backward Vis.		60	I.
60.	11:2	M	I	Fixat.	2 Sp.	Defect.	4 Sp.	65	I.
61.(3)	11:2	F	I	Fixat.	2 Sp.	Backward	4 Sp.	68	I.
62.	11:2	M	III/IV	Inter.	4 Obs. Diffic.	Microcephal.	4 Sp.	105	Normal
63.	11:2	M	IV	Normal	5 N. Diffic.	Epilep.	6 N.	98	Normal
64.(25)	11:2	M	II	Fixat.	3 Sp.	Delicate, Hystr.	Rem.	73	Retarded
65.	11:2	M	II	Fixat.	4 N. 2 R.C.	T.B., Ric.	5 Sp.	80	Retarded
66.	11:4	F	II	Fixat.	3 N. 2 R.C.	Little's Disease	5 N. 3 R.C.	75	Retarded
67.(21)	11:4	M	II	Fixat.	3 N. 1 R.C.	Backward	4 Sp.	70	Retarded
68.	11:5	M	II	Fixat.	3 Sp.	Ret. Dev.	6 Sp.	70	Retarded
69.(51)	11:7	F	(II)/III	Progr.	4 N. 1 R.C.	Backward	5 Sp.	82	Retardation Indicated (Slight)
70.	11:8	M	III	Fixat.	3 N. 1 R.C.	Ret. Dev.	6 Dev.	89	Retardation Indicated
71.	11:9	M	II	Fixat.	4 Sp. Diffic.	Defect. Environ.	Rem.	76	Retarded
72.	11:9	F	II	Fixat.	3 N. 2 R.C.	Ric., Alcoh.	6 Sp.	67	Retarded
73.	11:10	F	II	Fixat.	4 N. 2 R.C.	Backward	4 N. 3 R.C.	69	Retarded
74.	11:11	M	II	Fixat.	3 Sp.	Backward	5 Sp.	75	Retarded
75.	11:11	M	I	Fixat.	1 Sp.	Backward, Cong.	5 Sp.	61	I.

Case	Age	Sex	Grade	Course	Test	Condition	Placement	IQ	Diagnosis
76.	12:0	M	II	Fixat.	4 Sp.	Backward	6 Sp.	72	Retarded
77.	12:0	F	II	Fixat.	5 N. Diffic.	Hered. Defect	Rem.	78	Retardation Indicated
78.(10)	12:0	M	I	Fixat.	3 Sp.	N. Sp.	5 Sp.	68	—
79.(54)	12:0	F	(II)/III (IV)	Progr.	Obs.	Epilep.	8 N.	101	Disequilibrium
80.(52)	12:0	F	(I)–III	Progr.	Irregular	Trouble Endoc.	—	—	Retarded
81.	12:0	M	I	Fixat.	3 N. 3 R.C.	Backward	3 Sp.	60	—
82.	12:2	M	I	Fixat.	3 N. 2 R.C.	Backward Cong.	3 Sp.	64	—
83.	12:4	M	I	Fixat.	2 Sp. Diffic.	Backward	3 Sp.	58	—
84.	12:4	M	III	Fixat.	4 N. 1 R.C.	Unstable	6 Sp.	85	Retardation Indicated
85.(22)	12:6	F	II	Fixat.	2 Sp. Unstable	Backward	4 Sp.	35 / 60	Retardation Indicated
86.	12:6	M	II	Fixat.	4 N. 1 R.C.	Musc. Atroph. Ret.	R. Sch.	86	Retardation Indicated
87.	12:6	F	I	Fixat.	2 Sp.	Little's Disease		75	Retardation Indicated
88.	12:7	M	(II)–IV	Progr.	5 N. 1 R.C.	Microcephal.	3 Sp.	58	—
89.	12:8	F	I	Fixat.	3 N. 3 R.C.	Hearing Defect	6 N. 2 R.C.	79	Retardation Indicated
90.	12:8	M	III	Fixat.	5 N. 1 R.C.	Backward	3 Sp.	60	—
91.	12:11	M	III	Fixat.	6 N. 1 R.C., Thl.	Nervous	Obs.	85	Retardation Indicated
92.	12:11	M	III/IV	Inter.	4 Sp.	Abandoned	Rem.	82	Retardation Indicated
93.(4)	13:0	M	I	Fixat.	7 N. 1 R.C., Thl.	Defect. Environ.	Worker	80	Retardation Indicated
94.	13:0	F	III/IV	Inter.	2 Sp.	Backward, Unstab.	Workshop (Sheltered)	66	—
95.(1)	13:0	F	I	Fixat.	5 N. 1 R.C.	N. Sp.	Rem.	95	Retardation Indicated
96.	13:0	M	III	Fixat.	5 Sp.	Backward, Cong.	Rural	66	Retardation Indicated
97.	13:0	F	III	Inter.	5 N. Lang. Def.	Infant. Paral.	7 Dev.	84	Retardation Indicated
98.	13:0	F	III/IV	Inter.	5 R.C. Unstab.	Backward	7 Sp.	70	Retarded
99.	13:1	M	III	Fixat.	3 N. 3 R.C.	Cleft Palate	Tut.	84	Retardation Indicated
100.	13:2	F	II	Fixat.	5 Sp.	Defect. Environ.	7 R.C.	80	Retardation Indicated
101.	13:2	M	II	Fixat.	5 Sp.	Lordosis / Retarded	4 Sp.	61	Retarded
102.	13:2	M	II	Fixat.	4 N. 3 R.C.	Backward	5 Sp.	68	Retardation Indicated

No.	Age	Sex	Level	Form of Equilibrium	Class Assignment When Examined	Medical Information	Class Assignment Two Years After Examination	IQ	Reasoning
103.	13:2	F	I	Fixat.	3 N. 3 R.C.	N. Sp.	4 Sp.	58	—
104.(26)	13:3	F	II	Fixat.	3 Sp.	Backward	5 Sp.	67	Retardation Indicated
105.(23)	13:4	M	II	Fixat.	2 Sp. Slow	Backward Psychop.	4 Sp.	69	Retardation Indicated
106.	13:4	M	III/IV	Inter.	Irregular	Epilep.		76	Retarded
107.	13:4	F	II	Fixat.	4 Sp.	Backward	6 Sp.	67	Retardation Indicated
108.	13:4	M	(II)-IV	Progr.	5 N. Lang. Def.	Hearing Defect	7 N.	82	Retardation Indicated
109.(57)	13:5	M	II/(III)	Progr.	4 Sp.	Irritability	6 Sp.	74	Retardation Indicated Hesitant
110.	13:6	M	I	Fixat.	3 N. 3 R.C.	Backward	Rural	53	—
111.(53)	13:9	M	(II)/III (IV)	Progr.	Irregular	Defect. Environ. Hered.	6 Sp.	72	Retardation Indicated Inhibited
112.	13:9	M	III	Fixat.	6 Sp. Diffic.	Backward	Apprentice	72	Retardation Indicated
113.	13:9	M	I	Fixat.	Sp. Prep.	Mentally Defective	Institution	50 63	—
114.	13:10	M	III	Fixat.	4 N. 2 R.C. Thl.	Epilep.	Rem.	84	Retardation Suspected
115.	13:10	F	III	Fixat.	5 Sp.	Trouble Endoc.	7 Sp.	75	Retardation Indicated
116.	13:11	F	III	Fixat.	4 Sp.	Backward	6 Sp.	76	Retardation Indicated
117.	13:11	M	III/IV	Inter.	7 Sp. Unstab.	Backward Psychop.	Apprentice	98	Retardation Indicated
118.	14:0	F	I	Fixat.	2 Sp.	Backward	4 Sp.	56	—
119.	14:0	F	II	Fixat.	5 Sp.	Backward	Housework	60	Retarded
120.(58)	14:0	M	(II)/I	Retro.	3 Sp.	Imbecile, Perversion	Institution	—	—
121.	14:0	F	I	Fixat.	3 Sp. Diffic.	Backward, Hystr.	Housework	75	—

122.(27)	14:0	F	II	Fixat.	3 Sp.	Backward Cong.	Housework	69	Retarded
123.	14:1	M	I	Fixat.	3 Sp. Obs.	Imbecile, Epilep.	Institution	64	—
124.	14:3	M	I	Fixat.	3 N. 3 R.C.	Backward, Epilep.	R. Sch.	58	Suspected of Retardation
125.(39)	14:5	F	III	Fixat.	6 Obs.	Epilep., Traum.	Apprentice	94	Retardation Indicated
126.(47)	14:5	M	III/IV	Inter.	7 Sp. Diffic.	T.B., Retarded	Vagabond	80	—
127.	14:8	M	I	Fixat.	2 Sp.	Imbecile, Epilep.	Rural	45	
128.(38)	14:10	M	III	Fixat.	6 Sp.	Backward, Dis-equilibrium	Apprentice	83	Retardation Indicated
129.(60)	14:10	M	III/II	Decalage	4 Sp. Diffic.	Backward	—	—	Retardation Indicated / Disequilibrium
130.(42)	14:11	M	III/IV	Inter.	7 Sp. Diffic.	Hered. Psychop.	Apprentice	69	Retarded
131.	15:1	M	III	Fixat.	7 N. 1 R.C.	Rickets	Workshop, Sheltered	73	Retardation Indicated
132.	15:2	M	III/IV	Inter.	7 Sp. Lang. Def.	Cleft Palate	Military Service	80	Retardation Indicated
133.	15:3	M	III	Fixat.	7 Sp. Unstabl.	Backward	Apprentice	78	Retardation Indicated
134.(45)	15:3	M	III	Fixat.	6 Sp. Slow	Backward, Epilep.	Apprentice	74 / 104	Retardation Indicated
135.	15:4	M	III	Fixat.	3 Sp. Diffic.	Retarded, Epilep.	Institution	51	—
136.	15:7	M	(I)/III	Progr.	Apprentice	Retarded	Rem.	70	Retardation Indicated
137.	15:7	M	III	Fixat.	7 Sp. Diffic.	Retarded	—	68	Retarded
138.(43)	15:7	M	III	Fixat.	7 Sp.	Backward	Workshop, Sheltered	89	Retardation Indicated
139.(44)	15:11	M	III	Fixat.	7 Sp.	Hered. Defect.	—	85	Retardation Indicated
140.	16:0	F	I	Fixat.	3 Sp.	Retarded, Cleft Palate	Housework	68 / 72	
141.	16:2	F	I	Fixat.	4 Sp. Diffic.	Retarded	Institution	42	—
142.(11)	16:5	M	I	Fixat.	3 N. 3 R.D.	Retarded, Susp. Schiz.	Workshop, Sheltered	53	—
143.	16:5	M	III	Fixat.	7 Sp. Diffic.	Retarded, Aban-doned	Apprentice	63	Retarded

No.	Age	Sex	Level	Form of Equilibrium	Class Assignment When Examined	Medical Information	Class Assignment Two Years After Examination	IQ	Reasoning
144.	17:2	F	III	Fixat.	Sp. Schol.	Retarded, Epilep.	Housework	73	Retarded
145.	17:9	M	II	Fixat.	Apprentice	Retarded	Worker	67	Retarded
146.(28)	18:7	M	II	Fixat.	Sp. Schol.	Retarded, Susp. Schiz.	Workshop, Sheltered	65	Retarded
147.	19:1	M	II	Fixat.	N. Schol., R..	Retarded	Worker	70	Retarded
148.(29)	19:8	F	II	Fixat.	Irregular Schol.	Cong. Ret., Epilep.	Housework	—	Retarded
149.(59)	20:0	M	(III)/I	Retro.	Irregular Schol.	Little's Disease, Imbecile	Institution	51	—
150.	20:0	F	II	Fixat.	Sp. Schol. (Work)	Retarded, Cretin.	Housework	65	Retarded
151.(46)	22:0	M	III	Fixat.	Sp. Schol.	Retarded, Psychop.	Workshop, Sheltered	—	Retarded
152.(40)	23:0	F	III	Fixat.	N. Schol., Dev.	Retarded	Housework	79	Retardation Indicated
153.(41)	24:0	F	III	Fixat.	N. Schol.	Slight Cretin.	Apprentice	77	Retardation Indicated
154.(6)	24:3	F	I	Fixat.	N. R.C.	Retarded	Housework	58	—
155.	24:11	F	II	Fixat.	Sp. Schol.	Retarded, Epilep.	Housework	61	Retarded
156.	33:9	M	III	Fixat.	Sp. Schol.	Retarded	Workshop, Sheltered	—	Retarded
157.(30)	36:0	M	II	Fixat.	Sp. Schol.	Retarded	Workshop, Sheltered	—	Retarded
158.	38:1	M	II	Fixat.	Sp. Schol.	Retarded	Workshop, Sheltered	62	—
159.(12)	52:0	F	I	Fixat.	Schol. R.C.	Imbecile	Institution	—	—

Appendix B

Practical Directions

Techniques utilized in administering the examinations are given below. They are techniques which conform to the methods described in the text. The clinical method cannot be learned by mere written explanation, and the best methodological manual cannot replace the need for several months' training in the administration of these procedures. This point is emphasized in this book several different times. *The clinical method does not follow a definite pattern which is fixed in advance, and differs from the classical method of test by the importance it attributes to the reactions of the subject.* To systematize the intellectual exchange with the child would result in a loss of the essential part of the clinical method, or in modifying it to the point of falsifying the results.

The impossibility of communicating our methods of interrogation is the principal obstacle to the widespread use of the clinical method. Also, we may have been too influenced by concern for scientific method, and may have failed to adapt to the requirements of practical diagnosis. Rather than trying to simplify the method for the purpose of easy application, it seems preferable to point out its pitfalls.

Even though it is difficult to picture briefly a method which requires a continuous construction, several technical remarks may help those who are accustomed to questioning children to become familiar with the procedure which we have sought to adapt to the diagnosis of reasoning. The aim of the interrogation is to engage the child in a relatively free conversation concerning concrete experiences, and to direct a sort of intellectual exchange in a way which will show the level and equilibrium of the operations of reasoning. The material used, the nature of the questions around which the interrogation centers, and the order of succession of the problems will be stated briefly.

Again it is emphasized that the interrogation *in extenso* must be given as it is written. When recording responses, the questions of the examiner must be distinguished from the responses of the subject. If answers are recorded by a secretary, the examiner is able to concentrate on the questioning. However, if the presence of the third person interferes with the subject's performance, the child should be questioned with only the examiner present.

The comprehension of the facts common to the three experiments requires of the subject only a minimum of acquired knowledge: manipulation of a scale with two pans. Even without previous notions of weighing, a child whose mental age is five years or above will understand, during preliminary exercises, that the equal level of the two pans means equality of weight, whereas higher signifies lighter, and lower signifies heavier.

The measure of volume by the immersion of the ball of clay into water can also be explained very simply: the level of the water before and after the immersion of the ball is indicated by remarking, "You see the ball takes up space in the water. It makes the water rise to here [second mark]. Show me where the water will rise to if you transform the ball into a sausage," etc.

The Procedure for the Transformation of the Clay Ball

1. *Material:* clay, scales with two pans, straight glass jar filled three-fourths full of water, and two rubber bands to mark the water levels.

2. *Exploratory questions* which attempt to reveal the existence and structure of the notion in question:

"Is there the same, or more, or less clay in the ball than in the sausage [the pancake, the little pieces]?"

"Does the ball weigh the same, more, or less than the sausage [the pancake, the little pieces]?"

"Does the ball take the same, more, or less space than the sausage in the water [pancake, little pieces]?"

Or: "Will the ball make the water rise the same amount as the sausage?" etc.

One should carefully avoid suggestion of the answer by the intonation of the questions or the regularity of their form.

3. *Explanatory questions* urge the child to justify his point of view; either the child predicts addition or subtraction of substance, weight, or volume, or he confirms conservation. Each time he advances an opinion, he is asked why he thinks so, the examiner employing as far as possible the exact terms used by the child. For example: "Why do you think it always weighs the same in a long sausage as when it's in a ball?"

In the same way, the child is given the opportunity to check his predictions by experimentation. When the results of the experiment are not what he predicted, his attention can be drawn to this fact by saying, for example, "Why isn't it heavier in a ball, as you thought it would be?" "Why does the water rise the same for the ball as for the pancake?" It should be remembered that young children and certain retardates show some difficulty in justifying their reasoning. Don't be discouraged if the desired explanation is not obtained immediately, but try to vary the questions in order to stimulate the curiosity of the child, and to be able to determine if it is a case of true incapacity for explanation.

4. *Control questions* are used to look for coherence or contradiction in answers. Frequently a child will contradict himself during the questioning period. It is necessary to determine if it is a question of simple forgetting or a sign of progress stimulated by discussion and observation, or a sign of incoherent thought. For example, the examiner will ask: "Earlier you said the pancake was lighter than the ball because it was all thin, and now you think it weighs just the same. Can you say both, or which do you think is right?" etc.

The operatory construction underlying the verbal scheme should also be determined. The child who affirms conservation can be asked, "Doesn't it matter if there are so many little pieces . . . that they are so small?" "Doesn't it make any difference that the sausage hangs over both sides of the pan . . . that the small pieces are separated . . . that the pancake is too thin . . . that the sausage makes the water go up higher in the glass?" etc. In certain cases, the examiner can state "Other children thought . . . what do you think about it?" (The reasons used to encourage explanation should be taken from the child's vocabulary; avoid the artificial.)

If the child frankly denies one or the other of the principles of conservation, intuitive representations (such as possible return to the starting point) will be evoked: "Could you remake a ball with a sausage?" "Could you stick the little pieces together?" etc.

It should also be noted whether experimentation (showing constancy of weight or of water level) leads the child to revise his notions, or if he maintains his prediction of nonconservation. The more a child lacks spontaneity of thought, the more he will resort to verbal response; in this event, more control questions are required.

5. *The order of succession* of the questions is adapted to the child's reactions. He is asked to make two little balls the same size and the same weight. If he merely weighs them in his hands, he is asked to use the scales to verify their equality. Then he is asked to make a long sausage with one of the balls (or little pieces, or a thin pancake).

It is possible that the child reacts spontaneously. Questioning then starts on the topic that evoked the greatest interest. If he immediately predicts "it has become much lighter," the problem of weight is discussed first and then that of substance or volume. By contrast, if he asks no questions of his own accord, this fact will be noted and the discussion will start with the notions supposed to be most significant for his level of reasoning. In more evolved subjects, it can be interesting to start with questions pertaining to volume before passing to the other notions of conservation. In younger or more retarded subjects there would be an advantage in proceeding by order of acquisition in normal development (substance, weight, and volume).

One of the notions of conservation can be studied through several different transformations of the ball (sausage, pancake, and pieces), or else the child can be questioned successively on all three notions using only one transformation. If the child hesitates to affirm or deny conservation of substance when the clay is rolled into a sausage, then the experimenter immediately introduces sectioning to see if under other perceptive conditions the child will favor one solution over another. On the contrary, the order of questions will be varied as soon as verbal perseveration is noted, particularly under the form of a scheme of conservation.

The reactions of the subject will determine when verification by experimentation should be introduced; with a child who tends to affirm conservation, there is an advantage in collecting first of all a group of statements before verifying them. With a child frankly denying conservation it can be interesting to see if he is capable of assimilating such an observation in order to generalize it to other transformations of the ball.

Dissolution of Sugar Experiment

1. *Material:* one or two cubes of sugar, two straight glass jars identical in weight and capacity, each filled three-fourths full of water, two rubber bands to indicate the levels of water, spoon or stick, and scales with two pans.

2. *Pattern of interrogation:* The nature of the questions is exactly the same as in the preceding experiments so it will not be given detailed explanation. However, it seems useful to outline a pattern of interrogation whose sole aim is to show how the examiner's questions utilize the child's reactions, while at the same time centering on particular problems. A complete outline would have noted all questions suggested by the child's answers, but it was necessary for the writer to limit herself to asking a single question from among those which were possible; each time the question asked was indicated by the first responses of the child. The reader will fully understand this general approach after review of the interrogations recorded in this volume.

Initial question: What will happen if you put this sugar cube in the water?

Possible reactions: *It will melt,* it is sugary—It goes into little pieces— We won't see it any more—The water will rise—It will splash—The water goes lower because the sugar goes down—The sugar absorbs the water— It gets a bit heavy—The sugar gets lighter when it melts.

Question: *What does melt mean?*

Answer: *It means we don't see anything any more*—It isn't there any more—Turns into a liquid—It is like melting snow—When you drink tea. there is always something at the bottom—The sugar lump turns into little bits—It turns into dust, etc.

Question: *Why don't we see anything any more?*

Answer: *It gets so small*—It goes away—Only the taste is left—It turns into a clear liquid.

Question: *If someone drank this water, what taste would the water have?*

Answer: *The taste of sugar*—But after a few days it is like clear water —The taste goes away, etc.

Question: *Why can one still taste the sugar when you can't see anything?*

Answer: *Because there's always a little sugar left in the water*—The taste stays there the way it does in coffee—Taste is like a vapor, it stays when there is nothing left—I don't know.

Question: *Is there a way of getting the sugar back which stays in the water?*

Answer: *Perhaps with a strainer you could find little grains*—It is all in the water, only separated into tiny pieces—You can't find it again— What is in is in—You can't get it back again—When you don't see it any more you can't get it back again—etc.

Question: *Could you make the whole lump of sugar with what you find left in the bottom?*

Answer: *Of course; if you don't lose any, the sugar must still be in there*—Perhaps you can, perhaps you can't—There would be too little— No, the little grains are too small, and would only make a tiny lump of sugar.

Question: *Will the water level stay where it is, or will it move when we put the sugar in the jar [of water]?*

Answer: *It goes up, but comes down again at once*—The water goes down because the sugar absorbs the water—It only splashes; the water doesn't go up—It must go up because the sugar has been added.

Question: *Why will the water go up?*

Answer: *The sugar presses on the water: it is a bit heavy, so the water must go up*—The sugar takes up room; when I put my hand in the water goes up too—The sugar turns into water which is added to the water in the jar.

Question: *You see this bearing [metal ball] and the piece of sugar? Which is heavier?*

Answer: *The lump of metal.*

Question: *Which is bigger?*

Answer: *The sugar.*

Question: *Which will make the water go up higher?*

Answer: *The metal, because it is heavier*—The sugar, because it is bigger—It is the size that counts—I don't know.

3. *Experimental check:* The two jars are placed on the scales and the equality of their weight is observed. The water level is marked with a rubber band, and first the piece of metal is put in the water. The rise in the water level is marked with a second rubber band; the metal is removed and the sugar is put in the water.

Answer: *Oh! the sugar makes the water rise more.*

Question: *Why the sugar and not the metal?*

Answer: *The sugar is bigger*—I don't understand—It went more slowly to the bottom.

After the immersion of the sugar the water level is marked.

Question: *While the sugar is melting, what will happen to the water level?*

Answer: *It goes down to where it was before*—It goes down a little way, but not all the way—It goes up even higher—It stays where it is—etc.

Question: *Show me where it will go down to?*

Answer: *Indicates the lower level (i.e.,* the lower rubber band)—the upper level—an intermediate level—above the upper level.

Question: *Why will the water go down again?*

Answer: *Because the sugar in the water doesn't weigh anything any more*—the sugar isn't there any more—The little grains don't take up any more room—The little grains don't settle—The water goes into the sugar, and so the level goes down—It isn't heavy—It is like melting snow; only a little bit of water is left at the end.

Question: *So how much will this jar weigh on the scales?* (The pans of the scales are hidden behind a screen.) *The same as the other jar with pure water in it?*

Answer: *It is heavier because the sugar is always in it*—It weighs exactly the same as the other jar—If there was sugar in the other one it would be the same weight—It is heavier by just the weight of the sugar.

Question: *But just now you said that the sugar in the water didn't weigh anything any more?*

Answer: *Of course, it's still a bit heavier, but it isn't pressing on the water; it's floating*—I have changed my mind—It doesn't weigh anything any more—I don't know.

Question: *If you could take the water away, would the little grains weigh as much as the whole lump of sugar?*

Answer: *No, less*—Exactly the same as the whole lump of sugar—*More, because they have been in the water*—They are too small to be weighed.

Question: *Why don't they weigh as much as the whole lump of sugar?*

Answer: *The little grains are lighter when they are separated*—Part of the sugar has gone away—The floating grains don't have any weight— The water takes their weight away.

The level of the water is observed.

Answer: *Oh! It's still up!*—You have cheated (here the child may bend his head to observe the level from a different angle)—I think it has come down all the same.

Question: *Why has it stayed up?*

Answer: *The sugar is still in there*—The sugar is heavy even when it's in a powder—The sugar liquid takes up room—Melted or unmelted, it is still a lump of sugar—Because we put the rubber band there—If you stuck all the little grains together, it would take up the same room—I don't understand.

Question: *We are going to check it once more on the scales. On one side we will put the jar of pure water with the lump of sugar beside it, and on the other side the jar which has the melted sugar in it.* (Observe subject's reactions before actual check.)

Answer: *The jar which has the melted sugar in it is a bit lighter*—It is exactly the same thing because there is sugar on both sides—It is even heavier where the sugar has melted because the sugar has absorbed some water—The melted sugar doesn't weigh anything any more—Since the water level has not come down, the sugar must be still in there, so it weighs the same as a lump.

Check with the scales.

Answer: *Ah! I understand. It must be the same because if you put the little grains together, it would be like a whole lump*—I don't understand. Are you sure the scales are working properly?

Experiment with the Bars and the Cylinders
(Logico-Arithmetical Composition)

1. *Material:* three sets of objects—(1) four narrow brass bars of the same length and width, (1a, 1b, 1c, and 1d); (2) four bars similar to those of the first set, but colored black, red, blue and yellow respectively; (3) three or four objects, such as a lump of lead, a flat piece of coal, a

piece of dry wax, some clay in the shape of a sausage, all of which should weigh the same as the bars. Scales with two pans.

2. *The experiment:* The problems, in increasing order of difficulty, follow. If a child has shown that he might be at the third or fourth stage of reasoning, the experiment may begin directly with the third set, but always with the possibility of returning to the first or second set in cases of failure.

EQUIVALENCE OF WEIGHT BETWEEN BARS OF THE SAME COLOR

The first set of bars is presented and the child is asked to verify that 1a = 1b, and 1b = 1c. Notice whether the child is content with weighing the bars in his hands or on the scales, and also if he compares the bars by measuring them. After this the bars 1a and 1c are put obliquely on the table, and 1b is put on one side by itself. The question follows: "We have not yet weighed these two bars together; will they weigh the same, or will one be heavier than the other?" (For very young or severely retarded children the questions may be simplified: "Show me with your hands where the two pans of the scales would be?") According to his answer, the child will be asked, "Why do you think one is heavier?"; or, "How do you know they weigh the same?"; or, "Exactly the same or only about the same?"; etc. The procedure by which the child makes sure of the equivalence, will be noted (*i.e.*, whether he compared the bars, putting them on top of each other or side by side, whether he compares them just by looking, or through some mental operation). The child can then be asked whether he needs to check his statement by using the scales, or whether he is sure without doing so.

EQUIVALENCE OF WEIGHT BETWEEN BARS OF DIFFERENT COLORS

The procedure is exactly the same as that used in the first set, but the colored bars are used. Then additive compositions will be made: 1a + 1b = 1c + 1d? (After having established that 1d = 1c.) The bars will either be put on top of each other or separated.

EQUIVALENCE OF WEIGHT BETWEEN OBJECTS OF DIFFERENT FORMS AND COLORS

The child is asked to predict the relation of the weight between the bar 1a and the piece of lead, and to check the prediction by using the scales. Once this equivalence has been established, the child is asked if the lead is also equal to the bar 1b or the bar 1c, or if it is heavier or lighter. Again the child's procedure for making sure of the equivalence is noted. If in thought or in practice he substitutes one bar for the other, the following control questions will be asked: "Why do you think they are just the same weight? . . . Doesn't it matter if the lead is smaller? . . . Doesn't it matter that one should be of lead and the other of brass?"

If, however, he predicts inequality of weight, it is necessary to be sure that it is not a simple question of forgetting the facts, and these facts will be reviewed: "The lead weighed the same as which bar? . . . The two bars weighed how much?" The equivalence is checked on the scales, and the piece of coal is substituted for a bar, while the child is asked to predict whether the lead weighs the same, or more, or less than the piece of coal. At the same time, an effort must be made to understand the child's justification for his prediction. The same procedure will be followed for the wax and the clay sausage.

Finally, the additive compositions will be studied: "Are two bars equal, or not equal, to the piece of coal plus the wax?" Each time it must be made certain that the child has not forgotten the facts, and the compositions will be varied until the level of reasoning has been determined. If all the equivalences of weight have been successfully established, the child is ready to go on to the volume experiment.

Experiments Concerning Volume

Material: (1) three aluminum cylinders 1a, 1b, and 1c, of the same form, weight, and volume, and colored red, orange, and black respectively; (2) a brass cylinder, a lead cylinder, and a third of clay, all equal in size and volume, but of different weight; (3) a piece of dry wax and a sausage of clay, both equivalent in volume to the cylinders; (4) an aluminum cylinder double the height of the little cylinders, and one triple their height; (5) scales with two pans, two straight glass jars, identical in shape and weight to each other, filled three-quarters full and with rubber bands to mark the level of the water on each.

VOLUME EQUIVALENCE BETWEEN TWO CYLINDERS WHOSE FORM AND WEIGHT ARE THE SAME

The child is asked to immerse the cylinders, two by two, into the jars of water, marking the levels of the displaced water each time. When he has noticed that 1a and 1b, 1b and 1c "make the water rise the same amount" he must be asked to guess whether 1a and 1c will make the water rise the same amount, or whether one makes it rise more than the other. He must be told to mark where he thinks the level of the water will be by using the rubber band. The cylinders will be placed in the water sometimes vertically and sometimes obliquely or horizontally.

VOLUME EQUIVALENCE BETWEEN CYLINDERS WHOSE FORMS ARE IDENTICAL, BUT WHOSE WEIGHTS ARE DIFFERENT

The child is asked to say whether the lead cylinder "will make the water rise the same amount or higher," than the aluminum cylinder of the first set, and at the same time his attention will be drawn to the unequal weights. The reason for which he predicts an unequal rise in the water level will be noted, as will the way he discovers the relation between the rise of the water level and the volume of the object immersed. After the experimental check, the brass cylinder will be put in the place of an aluminum cylinder, and so on.

VOLUME EQUIVALENCE BETWEEN OBJECTS OF DIFFERENT SHAPES AND WEIGHTS

Alternately, the wax ball and the clay sausage will be put in the place of the "control" cylinder (one of the original aluminum cylinders). After this the experimenter will go on to the additive compositions, and the child will be made to say whether cylinders $1a + 1b = 1c + 1d$, while their positions in the jars of water will be varied.

The child can also be asked to guess how many little cylinders would have to be put in the water to make it rise as much as the long cylinder (using either the one which is double or the one which is triple the height of the little cylinder), etc. Once again, the experimenter must decide with care on whether the child corrects the perceptive illusions through reasoning effort or whether he remains wholly or partly dominated by them.

The experiment of bars and cylinders is an excellent means of control, and is useful in completing the conservation experiments. Taken separately, this experiment must be used with caution. The regularity of the questions easily leads to verbal perseveration. The experimenter must be careful to vary the form of the problems or, if necessary, to change their order.

Complete References*

Ajuriaguerra, J. de, Rey-Bellet, M., and Tissot, R.
    (In press) "With Respect to Some Problems Posed by Operating Deficits of Old People Affected by Degenerative Dementia at the Start of the Evolution."

Bachelard, G.
    1932   *Les Intuitions atomistiques.* Paris, Boivin.

Biäsch, H.
    1939   *Testreihen zur Prüfung von Schweizerkindern vom 3. bis 15. Altersjahr.* Frauenfeld und Leipzig, Huber.

Binet, A.
    1903   *L'Étude expérimentale de l'intelligence.* Bibliothèque de pédagogie et de psychologie, Paris, Schleicher.

    1909   "L'Intelligence des imbéciles," *Année psychologique,* vol. *15.*

    1913   *Les Idées modernes sur les enfants.* Paris, Flammarion.

Binet, A., and Simon, Th.
    1905   "Méthode nouvelle pour le diagnostic du nivau intellectuel des anormaux," *Année psychologique,* vol. *11.*

    1908   Le Développement de l'intelligence chez les enfants," *Année psychologique,* vol. *14.*

    1917   *La Mesure du développement de l'intelligence chez les jeunes enfants.* Paris, Société pour l'étude psychologique de l'enfant.

Blondel, Charles

* For the convenience of the American reader, the references appearing in the Translator's Introduction and the Glossary have been inserted in alphabetical order in the list of references that appeared in the 1963 edition of *Le Diagnostic du raisonnement chez les débiles mentaux,* in addition to their appearance in the Introduction and Glossary respectively. English-language versions have been listed when available, unless reference is made specifically to the French edition.

1914   *La Conscience morbide: Essai de psycho-pathologie générale.*
        Paris, Alcan.
Bruner, J. S.
    1961   *The Process of Education.* Cambridge, Harvard University
            Press.
Bühler, Charlotte
    1928   *Kindheit und Jugend (Genese des Bewusstseins).* Leipzig,
            Hirzel.
Bühler, Charlotte, and Hetzer, Hildegard
    1932   *Kleinkindertests: Entwicklungstests vom 1. bis 6. Lebensjahr.*
            Leipzig, Barth.
Burt, C.
    1919   "The Development of Reasoning in School Children," *Journal
            of Educational Psychology.*
Chandler, Michael J.
    1967   "Definition of Terms Found in Piaget's Writings" (personal
            communication). Geneva, University of Geneva.
Claparède, Edouard
    1917   "Profils psychologiques gradués d'après l'ordination des sujets,
            avec quelques mots sur l'utilité des profils en psychologie
            légale," *Archives de psychologie,* vol. *16.*
    1924   *Comment diagnostiquer les aptitudes chez les écoliers.* Paris,
            Flammarion.
Claparède, Édouard, and Schuler, A.
    1917   "Le Test des phrases absurdes," *Intermédiaire éducateurs, 49.*
Decroly, O.
    1932   *Études de psychogenèse. (Observations, expériences, et en-
            quêtes sur le développement des aptitudes de l'enfant).* Paris,
            Lamartine.
Decroly, O., and Buyse
    1928   *La Pratique des tests mentaux.* Paris, Alcan.
Descœudres, Alice
    1917   "Enquête sur l'évaluation subjective de quelques tests de Binet
            et Simon," *Archives de psychologie,* vol. *16.*
    1920   *Le Développement de l'enfant de 2. à 7 ans.* Neuchâtel, Dela-
            chaux and Niestlé.
Fraisse, Paul, and Piaget, Jean, eds.
    1963   *Traité de psychologie expérimentale, vol. 1.* Paris, Presses
            Universitaires de France.
Gesell, Arnold
    1925   *The Mental Growth of the Pre-school Child: A Psychological
            Outline of Normal Development from Birth to the Sixth Year,*

Including a System of Development Diagnosis. New York, Macmillan.

Hunt, J. McV.
    1961 *Intelligence and Experience.* New York, Ronald Press.

Hurtig, M.
    1960 "Études expérimentales des possibilités d'apprentissage intellectuel d'enfants débiles et d'enfants normaux," *Enfance.*

Inhelder, Bärbel
    1962 "Piaget's Genetic Approach to Cognition," *in* "Thought in the Young Child," William Kessen and Clementina Kuhlmann, eds., *Monographs of the Society for Research in Child Development, 83.*

Inhelder, Bärbel, and Piaget, Jean
    1958 *The Growth of Logical Thinking from Childhood to Adolescence.* (French 1955, English 1958), New York, Basic Books.
    1963 *The Early Growth of Logic.* (French 1959, English 1963), London, Routledge and Kegan Paul.

Janet, Pierre
    1894 *L'Automatisme psychologique: Essai de psychologie expérimentale sur les formes inférieures de l'activité humaine.* Bibliothèque de philosophie contemporaine. Paris, Alcan.
    1926 *De l'Angoisse à l'extase: Études sur les croyances et les sentiments,* vol. *1.* Paris, Maloine.
    1928 *L'Évolution de la mémoire et la notion du temps.* Paris, Maloine.
    1929 *L'Évolution psychologique de la personnalité.* Paris, Maloine.
    1935 *Les Débuts de l'intelligence.* Paris, Maloine.
    1936 *L'Intelligence avant le langage.* Paris, Maloine.

Lehrbuch de Psychopathologie des Kindersalters.
    1938 Erlenbach-Zurich-Leipzig, Rotapfelverlag.

Meili, R.
    1937 *Psychologische Diagnostik.* Schaffhausen, Verlag Meili.

Nassefat, N.
    1963 *Étude quantitative sur l'évolution des operations intellectuelles.* Neuchâtel, Delachaux and Niestlé.

Piaget, Jean
    1923 "Une Forme verbale de comparaison chez l'enfant (Un Cas de transition entre le jugement prédicatif et le jugement de relation)," *Archives de psychologie,* vol. *18.*
    1926 *The Language and Thought of the Child.* (French 1923, 4th ed. 1956), New York, Harcourt, Brace.

1928a *Judgment and Reasoning in the Child.* (French 1924, 4th ed. 1956), New York, Harcourt, Brace.

1928b "Les Trois systèmes de la pensée de l'enfant," *Bulletin de la société française de philosophie.* Paris, A. Colin.

1929   *The Child's Conception of the World.* (French 1926), New York, Harcourt, Brace.

1930   *The Child's Conception of Physical Causality.* (French 1927), London, Kegan Paul.

1932   *The Moral Judgment of the Child.* (French 1932), London, Kegan Paul.

1941a "Communications dans le comptes rendus de la Société de Physique de Genève," vol. *58.*

1941b "Le Mécanisme du développement mental et les lois du groupement des opérations: Esquisse d'une théorie opératoire de l'intelligence," *Archives de psychologie, 28,* 215–85.

1942   *Classes, relations et nombres: Essai sur les groupements de la logistique et sur la réversibilité de la pensée.* Paris, Vrin.

1943   "Recherches sur le développement des perceptions. I. Introduction a l'étude des perceptions chez l'enfant et analyse d'une illusion relative à perception visuelle de cercles concentriques (Delbœuf)," *Archives de psychologie,* vol. *29,* no. 113.

1947   *La Psychologie de l'intelligence.* (English 1950), Paris, A. Colin.

1949a *Introduction à l'épistémologie génétique: 1. La Pensée mathématique.* Paris, Presses Universitaires de France.

1949b *Traité de logique: Essai de logistique opératoire.* Paris, A. Colin.

1950a *La Construction du réel chez l'enfant,* 2d ed. (1st ed. 1937–38, English 1954), Neuchâtel, Delachaux and Niestlé.

1950b *The Psychology of Intelligence.* (French 1947), New York, Harcourt, Brace.

1952   *The Origins of Intelligence in Children.* (French 1936), New York, International Universities Press.

1954   *The Construction of Reality in the Child.* (French 1937–38, 2d ed. 1950), New York, Basic Books.

1956a *Le Jugement et le raisonnement chez l'enfant,* 4th ed. (1st ed. 1924, English 1928), Neuchâtel, Delachaux and Niestlé.

1956b *Le Langage et la pensée chez l'enfant,* 4th ed. (1st ed. 1923, English 1926), Neuchâtel, Delachaux and Niestlé.

Piaget, Jean, Apostel, L., and Mandelbrot, B.

1957   "Logique et équilibre," *Études d'épistémologie génétique, 2,* Paris, Presses Universitaires de France.

Piaget, Jean, and Beth, Evert W.

  1961   "Épistémologie mathématique et psychologie: Essai sur les relations entre la logique formelle et la pensée réelle," *Études d'épistémologie génétique, 14,* Paris, Presses Universitaires de France.

Piaget, Jean, Beth, Evert W., and Mays, W.

  1957   "Épistémologie génétique et recherche psychologique," *Études d'épistémologie génétique, 1,* Paris, Presses Universitaires de France.

Piaget, Jean, and Greco, Pierre

  1959   "Apprentissage et connaissance," *Études d'épistémologie génétique, 7,* Paris, Presses Universitaires de France.

Piaget, Jean, and Inhelder, Bärbel

  1941   *Le Développement des quantités physiques chez l'enfant.* (2d ed. 1962), Neuchâtel, Delachaux and Niestlé.

  1951   *La Genèse de l'idée de hasard chez l'enfant.* Paris, Presses Universitaires de France.

  1956   *The Child's Conception of Space.* (French 1947, English 1956), London, Routledge and Kegan Paul.

  1962   *Le Développement des quantités physiques chez l'enfant,* 2d ed. (1st ed. 1941), Neuchâtel, Delachaux and Niestlé.

  1966a   *L'Image mentale chez l'enfant.* Paris, Presses Universitaires de France.

  1966b   *La Psychologie de l'enfant: Collection "Que Sais-je."* Paris, Presses Universitaires de France.

  (In press) *Mémoire à intelligence.*

Piaget, Jean, Inhelder, Bärbel, and Szeminska, Alina

  1960   *The Child's Conception of Geometry.* (French 1948, English 1960), London, Routledge and Kegan Paul.

Piaget, Jean, and Krafft

  1960   "La Notion de l'ordre des événements et le test des images en désordre chez l'enfant de 6. à 10. ans," *Archives de psychologie,* vol. *19.*

Piaget, Jean, and Szeminska, Alina

  1952   *The Child's Conception of Number.* (French 1941, English 1952), London, Routledge and Kegan Paul.

Ranson, J.

  1950   *Application des épreuves de Piaget-Inhelder à une group de debiles mentaux.* Lyon, Bosc.

Rey, A.

  1930   "De l'Illusion de poids chez les anormaux," *Archives de psychologie,* vol. *22.*

1934   "D'un Procédé pour évaluer l'éducabilité. (Quelques explica-
tions en psychopathologie)," *Archives de psychologie*, vol. *24.*

1935   "Réflexions sur le problème du diagnostic mental," *Cahiers de
pédagogie expérimentale et de psychologie de l'enfant* No. 5.
Geneva, L'Institut des Sciences de l'Éducation.

Rossolimo, G.

1926   *Das psychologische Profil.* Halle an der Saale, Carl Marhold.

Stern, W.

1928   *Die Intelligenz der Kinder und Jugendlichen und die Methoden
ihrer Untersuchung.* Leipzig, Barth.

Terman, L. M.

1919   *The Measurement of Intelligence.* London, Harrap.

Tramer, M.

1942   *Lehrbuch der allgemeinen Kinderpsychiatrie.* Basel, Benno
Schwabe.

Vermeylen, G.

1922   "Les Débiles mentaux. Étude expérimentale et clinique," *Bulletin de l'Institut général psychologique.*

Vihn-Bang

1959   "Evolution des conduits et apprentissage," *Études d'episté-
mologie génétiques, 9,* Paris, Presses Universitaires de France.

Wallon, H.

1925   *L'Enfant turbulent. Étude sur les retards et les anomalies du
développement moteur et mental.* Paris, Alcan.

1934   *Les Origines du caractère.* Paris, Boivin.

1937   "Le Développement moteur et mental chez l'enfant," *Actes du
XIᵐᵉ Congrès International de Psychologie.* Paris, Imprimerie
Moderne.

1942   *De l'Acte à la pensée.* Paris, Flammarion.

Zazzo, René

1960a "Nouvelles recherches sur la débilté mentale," *Enfance,* No.
4–5.

1960b *Manuel pour l'etude psychologique de l'enfant.* Neuchâtel,
Delachaux and Niestlé.

Index